Resumes And Cover Letters That Have Worked, Revised Edition

Anne McKinney, Editor

PREP PUBLISHING

FAYETTEVILLE, NC

PREP Publishing
1110½ Hay Street
Fayetteville, NC 28305
(910) 483-6611

Library of Congress Cataloging-in-Publication Data

Resumes and Cover Letters that have worked, Revised Edition / Anne McKinney, editor. --2nd ed.
        p. cm. -- (Real-resumes series)
        ISBN 978-1475094367; 1475094361 (pbk.)
    1. Resumes (Employment) 2. Cover Letters. I. McKinney, Anne, 1948- . II. PREP Publishing.
    HF5383.R424 1995
    808′.06665--dc20   95-19458
                                                                           CIP

Printed in the United States of America
Second Edition

By PREP Publishing

Business and Career Series:

RESUMES AND COVER LETTERS THAT HAVE WORKED, Revised Edition

RESUMES AND COVER LETTERS THAT HAVE WORKED FOR MILITARY PROFESSIONALS

GOVERNMENT JOB APPLICATIONS AND FEDERAL RESUMES

COVER LETTERS THAT BLOW DOORS OPEN

LETTERS FOR SPECIAL SITUATIONS

RESUMES AND COVER LETTERS FOR MANAGERS

REAL-RESUMES FOR COMPUTER JOBS

REAL-RESUMES FOR MEDICAL JOBS

REAL-RESUMES FOR FINANCIAL JOBS

REAL-RESUMES FOR TEACHERS

REAL-RESUMES FOR STUDENTS

REAL-RESUMES FOR CAREER CHANGERS

REAL-RESUMES FOR SALES

REAL ESSAYS FOR COLLEGE & GRADUATE SCHOOL

REAL-RESUMES FOR AVIATION & TRAVEL JOBS

REAL-RESUMES FOR POLICE, LAW ENFORCEMENT & SECURITY JOBS

REAL-RESUMES FOR SOCIAL WORK & COUNSELING JOBS

REAL-RESUMES FOR CONSTRUCTION JOBS

REAL-RESUMES FOR MANUFACTURING JOBS

REAL-RESUMES FOR RESTAURANT, FOOD SERVICE & HOTEL JOBS

REAL-RESUMES FOR MEDIA, NEWSPAPER, BROADCASTING & PUBLIC AFFAIRS JOBS

REAL-RESUMES FOR RETAILING, MODELING, FASHION & BEAUTY JOBS

REAL-RESUMES FOR HUMAN RESOURCES & PERSONNEL JOBS

REAL-RESUMES FOR NURSING JOBS

REAL-RESUMES FOR AUTO INDUSTRY JOBS

REAL RESUMIX AND OTHER RESUMES FOR FEDERAL GOVERNMENT JOBS

REAL KSAS--KNOWLEDGE, SKILLS & ABILITIES--FOR GOVERNMENT JOBS

REAL BUSINESS PLANS AND MARKETING TOOLS

Judeo-Christian Ethics Series:

SECOND TIME AROUND

BACK IN TIME

WHAT THE BIBLE SAYS ABOUT...Words that can lead to success and happiness

A GENTLE BREEZE FROM GOSSAMER WINGS

BIBLE STORIES FROM THE OLD TESTAMENT

TABLE OF CONTENTS

Resumes And Cover Letters That Have Worked, Revised Edition

Anne McKinney, Editor

A WORD FROM THE EDITOR:
ABOUT THE REAL-RESUMES SERIES

We hope the superior samples will help you manage your current job campaign and your career so that you will find work aligned to your career interests.

Welcome to the Real-Resumes Series. The Real-Resumes Series is a series of books which have been developed based on the experiences of real job hunters and which target specialized fields or types of resumes. As the editor of the series, I have carefully selected resumes and cover letters (with names and other key data disguised, of course) which have been used successfully in real job hunts. That's what we mean by "Real-Resumes." What you see in this book are *real* resumes and cover letters which helped real people get ahead in their careers.

The Real-Resumes Series is based on the work of the country's oldest resume-preparation company known as PREP Resumes. If you would like a free information packet describing the company's resume preparation services, call **910-483-6611** or write to PREP at 1110½ Hay Street, Fayetteville, NC 28305. If you have a job hunting experience you would like to share with our staff at the Real-Resumes Series, please contact us at preppub@aol.com or visit our website at http://www.prep-pub.com.

The resumes and cover letters in this book are designed to be of most value to people already in a job hunt or contemplating a career change. If we could give you one word of advice about your career, here's what we would say: Manage your career and don't stumble from job to job in an incoherent pattern. Try to find work that interests you, and then identify prosperous industries which need work performed of the type you want to do. Learn early in your working life that a great resume and cover letter can blow doors open for you and help you maximize your salary.

As the editor of this book, I would like to give you some tips on how to make the best use of the information you will find here. Because you are considering a career change, you already understand the concept of managing your career for maximum enjoyment and self-fulfillment. The purpose of this book is to provide expert tools and advice so that you *can* manage your career. Inside these pages you will find resumes and cover letters that will help you find not just a job but the type of work you want to do.

Overview of the Book
Every resume and cover letter in this book actually worked. And most of the resumes and cover letters have common features: most are one-page, most are in the chronological format, and most resumes are accompanied by a companion cover letter. In this section you will find helpful advice about job hunting. Step One begins with a discussion of why employers prefer the one-page, chronological resume. In Step Two you are introduced to the direct approach and to the proper format for a cover letter. In Step Three you learn the 14 main reasons why job hunters are not offered the jobs they want, and you learn the six key areas employers focus on when they interview you. Step Four gives nuts-and-bolts advice on how to handle the interview, send a follow-up letter after an interview, and negotiate your salary.

The cover letter plays such a critical role in a career change. You will learn from the experts how to format your cover letters and you will see suggested language to use in particular career-change situations. It has been said that "A picture is worth a thousand words" and, for that reason, you will see numerous examples of effective cover letters used by real individuals to change fields, functions, and industries.

The most important part of the book is the Real-Resumes section. Some of the individuals whose resumes and cover letters you see spent a lengthy career in an industry they loved. Then there are resumes and cover letters of people who wanted a change but who probably wanted to remain in their industry. Many of you will be especially interested by the resumes and cover letters of individuals who knew they definitely wanted a career change but had no idea what they wanted to do next. Other resumes and cover letters show individuals who knew they wanted to change fields and had a pretty good idea of what they wanted to do next.

Whatever your field, and whatever your circumstances, you'll find resumes and cover letters that will "show you the ropes" in terms of successfully changing jobs and switching careers.

Before you proceed further, think about why you picked up this book.
- Are you dissatisfied with the type of work you are now doing?
- Would you like to change careers, change companies, or change industries?
- Are you satisfied with your industry but not with your niche or function within it?
- Do you want to transfer your skills to a new product or service?
- Even if you have excelled in your field, have you "had enough"? Would you like the stimulation of a new challenge?
- Are you aware of the importance of a great cover letter but unsure of how to write one?
- Are you preparing to launch a second career after retirement?
- Have you been downsized, or do you anticipate becoming a victim of downsizing?
- Do you need expert advice on how to plan and implement a job campaign that will open the maximum number of doors?
- Do you want to make sure you handle an interview to your maximum advantage?

Introduction:
The Art of
Changing
Jobs...
and Finding
New Careers

- Would you like to master the techniques of negotiating salary and benefits?
- Do you want to learn the secrets and shortcuts of professional resume writers?

Using the Direct Approach

As you consider the possibility of a job hunt or career change, you need to be aware that most people end up having at least three distinctly different careers in their working lifetimes, and often those careers are different from each other. Yet people usually stumble through each job campaign, unsure of what they should be doing. Whether you find yourself voluntarily or unexpectedly in a job hunt, the direct approach is the job hunting strategy most likely to yield a full-time permanent job. The direct approach is an active, take-the-initiative style of job hunting in which you choose your next employer rather than relying on responding to ads, using employment agencies, or depending on other methods of finding jobs. You will learn how to use the direct approach in this book, and you will see that an effective cover letter is a critical ingredient in using the direct approach.

The "direct approach" is the style of job hunting most likely to yield the maximum number of job interviews.

Lack of Industry Experience Not a Major Barrier to Entering New Field

"Lack of experience" is often the last reason people are not offered jobs, according to the companies who do the hiring. If you are changing careers, you will be glad to learn that experienced professionals often are selling "potential" rather than experience in a job hunt. Companies look for personal qualities that they know tend to be present in their most effective professionals, such as communication skills, initiative, persistence, organizational and time management skills, and creativity. Frequently companies are trying to discover "personality type," "talent," "ability," "aptitude," and "potential" rather than seeking actual hands-on experience, so your resume should be designed to aggressively present your accomplishments. Attitude, enthusiasm, personality, and a track record of achievements in any type of work are the primary "indicators of success" which employers are seeking, and you will see numerous examples in this book of resumes written in an all-purpose fashion so that the professional can approach various industries and companies.

Using references in a skillful fashion in your job hunt will inspire confidence in prospective employers and help you "close the sale" after interviews.

The Art of Using References in a Job Hunt

You probably already know that you need to provide references during a job hunt, but you may not be sure of how and when to use references for maximum advantage. You can use references very creatively during a job hunt to call attention to your strengths and make yourself "stand out." Your references will rarely get you a job, no matter how impressive the names, but the way you use references can boost the employer's confidence in you and lead to a job offer in the least time.

You should ask from three to five people, including people who have supervised you, if you can use them as a reference during your job hunt. You may not be able to ask your current boss since your job hunt is probably confidential.

A common question in resume preparation is: "Do I need to put my references on my resume?" No, you don't. Even if you create a references page at the same time you prepare your resume, you don't need to mail, e-mail, or fax your references page with the resume and cover letter. Usually the potential employer is not interested in references until he meets you, so the earliest you need to have references ready is at the first interview. Obviously there are exceptions to this standard rule of thumb; sometimes an ad will ask you to send references with your first response. Wait until the employer requests references before providing them.

An excellent attention-getting technique is to take to the first interview not just a page of references (giving names, addresses, and telephone numbers) but an actual letter of reference written by someone who knows you well and who preferably has supervised or employed you. A professional way to close the first interview is to thank the interviewer, shake his or her hand, and then say you'd like to give him or her a copy of a letter of reference from a previous employer. Hopefully you already made a good impression during the interview, but you'll "close the sale" in a dynamic fashion if you leave a letter praising you and your accomplishments. For that reason, it's a good idea to ask supervisors during your final weeks in a job if they will provide you with a written letter of recommendation which you can use in future job hunts. Most employers will oblige, and you will have a letter that has a useful "shelf life" of many years. Such a letter often gives the prospective employer enough confidence in his opinion of you that he may forego checking out other references and decide to offer you the job on the spot or in the next few days.

With regard to references, it's best to provide the names and addresses of people who have supervised you or observed you in a work situation.

Whom should you ask to serve as references? References should be people who have known or supervised you in a professional, academic, or work situation. References with big titles, like school superintendent or congressman, are fine, but remind busy people when you get to the interview stage that they may be contacted soon. Make sure the busy official recognizes your name and has instant positive recall of you! If you're asked to provide references on a formal company application, you can simply transcribe names from your references list. In summary, follow this rule in using references: If you've got them, flaunt them! If you've obtained well-written letters of reference, make sure you find a polite way to push those references under the nose of the interviewer so he or she can hear someone other than you describing your strengths. Your references probably won't ever get you a job, but glowing letters of reference can give you credibility and visibility that can make you stand out among candidates with similar credentials and potential!

The approach taken by this book is to (1) help you master the proven best techniques of conducting a job hunt and (2) show you how to stand out in a job hunt through your resume, cover letter, interviewing skills, as well as the way in which you present your references and follow up on interviews. Now, the best way to "get in the mood" for writing your own resume and cover letter is to select samples from the Table of Contents that interest you and then read them. A great resume is a "photograph," usually on one page, of an individual. If you wish to seek professional advice in preparing your resume, you may contact one of the professional writers at Professional Resume & Employment Publishing (PREP) for a brief free consultation by calling 1-910-483-6611.

Part One: Some Advice About Your Job Hunt

What if you don't know what you want to do?

Your job hunt will be more comfortable if you can figure out what type of work you want to do. But you are not alone if you have no idea what you want to do next! You may have knowledge and skills in certain areas but want to get into another type of work. What *The Wall Street Journal* has discovered in its research on careers is that most of us end up having at least three distinctly different careers in our working lives; it seems that, even if we really like a particular kind of activity, twenty years of doing it is enough for most of us and we want to move on to something else!

That's why we strongly believe that you need to spend some time figuring out ***what interests you*** rather than taking an inventory of the skills you have. You may have skills that you simply don't want to use, but if you can build your career on the things that interest you, you will be more likely to be happy and satisfied in your job. Realize, too, that interests can change over time; the activities that interest you now may not be the ones that interested you years ago. For example, some professionals may decide that they've had enough of retail sales and want a job selling another product or service, even though they have earned a reputation for being an excellent retail manager. We strongly believe that interests rather than skills should be the determining factor in deciding what types of jobs you want to apply for and what directions you explore in your job hunt. Obviously one cannot be a lawyer without a law degree or a secretary without secretarial skills; but a professional can embark on a next career as a financial consultant, property manager, plant manager, production supervisor, retail manager, or other occupation if he/she has a strong interest in that type of work and can provide a resume that clearly demonstrates past excellent performance in *any* field and *potential* to excel in another field. As you will see later in this book, "lack of exact experience" is the last reason why people are turned down for the jobs they apply for.

How can you have a resume prepared if you don't know what you want to do?

You may be wondering how you can have a resume prepared if you don't know what you want to do next. The approach to resume writing which PREP, the country's oldest resume-preparation company, has used successfully for many years is to develop an "all-purpose" resume that translates your skills, experience, and accomplishments into language employers can understand. What most people need in a job hunt is a versatile resume that will allow them to apply for numerous types of jobs. For example, you may want to apply for a job in pharmaceutical sales but you may also want to have a resume that will be versatile enough for you to apply for jobs in the construction, financial services, or automotive industries.

Based on more than 20 years of serving job hunters, we at PREP have found that your best approach to job hunting is **an all-purpose resume** and **specific cover letters tailored to specific fields** rather than using the approach of trying to create different resumes for every job. If you are remaining in your field, you may not even need more than one "all-purpose" cover letter, although the cover letter rather than the resume is the place to communicate your interest in a narrow or specific field. An all-purpose resume and cover letter that translate your experience and accomplishments into plain English are the tools that will maximize the number of doors which open for you while permitting you to "fish" in the widest range of job areas.

Figure out what interests you and you will hold the key to a successful job hunt and working career. (And be prepared for your interests to change over time!)

"Lack of exact experience" is the last reason people are turned down for the jobs for which they apply.

Your resume will provide the script for your job interview.
When you get down to it, your resume has a simple job to do: Its purpose is to blow as many doors open as possible and to make as many people as possible want to meet you. So a well-written resume that really "sells" you is a key that will create opportunities for you in a job hunt.

This statistic explains why: The typical newspaper advertisement for a job opening receives more than 245 replies. And normally only 10 or 12 will be invited to an interview.

But here's another purpose of the resume: it provides the "script" the employer uses when he interviews you. If your resume has been written in such a way that your strengths and achievements are revealed, that's what you'll end up talking about at the job interview. Since the resume will govern what you get asked about at your interviews, you can't overestimate the importance of making sure your resume makes you look and sound as good as you are.

So what is a "good" resume?
Very literally, your resume should motivate the person reading it to dial the phone number or e-mail the screen name you have put on the resume. When you are relocating, you should put a local phone number on your resume if your physical address is several states away; employers are more likely to dial a local telephone number than a long-distance number when they're looking for potential employees.

If you have a resume already, look at it objectively. Is it a limp, colorless "laundry list" of your job titles and duties? Or does it "paint a picture" of your skills, abilities, and accomplishments in a way that would make someone want to meet you? Can people understand what you're saying? If you are attempting to change fields or industries, can potential employers see that your skills and knowledge are transferable to other environments? For example, have you described accomplishments which reveal your problem-solving abilities or communication skills?

How long should your resume be?
One page, maybe two. Usually only people in the academic community have a resume (which they usually call a *curriculum vitae*) longer than one or two pages. Remember that your resume is almost always accompanied by a cover letter, and a potential employer does not want to read more than two or three pages about a total stranger in order to decide if he wants to meet that person! Besides, don't forget that the more you tell someone about yourself, the more opportunity you are providing for the employer to screen you out at the "first-cut" stage. A resume should be concise and exciting and designed to make the reader want to meet you in person!

Should resumes be functional or chronological?
Employers almost always prefer a chronological resume; in other words, an employer will find a resume easier to read if it is immediately apparent what your current or most recent job is, what you did before that, and so forth, in reverse chronological order. A resume that goes back in detail for the last ten years of employment will generally satisfy the employer's curiosity about your background. Employment more than ten years old can be shown even more briefly in an "Other Experience" section at the end of your "Experience" section. Remember that your intention is not to tell everything you've done but to "hit the high points" and especially impress the employer with what you learned, contributed, or accomplished in each job you describe.

Your resume is the "script" for your job interviews. Make sure you put on your resume what you want to talk about or be asked about at the job interview.

The one-page resume in chronological format is the format preferred by most employers.

Once you get your resume, what do you do with it?

You will be using your resume to answer ads, as a tool to use in talking with friends and relatives about your job search, and, most importantly, in using the "direct approach" described in this book.

When you mail your resume, always send a "cover letter."

A "cover letter," sometimes called a "resume letter" or "letter of interest," is a letter that accompanies and introduces your resume. Your cover letter is a way of personalizing the resume by sending it to the specific person you think you might want to work for at each company. Your cover letter should contain a few highlights from your resume—just enough to make someone want to meet you. Cover letters should always be typed or word processed on a computer—never handwritten.

Never mail or fax your resume without a cover letter.

1. Learn the art of answering ads.

There is an "art," part of which can be learned, in using your "bestselling" resume to reply to advertisements.

Sometimes an exciting job lurks behind a boring ad that someone dictated in a hurry, so reply to any ad that interests you. Don't worry that you aren't "25 years old with an MBA" like the ad asks for. Employers will always make compromises in their requirements if they think you're the "best fit" overall.

What about ads that ask for "salary requirements?"

What if the ad you're answering asks for "salary requirements?" The first rule is to avoid committing yourself in writing at that point to a specific salary. You don't want to "lock yourself in."

There are two ways to handle the ad that asks for "salary requirements."

What if the ad asks for your "salary requirements?"

First, you can ignore that part of the ad and accompany your resume with a cover letter that focuses on "selling" you, your abilities, and even some of your philosophy about work or your field. You may include a sentence in your cover letter like this: "I can provide excellent personal and professional references at your request, and I would be delighted to share the private details of my salary history with you in person."

Second, if you feel you must give some kind of number, just state a range in your cover letter that includes your medical, dental, other benefits, and expected bonuses. You might state, for example, "My current compensation, including benefits and bonuses, is in the range of $30,000-$40,000."

Analyze the ad and "tailor" yourself to it.

When you're replying to ads, a finely tailored cover letter is an important tool in getting your resume noticed and read. On the next page is a cover letter which has been "tailored to fit" a specific ad. Notice the "art" used by PREP writers of analyzing the ad's main requirements and then writing the letter so that the person's background, work habits, and interests seem "tailor-made" to the company's needs. Use this cover letter as a model when you prepare your own reply to ads.

Date

Mr. Arthur Wise
PYA Monarch
9439 Goshen Lane
Dallas, TX 22105

Dear Mr. Wise:

I would appreciate an opportunity to show you in person, soon, that I am the energetic, dynamic individual you are looking for as your Sales Representative and Food Broker for PYA Monarch in the Dallas area.

Here are just three reasons why I believe I am the effective young professional you seek:

- *I am a proven salesperson* with a demonstrated ability to "prospect" and produce sales. In my current job as a sales representative, I contact more than 150 business professionals per week and won my company's annual award for outstanding sales performance.

- *I enjoy traveling and am eager to assist in the growth of your business.* I am fortunate to have the natural energy, industry, and enthusiasm required to put in the long hours necessary for effective sales performance.

- *I understand the food brokerage business and my lifestyle is suited to the long hours and weekend work.* I am single and available to meet customers at their convenience.

I am fortunate to have the natural energy, industry, and enthusiasm required to put in the long hours necessary for effective sales performance. You will find me, I am certain, a friendly, good-natured person whom you would be proud to call part of your "team." I would enjoy the opportunity to share my proven sales techniques and extensive knowledge with other junior sales professionals in a management and development position.

I hope you will call or write me soon to suggest a convenient time when we might meet to discuss your needs further and how I might serve them.

Yours sincerely,

Your Name

Employers are trying to identify the individual who wants the job they are filling. Don't be afraid to express your enthusiasm in the cover letter!

2. Talk to friends and relatives.

Don't be shy about telling your friends and relatives the kind of job you're looking for. Looking for the job you want involves using your network of contacts, so tell people what you're looking for. They may be able to make introductions and help set up interviews.

About 25% of all interviews are set up through "who you know," so don't ignore this approach.

3. Finally, and most importantly, use the "direct approach."

The "direct approach" is a strategy in which you choose your next employer.

More than 50% of all job interviews are set up by the "direct approach." That means you actually mail, e-mail, or fax a resume and a cover letter to a company you think might be interesting to work for.

To whom do you write?

In general, you should write directly to the *exact name* of the person who would be hiring you: say, the vice-president of marketing or data processing. If you're in doubt about to whom to address the letter, address it to the president by name and he or she will make sure it gets forwarded to the right person within the company who has hiring authority in your area.

How do you find the names of potential employers?

You're not alone if you feel that the biggest problem in your job search is finding the right names at the companies you want to contact. But you can usually figure out the names of companies you want to approach by deciding first if your job hunt is primarily geography-driven or industry-driven.

In a **geography-driven job hunt,** you could select a list of, say, 50 companies you want to contact **by location** from the lists that the U.S. Chambers of Commerce publish yearly of their "major area employers." There are hundreds of local Chambers of Commerce across America, and most of them will have an 800 number which you can find through 1-800-555-1212. If you and your family think Atlanta, Dallas, Ft. Lauderdale, and Virginia Beach might be nice places to live, for example, you could contact the Chamber of Commerce in those cities and ask how you can obtain a copy of their list of major employers. Your nearest library will have the book which lists the addresses of all chambers.

In an **industry-driven job hunt,** and if you are willing to relocate, you will be identifying the companies which you find most attractive in the industry in which you want to work. When you select a list of companies to contact **by industry,** you can find the right person to write and the address of firms by industrial category in *Standard and Poor's, Moody's,* and other excellent books in public libraries. Many Web sites also provide contact information.

Many people feel it's a good investment to actually call the company to either find out or double-check the name of the person to whom they want to send a resume and cover letter. It's important to do as much as you feasibly can to assure that the letter gets to the right person in the company.

On-line research will be the best way for many people to locate organizations to which they wish to send their resume. It is outside the scope of this book to teach Internet research skills, but librarians are often useful in this area.

What's the correct way to follow up on a resume you send?

There is a polite way to be aggressively interested in a company during your job hunt. It is ideal to end the cover letter accompanying your resume by saying, "I hope you'll welcome my call next week when I try to arrange a brief meeting at your convenience to discuss your current and future needs and how I might serve them." Keep it low key, and just ask for a "brief meeting," not an interview. Employers want people who show a determined interest in working with them, so don't be shy about following up on the resume and cover letter you've mailed.

STEP THREE: Preparing for Interviews

It pays to be aware of the 14 most common pitfalls for job hunters.

But a resume and cover letter by themselves can't get you the job you want. You need to "prep" yourself before the interview. Step Three in your job campaign is "Preparing for Interviews." First, let's look at interviewing from the hiring organization's point of view.

What are the biggest "turnoffs" for potential employers?

One of the ways to help yourself perform well at an interview is to look at the main reasons why organizations *don't* hire the people they interview, according to those who do the interviewing.

Notice that "lack of appropriate background" (or lack of experience) is the *last* reason for not being offered the job.

The 14 Most Common Reasons Job Hunters Are Not Offered Jobs (according to the companies who do the interviewing and hiring):

1. Low level of accomplishment
2. Poor attitude, lack of self-confidence
3. Lack of goals/objectives
4. Lack of enthusiasm
5. Lack of interest in the company's business
6. Inability to sell or express yourself
7. Unrealistic salary demands
8. Poor appearance
9. Lack of maturity, no leadership potential
10. Lack of extracurricular activities
11. Lack of preparation for the interview, no knowledge about company
12. Objecting to travel
13. Excessive interest in security and benefits
14. Inappropriate background

Department of Labor studies have proven that smart, "prepared" job hunters can increase their beginning salary while getting a job in *half* the time it normally takes. (4½ months is the average national length of a job search.) Here, from PREP, are some questions that can prepare you to find a job faster.

Are you in the "right" frame of mind?

It seems unfair that we have to look for a job just when we're lowest in morale. Don't worry *too* much if you're nervous before interviews. You're supposed to be a little nervous, especially if the job means a lot to you. But the best way to kill unnecessary fears about job hunting is through 1) making sure you have a great resume and 2) preparing yourself for the interview. Here are three main areas you need to think about before each interview.

Do you know what the company does?

Don't walk into an interview giving the impression that, "If this is Tuesday, this must be General Motors."

Find out before the interview what the company's main product or service is. Where is the company heading? Is it in a "growth" or declining industry? (Answers to these questions may influence whether or not you want to work there!)

Information about what the company does is in annual reports, in newspaper and magazine articles, and on the Internet. If you're not yet skilled at Internet research, just visit your nearest library and ask the reference librarian to guide you to printed materials on the company.

Do you know what you want to do for the company?

Before the interview, try to decide how you see yourself fitting into the company. Remember, "lack of exact background" the company wants is usually the last reason people are not offered jobs.

Understand before you go to each interview that the burden will be on you to "sell" the interviewer on why you're the best person for the job and the company.

How will you answer the critical interview questions?

Put yourself in the interviewer's position and think about the questions you're most likely to be asked. Here are some of the most commonly asked interview questions:

Q: *"What are your greatest strengths?"*
A: Don't say you've never thought about it! Go into an interview knowing the three main impressions you want to leave about yourself, such as "I'm hard-working, loyal, and an imaginative cost-cutter."

Q: *"What are your greatest weaknesses?"*
A: Don't confess that you're lazy or have trouble meeting deadlines! Confessing that you tend to be a "workaholic" or "tend to be a perfectionist and sometimes get frustrated when others don't share my high standards" will make your prospective employer see a "weakness" that he likes. Name a weakness that your interviewer will perceive as a strength.

Q: *"What are your long-range goals?"*
A: If you're interviewing with Microsoft, don't say you want to work for IBM in five years! Say your long-range goal is to be *with* the company, contributing to its goals and success.

Q: *"What motivates you to do your best work?"*
A: Don't get dollar signs in your eyes here! "A challenge" is not a bad answer, but it's a little cliched. Saying something like "troubleshooting" or "solving a tough problem" is more interesting and specific. Give an example if you can.

Research the company before you go to interviews.

Anticipate the questions you will be asked at the interview, and prepare your responses in advance.

Q: "What do you know about this organization?"

A: Don't say you never heard of it until they asked you to the interview! Name an interesting, positive thing you learned about the company recently from your research. Remember, company executives can sometimes feel rather "maternal" about the company they serve. Don't get onto a negative area of the company if you can think of positive facts you can bring up. Of course, if you learned in your research that the company's sales seem to be taking a nose-dive, or that the company president is being prosecuted for taking bribes, you might politely ask your interviewer to tell you something that could help you better understand what you've been reading. Those are the kinds of company facts that can help you determine whether or not you want to work there.

Q: "Why should I hire you?"

A: "I'm unemployed and available" is the wrong answer here! Get back to your strengths and say that you believe the organization could benefit by a loyal, hard-working cost-cutter like yourself.

In conclusion, you should decide in advance, before you go to the interview, how you will answer each of these commonly asked questions. Have some practice interviews with a friend to role-play and build your confidence.

STEP FOUR: Handling the Interview and Negotiating Salary

Now you're ready for Step Four: actually handling the interview successfully and effectively. Remember, the purpose of an interview is to get a job offer.

Eight "do's" for the interview

According to leading U.S. companies, there are eight key areas in interviewing success. You can fail at an interview if you mishandle just one area.

1. **Do wear appropriate clothes.**
   You can never go wrong by wearing a suit to an interview.

2. **Do be well groomed.**
   Don't overlook the obvious things like having clean hair, clothes, and fingernails for the interview.

3. **Do give a firm handshake.**
   You'll have to shake hands twice in most interviews: first, before you sit down, and second, when you leave the interview. Limp handshakes turn most people off.

4. **Do smile and show a sense of humor.**
   Interviewers are looking for people who would be nice to work with, so don't be so somber that you don't smile. In fact, research shows that people who smile at interviews are perceived as more intelligent. So, smile!

5. **Do be enthusiastic.**
   Employers say they are "turned off" by lifeless, unenthusiastic job hunters who show no special interest in that company. The best way to show some enthusiasm for the employer's operation is to find out about the business beforehand.

Go to an interview prepared to tell the company why it should hire you.

A smile at an interview makes the employer perceive of you as intelligent!

6. Do show you are flexible and adaptable.

An employer is looking for someone who can contribute to his organization in a flexible, adaptable way. No matter what skills and training you have, employers know every new employee must go through initiation and training on the company's turf. Certainly show pride in your past accomplishments in a specific, factual way ("I saved my last employer $50.00 a week by a new cost-cutting measure I developed"). But don't come across as though there's nothing about the job you couldn't easily handle.

7. Do ask intelligent questions about the employer's business.

An employer is hiring someone because of certain business needs. Show interest in those needs. Asking questions to get a better idea of the employer's needs will help you "stand out" from other candidates interviewing for the job.

8. Do "take charge" when the interviewer "falls down" on the job.

Employers are seeking people with good attitudes whom they can train and coach to do things their way.

Go into every interview knowing the three or four points about yourself you want the interviewer to remember. And be prepared to take an active part in leading the discussion if the interviewer's "canned approach" does not permit you to display your "strong suit." You can't always depend on the interviewer's asking you the "right" questions so you can stress your strengths and accomplishments.

An important "don't": Don't ask questions about salary or benefits at the first interview.
Employers don't take warmly to people who look at their organization as just a place to satisfy salary and benefit needs. Don't risk making a negative impression by appearing greedy or self-serving. The place to discuss salary and benefits is normally at the second interview, and the employer will bring it up. Then you can ask questions without appearing excessively interested in what the organization can do for you.

Now...negotiating your salary
Even if an ad requests that you communicate your "salary requirement" or "salary history," you should avoid providing those numbers in your initial cover letter. You can usually say something like this: "I would be delighted to discuss the private details of my salary history with you in person."

Once you're at the interview, you must avoid even appearing *interested* in salary before you are offered the job. Make sure you've "sold" yourself before talking salary. First show you're the "best fit" for the employer and then you'll be in a stronger position from which to negotiate salary. **Never** bring up the subject of salary yourself. Employers say there's no way you can avoid looking greedy if you bring up the issue of salary and benefits before the company has identified you as its "best fit."

Don't appear excessively interested in salary and benefits at the interview.

Interviewers sometimes throw out a salary figure at the first interview to see if you'll accept it. You may not want to commit yourself if you think you will be able to negotiate a better deal later on. Get back to finding out more about the job. This lets the interviewer know you're interested primarily in the job and not the salary.

When the organization brings up salary, it may say something like this: "Well, Mary, we think you'd make a good candidate for this job. What kind of salary are we talking about?" You may not want to name a number here, either. Give the ball back to the interviewer. Act as though you hadn't given the subject of salary much thought and respond something like this: "Ah, Mr. Jones, I wonder if you'd be kind enough to tell me what salary you had in mind when you advertised the job?" Or ... "What is the range you have in mind?"

Don't worry, if the interviewer names a figure that you think is too low, you can say so without turning down the job or locking yourself into a rigid position. The point here is to negotiate for yourself as well as you can. You might reply to a number named by the interviewer that you think is low by saying something like this: "Well, Mr. Lee, the job interests me very much, and I think I'd certainly enjoy working with you. But, frankly, I was thinking of something a little higher than that." That leaves the ball in your interviewer's court again, and you haven't turned down the job either, in case it turns out that the interviewer can't increase the offer and you still want the job.

Salary negotiation can be tricky.

Last, send a follow-up letter.

Mail, e-mail, or fax a letter right after the interview telling your interviewer you enjoyed the meeting and are certain (if you are) that you are the "best fit" for the job. The people interviewing you will probably have an attitude described as either "professionally loyal" to their companies, or "maternal and proprietary" if the interviewer also owns the company. In either case, they are looking for people who want to work for *that* company in particular. The follow-up letter you send might be just the deciding factor in your favor if the employer is trying to choose between you and someone else. You will see an example of a follow-up letter on page 16.

A follow-up letter can help the employer choose between you and another qualified candidate.

A cover letter is an essential part of a job hunt or career change.

Many people are aware of the importance of having a great resume, but most people in a job hunt don't realize just how important a cover letter can be. The purpose of the cover letter, sometimes called a **"letter of interest,"** is to introduce your resume to prospective employers. The cover letter is often the critical ingredient in a job hunt because the cover letter allows you to say a lot of things that just don't "fit" on the resume. For example, you can emphasize your commitment to a new field and stress your related talents. The cover letter also gives you a chance to stress outstanding character and personal values. On the next two pages you will see examples of very effective cover letters.

A cover letter is an essential part of a career change.

Please do not attempt to implement a career change without a cover letter. A cover letter is the first impression of you, and you can influence the way an employer views you by the language and style of your letter.

Special help for those in career change

We want to emphasize again that, especially in a career change, the cover letter is very important and can help you "build a bridge" to a new career. A creative and appealing cover letter can begin the process of encouraging the potential employer to imagine you in an industry other than the one in which you have worked.

As a special help to those in career change, there are resumes and cover letters included in this book which show valuable techniques and tips you should use when changing fields or industries. The resumes and cover letters of career changers are identified in the table of contents as "Career Change" and you will see the "Career Change" label on cover letters in Part Two where the individuals are changing careers.

Date

**Addressing the Cover
Letter:** Get the exact
name of the person to
whom you are writing. This
makes your approach
personal.

Exact Name of Person
Exact Title of Person
Company Name
Address
City, State Zip

Dear Sir or Madam:

With the enclosed resume, I would like to make you aware of my strong desire to become a part of your organization's management trainee program.

Second Paragraph: You
have a chance to talk
about whatever you feel is
your most distinguishing
feature.

As you will see from my resume, I recently earned my Bachelor of Science in Hotel Management degree at Cornell University. Since it has always been my childhood dream to become a General Manager for a hospitality industry firm, my college graduation was an especially meaningful event in my life. My parents operated a "mom-and-pop" restaurant throughout my youth, and a love for the industry "got in my blood."

Third Paragraph: You
bring up your next most
distinguishing qualities and
try to
sell yourself.

While earning my college degree, I recently completed internships with major hospitality industry firms, and I successfully assumed all the duties of an assistant catering manager. During those internships, under the guidance of experienced restaurant and hotel professionals, I wrote a project development plan, and I also developed a new vegetarian menu for an established restaurant. The menu has been test marketed in five select cities, and the preliminary results indicate that the menu will be adopted nationally.

Fourth Paragraph: Here
you have another
opportunity to reveal
qualities or achievements
which will impress your
future employer.

In summer jobs while earning my college degree, I worked in all aspects of the hospitality industry as I held part-time jobs as a waitress and hostess. I am highly skilled at working as part of a team on restaurant crews, and I am dedicated to the highest standards of profitability and customer service.

Final Paragraph: She
asks the employer to
contact her. Make sure
your reader knows what
the "next step" is.

If you can use a highly motivated young professional with unlimited personal initiative as well as strong personal qualities of dependability and trustworthiness, I hope you will contact me to suggest a time when we might meet to discuss your needs. I can provide excellent personal and professional references, and I am eager to apply my natural creativity and industry knowledge to benefit a hospitality industry firm.

Sincerely,

**Alternate Final
Paragraph:** It's more
aggressive (but not too
aggressive) to let the
employer know that you
will be calling him or her.
Don't be afraid to be
persistent. Employers are
looking for people who
know what they want to
do.

Melanie Thompson

Alternate final paragraph:
I hope you will welcome my call soon when I contact you to try to arrange a brief meeting to discuss your needs and how my talents might help you. I appreciate whatever time you could give me in the process of exploring your needs.

Date

Exact Name of Person
Title or Position
Name of Company
Address (number and street)
Address (city, state, and zip)

Dear Exact Name of Person: (or Dear Sir or Madam if answering a blind ad)

I would appreciate an opportunity to talk with you soon about how I could contribute to your organization through my experience as a Waitress and Hostess along with my knowledge of the restaurant business. Mr. Thomas Crane, a General Manager with the Princess Cruise Lines, recently made me aware of the career opportunities available within your organization, and he strongly encouraged me to approach you. I am interested in discussing employment opportunities with you.

You will see from my resume that I began working when I was 16 years old while I was in high school. I have become a skilled waitress while working in various restaurants, and I had an opportunity to learn from veteran industry professionals.

Most recently I have worked as a Hostess for an upscale restaurant, and I am respected for my gracious style of interacting with the public. I have become skilled at hiring, training, and supervising restaurant personnel, including waitstaff and kitchen prep workers.

Although I am held in the highest regard by my current employer, I have decided to explore career opportunities outside my current firm. I am seeking an employer who can use a highly motivated individual with strong communication skills and an outstanding employment record. I am aware that becoming a part of a cruise line would involve extensive travel, and I am ready for that challenge. I am single and available for frequent and extended travel as your needs require.

If you can use a self-starter who could rapidly become a valuable part of your organization, I hope you will contact me to suggest a time when we might meet to discuss your needs and how I might serve them. I can provide outstanding references.

Sincerely,

Lonnie Patton

cc: Thomas Crane

Date

Exact Name of Person
Title or Position
Name of Company
Address (number and street)
Address (city, state, and zip)

Dear Exact Name:

I am writing to express my appreciation for the time you spent with me on 9 December, and I want to let you know that I am sincerely interested in the position of Controller which we discussed.

I feel confident that I could skillfully interact with your 60-person work force, and I would cheerfully travel as your needs require. I want you to know, too, that I would not consider relocating to Salt Lake City to be a hardship! It is certainly one of the most beautiful areas I have ever seen.

As you described to me what you are looking for in the person who fills this position, I had a sense of "déjà vu" because my current boss was in a similar position when I went to work for him. He needed someone to come in and be his "right arm" and take on an increasing amount of his management responsibilities so that he could be freed up to do other things. I have played a key role in the growth and profitability of his multiunit business, and he has come to depend on my sound financial and business advice as much as my day-to-day management skills. Since Christmas is the busiest time of the year in the restaurant business, I feel that I could not leave him during that time. I could certainly make myself available by mid-January.

It would be a pleasure to work for a successful individual such as yourself, and I feel I could contribute significantly to your hotel chain not only through my accounting and business background but also through my strong qualities of loyalty, reliability, and trustworthiness. I am confident that I could learn Quick Books rapidly, and I would welcome being trained to do things your way.

Yours sincerely,

Jacob Evangelisto

PART TWO:

Experienced Professionals

ACCOUNTING, BANKING, CREDIT & INSURANCE

Date

Exact Name of Person
Title or Position
Name of Company
Address (no., street)
Address (city, state, zip)

Accounting/Auditing

Dear Exact Name of Person: (or Dear Sir or Madam if answering a blind ad.)

I would appreciate an opportunity to talk with you soon about how I could contribute to your organization through my experience in a "Big 6" accounting firm, my strong analytical and communication skills, as well as my proven management ability and executive potential.

You will see from my enclosed resume that I am presently a Staff Auditor with Cooper & Lybrands in Charlotte, NC. I have learned a great deal working with this national CPA firm and feel that I am at a point in my life where I would like to make the move to private industry. I have been given the opportunity to complete an audit on my own — from planning to preparing the financial statements — and have traveled throughout the state as well as to clients outside of North Carolina to participate in audits. Having worked with banks, retail operations, and manufacturing firms I feel that I have become adept at dealing with senior management with professionalism and maturity. I graduated **summa cum laude** with a B.S. in Accounting.

Through my earlier summer/seasonal jobs as a Bank Teller and retail Sales Associate/ Cashier, I gained skills related to inventory control, sales, and customer service, thereby displaying my adaptability and willingness to try new things.

Since earning my B.S. in Accounting with honors, I have become familiar with computer applications and am proficient in Word, PageMaker, Powerpoint and Excel software.

Certain that I offer the educational background and experience necessary to make significant contributions to your organization, I also offer strong personal qualities that include persistence, dependability, and initiative. A proven team player, I work well independently or contribute to group efforts. I can provide exceptionally strong personal and professional references. I am known for my strong decision-making skills and common sense.

I hope you will welcome my call soon to arrange a brief meeting at your convenience to discuss your current and future needs and how I might serve them. Thank you in advance for your time.

Sincerely yours,

Monique Uzuega

Alternate last paragraph:
I hope you will call or write me soon to suggest a time convenient for us to meet and discuss your current and future needs and how I might serve them. Thank you in advance for your time.

MONIQUE UZUEGA

1110½ Hay Street, Fayetteville, NC 28305   •   preppub@aol.com   •   (910) 483-6611

OBJECTIVE

To offer my experience and education in accounting to an organization that can use a self disciplined and mature young professional with a strong interest in making contributions through my talents, drive, and dedication to excellence.

EDUCATION

B.S., Accounting, Hampton University, Hampton, VA, 2003.
- Graduated *summa cum laude* with a 3.5 GPA.
- Placed on the Dean's List and was named to Alpha Kappa Mu Honor Society.
- Was inducted into the Accounting Honor Society.
- Was selected by faculty members to tutor other students in the department.

PROFESSIONAL TRAINING

Attended Coopers & Lybrand corporate training programs in the following areas:
depository institution auditing — procedures for auditing banks
advanced auditing — planning the audit
introduction to auditing

SPECIAL SKILLS

Offer proficiency with software including:
Word   PageMaker   Powerpoint   Excel

EXPERIENCE

STAFF AUDITOR. Coopers & Lybrand, L.L.P., Charlotte, NC (2003-present). Have earned a reputation as a talented and proficient professional who can handle the responsibilities of taking charge of large projects and bringing them to completion while building strong working relations with senior personnel in various industries.
- Was aggressively recruited by this "Big 6" accounting firm and other companies in my senior year; have excelled in every task I have undertaken and am being groomed for further rapid promotion by this national CPA firm.
- Planned audits for clients in industries including banking, retail, and manufacturing.
- Provided valuable insights into the development of individual audit plans, evaluation of internal accounting controls, and preparation of each audit program.
- Became knowledgeable of the proper techniques for auditing accounts ranging from cash, fixed assets, accounts receivable, accounts payable, and investment accounts.
- Used my sharp analytical skills to determine and document changes in accounts.
- Learned to obtain information from clients in an unobtrusive way so that the audit could be completed and to make suggestions which would improve their work flow.
- Performed tests used to determine that the clients had control over their internal accounting systems and that they were working properly.
- Contributed to team efforts in the preparation of client financial statements.
- Traveled throughout the state and made visits to clients outside NC.

Gained practical work experience and earned a reputation for dedication, honesty, and dependability in summer jobs including the following:
BANK TELLER. NationsBank, Charlotte, NC (2001-03). Polished my public relations skills while processing customer transactions including accepting deposits, cashing checks, processing withdrawals, and selling savings bonds and money orders. Received on-the-job training in the bank's on-line computer system.

SALES ASSOCIATE and CASHIER. Germany (1999-00). Learned customer service and sales skills in two different retail locations: worked in a shore store and then in a record, video, and electronics outlet.
- Gained experience in a range of activities including: stocking incoming merchandise, closing registers at the end of the day, balancing daily receipts, and setting up display.
- Displayed maturity which resulted in my selection to train other employees as cashiers.

PERSONAL

An avid sports enthusiast, was active in sports management in high school : managed the track and field as well as basketball teams; traveled in Europe on the school dance, basketball, and football teams. Was specially selected treasurer of my high school yearbook. Was elected sophomore class vice president. Enjoy travel and find it easy to join a team.

ACCOUNTING, BANKING, CREDIT & INSURANCE

Date

Exact Name of Person
Title or Position
Name of Company
Address (no., street)
Address (city, state, zip)

Banking Management

Dear Exact Name of Person: (or Dear Sir or Madam if answering a blind ad.)

I would appreciate an opportunity to talk with you soon about how I could contribute to your organization through my extensive management experience in most functional areas of banking.

As you will l see from my resume, I have enjoyed a track record of promotion within one of the leading financial institutions in the South. I have often worn multiple "hats" and am known for my ability to oversee complex responsibilities in numerous areas simultaneously. For example, in my current position as a vice president, I oversee the Operations, Human Resources, and Compliance areas for the bank, and I have actually developed the bank's Deposit Compliance Program.

If you feel your management team could benefit from my in-depth experience, creative problem-solving style, and reputation as a strategist and visionary, I would be delighted to make myself available at your convenience to discuss your needs and goals and how I might help you achieve them. I am very highly regarded by my current employer and, although I can provide exceptionally strong references, I would appreciate your not contacting my employer until after we meet.

I hope you will welcome my call soon to arrange a brief meeting at your convenience to discuss your current and future needs and how I might serve them. Thank you in advance for your time.

Sincerely yours,

Karen Brice

Alternate last paragraph:
I hope you will call or write me soon to suggest a time convenient for us to meet and discuss your current and future needs and how I might serve them. Thank you in advance for your time.

KAREN BRICE

1110½ Hay Street, Fayetteville, NC 28305 • preppub@aol.com • (910) 483-6611

OBJECTIVE	To contribute to an organization that can use an innovative manager who believes that "the sky is the limit" when persistence, creativity, and attention to detail are combined with superior planning, time management, organizational, communication, and problem-solving skills.
SUMMARY OF EXPERIENCE	*For more than 12 years, have built a "track record" of accomplishment in positions of increasing responsibility at Southern Citizen Bank, Atlanta, GA; have earned a reputation as a dynamic motivator, skilled trainer, and creative organizer.*

EXPERIENCE

VICE PRESIDENT, OPERATIONS/HUMAN RESOURCES/COMPLIANCE. (2003-present). Was promoted to handle additional responsibilities related to consumer compliance while continuing to handle responsibilities described in the Assistant Vice President job below.
- Developed Deposit Compliance Program for consumer law and regulation.
- Personally conduct compliance testing (audits) and the training program; have trained approximately 25 employees in this specific area.
- Have become very experienced in internal auditing for compliance.

ASSISTANT VICE PRESIDENT, OPERATIONS/HUMAN RESOURCES. (2001-03). In this highly visible, fast-paced position reporting to bank president, am wearing "three hats," balancing responsibilities in human resources, operations, and investments.
- **Management:** Directly supervise five people, ensuring that assigned responsibilities are executed in a systematic and effective manner.
- **Operations:** In coordination with top management, develop and implement plans and policies that affect accounting, bookkeeping, and data processing of the main office and two branches.
- **Human Resources:** Apply my expert knowledge to develop, maintain, and administer all personnel policies as they apply to 25 bank employees; oversee EEO compliance, recruitment, safety & health.
- **Benefits Administration:** Oversee all salary and benefit functions, including 401(k) pension plan and Blue Cross/Blue Shield health plan.
- **Finances:** Manage an investment portfolio utilizing excess funds per day while efficiently planning and administering the department's budget.
- **Training:** In addition to coordinating in-house programs on personnel policies, organize and conduct training on compliance with demand deposit, regular direct deposit, bank privacy and other regulations.

OPERATIONS OFFICER. (1996-01). Excelled in directing all aspects of the Operations Department because of my versatile management skills.
- After thoroughly researching computer hardware/software programs, introduced NCR 77 proof machines to improve the efficiency of bank transactions.
- Reviewed surveys of community banks and made recommendations on competitively pricing products.
- As a member of the Strategic Planning Committee, offered input on personnel and operational issues.
- Managed all day-to-day bookkeeping functions and monitored the bank's cash position, making investments or borrowing funds as appropriate. Supervised five employees.

HEAD BOOKKEEPER. (1995-1996). Ensured the highest standards of customer service while supervising and reviewing the work of five assistants. Balanced general ledger accounts.
- Processed overdrafts, returns items, and ACH debits and credits.
- Opened checking, savings, and certificate of deposit accounts.

PROOF OPERATOR. (1994-1995). While learning the basics of office management, acquired precise habits balancing, encoding, endorsing, and filming all items related to deposits with a proof machine.

EDUCATION & TRAINING

B.S., **Accounting**, Fayetteville State University; expected in 2004.
Excelled in the following courses:

Principles of Management	Introduction to Computers	Supervision
Business Communication	Banking and Finance	Accounting

Attended seminars on sexual harassment, interviewing & hiring, state and federal wages, personnel policies (developing/implementing), public speaking, and check processing.

PERSONAL

Knowledge of Word, Excel, and Twin. Self motivated professional with a reputation as a team leader.

ACCOUNTING, BANKING, CREDIT & INSURANCE

Date

Exact Name of Person
Title or Position
Name of Company
Address (no., street)
Address (city, state, zip)

Customer Service

Dear Exact Name of Person: (or Dear Sir or Madam if answering a blind ad.)

I would appreciate an opportunity to talk with you soon about my strong interest in receiving consideration for a position in Public Relations. I believe I offer the enthusiasm, talent, and knowledge that make me a professional who can make important contributions to First Union National Bank in this area.

As you will see from my enclosed resume, I am presently a Client Services Representative who consistently places at the top of my peer group in internal performance evaluations. I rapidly advanced from Administrative Assistant in the consumer banking department, gained experience as a Teller, and then advanced to this position where I represent the bank while opening new accounts and selling bank products to our clients.

My ability to develop interesting and informative written materials was discovered in high school when I edited the yearbook. While attending Peace College in Raleigh for my first two years of studies, I was selected to edit the college yearbook and was credited with producing an attractive and well-organized publication. I went on to earn a degree in Mass Communications from the University of North Carolina at Chapel Hill where I wrote for the college newspaper and was active in leadership roles in the student government. I have become involved in the Junior League and am now serving this organization as the Public Relations chairman in a role which includes preparing all newspaper releases about the organization and its civic activities.

I believe that through my enthusiasm, experience, and talent I can make valuable contributions in preparing products which will enhance the bank's ability to sell services to the public and gain new clients through informative and interesting written materials.

I hope you will call or write me soon to suggest a time convenient for us to discuss how I would fit into the bank's public relations efforts and how I might continue to serve most effectively. Thank you in advance for your time.

Sincerely,

Kerry Zaeske

KERRY ZAESKE

1110½ Hay Street, Fayetteville, NC 28305 • preppub@aol.com • (910) 483-6611

OBJECTIVE

To offer my strong verbal and written communication skills along with my knowledge of and experience in banking and finance to an organization that can benefit from my ability to translate ideas and concepts into interesting and informative materials.

EDUCATION

B.S. in Mass Communications, University of North Carolina at Chapel Hill, NC, 2001.
- Maintained a cumulative GPA of above 3.0.
- Wrote articles for the college newspaper.
- Contributed my organizational and leadership abilities while coordinating functions, arranging for speakers, and planning festivals, pageants, and other social events as the elected secretary of the student government's Student Activities Committee.
Attended Peace College, Raleigh, NC, for my first two years of basic studies in the Liberal Arts.
- Selected by faculty advisors to edit the college yearbook during my sophomore year, applied my communication skills and creativity to write copy for and produce a well-organized and attractive publication.
- Polished skills gained while editing my high school yearbook.

EXPERIENCE

CLIENT SERVICES REPRESENTATIVE. First Union National Bank, Charlotte, NC (2003-present). After a short period of time as an Administrative Assistant in the consumer banking department, was soon selected to gain experience as a Teller before advancing to this highly visible role as the public's first contact with the bank and its services.
- Consistently placed at the top of my peer group within the region according to the bank's system of internal performance ratings.
- Displayed the ability to listen to people's financial needs and requirements in order to recommend products such as Certificates of Deposit, MasterCard and VISA credit cards, and savings accounts and to open accounts.

SALES REPRESENTATIVE. Carlyle & Co., Fayetteville, NC (2001-03). Consistently met aggressive sales goals through both my patience and persistence in public relations and customer service.
- Became known as a goal-driven, skilled professional who could be counted to always deliver customer satisfaction.

ADMINISTRATIVE ASSISTANT. First Union National Bank, Fayetteville, NC (2001-02). Gained valuable experience in banking procedures and all phases of the loan process while providing clerical and administrative support to two regional vice presidents specializing in the area of consumer credit.
- Used my talent for organization and attention to detail while creating spreadsheets, typing, and maintaining files for two busy executives.
- Improved the filing system for increased efficiency.
- Refined my communication skills dealing with banking professionals on a regular basis.
- Polished my knowledge of computer operations using Word and Excel software while typing memos and correspondence as well as handling financial record keeping.

LEGAL OFFICE INTERN. Office of the District Attorney, Fayetteville, NC (1998-99). Gained valuable exposure to the workings of the law while aiding assistant district attorneys in such activities as contacting witnesses to remind them of court appearances; became familiar with the court system and legal procedures while learning to work with elected officials.
- Ensured persons pleading "not guilty" were aware of how to respond to questioning; learned to write guilty pleas.
- Earned a reputation for my maturity and judgment displayed while relating to a variety of people from all socioeconomic and age groups.

PERSONAL

Am an articulate speaker and skilled writer. Offer a creative and enthusiastic approach to project development and the organizational skills to see them to completion. Enjoy dealing with the public and making contributions to my community.

ACCOUNTING, BANKING, CREDIT & INSURANCE

Date

Mr. Jerry Vestry
American Express Financial Services
Suite 2220
Tampa, FL 33062

Financial Consulting

Dear Mr. Vestry:

With the enclosed resume, I am responding to your ad in the *Wall Street Journal* for a Financial Services Coordinator.

As you will see from my resume, I have most recently excelled as a Financial Consultant with one of the leading financial services companies in the nation.

Your ad mentioned that your ideal candidate "will have some understanding of commodities markets and will possess a proven ability to use technical knowledge in a creative way." Prior to becoming a Financial Consultant, I worked as a Commodities Broker, and I possess an expert understanding of commodities markets. After years of studying different markets and many charts, I have noticed all markets exhibit the same natural recurring tendencies. My ideas and systems revolve around these principles. My investment objectives are simple; to make as much money as the markets will yield during a given time frame. Constantly evolving and changing, markets go through lively phases and dead, illiquid phases. While some markets are best daytraded, others are good for position trades only. Other markets are good for being short option premium and nothing else. No one trading system works all the time. Conditions must be appraised before any objective, strategy, or individual trading tactic can be employed. I have devised systems and principles to be used during different market environments, and I have used them successfully in reaping huge financial rewards.

If you are seeking someone who offers extensive experience in nearly every type of financial market, I would enjoy the opportunity to meet with you in person to discuss further details of the position you advertised. I can provide excellent personal and professional references, including from my current employer, but I would prefer if you did not contact my current employer until after we meet in person to discuss your needs. Thank you in advance for your time and your consideration.

Sincerely yours,

Hugh Dudley

HUGH DUDLEY

1110½ Hay Street, Fayetteville, NC 28305 • preppub@aol.com • (910) 483-6611

OBJECTIVE   To benefit an organization that can use an experienced manager with strong consulting skills along with expert knowledge of financial products including investments, savings, and protection and credit products.

LICENSES   Have the following NASD licenses:
  Series 7 — General Securities Agent
  Series 65 — Uniform Investment Adviser
  Series 63 — Uniform Securities Agent
Became a registered Commodities Broker as of February, 2001.
Became a member, Chicago Board of Trade and the Chicago Board Options Exchange, 1996; acquired seats on and received my license to trade on both exchanges.

EDUCATION   Graduated *cum laude* with a B.A. degree in Business Administration and Accounting, Tufts University, Medford, MA, 1994; member, Alpha Chi National Honorary.
  • Entered college as a biology major; upon taking my first investment course, discovered my love of the investment business, and made 37 A's out of 38 courses through my senior year.

ELECTED & ACADEMIC HONORS
  • Received 1994 *Wall Street Journal* award given annually to top Business Administration student.
  • Elected President, Business and Economics Club.
  • Was the honored recipient of the award given to the top business student.
  • Won scholarships from two major corporations/institutions.

EXPERIENCE   **FINANCIAL CONSULTANT.** Smith Barney, Panama City, FL (2002-03). Developed a base of clients for whom I devised financial strategies to help them achieve the long-term financial goals which I had helped them identify.
  • Established portfolios for clients and selected appropriate investments based on client age, desire for asset growth, need for diversification, risk profile, and other factors.
  • Helped several clients realize very large increases in their total asset base.
  • Refined my ability to assess financial needs, provide prudent advice, and close a sale.
  • Excelled in building relationships and cementing trust while gaining valuable sales and customer relations experience in a financial services environment.

COMMODITIES BROKER. LaFayette Commodities, Chicago, IL (1998-02). Placed customer orders directly to trading pits and worked with customers on investment strategies; became familiar with many "do's and don'ts" of trading by observing customer trading tendencies and through my own experiences.
  • As a Broker, learned what type of order to use during different market environments.
  • Have been trading my own account from a home office since July, 2002; have full equipment setup, instant quotes, and direct access to the trading pits by phone.

OEX MARKET MAKER. CBC Options, Chicago Board Options Exchange, Chicago, IL (1996). Trained to become a floor trader and learned how to execute trades and manage investment/portfolio risks; applied different strategies while managing an equity trading account and refined my ability to make sound investment decisions in a fast-paced environment; became regarded as an "expert" on the options market and its strategies.

PERSONAL   Extremely computer literature. Highly motivated self starter. Excellent references.

ACCOUNTING, BANKING, CREDIT & INSURANCE

Date

Exact Name of Person
Title or Position
Name of Company
Address (no., street)
Address (city, state, zip)

Financial Services Support

Dear Exact Name of Person: (or Dear Sir or Madam if answering a blind ad.)

I would appreciate an opportunity to talk with you soon about how I could benefit your organization through my experience in sales, customer service, marketing, and management. I have just relocated to the Palm Beach area, and I feel my experience and skills could be of considerable value to your organization.

Most recently I have excelled as an Administrative Assistant for a financial services firm, and I excelled in handling a variety of tasks in areas which included pre-sale, underwriting, customer service, computer operation, accounts payable/receivable, and health insurance processing. In prior jobs, I gained excellent time-management and organizational skills while working at a variety of jobs while attending school full-time. I have experience in handling a wide range of financial procedures and possess excellent communication, planning, and time-management abilities.

I have earned a reputation for my ability to rapidly master new tasks and solve thorny problems. I am accustomed to operating on the "front line," making decisions and maximizing resources while handling a wide range of financial transactions in a fast-paced environment. You would find me to be a congenial person who prides myself on my ability to rapidly become a valuable part of a team.

The address and phone number on my resume are those of my parents, because my husband and I are in the process of househunting in the Palm Beach area and do not yet have a telephone connected. My parents will be able to get messages to me reliably and quickly, so please call them and leave a message and I will get in touch with you right away. I hope I will have an opportunity to meet with you to discuss your needs and how I might serve them. I can guarantee that you would be getting a very valuable employee, and I can provide outstanding personal and professional references which will attest to that fact.

Sincerely yours,

Carmen Lopez

Financial Services Support

CARMEN LOPEZ

1110½ Hay Street, Fayetteville, NC 28305 • preppub@aol.com • (910) 483-6611

OBJECTIVE

To benefit an organization seeking a hard-working, results-oriented business and financial professional with top-notch skills in accounting, marketing, and sales as well as excellent organizational and time-management skills.

EDUCATION

B.S. in Business Administration with a minor in Marketing, Fayetteville State University, Fayetteville, NC, May 2002; consistently made both Dean's List and Chancellor's List.

COMPUTERS

Proficient in Microsoft Word, Excel, PowerPoint, and software specific to insurance industry or The Principal including Quicken.

EXPERIENCE

ADMINISTRATIVE ASSISTANT. Prudential Financial Group, Raleigh, NC (2003-present). Have excelled in several functional areas while working with this financial services firm.

- *Pre-sale*: Handle correspondence including mass mailings to prospects, letters to individual prospects, or referrals from existing clients.
- *Underwriting*: Process new business applications; review applications for completion, complete Field Office Report, order underwriting requirements, submit application to appropriate Home Office service team, communicate with case coordinator and/or underwriter as case proceeds through underwriting.
- *Customer service*: Perform extensive customer service.
- *Quicken/AR/AP*: Handle accounts receivable, accounts payable, and/or Quicken entries for bookkeeping.
- *Health insurance*: Assemble quotes from different health carriers or prepare quotes using carriers' rate book, process applications, and prepare policies for delivery.

CHILD SUPPORT INTERN. Superior Clerk of Court, Cumberland County, NC (2002). Served a three month internship providing financial, clerical, and administrative support to the Child Support Division; performed general clerical and data entry functions.

- Handled a wide range of financial transactions, including processing bad checks.
- Prepared docket sheets for use by the Cumberland County District Attorney.

Paid for my college education and refined my time-management and organizational skills working various part-time and full-time jobs while attending school full-time.
CASHIER/WAITRESS/HOSTESS. Peaden's Seafood, Fayetteville, NC (2002). Wore several hats in this popular and fast-paced restaurant, including seating customers, waiting on customers, and serving as cashier.

CASHIER/SALES ASSOCIATE. Sam's Club, Fayetteville, NC (1998-02). Performed a wide range of cash-handling procedures in addition to promoting and selling both individual and commercial discount club memberships.

- Provided accurate cash-flow, register reconciliation, and refunds, as well as answering and resolving customer questions and complaints.
- Assisted new members in choosing appropriate membership, completing necessary forms, and inputting data to generate membership cards and accounts.
- Provided product information and recommendations while assisting in purchases.

ADMINISTRATIVE ASSISTANT. Hillcrest Junior High School, Fayetteville, NC (1993-98). Acted as school's "front-line," providing a wide range of administrative and clerical procedures working in this busy office.

- Registered new students, processed and updated student files, sorted and distributed incoming mail, scheduled parent-teacher conferences, and performed clerical tasks.
- Processed purchase orders, managed inventory, made deposits, maintained petty cash.
- Prepared 5-year school review report for school officials and community leaders.
- Assisted in coordinating school events and activities.

PERSONAL

Excellent personal and professional references available on request. Am a flexible, versatile professional who enjoys challenges, problem-solving, and maximizing resources. Have received numerous outstanding work performance evaluations.

ACCOUNTING, BANKING, CREDIT & INSURANCE:
Financial Services

JESSICA LYNCH

1110½ Hay Street, Fayetteville, NC 28305 • preppub@aol.com • (910) 483-6611

OBJECTIVE	To benefit an organization that can use a hard-working, detail-oriented professional who is proficient in all areas of financial accounting and data management and has a demonstrated ability to enhance cost efficiency.

EXPERIENCE

CUSTOMER SERVICE SPECIALIST. Citizens and Southern Bank, Fayetteville, NC (2003-present). Applied my analytical skills and financial expertise to troubleshoot customer problems in a courteous and efficient manner while cross selling bank products.

- Sell cashiers checks, money orders, travelers checks, EE bonds, and foreign currency.
- Manage paying and receiving functions, including loan payments, night deposits, and ATM deposits.
- Prepare large currency transaction and safeguard reports.
- Balance cash box and process cash advances.

BRANCH SERVICE ASSISTANT and **DEALER OPERATIONS CLERK.** First Interstate Bank of Arizona, Tucson, AZ (1990-2002). Refined my ability to manage time and resources in these customer service and finance positions; researched and revised customer problems in a courteous and efficient manner while managing administrative functions of the branch.

- Opened checking, saving, and certificate of deposit accounts.
- Maintained loan files and reports, as well as signature cards.
- Processed name/address changes and "hot" card requests.
- Conducted fund transfers by telephone.
- Excelled in the administration of flooring loans inventory, totaling $40 million.
- Balanced and verified contracts.
- Performed credit checks and validations.
- Input data in computer for flooring payments and payoffs.
- Typed security agreements and notes for leasing loans.

ADMINISTRATIVE ASSISTANT. U.S. Life Title Company, Tucson, AZ (1988-1990). Learned to use a wide range of office machines and acquired precise habits typing Alta/Standard policies and preliminary title reports.

SALESPERSON. Lerner Shop, Tucson, AZ (1987-1988). Acquired top customer-service abilities in this direct contact role selling women's sportswear at this popular retail store.

CORPORATE OFFICE TRAINEE. Valley National Bank of Arizona, Tucson, AZ (1986-1987). While learning the basics of office management, acquired valuable bookkeeping experience including posting payments, telephone transfers, stop payments, balance verifications, and customer assistance.

EDUCATION & TRAINING

Successfully completed the following finance and accounting courses at Pima Community College, Tucson, AZ: Installment Credit, Accounting I, and Principles of Bank Operations.

Attended training at the American Banking Institute, Tucson, AZ: Commercial Loan Documentation and Real Estate Documentation.

EQUIPMENT SKILLS

Have a strong working knowledge of the following office equipment and software:

TIPS Machine	EPSON Computer (ACAPS)	RJE Credit Bureau Machine
Monroe Calculator	Encoder	Typewriter (45 wpm)
Sharp-Electronic Audit Machine		Microsoft Word software

PERSONAL

Am known for my professionalism, keen judgement, and innovative ideas. Offer a proven ability to get along with people from all backgrounds. Outstanding references on request.

ACCOUNTING, BANKING, CREDIT & INSURANCE: Insurance Adjusting

DANIEL NAIDO

1110½ Hay Street, Fayetteville, NC 28305 • preppub@aol.com • (910) 483-6611

OBJECTIVE

To benefit a company that can use an expert automobile appraiser and licensed insurance adjuster who offers a proven commitment to outstanding customer service along with a reputation for unquestioned honesty, strong negotiating skills, and technical knowledge.

LICENSE

Licensed by the state of South Carolina as an Auto Damage Adjuster and Auto Appraiser; also licensed as a Notary Public.
- Was previously licensed in New York as an Automobile Damage Adjuster/Appraiser.
- Hold a valid North Carolina Driver's License with a violation-free record.

EXPERIENCE

AUTO DAMAGE ADJUSTER. Nationwide Insurance Company, Columbia, SC (2003-present) and New York State (1994-03). Began with Nationwide as a part-time security guard on weekends, and was offered a chance to train as an adjuster; excelled in all schools and training programs, and have exceeded corporate goals and expectations in every job I have held within Nationwide.

- *1993-95*: After initial training as an adjuster, worked in Brooklyn and the Bronx, NY: averaged five claims per day while helping the company earn a reputation for outstanding customer service.
- *1995-97*: Relocated to Nassau County, Long Island, where I trained new adjusters while also working the field and drive-in.
- *1997-00*: Worked in Suffolk County, a huge territory 30 miles wide and 100 miles long, where I made a significant contribution to building the territory; when I left as the only adjuster in Suffolk County, I was replaced with four adjusters in this rapidly expanding territory where I had helped Nationwide earn a name for excellent service.
- *1900-03*: Built a six-adjuster territory into a 14-adjuster territory in Queens.
- *2003-present*: Was the first adjuster sent into South Carolina, and have played a key role in implementing the company's strategic plan to do more business inland selling auto policies; in a highly competitive market, opened the Columbia office "from scratch," which now includes two drive-in locations as well as a guaranteed repair shop which I monitor while averaging 100-125 claims monthly as the only adjuster within a 50-mile area.

Technical knowledge: Skilled at utilizing Mitchell Estimate Sys and CCC Total Loss Evaluation as well as guide books including NADA and the Red Book; routinely use equipment including a CRT and personal computer.
- Known for my excellent negotiating skills and ability to settle claims quickly and fairly.
- In the Columbia area, have improved customer relations and reduced loss ratio 15%.
- Skilled at evaluating total losses, coordinating removal of salvage, and handling titles.

Other experience: **AUTO & FURNITURE UPHOLSTERER.** New York City (1993-94). Worked in upholstery of auto seats, vinyl tops, convertible tops, and interior trim while customizing automobile and boat interiors; learned how to custom cut and sew fabric to fit and learned to re-create original factory trim.

NAVAL PETTY OFFICER. (1988-92). After joining the Navy, advanced rapidly through the ranks to E-5 in four years while managing people as well as inventories of ammunition, missiles, and nuclear fuel; was strongly urged to make a career out of the Navy because of my exceptional management ability, leadership skills, human relations know-how, and technical knowledge of supply and logistics.

EDUCATION & TRAINING

Completed college course work in Business Administration and Management, Farmingdale State University, NY, 2001-02.
Completed technical training in Insurance Law and Risk & Insurance as well as numerous courses conducted by companies such as General Motors and Honda pertaining to refinishing, principles of four-wheel steering, transmission repair, computer operation, and other areas.

PERSONAL

Offer an unusual combination of exceptional organizational and communication skills, along with technical knowledge of auto adjusting and the insurance industry. Strongly believe in delivering outstanding customer service.

ACCOUNTING, BANKING, CREDIT & INSURANCE

Date

Exact Name of Person
Title or Position
Name of Company
Address (no., street)
Address (city, state, zip)

Loan, Credit, and Collections

Dear Exact Name of Person: (or Dear Sir or Madam if answering a blind ad.)

I would appreciate an opportunity to talk with you soon about how I could contribute to your organization through my exceptionally strong skills in management, finance, sales, and customer service.

You will see from my resume that I have excelled in jobs which required excellent interpersonal skills and the ability to deal well with people while also overseeing financial administration and determining credit and lending policies. Most recently, I have managed the credit department (which I also established "from scratch") for a construction industry supply firm which has nearly tripled sales in the last five years. The policies I established and implemented played a key role in the profitability of the company during a period of rapid growth.

In previous jobs I worked for East Coast Federal Savings & Loan and for NCNB National Bank of North Carolina. I am skilled in handling consumer lending, directing collections activities, marketing consumer credit, and performing credit investigations.

I have frequently been commended for my natural "sales" skills, and I have refined my sales abilities in commercial banking environments as well as in the building industry. I feel certain I could aggressively market any product line or service that I believe in, and I feel that most successful managers "think sales" during most of their business day.

You would find me to be a congenial individual who is known for integrity, honesty, and reliability. I enjoy tackling new challenges and always give my best to any job I undertake, and I can provide outstanding personal and professional references.

I hope you will welcome my call soon to arrange a brief meeting at your convenience to discuss your current and future needs and how I might serve them. Thank you in advance for your time.

Sincerely yours,

Phillip Harris

Alternate last paragraph:
I hope you will call or write me soon to suggest a time convenient for us to meet and discuss your current and future needs and how I might serve them. Thank you in advance for your time.

PHILLIP HARRIS

1110½ Hay Street, Fayetteville, NC 28305 • preppub@aol.com • (910) 483-6611

OBJECTIVE

To add value to an organization that can use a well organized manager who is skilled in developing new systems and procedures for profitability enhancement, establishing new accounts and managing existing ones, and administering finances at all levels.

EDUCATION

Bachelor of Science in Business Administration (B.S.B.A.) degree, concentration in Finance, East Carolina University, 1991.
- Member, Beta Kappa Alpha Banking and Finance Fraternity.
- Was active in intramural softball, basketball, and arm wrestling.
- Worked throughout college in order to finance my college education.
  Completed A.I.B. in Consumer Lending, Pitt Community College.

EXPERIENCE

CREDIT MANAGER. All Purpose Building Supply, Raleigh, NC (1998-03). Was specially recruited by the company to assume this position which involved establishing a credit department with three employees.

- Played a key role in the growth of the company from two stores with sales of less than $15 million to five stores with sales of more than $40 million.
- Reduced the number of days of sales outstanding by 20+ days in 2002.
- Was in charge of approving all new accounts for five stores.
- Developed and maintained an excellent working relationship with all customers.
- Formulated and implemented key areas of company policy by authoring the credit policies; directed activities including account adjustments, skip tracing, liening, and billing.
- Coordinated with the corporate attorney; prepared cash flow projections and provided the controller with financial information for profit-and-loss statements and balance sheets for the company owners.
- Implemented procedures that lowered chargeoffs and increased collection activity while accounts receivables grew from $2 million to $7.5 million.

CONSUMER LOAN OFFICER. East Coast Federal Savings & Loan, Fayetteville, NC (1994-98). Was promoted to responsibilities for handling activities in these areas:

commercial lending	consumer lending
collections	credit card approval
credit investigations	marketing of consumer loans

LOAN OFFICER & COLLECTION REPRESENTATIVE. NCNB National Bank of North Carolina, Fayetteville, NC (1991-94). After excelling as a Collection Representative from 1991-94, was promoted to Loan Officer, in charge of lending money for consumer purchases and performing credit investigations.
- As a Collection Representative, collected past due accounts, cross referenced bank records versus automobile dealerships' records, and investigated consumer account payment records while also handling foreclosures, repossessions, insurance claims, and skip tracing of delinquent accounts.
- Performed liaison with banking auditors and legal personnel.
- Gained expertise in all aspects of banking and lending.

SALESMAN/ACCOUNT REPRESENTATIVE. Triangle Building Supply, Fayetteville, NC (1985-91). Worked at this construction industry supply company in the summers and breaks during the years when I was earning my college degree.
- Learned to deal with people while selling firearms, building materials, light fixtures, garden supplies, and hardware.
- Graduated into responsibilities for handling major accounts.

PERSONAL

In high school was a member of the National Math Honor Society and the Science Club and set my school's record in the shot put while also excelling in football and wrestling.

CITY SERVICES: Firefighting

LLOYD BYRD

1110½ Hay Street, Fayetteville, NC 28305 • preppub@aol.com • (910) 483-6611

OBJECTIVE

To offer my strong working knowledge of emergency services to an organization that can benefit from my abilities related to administration and supervision of emergency services operations through my well-developed communication skills.

CERTIFICATIONS

Completed training programs leading to certification in the following areas:

NC Fire Fighter Level I	NC Fire Fighter Level II
NC Level II Fire Service Instructor	NC Fire Fighter Level III
NC Emergency Medical Technician (EMT)	Basic Vehicle Extraction
NC Hazardous Materials Operation Level I	Basic Trauma Life Support

EDUCATION

Attend continuing education courses in **Fire/Emergency Services,** Fayetteville Technical Community College (FTCC), NC.

Am knowledgeable of a wide range of fire fighting activities including:

hazardous material control	scene evaluation	building inspection
advanced rescue techniques	incident command system	equipment inspection

EXPERIENCE

Have developed the ability to manage my time for maximum productivity while holding multiple jobs and volunteer roles simultaneously:

FIRE FIGHTER and **EMERGENCY MEDICAL TECHNICIAN.** Vander Fire Department, Fayetteville, NC (2001-present). Have developed a working knowledge of PROBE Chief and Microsoft Word software and how to use these computer programs for record keeping and preparing reports.

INSTRUCTOR. Sampson Community College, Clinton, NC (2003-present). Serve as the Lead Instructor for the Fire Academy portion of the school's curriculum.

VOLUNTEER FIRE FIGHTER. Vander Fire Department, Fayetteville, NC (2003-present).

FIRE FIGHTER. Eastover Fire Department, Fayetteville, NC (2002-03). Made important contributions to this station's operations including doing extensive public relations work and was promoted to hold a captain's slot.
- Developed and implemented a HAZ-COM policy in accordance with NC General Statutes 95-173-95-218 of the Hazardous Chemicals Right-to-Know Act — also included information from OSHA and SARHA regulations.
- Implemented a fire prevention program after developing information geared to hold the interest of elementary school children.
- Presented fire prevention programs to nursing homes serviced by this station.

VOLUNTEER FIRE FIGHTER. Eastover Fire Department, Fayetteville, NC (1997-03).

SQUAD SERGEANT. Cumberland County Rescue Squad, Fayetteville, NC (1996-97). Supervised a six-person squad at substation #60, Cedar Creek Road.

AFFILIATIONS

Hold membership in the following professional organizations:
NC Fire Fighters Association
NC Fire Instructors Association
NC Association of Rescue Squads

PERSONAL

Am highly self-motivated. Offer outstanding communication skills. Am very effective in calming people and dealing with people of all ages under difficult and dangerous conditions.

REFERENCES

Richard K. Bradshaw	Mark McLaurin
Assistant Chief	Assistant Chief
Vander Fire Department	Eastover Fire Department
Route 2, Box 457-C Sapona Road	Route 1, Box 121-A Highway 301 N.
Fayetteville, NC 28301	Fayetteville, NC 28301

ROBERT ZINGERY

1110½ Hay Street, Fayetteville, NC 28305 • preppub@aol.com • (910) 483-6611

OBJECTIVE

To offer a background of progression in managerial roles based on outstanding analytical skills and sensitivity to customer comments and needs as well as extensive knowledge of solid waste operations to an organization in need of a mature professional.

EXPERIENCE

Advanced in this track record of accomplishments with the City of Savannah, GA, while becoming known as a professional who could build teams and make the most of outdated and inadequate equipment:
SANITATION SUPERINTENDENT. (2003-present). Manage approximately 130 employees operating a fleet of 45 vehicles used in solid waste collection and disposal for this progressive and growing city with a current population of over 113,000.

- Achieved an 87.9% customer satisfaction rate in a survey of city residents, a rate of satisfaction almost unheard of in any city; reached this high level despite the drawbacks of using outdated equipment.
- Earned frequent praise for my ability to listen to customer concerns and questions and find the solutions to difficult and sensitive issues.
- Planned, directed, and coordinated the department's work flow including scheduling, reviewing and evaluating work performance areas, and working with staff members to solve problems.
- Made hiring decisions; trained and evaluated employee performance; handled disciplinary actions and terminations.
- Participated in budget development and administration including forecasting future needs and approving expenditures.
- Was commended for my sound judgment and superb understanding of how to move equipment and personnel around in order to meet the greatest needs and for overcoming such handicaps as backups and delays caused by renovation at one landfill.

SANITATION ROUTE INSPECTOR. (1999-03). Was promoted to the superintendent's position on the basis of my professionalism and accomplishments while supervising 14 employees responding to meeting the solid waste collection needs of city residents.
- Managed a fleet of four Packer body trucks and one Knuckle boom in a sanitation operation.
- Known for my dependability, helped ensure that my route personnel maintained a reputation with the public for always being on schedule and providing efficient service.
- Selected to serve on a merit pay review committee, made suggestions based on my concerns, which were investigated and resulted in more equitable distributions.

MEDIUM EQUIPMENT OPERATOR. (1998-99). Joined this organization with no prior knowledge or experience in solid waste collecting and quickly became known for my hard work and willingness to learn while providing city residents with timely service
- Operated a truck with two crew members following a scheduled route within the city and learned the different types of vehicles and equipment used in the solid waste collection industry.

Highlights of earlier experience: Refined managerial and supervisory skills in a distinguished career in the U.S. Army.
- Supervised, counseled, and advised as many as 180 employees in a maintenance company while also acting as the staff liaison for logistics support activities.
- Excelled in motivating people to accomplish seemingly impossible assignments with inferior, outdated equipment in organizations which had serious morale problems.

TRAINING

Completed several City of Savannah-sponsored seminars and training programs emphasizing such topics as employee/management relations, customer relations and service, and how to prevent abuse of leave policies. Studied General Education at a campus of the University of Maryland in Germany.

PERSONAL

Excel in providing leadership by example: make it personal policy to never expect any employee to do anything I am not wiling to do myself. Thrive on challenge and pressure.

COMPUTER OPERATIONS & MIS SYSTEMS

Date

Exact Name of Person
Title or Position
Name of Company
Address (number and street)
Address (city, state, and ZIP)

Data Entry   Dear Exact Name of Person: (or Dear Sir or Madam if answering a blind as.)

Can you use a hard-working and energetic young professional who offers outstanding office operations and management skills with an especially strong background in customer service and data entry?

As you will see by my enclosed resume, I most recently contributed my abilities in the administrative offices of the Target Stores location in Fayetteville, NC. As the Assistant Personnel Manager, I played a role in setting up the procedures for and organizing the personnel department. I oversaw the management of personnel records, time cards, and scheduling for around 150 employees with direct supervision over six people.

In earlier jobs, I was cited for my customer service and managerial abilities and placed in positions of responsibility usually reserved for older, more experienced managers. For instance, at the Peachtree Plaza Hotel in downtown Atlanta, GA, I directed a staff of 18 people at one of the hotel's popular restaurants. While serving my country in the U.S. Army I used state-of-the-art automated equipment to maintain personnel records for over 15,000 people at Ft. Bragg, NC, the world's largest U.S. military base.

I feel that I offer exceptional organizational, motivational, and communication skills. With a reputation as a fast learner, I am very comfortable with using computer systems and with rapidly mastering new ones as they are available.

I hope you will welcome my call soon to arrange a brief meeting at your convenience to discuss your current and future needs and how I might serve them. Thank you in advance for your time.

Sincerely yours,

Gail Davies

Alternate last paragraph:
I hope you will call or write me soon to suggest a time convenient for us to meet and discuss your current and future needs and how I might serve them. Thank you in advance for your time.

GAIL DAVIES

1110½ Hay Street, Fayetteville, NC 28305 • preppub@aol.com • (910) 483-6611

OBJECTIVE	To contribute through my reputation as a hard-working, enthusiastic, and energetic young professional with a broad base of experience related to data entry, computer operations, personnel management, and customer service.
SPECIAL SKILLS	Offer outstanding office skills such as the following: **Computer skills:** am familiar with Microsoft Word, Access and Powerpoint software programs. **General office skills:** type approximately 55 wpm and am experienced in filing and using standard office equipment including multi-line phones, faxes, and copiers.
EXPERIENCE	**ASSISTANT PERSONNEL MANAGER.** Target Stores, Fayetteville, NC (2003). Was cited for my planning and organizational skills as well as my detail orientation while contributing to the smooth operation of internal personnel activities along with customer service for this business in its first year in this city.

- Directly supervised six people; maintained personnel records for over 150 employees along with scheduling, timekeeping, and preparing the payroll.
- Contributed to the store's reputation for customer service by seeing that rain checks were issued promptly when advertised merchandise became available and while assisting with check cashing.
- Played an important role in the establishment of personnel department organization.
- Learned ISIS and HOST computer systems which are specialized systems with pricing, e-Mail, and merchandising information for the retail industry.

ADMINISTRATIVE ASSISTANT. U.S. Army, Ft. Bragg, NC (2001-03). Fine tuned my general office, administrative, and customer service skills while handling dual roles as an Administrative Assistant and Personnel Information Systems Management Specialist in a department maintaining personnel records for more than 15,000 people.

- Received, analyzed, and entered data into an army-wide data base at a personnel headquarters located at the nation's largest military base.
- Was singled out for my exceptional public relations skills demonstrated while assisting customers with various needs.
- Applied a range of writing, proofreading, and typing/word processing abilities while preparing correspondence, documentation to explain awards, and narratives for various personnel efficiency reports.

ASSISTANT MANAGER. The Cafe, Westin Hotels, Atlanta, GA (2000-01). Was hired at the age of 20 to manage a staff of 18 people and a wide range of daily activities in the restaurant at Peachtree Plaza, a major downtown hotel.

- Learned what to look for and how to investigate any overages or shortages in cash drawers or in stock and supply levels.
- Trained, scheduled, and supervised employees.

ASSISTANT MANAGER. Burger King, Decatur, GA (1996-97). Originally hired as a Cashier, was soon promoted on the basis of my maturity and ability to lead others and contribute to the sense of team work that is necessary in the fast-paced environment of fast food.

- Supervised nine people while overseeing day-to-day activities including an emphasis on quick, friendly customer service.
- Was entrusted with the security of cash deposits as well as with handling cash drops and balancing cash drawers.

EDUCATION & TRAINING	Completed three years of college course work in Biology. Excelled in approximately 724 hours of professional development training in the areas of computer systems information analyzation and personnel information systems management.
PERSONAL	Am a quick learner who strongly believes in always giving 100%. Have an outgoing personality and well-developed motivational abilities.

COMPUTER OPERATIONS & MIS SYSTEMS

JOSEPH GENTER

1110½ Hay Street, Fayetteville, NC 28305 • preppub@aol.com • (910) 483-6611

OBJECTIVE

To offer my creative problem-solving approach and my extensive experience in management information systems design and implementation to an organization that can use a resourceful technical expert with highly refined supervisory, communication, strategic thinking, and customer service skills.

EXPERIENCE

MANAGEMENT INFORMATION SYSTEMS (MIS) MANAGER. Seven-Eleven Stores, Sanford, NC (2003-present). Was recruited by this fast-growing corporation which employs more than 500 people and operates 85 stores grossing over $150 million annually to analyze its current MIS structure and to design MIS systems which would be compatible with strategic goals and accommodate continued rapid growth.

- In 2003 determined that the company's current computer system consisting of an IBM S/36 and store PCs would not facilitate the company's objectives; implemented a Novell Network on a UNIX system for corporate accounting.
- Performed extensive research on systems and networks available; selected potential vendors and negotiated the final contract.
- Functioned as co-developer of the implementation strategy with the software vendor in order to reduce standard implementation time by 32%.
- Replaced store computers with a Windows-based system that reduced manual record keeping by store managers while providing for the daily transmittal of sales, purchases, cash, and inventory levels to the corporate office.
- Have designed and am directing the implementation of the next phase of this reengineering project, integrating the gas console, fuel tanks, credit cards, money orders, time clock, and cash registers.
- Have gained valuable skills in implementing change within an organization where there are many first-line supervisors who must be trained, coached, and persuaded in order for the new system to be truly successful.
- Cut costs in the computer department by 28% while improving productivity of all stores.
- Have enhanced the job satisfaction of store managers in a high-turnover industry through the style in which I implemented the changes; increased both the confidence and competence levels of supervisory staff while eliminating hours of paperwork weekly.
- Personally designed and conducted training and support for all job levels.

Capability Computer Systems, Spartanburg, SC (1995-03). *Was promoted in the following "track record" of advancement by a $20 million company providing computer software and services to the building materials and home building industry.*
DIRECTOR OF DEVELOPMENT. (1998-03). Was promoted to oversee product development related to software for building materials companies; stepped into a situation where we were losing customers and sales because of poor product design and delivery.

- Transformed a failing operation which was losing money and customers into an efficient and profitable business which enjoyed four consecutive years of steady growth under my direction; the Building Material System product I reengineered is now the #1 product in its industry.
- After I reengineered and stabilized the product, initiated the development of the Next Generation System with a 4th Generation language system running on a client server environment.
- Managed a budget of $1.2 million and a development staff of 25 programmers plus two contract programmers.
- Led my team to receive the company award in 1999 for "Department Comeback of the Year;" improved productivity of the development staff by over 34 percent in the first year.
- Served on a quality team for improving customer service and software development processes while managing the design, programming, testing, and documentation of Builder Management and Building Material products.

PROGRAMMING MANAGER. (1998). Was promoted to manage all projects for the Builder Management System; managed six development personnel while implementing a complete multi-user version of the software that worked on Novell, IBM Token Ring, and other networks.

- Became skilled in creating a multi-user version of software that could run on any Network.

PROJECT LEADER. (1996-98). Received the company's "Department of the Year" award for my creativity and management skills in overseeing the rewriting of the Home Builder System, a project given to me with a five-month deadline which required development of software in a new language and which included 50 major enhancements.

- Completed the project on time and with "bug free" software according to customers.
- Played a major role in the success of a product which is still selling today and which has been as high as second in market share.

SYSTEM PROGRAMMER. (1995-96). Was hired to increase the speed and performance of the Home Building System; developed and maintained an ISAM 20% faster than the existing one while also developing "C" and Assembler Code that made the interfaces-to-applications run faster.
- Was rapidly promoted into management because of my versatile abilities.

VICE-PRESIDENT OF DEVELOPMENT. Accounting Systems and Analysis, Inc., Jacksonville, FL (1991-95). For a company providing custom software for home builders, contractors, auto dealers, and home health care companies, was responsible for the analysis, design, programming, testing, and support of all products.
- Developed fully integrated accounting systems for all the industries mentioned above.
- Managed 15 programmers and testers.
- Worked closely with customers and then designed software to meet their needs.

SKILLS

Software: Visual Basic, Visual C++, C, Progress, Informix, Access, Pascal, Cobol, Micro-Focus Cobol, Acucobol, Assembler, Basic, Fortran

Hardware: HP, Data General AViiONs, IBM RS6000, NCR Tower, NCR 3000 series, Data General MV series, IBM S/36, IBM-PC compatibles

Operating Systems: Literate in most operating systems, with extensive experience in Windows 95, Window NT, Novell, Windows, UNIX, AIX, HP/UX, DG/UX, XENIX, AOS/VS, MVS, DOS

EDUCATION

Mercer University, Macon, GA. BS in Computer Science, 1991.

AFFILIATIONS

Past member of the North Greenville Rotary Club
Past member of the National Forest Product Task Force on EDI
Who's Who of Business Leaders

COMPUTER OPERATIONS & MIS SYSTEMS

Date

Exact Name of Person
Title or Position
Name of Company
Address (number and street)
Address (city, state, and ZIP)

Systems Analyst   Dear Exact Name of Person: (or Dear Sir or Madam if answering a blind ad.)

I would appreciate an opportunity to talk with you soon about how I could contribute to your organization through my technical expertise, managerial experience, and supervisory skills.

As you will see from my enclosed resume, I am knowledgeable of and highly proficient in areas which include analyzing requirements, systems, and software; maintaining software and systems; designing systems; quality assurance; operations planning; and automated message handling systems.

At the present time I am the sole representative of Sterling Software at the Joint Special Operations Command at Ft. Bragg, NC. Having held this position since 2000, I have been successful in increasing customer satisfaction and reducing system downtime.

I have developed a reputation as an articulate and intelligent professional who can be counted on to find ways to maximize the use of the most advanced telecommunications and computer operating systems.

I hope you will welcome my call soon to arrange a brief meeting at your convenience to discuss your current and future needs and how I might serve them. Thank you in advance for your time.

Sincerely yours,

Lawrence Zimmerman

Alternate last paragraph:
I hope you will call or write me soon to suggest a time convenient for us to meet and discuss your current and future needs and how I might serve them. Thank you in advance for your time.

Systems Analyst

LAWRENCE ZIMMERMAN
1110½ Hay Street, Fayetteville, NC 28305   •   preppub@aol.com   •   (910) 483-6611

OBJECTIVE
To offer an extensive background of experience as a systems analyst with excellent management skills and the capability of working with large systems with multiple data bases.

SUMMARY
Offer knowledge of areas of application including, but not limited to, the following:

requirement analysis	software maintenance	systems analysis
systems configuration	operations planning	software development
facilities management	quality assurance	intelligence systems
communications systems	automated message handling	
systems design/engineering	command and control systems weather	

EDUCATION
Bachelor's degree in Business Administration, Campbell University, Buies Creek, NC, 2003.
A.A.S., Management Information Systems, Community College of the Air Force, 1999.

CLEARANCE
Currently hold a Top Secret security clearance with SCI access.

EXPERIENCE
SENIOR SYSTEMS ANALYST. Sterling Software ITD, Bellevue, NE (2000-present). As the company's representative at the Joint Special Operations Command (JSOC) at Ft. Bragg, NC, perform software engineering and software maintenance on DoD (Department of Defense) telecommunications computer systems while ensuring the quality of line protocols for a system with multiple long distance and local users.
* Maintained the operational status of the Communications Support Processor (CSP) system by identifying, analyzing, reporting, and resolving software problems.
* Installed, integrated, and implemented new software releases or baseline modifications.
* Tailored systems to customer specifications and provided both temporary and permanent enhancements.
* Set up and maintained multiple data bases and tables; performed systems analysis.
* Programmed data using parameters with applications high-level routing keyword techniques.
* Worked in close cooperation with systems programmers, maintenance personnel, systems managers, and operations personnel.
* Significantly increased customer satisfaction while providing continuous training and keeping users informed of new enhancements.

SYSTEMS MANAGER. U.S. Air Force, Offutt AFB, Omaha, NE (1996-00). Met the demands of multiple simultaneous responsibilities as **Programmer/Analyst, Project Management Monitor,** and **Coordinator/ Analyst** while using my knowledge of multiple data base management to maintain record history in more than 90 projects and 130 resources within a Strategic Information Systems Division.
* Expanded my knowledge of data base management as well as refining my written communication skills while writing reports.
* Managed a front-end telecommunications processor including software maintenance.
* Tested, evaluated, reported, and provided accurate and reliable quality assurance of new software products prior to the installation of new versions.
* Maintained multiple table driven and multiple data base systems.
* Provided support for a dual-homed, multichannel communications processor while increasing the knowledge level of my subordinates on systems and systems integration.

TECHNICAL EXPERTISE
Protocols: Proficient with TCP/IP, NWLINK (IPX/SPX), NETBUEI (16 and 32 bits), SLIP, PPP, PPTP, Frame Relay, Token Ring, SNA.
Network design: Install, configure, and maintain LANs, WANs, and Windows NT systems.
Software, operating systems, platforms: Windows 95/98/Me/NT/2000; Novell Netware, OS/2; UNIX/AIX, DOS, Token-Ring/Ethernet NICs, CISCO routers/switches, RS/6000, dBase III/IV, CA-CLIPPER, servers, bridges, hubs; MS Outlook, MS Office 95/97/2000; Lotus Notes; Lotus SmartSuite.

PERSONAL
Offer excellent interpersonal communication abilities along with supervisory, managerial, and technical knowledge. Can provide outstanding personal and professional references.

CONSTRUCTION INDUSTRY

Date

Exact Name of Person
Title or Position
Name of Company
Address (no., street)
Address (city, state, zip)

Construction Foreman

Dear Exact Name of Person: (or Dear Sir or Madam if answering a blind ad.)

Can you use a resourceful young professional with extensive operations and project management experience along with a "track record" of outstanding results in safety, cost reduction, and other areas?

As you will see from my resume, I am currently excelling as a project manager/foreman for a multimillion-dollar company operating all over the east coast. My results in 2004 have been impressive; I have greatly exceeded my targeted 20% profit margin by actually performing 32% above profit while finishing all jobs within or ahead of schedule and with no accidents.

In both my current job and in a previous job as Manager of Operations with a major fire prevention company working under contract to GE, IBM, and other industrial giants, I have acquired expert knowledge of OSHA, EPA, and other regulations. I have been trained and certified by OSHA in soil testing and I have worked closely with OSHA officials regarding HAZMAT, MSDS, and other areas.

I am particularly proud of the contributions I have made to my employers in the areas of cost reduction. On numerous occasions I have discovered ways to free up working capital by decreasing inventory carrying costs, automating manual functions, and monitoring everyday activities to find new ways to streamline operations and decrease both overhead and variable costs.

You would find me in person to be a congenial individual who prides myself on my ability to get along well with people at all levels. I can provide excellent references from all previous employers, including from my current company.

I hope you will write or call me soon to suggest a time when we might meet to discuss your current and future goals and how I might help you achieve them. Thank you in advance for your time.

Sincerely yours,

Napoleon Radosevich

Alternate last paragraph:
I hope you will welcome my call soon to arrange a brief meeting at your convenience to discuss your current and future needs and how I might serve them. Thank you in advance for your time.

NAPOLEON RADOSEVICH

1110½ Hay Street, Fayetteville, NC 28305   •   preppub@aol.com   •   (910) 483-6611

OBJECTIVE
To benefit an organization that can use a skilled operations manager who offers extensive knowledge of OSHA requirements, in-depth experience in project management and cost/inventory control, as well as expertise in recruiting, training, and managing personnel.

EDUCATION
B.S. degree in Business Administration, Temple University, Ambler, PA, 1996.
- Concentrated in courses in Finance, Management, and Human Resources.

CERTIFICATION
Have been trained and certified by OSHA in soil testing; have worked closely with OSHA and am very familiar with OSHA, EPA, and other safety guidelines.

EXPERIENCE
FOREMAN/PROJECT MANAGER. DKS Construction, Charlotte, NC (2003-present). Am being groomed for further promotion by this multimillion-dollar company which operates in states from GA, across to FL, and into VA; manage projects which involve laying utility lines, erecting overhead lines, and installing transformer boxes in commercial/industrial projects such as factories, shopping malls, and large-scale housing developments.
- Am considered one of the company's most knowledgeable managers on OSHA.
- Work with representatives of all the building trades while essentially operating as a profit center; in the past year, exceeded my goal of producing a 20% profit margin by actually performing 32% above profit.
- As required, operate backhoe and boom truck; read blueprints; perform all terminating in hot boxes.
- Finished all jobs on time or early while establishing a perfect safety record of no accidents on the projects I managed.

ASSISTANT OF OPERATIONS. Brooks Brothers, Utica, NY (2000-02). Made impressive contributions to this company which, upon the ratification of NAFTA in 2002, immediately moved its manufacturing facilities to lower-cost Mexico.
- For this company which manufactures expensive men's suits, worked side-by-side with the Operations Manager; personally discovered an over ordering bias and made changes which reduced excess inventory by $150,000 per year.
- For more than 500 employees, established production schedules, assured optimum use of production capacity, and coordinated raw materials and labor.
- Played a key role in developing a computer program which improved inventory control.

MANAGER OF OPERATIONS. Caution Equipment, Waterville, NY (1997-00). Shortly after college graduation, excelled in a position which was created for me by this fast-growing company; rapidly automated all office communication and thereby greatly improved overall decision making and the working relationships among sales, transportation, administrative, and other personnel.
- Played a key role in obtaining the first million-dollar sale for this fire prevention company working under contract to IBM, GE, and major wire manufacturers.
- Prudently reduced a $1 million excess inventory to a safe $300,000 level.
- On my own initiative, established excellent working relationships with OSHA and authored company policy/procedures related to HAZMAT, MSDS, and other areas; assured that company vehicles met DOT standards for carrying Halon.
- Monitored policies and procedures in all company areas, from personnel training to safety management, in order to identify new ways to improve efficiency and lower costs.
- Directed inventory and warehouse stock control, warehousing, sales order entry, customer service, traffic and shipping, and other areas.

MANAGER OF PERSONNEL. Tele-Tector of Montgomery County, Plymouth Meeting, PA (1992-97). Left this 40-person security alarm company where I worked while in high school and college when the owner sold it to Wells Fargo; after beginning in an entry-level job, advanced to handle the development and management of personnel policies and programs, wage and salary administration, employee recruiting and training, safety and health.

PERSONNEL
Offer an ability to use computers to solve management problems. Excellent references.

CONSTRUCTION INDUSTRY

March 15, 2003

Exact Name of Person
Title or Position
Name of Company
Address (no., street)
Address (city, state, zip)

Construction Manager   Dear Sir or Madam:

I would appreciate an opportunity to talk with you soon about how I could contribute to The Mayo Clinic. I am responding to your ad for a Construction Manager with this <u>confidential</u> resume and cover letter to express my interest in receiving your consideration for this position.

As you will see from my enclosed resume, I offer approximately 18 years of progressively increasing responsibility in construction management with the specialized knowledge in a hospital environment that you require.

I would like to point out that I am experienced in working within JCAHO (Joint Commission on Accreditation of Health-Care Organizations), DFS (Division of Facility Services), and Interim Life Safety guidelines through my extensive background in construction management in a hospital environment.

Known for my dedication to high quality and compliance with safety standards, I have always been effective in supervising projects and seeing that work is completed on schedule.

I hope you will welcome my call soon to arrange a brief meeting at your convenience to discuss the current and future needs of Moore Regional Hospital and how I might serve them. Thank you in advance for your time. I can provide outstanding personal and professional references.

Sincerely yours,

Christopher Oxendine

CHRISTOPHER OXENDINE

1110½ Hay Street, Fayetteville, NC 28305 • preppub@aol.com • (910) 483-6611

OBJECTIVE
To offer a background of 18 years experience in construction including six in construction management and eight in health care facility construction projects with proven strengths in inspiring the confidence and trust of others and effective negotiating skills.

TRAINING
Currently enrolled in an AUTO CAD V-12 class, Wake County Technical Community College.
Completed training leading to certification in the following areas:
OSHA Construction Safety and Health, 2003   Mechanical Blueprinting
Institute of Government Contracting for Professional Services, 2003 ITT Cable Repair

EXPERIENCE
CONSTRUCTION MANAGER. Duke University Hospital, Durham, NC (2002-present). Completed construction and renovation projects while taking care of operational aspects including preparing cost estimates, preparing and monitoring schedules for in-house projects, and overseeing quality control to ensure the highest quality workmanship.
- Further enhanced my knowledge of JCAHO (Joint Commission on Accreditation for Health-Care Organizations), DFS (Division of Facility Services), and Interim Life Safety.
- Evaluated and approved/disapproved design changes; made recommendations which led to cost reductions.
- Applied communication skills as liaison between administration, staff, and architects as well as while working closely with staff members to coordinate in-house projects.
- Resolved complex contractual issues in close cooperation with architects and engineers.
- Developed phasing requirements and ensured that construction did not disrupt medical center operations.

Completed numerous projects for Bechtel Corporation, San Francisco, CA (1998-01):
SITE MANAGER. (1999-01). Oversaw the $19 million project to construct a 187,000-sq. ft. four-story Patient Services Tower (with full mechanical basement) which housed eight operating rooms, intensive care units, fifteen LDR, three delivery rooms, a coffee shop, pharmacy, and additional support services.
- Coordinated daily field activities of individual prime contractors while also reviewing contractor quotes and monthly billings.
- Handled the resolution of design and coordination conflicts, monitored contract compliance, and provided quality control oversight.
- Maintained contact with architects and engineers; completed project documentation.
- Prepared and maintained correspondence with the owner, architect, and contractors.
- Participated in project scheduling, job progress meetings, and monitored safety.

SITE MANAGER. (1999-01). Managed a contract to build a $5.5 million two-floor 31,000-sq. ft. vertical expansion of an existing six-floor patient tower complete with an 8,000-sq. ft. penthouse mechanical room; the project also included adding two elevators and renovating four elevators to serve the two new floors.
- Handled all aspects of contract management: supervised daily activities, completed documentation and correspondence, reviewed changes and billing, formulated schedules, ensured contract compliance, and ensured safety compliance.

SITE MANAGER. (1999). Directed the construction of a $3.2 million, 15,000-sq. ft. Central Energy Plant which housed boilers, chillers, cooling towers, pumps, emergency generators, and other major mechanical and electrical equipment capable of servicing the South Patient Tower and future Patient Service Tower.
- Coordinated daily contractor field activities with a primary focus on structural and architectural, excavation/tunnel connection construction, piping installation, and electrical.

PROJECT SUPERINTENDENT. Lawrence Kaplan and Associates, Madison, WI (1997-99). Provided managerial support in areas including the following: documentation, review and awarding of subcontracts, supervision of an adequate work force, scheduling, quality control, inspection, monitoring safety compliance, and ensuring contract compliance.
- Completed the following projects: 27,000-sq. ft. expansion and 3,700-sq. ft. Linear Accelerator addition to a medical office building, Winchester, VA; 4,200-sq. ft. cat scan and ophthalmology addition for Kaiser Permanente, Raleigh, NC; 28,000-sq. ft. Kaiser Permanente, Durham, NC.

PERSONAL
Offer computer experience with Microsoft Word, Excel, and Access software programs.

ENTREPRENEURS SEEKING CORPORATE POSITIONS

Date

Exact Name of Person
Title or Position
Name of Company
Address (no., street)
Address (city, state, zip)

Management in Any Industry

Dear Exact Name of Person: (or Dear Sir or Madam if answering a blind ad.)

I would appreciate an opportunity to talk with you soon about how I could contribute to your organization through my business management, sales, and communication skills.

As you will see from my resume, I have founded successful businesses, tripled the sales volume of an existing company, and directed projects which required someone who could take a concept and turn it into an operating reality. While excelling as a retailer and importer of products that included oriental rugs and English antiques, I have become accustomed to working with a discriminating customer base of people regionally who trust my taste and character. In addition to a proven "track record" of producing a profit, I have earned a reputation for honesty and reliability. I believe there is no substitute in business for a good reputation.

I am ready for a new challenge, and that is why I have, in the last several months, closed two of my business locations and turned over the management of the third operation to a family member. I want to apply my seasoned business judgement, along with my problem-solving and opportunity-finding skills, to new areas.

If you can use the expertise of a savvy and creative professional who is skilled at handling every aspect of business management, from sales and marketing to personnel and finance, I would enjoy talking with you informally about your needs and goals. A flexible and adaptable person who feels comfortable stepping into new situations, I am able to "size up" problems and opportunities quickly through the "lens" of experience. I pride myself on my ability to deal tactfully and effectively with everyone.

I hope you will welcome my call soon to arrange a brief meeting at your convenience to discuss your current and future needs and how I might serve them. Thank you in advance for your time.

Sincerely yours,

Desmond Vaughn

Alternate last paragraph:
I hope you will call or write me soon to suggest a time convenient for us to meet and discuss your current and future needs and how I might serve them. Thank you in advance for your time.

DESMOND VAUGHN

1110½ Hay Street, Fayetteville, NC 28305　　•　　preppub@aol.com　　•　　(910) 483-6611

OBJECTIVE　　To add value to an organization that can use a resourceful entrepreneur and manager who offers a proven ability to start up successful new ventures and transform ailing operations into profitable ones through applying my sales, communication, and administrative skills.

EDUCATION　　Earned a **B.A. degree in Sociology**, University of North Carolina at Chapel Hill, NC.
Completed numerous executive development courses in business management and sales.

LICENSE　　Licensed as a real estate broker since 1972; current on continuing education through 2003.

AFFILIATIONS & COMMUNITY LEADERSHIP　　Have served by invitation on the Board of Directors of the following organizations:

Pinehurst Business Guild	Heart Association
Olde Fayetteville Association	Fayetteville Family Life Center
Bowman Gray Hospital Pastoral Foundation	New South River Association
City of Fayetteville Downtown Revitalization Commission	

- Have earned a reputation as a creative strategist with the ability to transform ideas into operating realities and with the communication and leadership skills necessary to instill enthusiasm in others.

EXPERIENCE　　**FOUNDER/MANAGER.** The Captain's Den, Raleigh, Pinehurst, and Southern Pines, NC (1986-02). Established "from scratch" this business which grew to two locations with sales in the mid six figures; developed a product line of oriental rugs which I bought from sources worldwide, and developed a customer base which included discriminating purchasers from all over the southeast.

- Refined my expertise in all aspects of business management, including financial planning and reporting, hiring and training personnel, designing advertising and marketing plans, selling products valued at up to thousands of dollars, and overseeing accounts payable and receivable.
- From 1988-92, simultaneously acted as an **Importer** and management consultant for an English antiques business; traveled to England three times a year as an importer.
- From 1986-88, after being specially recruited as Development Director by the Methodist State Convention, took on the paid job of coordinating the pledging and collection of $1.5 million to construct a dormitory and cafeteria for the Methodist State Convention; set up all systems and procedures and managed funds until construction was finished.
- Recently closed down the Pinehurst and Raleigh locations, and have turned over the Southern Pines location to a family member.

ENTREPRENEUR. Desmond Vaughn, Inc., Pinehurst, NC (1997-02). After extensive market research to determine the viability of establishing a business in the gifts and accessories niche, set up a store in the affluent Pinehurst community which rapidly became successful through innovative promotions, vigorous marketing, and word of mouth.

- Recently turned the full-time management of this business over to a family member.
- In less than two years, the business was producing sales in the low six figures.

EXECUTIVE VICE PRESIDENT & SALES MANAGER. Solomon's Carpet Co., Inc., Raleigh, NC (1978-86). Took over the management of an existing business and, in five years, tripled the sales volume while increasing the staff from four to 11 employees.

- Used radio and newspaper in innovative and memorable ways.
- Supervised a five-person sales staff and trained them in techniques related to prospecting, closing the sale, overcoming objections, and solving customer concerns.

Other experience: CAPTAIN/COMPANY COMMANDER. U.S. Army. Was promoted rapidly to lead a military police company; was awarded the Bronze Star and Army Commendation Medal for service in Vietnam.

PERSONAL　　Offer a proven ability to manage several functional areas and projects at the same time. Am confident that I can turn any solid concept into a profitable business through the knowledge and experience I have acquired. Am creative, and enjoy the thrill of "making things happen."

ENTREPRENEURS SEEKING CORPORATE POSITIONS

Date

Mr. Johnathan Wydell
Quality King Pest Control Services
354 San Francisco Avenue
Los Angeles, CA 92384

**Pest Control
Industry**

Dear Mr. Wydell:

I would appreciate an opportunity to talk with you soon about how I could contribute to your organization through my demonstrated ability to pinpoint new business opportunities and to develop business activities that address those opportunities.

As you will see from my resume, I have most recently been a successful entrepreneur and recently sold a pest control business which I founded to one of the largest pest elimination service companies in the country. It was not viable for me to remain with the company since its "promotion from within" policy would have required me to accept an entry-level position within the corporation, and I feel that my extensive management and sales skills would not be fully utilized at such a level.

Essentially I obtained my pest control license at the age of 21 and then, on my own initiative, transformed myself, through education and hard work, into a highly knowledgeable service professional. At 33 years of age, I am ready to tackle new challenges and opportunities.

I feel confident I could succeed in your organization because of my proven ability to communicate ideas to others, my exceptionally strong problem-solving skills, and my ability to formulate new ideas based on information obtained from multiple sources. I have an outgoing and self-confident personality that enables me to rapidly earn the trust of others.

I hope you will review my skills and experience in order to determine if they could be of value to you. I am a proven performer and I will add considerable value to any company I am a part of. I am writing to you because I know of your company's fine reputation, and I believe I could contribute significantly to your bottom line. Please give me a call if you feel there is a fit between your needs and what I offer. Thank you in advance for your time, and I shall look forward to the possibility of meeting you.

Yours sincerely,

Thomas Westberry

THOMAS WESTBERRY

1110½ Hay Street, Fayetteville, NC 28305 • preppub@aol.com • (910) 483-6611

OBJECTIVE

To contribute to an organization that can use a dynamic professional who offers exceptionally strong sales and management abilities which could be valuable to any industry.

HIGHLIGHTS OF BUSINESS SKILLS

Am an extremely versatile professional with skills/experience in the following areas:

starting up new business operations	purchasing materials
selecting and training employees	controlling inventory
writing reports and proposals	accounting/preparing financial reports
handling sales, marketing, public relations	dealing with regulatory agencies

TECHNICAL EDUCATION

- Completed specialized education at **City College of Chicago** in Pest Control Technology.
- Excelled in extensive pest control course work at **California State University**.
- Completed advanced courses at **California State University** at the Wood Destroying Organisms Institute.
- Completed corporate training sponsored by leading industry firms including Stephensen Chemicals, Forshaw Distribution, and Whitmire Research Laboratories.

QUALIFICATIONS

California Structural Pest Control Certification in Household Pests and Wood Destroying Organisms, May 1989; California Structural Pest Control License in Household Pests and Wood Destroying Organisms, December 1990.

EXPERIENCE

FOUNDER/PRESIDENT. Quality Pest Control Services, Inc., San Francisco, CA (1997-03). Started "from scratch" a company which was recently bought out by one of the largest pest elimination service companies in the country; did not remain with the company because its policy of "promotion from within" would have required me to accept an entry-level position in the corporation.

- Succeeded as an entrepreneur and business manager in a highly competitive industry because of my ability to communicate ideas to others, my problem-solving skills, my ability to formulate new ideas based on information obtained from multiple sources, and my outgoing and self-confident nature.
- Established the company in San Francisco and then expanded the service area from Oakland to Palo Altos. Handled all financial matters including budgets, profit-and-loss quotas, tax planning, insurance, and purchasing.
- In June and July 2003, was involved in a project with a large supermarket chain which involved performing quality assurance inspections throughout each store; evaluated the chain's pest control program, assessed food handling and storage procedures, and monitored temperature control in critical areas such as deli/bakeries, meat and seafood shops, and cooler/freezer; also evaluated employee adherence to local health codes.
- Have acquired considerable experience in dealing with government regulatory agencies and in preparing the paperwork necessary to document programs in critical situations.

SERVICE SPECIALIST. Lab Technologies Inc., Miami, FL (1997). Serviced a variety of commercial and institutional accounts.

- Developed expertise in treating sensitive accounts such as hospitals and nursing homes.
- Played a key role in stabilizing new accounts during a period of rapid growth.

EXTERMINATOR. Safeguard Exterminating Company, Inc., Chicago, IL (1989-97). Was a major force in the company's growth over eight years of 15% yearly; helped establish formal training and hiring policies; began in sales and in my fourth year was promoted to supervisor overseeing clean-out coordination, termite control coordination, equipment maintenance, and troubleshooting in all areas of service.

- In my fifth year was promoted to **Vice President of Sales and Training**; had responsibility for setting/achieving branch goals and for defining/implementing training programs covering residential and commercial pest control while also overseeing safety procedures, vehicle maintenance, and equipment maintenance.

EDUCATION

Completed general courses at City College of Chicago.

PERSONAL

Offer experience in using and repairing a wide range of equipment including compressed air sprayers, air atomization units, dusters, power spray units, respirators, and gas and electric motors.

ENTREPRENEURS SEEKING CORPORATE POSITIONS

Date

Mrs. Sylvia Ray
Pfeifer Supply Company
2930 Southern Avenue
Meredith, GA 30093

Plumbing, Heating, & Cooling

Dear Mrs. Ray:

I would sincerely enjoy the opportunity to meet and talk with you about my desire to contribute to the growth and profitability of Pfeifer Supply Company.

On the enclosed resume I have described my expertise related to wholesale plumbing, heating, and industrial supplies, including my extensive personnel and operations management experience.

Regarded within the industry as an innovator and leader, I have developed the ability to "build a team" of highly motivated and productive employees.

I believe you would find me personally to be a warm professional who enjoys sharing my "wealth" of experience with other managers.

I am looking forward to our January 5 meeting when we can discuss your current and future needs and how I might serve them. Thank you in advance for your time.

Sincerely yours,

Hilton Walters

HILTON WALTERS

1110½ Hay Street, Fayetteville, NC 28305   •   preppub@aol.com   •   (910) 483-6611

OBJECTIVE

To contribute to corporate growth and profitability through my expertise related to wholesale plumbing, heating, and industrial supplies, including my superior product knowledge and extensive personnel management experience.

HONORS

Because of my executive ability, financial savvy, and decision-making skills, was selected for these and other honors in my community:
- Board of Directors: First Citizen's Bank, Guaranty Savings and Loan Association, Occoneechee Boy Scouts Council.
- Board of Directors: University of North Carolina at Chapel Hill.
- Board of Trustees: Fayetteville Exchange Club, Lions Club, Chamber of Commerce, Rotary Club.

EXPERIENCE

BRANCH OPERATIONS MANAGER. Hilton Walters Supply Company, Raeford headquarters and other branches in SC and NC (1969-02). Over a 32-year period, developed "from scratch" a wholesale distributor company that eventually had $10 million in annual sales, 1,800 customers, and branches in NC and SC.
- Established a loyal clientele of satisfied customers including:

Plumbing contractors	Industrial customers
Heating and A/C contractors	Motels and hotels
Refrigeration contractors	Schools and colleges
Mechanical contractors	Water and sewer contractors
Hospitals	Electrical contractors

- Warehoused and sold a complete line of plumbing, heating, electrical, air conditioning, refrigeration, and industrial supplies/equipment.
- Managed aspects of operations, including hiring branch managers and sales personnel.
- Boosted sales and productivity through implementing an employee credit union as well as bonus incentive/profit sharing plans.
- Maintained continuous growth and profitability through my expert sales and purchasing techniques.
- Assured excellent control at all times of accounts receivable as well as a $1.6 million average inventory.
- Became regarded as an industry leader because of my ability to "build a team" of dedicated employees.
- Acquired a real "knack" for recruiting, hiring, and motivated and talented employees.

AFFILIATIONS

Dedicated personally and professionally to Christian principles, have served my industry in these and other ways:
- President: East Carolina Wholesalers.
- President and co-founder: East Coast Wholesaler's Association.
- Member and Board of Directors: Southern Wholesaler's Association.
- Member: National Association of Wholesale Distributors.
- Member: National Plumbing, Heating, and Cooling Information Bureau.
- Member: Fayetteville Area Master Plumber's Association.
- Associate Member: NC Plumbing, Heating, Cooling Contractors.

PERSONAL

Enjoy the challenge of putting together a highly motivated team of employees who are determined to make a profit while serving satisfied customers. Have a private pilot's license. Am flexible and willing to relocate.

HOSPITALITY INDUSTRY

Date

Exact Name of Person
Title or Position
Name of Company
Address (no., street)
Address (city, state, zip)

Bartender   Dear Exact Name of Person: (or Dear Sir or Madam if answering a blind ad.)

I would appreciate an opportunity to talk with you soon about how I could contribute to your organization through my vast knowledge of the food and beverage business.

As you will see from my resume, after serving my country in the U.S. Army as a military policeman and counterintelligence/special agent, I have contributed to the success of businesses serving the entertainment/recreational needs of people. Most recently as a bartender I have played a key role in building the clientele of a popular bar and grill. I am considered an expert on mixology and have even created my own "signature" drinks.

In other jobs I have supervised lifeguards, instructed fishing and water skiing activities, and controlled inventories of recreational equipment.

I hope we will have the opportunity to talk in person about how I could be of value to your business. I can provide outstanding personal and professional references, and I was entrusted while in military service with one of the nation's highest security clearances. You would find me to be someone of the highest character who is known for my willingness to "pitch in" and work as needed when other workers encounter unexpected problems.

I will be in Dillon, Colorado, from Tuesday 20th September through Saturday, 24th September, and I will call when I get into town to see if your schedule will permit us to meet. Thank you in advance for your time.

Sincerely yours,

Glen Leamons

GLEN LEAMONS

1110½ Hay Street, Fayetteville, NC 28305 • preppub@aol.com • (910) 483-6611

OBJECTIVE

To benefit an organization that can use a hard-working and reliable individual who offers a background in the hospitality industry along with experience as a military professional.

EXPERIENCE

BARTENDER/FOOD SERVER. Big Daddy's Bar & Grill, Fayetteville, NC (2003-04). Am involved in all aspects of operating and managing this popular bar and grill serving a loyal clientele in a town adjacent to the world's largest U.S. military base; assure that the bar is perfectly cleaned and well stocked at all times.

- *Mixology*: Considered an expert on mixology, have become knowledgeable of more than 80 different import beers and demonstrated my comprehensive knowledge of mixed drinks; created my own "signature" drinks which became favorites.
- *Management*: Act as assistant manager in his absence; became known for my professionalism and willingness to work "on call, no questions asked."
- *Food preparation*: Responsible for food orders and food preparation.
- *Purchasing/inventory control*: Accountable for beer and liquor inventory; determine product line and order beverages and some foodstuffs.
- *Finances*: Assure proper pricing and handling of in excess of $2,000 daily.
- *Customer relations*: Play a key role in building the clientele.
- *Technical knowledge*: Implement all state laws on alcohol consumption.

SKI MACHINE OPERATOR/MAINTENANCE COORDINATOR. Ski Rixen, Ft. Bragg, NC (2000-04). While simultaneously excelling in the job above, was in charge of lifeguards and ski machine on a busy lake used by swimmers, boaters, and water skiers; monitored skiers' safety and assured proper maintenance of equipment.

- As a water skiing instructor, taught thousands of people to water ski.

COUNTERINTELLIGENCE/SPECIAL AGENT. U.S. Army, Ft. Bragg, NC (2000-03). Was promoted ahead of my peers into "mid-management" and achieved the rank of E-5 in record time due to my disciplined hard work, reliability, and highly motivated nature.

- Won numerous awards including "Soldier of the Year," "Soldier of the Quarter," and "Non-Commissioned Officer of the Year."
- Advanced into supervision and was in charge of a platoon of up to 30 people.

INVENTORY CONTROLLER and **CUSTOMER SALES REPRESENTATIVE.** Graybar Electric, Orlando, FL (1997-00). Began as a truck driver and became very knowledgeable of Central Florida's road system while loading and driving trucks filled with electrical equipment; was promoted to an inside warehouse job and then to a sales position.

- Controlled and accounted for $16 million in inventory while overseeing warehouse sanitation and internal organization.
- Also excelled in a sales position; handled sales of $200,000 monthly and helped increase sales by my ability to communicate with customers by telephone and in person.

LIFEGUARD/SKI INSTRUCTOR/FISHING GUIDE. Walt Disney World, Orlando, FL (1997). Supervised large groups of people and was responsible for the safety of hundreds of people daily while maintaining a 100-person pool and overseeing swimming and water activities.

- Instructed water skiing and drove a boat; instructed fishing.

MILITARY POLICEMAN. U.S. Army, various locations (1994-00). Gained computer operations and video monitoring/surveillance skills and learned to operate and maintain firearms while serving my country as a Special Reaction Team Leader, Squad Leader, and Platoon Leader.

EDUCATION

Completed more than two years of college-level courses related to computer programming, law enforcement, criminal investigations, counterterrorism and surveillance, lifesaving and emergency medical treatment, and supervision/management.

PERSONAL

While serving my country, held one of the country's highest security clearances, Top Secret based on a Special Background Investigation. Vast knowledge of food/beverage business.

HOSPITALITY INDUSTRY

Date

Exact Name of Person (if known)
Title or Position
Name of Company
Address (no., street)
Address (city, state, zip)

**Dietetics and
Institutional
Food Service
Management**

Dear Exact Name of Person: (or Dear Sir or Madam if answering a blind ad.)

Could your organization use an experienced manager, supervisor, and trained dietitian who offers a background of working from the ground floor up in the food service industry? If so, I would appreciate an opportunity to talk with you soon about how I could contribute to your organization through my experience and personal qualities.

As you will see from my resume, I have skills and abilities that could make me a valuable part of your team. In addition, I feel certain that you would find me to be a hard-working and reliable professional who prides myself on doing any job to the best of my ability. I can provide excellent personal and professional references if you request them.

I hope you will call or write me soon to suggest a time convenient for us to meet and discuss your current and future needs and how I might serve them. Thank you in advance for your time.

Sincerely yours,

Brad Ward

Dietetics and Institutional Food Service Management
BRAD WARD

1110½ Hay Street, Fayetteville, NC 28305   •   preppub@aol.com   •   (910) 483-6611

OBJECTIVE

To benefit an organization that can use an experienced manager, supervisor, and trained dietitian who offers a background of working from the ground floor up in the food service industry.

EXPERIENCE

Offer a track record of promotion with Second Home, Charlotte, NC (1994-03):
FOOD SERVICE DIRECTOR. Demonstrated knowledge of foods, their nutritional value, and methods of preparation; applied principles of personnel management, recordkeeping, and sanitation/safety.

Meal Planning: Carefully studied menus to ensure diets were nutritionally adequate.
Purchasing and Storage: Made decisions on quality and quantity in purchasing; maintained adequate and safe storage for supplies and equipment.
Recordkeeping: Compiled menu file for possible review; maintained equipment file for keeping operating instructions and directions for routine maintenance; prepared monthly meal cost report for submission to the Administrator.
Employee Supervision: Supervised the kitchen staff and the operation of dietary laws; observed for overproduction of food and improper preparation; hired, counseled, and disciplined, if necessary, all dietary employees.
Sanitation and Safety: Ensured cleanliness of kitchen including food, equipment, personnel, and physical environment; established and maintained a routine cleaning schedule.

DIETITIAN. Prepared a variety of dietary meals for 85 people; worked with Food Service Supervisor on budget control and inventory.

SHIFT MANAGER. Captain D's Restaurant, Chapel Hill, NC (1993-94). Responsible for deposits, cash reports, scheduling and time cards, food orders, supplies, inventory, budget control, and ensuring sanitation regulations were strictly followed.

KITCHEN MANAGER. Bronte Brothers Restaurant, Pinehurst, NC (1992-93). Ensured that all meals in a full-service restaurant were prepared properly including seafood, steaks, full salad bar, and buffet-style meals seven days per week; ordered all supplies and maintained accurate inventory.

Advanced through promotions with the U.S Air Force, various worldwide locations (1983-92):
DINING HALL SUPERVISOR. Opened food service operation on a new military base supervising 50 people, both military and civilian; maintained budget control and handled civilian payroll for 34 Korean nationals.

FOOD SERVICE SUPERVISOR. Was in charge of the dining hall and 25 personnel working directly under my supervision.

COOK/SHIFT LEADER. Prepared daily meals while also scheduling personnel, ordering food, and reconciling cash drawers.

FIRST COOK. Ensured all meals were prepared to taste and met specific military standards; trained apprentice cooks; and assisted with menu preparation.

EDUCATION & TRAINING

Majored in Business Administration, Methodist College, Fayetteville, NC.
Studied Sociology, Methodist College, Fayetteville, NC.
Successfully completed a six-week food service course studying basic cooking, baking, sanitation, budget control, purchasing, and stock control.

PERSONAL

Strongly believe that the appearance of the employee and the manner in which food is served is an important factor determining the way in which the food is accepted. Am a hard working team player with a "do whatever it takes" attitude.

HOSPITALITY INDUSTRY

Date

Exact Name of Person
Title or Position
Name of Company
Address (no., street)
Address (city, state, zip)

Food Service Management

Dear Exact Name of Person: (or Dear Sir or Madam if answering a blind ad.)

I would appreciate an opportunity to talk with you soon about how I could contribute to your organization through my experience in the food service industry, including my knowledge of the administrative aspects of this industry.

You will see from my resume that I earned a reputation as a knowledgeable, dependable, and respected professional while serving in the U.S. Army. I have overseen operations of dining facilities serving three meals a day to as many as 800 people. I have become skilled at managing the details of inventory control, quality control, sanitation, and production operations while also training employees, maintaining excellent customer relations, and solving difficult and unexpected supply problems.

Especially effective at training others, I am skilled at motivating personnel and developing them into productive teams of workers who are known for providing attractive and nourishing meals. My experience also includes ensuring sanitation and health standards are met and controlling inventories of perishable and non-perishable foods. During the war in the Middle East, I was singled out to manage a dining facility and was commended for my organizational and leadership skills during this trying period.

I hope you will welcome my call soon to arrange a brief meeting at your convenience to discuss your current and future needs and how I might serve them. Thank you in advance for your time.

Sincerely yours,

Helen Tyson

Alternate last paragraph:
I hope you will call or write me soon to suggest a time convenient for us to meet and discuss your current and future needs and how I might serve them. Thank you in advance for your time.

HELEN TYSON

1110½ Hay Street, Fayetteville, NC 28305   •   preppub@aol.com   •   (910) 483-6611

OBJECTIVE   To offer my management experience, motivational skills, and organizational abilities to a company that can use a hard-working professional with extensive knowledge related to quality control, inventory control, production operations, and service operations.

COMPUTERS   Knowledgeable of computer software including Microsoft Word and Excel.

EXPERIENCE   **COOK.** Bandolino's Restaurant, Fayetteville, NC (2003-present). Am contributing to the high quality of food served in this full-service restaurant by producing fine baked goods while also preparing/cooking a wide range of items for the brunch buffet; prepare salads, sandwiches, and desserts according to customers' orders.

COOK. Lewison's Kitchen, Ft. Bragg, NC (2003). Prepared and cooked meats, gravies, sauces, and soups; acted as supervisor in the absence of the manager.

PACKAGE HANDLER. United Parcel Service (UPS), McAllen, TX (2002). Earned a reputation as an extremely hard worker while lifting/loading an average of 120 packages an hour.
* Set records for the number of packages loaded during the hectic Christmas season.
* Simultaneously served in the Army Reserve as a Baker Supervisor/Section Leader.

Refined my supervisory and managerial skills in food service operations, U.S. Army:
SUPERVISORY BAKER. Ft. Hood, TX (2001). As a night-shift baker, prepared pastries, pies, cakes, and cookies for a dining facility which fed approximately 1,500 meals a day.
* Taught personnel proper procedures for preparing meals using mobile kitchen systems as well as the recommended methods for handling cash and ordering supplies.

FACILITY SUPERVISOR. Germany (1999-01). Advanced to higher supervisory levels in an operation serving two meals a day to around 500 people; handled responsibilities including ordering supplies, planning meals, training personnel, and preparing reports.
* Reduced the facility's account status to within 3% of allocations; maintained this level.

SERVICE OPERATIONS MANAGER. Saudi Arabia (1999-00). Singled out for my demonstrated knowledge and leadership abilities, oversaw ordering supplies and planning menus as well as controlling record keeping and supervising 32 employees.
* Ensured that my organization's personnel were enjoying fresh nutritious meals despite the drawbacks of operating in an inhospitable climate under combat pressures.

ASSISTANT MANAGER. Ft. Bragg, NC (1996-99). Planned menus, prepared reports, and maintained accounts for the dining facility at Simmons Army Airfield.

OFFICE MANAGER. Germany (1992-96). Earned the respect of the facility's general manager and was frequently entrusted to manage day-to-day operations.
* Set up the office system and took care of maintaining accounts, handling cash transactions, and planning menus.

Highlights of earlier experience: Learned scheduling, accounting for food items, and health and safety guidelines in U.S. Army assignments as a Shift Supervisor and Cook.
* Was commended for my instrumental role in helping a Ft. Hood, TX, dining facility win the prestigious Connelly Award as "best overall field mess in the U.S. Army" for 1990.
* Earned the honor of "Culinary Specialist of the Quarter" at one facility in Germany.

EDUCATION   Currently am studying for an associate's degree in Business Administration, National Education Corporation,
&   Scranton, PA.
TRAINING   Completed training related to inventory management, accounting, supervision, and supply.

PERSONAL   Work well under pressure. Excel at motivating and training other employees. Familiar with team kettles, convection ovens, food slicers, and food processors.

HOSPITALITY INDUSTRY

Date

Exact Name of Person
Title or Position
Name of Company
Address (no., street)
Address (city, state, zip)

Restaurant Multi-Unit Management

Dear Exact Name of Person: (or Dear Sir or Madam if answering a blind ad.)

I would appreciate an opportunity to meet with you confidentially to discuss the possibility of my joining your organization. As you will see from my resume, I have excelled in a variety of roles within the Family Steak & Seafood Corporation, and I have the highest regard for our management team and for my associates. Although I am essentially happy in my current organizational home, I am interested in learning more about your company's strategic direction, because I feel I could contribute to your goals and add value to your company.

While working with Family Steak & Seafood Corporation for the past eight years, I have had an opportunity to acquire skills in every functional area of restaurant operations. Most recently I played a key role in opening a restaurant which has become the highest-volume unit in the chain's history. While overseeing every aspect of operation in this 235-person restaurant, I have instilled in employees an attitude of "attention to detail" which has produced an exceptionally strong commitment to quality standards.

With a reputation as a dynamic motivator and trainer, I have been commended for my ability to hire, train, develop, and motivate some of the industry's finest human resources. I believe strongly that it is the quality of your people and the way you train them that is the key to success in our highly competitive industry. You will see from my resume that I have won numerous awards and honors, including awards for closing down strong competitors.

You would find me in person to be a gregarious and outgoing fellow who offers a proven ability to relate well to customers and to employees at all levels. I have won numerous awards for my exceptional results in the areas of training, profit, sales, and operations.

I hope you will welcome my call soon to arrange a brief meeting at your convenience to discuss your current and future needs and how I might serve them. Thank you in advance for your time.

Sincerely yours,

Belinda Oliver

Alternate last paragraph:
I hope you will call or write me soon to suggest a time convenient for us to meet and discuss your current and future needs and how I might best serve them. Thank you in advance for your time.

Restaurant Multi-Unit Management

BELINDA OLIVER
1110½ Hay Street, Fayetteville, NC 28305 • preppub@aol.com • (910) 483-6611

OBJECTIVE

To benefit an organization that can use a dynamic and resourceful general manager who offers expertise in restaurant operations including experience in starting up new units, overseeing multiple locations, and troubleshooting problems in existing establishments.

ACHIEVEMENTS & DISTINCTIONS

- 2003; Started up a restaurant that is the highest-volume restaurant in the chain's history.
- **Top Training Manager** award, 2002; have been recognized for my expertise in training employees and developing human resources considered the best in the industry.
- **Top Ten Award**, 2002; through my management skills, transformed an average operation into a restaurant in the "top 10%" of the company's units in sales/profits.
- Two **Notch in the Gun** awards, 2002 and 1999; for closing down two competitors (Western Sizzler and Golden Corral).
- **ServSafe**, 2003; received this award from the National Restaurant Association for my impeccable sanitation and health practices.

SUMMARY OF EXPERIENCE

For the past eight years, worked at Family Steak & Seafood Restaurant, the largest restaurant chain in North Carolina; have earned a reputation as a dynamic motivator, skilled trainer, creative organizer, and innovative manager.

EXPERIENCE

ASSOCIATE MANAGER. Family Steak & Seafood Corporation, Charlotte, NC (2002-present). Relocated to Charlotte after completing an extensive executive development training session in the operation of metropolitan units from December 2002 - April 2003; then opened a restaurant which has become the chain's highest-volume unit.

- *Employee training and supervision*: Oversee hiring, training, and scheduling of the restaurant's 235 employees; reduced labor costs 6% within three months after opening.
- *Inventory control*: Cost-effectively manage the purchasing, receipt, and utilization of an inventory of perishable and non-perishable items.
- *Finances*: Prepare profit-and-loss statements; monitor invoicing; oversee payroll administration.
- *Quality control*: Have instilled in employees an attitude of "attention to detail" that has produced a strong commitment to quality standards.
- *Sales and profitability*: Have exceeded every monthly record established for sales since opening in May, 2003.

PARTNER/MANAGER. Family Steak & Seafood Corporation, Wilmington, NC (1996-02). Excelled in a variety of roles because of my versatile management skills.

- *Operations management*: Increased sales in off-season by 35% over a six-year period; learned that persistence and hard work are the keys to achieving sales goals in the restaurant industry.
- *Competitive spirit*: Despite the disadvantage of having to compete with limited seating space, closed down two competitors and increased sales by 26%.
- *Training and development*: Trained district managers, partner managers, franchise service consultants, and assistant managers.
- *Area supervision*: Functioned as a Temporary Area Supervisor and helped selling units with a variety of problems when the district supervisor was overloaded.
- *Coordination*: Became skilled in every aspect of unit operations management including sales/profit control, hiring/training, scheduling, and food cost control/ordering.

ASSISTANT MANAGER. Family Steak & Seafood Corporation, Roanoke Rapids, NC (1995-96). Was commended for my creative approach to community involvement and acquired expertise in guest services while training employees and controlling food/labor costs.

EDUCATION

Business Administration studies, North Carolina State University, Raleigh, NC, 1991-94.
Completed extensive executive/management training, Family Steak & Seafood, 1995-03.

PERSONAL

Offer extensive expertise in setting up menu matrices, completing sanitation paperwork, handling purchasing, and performing every job and task in restaurant operations.

HOSPITALITY INDUSTRY

Date

Exact Name of Person
Title or Position
Name of Company
Address (no., street)
Address (city, state, zip)

Seeking Advancement into Hotel/Restaurant Management

Dear Exact Name of Person: (or Dear Sir or Madam if answering a blind ad.)

I would appreciate an opportunity to talk with you soon about how I could contribute to your organization through my education and experience related to the field of restaurant and hotel management.

In 2002 I received an Associate's degree in Hotel and Restaurant Management from Pennsylvania State University. I have been working since the summer of 1997 as a hostess, waitress, and banquet coordinator. After starting with a family-style restaurant at age 14, I quickly earned a reputation as a mature and responsible young person. I earned the trust of the owner and was soon working all shifts and filling in during the manager's absence.

Very customer-service oriented, I am known for my ability to remain calm and in control even when things are very hectic and busy. I am a team player who motivates others to follow my example of professionalism and dedication to quality service.

I hope you will welcome my call soon to arrange a brief meeting at your convenience to discuss your current and future needs and how I might serve them. Thank you in advance for your time.

Sincerely yours,

Teresa Abbott

Alternate last paragraph:
I hope you will call or write me soon to suggest a time convenient for us to meet and discuss your current and future needs and how I might serve them. Thank you in advance for your time.

Seeking Advancement into Hotel/Restaurant Management

TERESA ABBOTT

1110½ Hay Street, Fayetteville, NC 28305 • preppub@aol.com • (910) 483-6611

OBJECTIVE

To contribute through my education and experience related to restaurant and hotel management by offering my motivational and communication skills along with my energy, enthusiasm, and reputation as a dependable and knowledgeable young professional.

EDUCATION

Associate's degree in **Hotel and Restaurant Management,** Pennsylvania State University, Berks Campus in Wyomissing, PA, 2002.
- Supervised up to seven people while planning, organizing, cooking for, and serving at campus special events, thereby gaining an opportunity to manage details while remaining in control when problems arose (college-sponsored Hotel/Restaurant Society).

Studied **Marketing and Small Business Management,** Lebanon County Vo-Tech, Lebanon, PA.

TRAINING

Completed the following additional programs:
Sanitation Certification, learned food diseases, bacteria prevention, proper water temperatures, and insect control, Pennsylvania State University, Wyomissing, PA, 2002.
Cooking Course, emphasis on preparing, measuring, cooking, and serving food, Wyomissing Vo-Tech, Wyomissing, PA, 2001.

SPECIAL KNOWLEDGE

Through training and experience, have gained knowledge of the restaurant business from concept to operation including the following areas:

break-even point analysis	forecasting sales	job descriptions
cleaning/operating supplies	positions and tasks	profit management
preparation and portion control	personnel management	task and job analysis

staffing: recruitment, selection, interviewing, orientation, training
food purchasing: purchasing, storage of different types of food
sanitation: acidity and bacterial growth, food protection, pest control

Use Macintosh computers with Microsoft Works for word processing and spreadsheets.

EXPERIENCE

FOOD SERVICE TEAM MEMBER. McDonald's Hamburgers, Spring Lake, NC (2003-present). Because of my education and experience in the restaurant business was able to quickly become familiar with the variety of positions it takes to make a fast food restaurant operate smoothly; provided courteous service in all areas.
- Ensured that customers were served rapidly while taking food and drink orders, entering items into the computer, bagging the food, and making change.
- Gained practical kitchen experience cooking meat and assembling sandwiches as well as frying French fries, fish, and chicken nuggets.

HOSTESS and **WAITRESS.** Big Boy East of Lebanon, Lebanon, PA (2002). Expanded my knowledge of food service by handling functions ranging from greeting customers and seating them, to explaining menu choices, to taking orders, to serving food, to stocking servers' stations, to totaling bills and collecting payments.
- Learned to use the Omron computer system for adding bills.
- Was able to work with the restaurant's bakers while learning to make speciality goods such as strawberry pies, muffins, and cornbread.

HOSTESS and **WAITRESS.** The Hearth Family Restaurant, Lebanon, PA (1997-02). Began working at age 14 and while still in high school gained a reputation as a mature and responsible young person who learned quickly and could be counted on to work hard to ensure customer satisfaction even when things were very busy and hectic.
- Became known for my maturity and willingness to work long hours and was placed in charge to oversee operations during all shifts and in the absence of the owner.
- Was singled out for training in serving banquets which included setting up and preparing for large groups and ensuring fast, efficient service.
- Learned to take charge and tactfully manage workers who were older and often more experienced.

Highlights of other experience: While attending a vocational-technical high school, managed a school store run by students: used my computer knowledge to input inventory data into a new system that had just been obtained that year.

PERSONAL

Am a positive and optimistic individual. Offer an energetic, enthusiastic, and outgoing personality. Enjoy contributing to team efforts and seeing customers enjoy services.

INDUSTRIAL

Exact Name of Person
Title or Position
Name of Company
Address (no., street)
Address (city, state, zip)

Industrial Engineering

Dear Exact Name of Person: (or Dear Sir or Madam if answering a blind ad.)

I would appreciate an opportunity to talk with you soon about how I could contribute to your organization through my industrial engineering background including my experience in managing cost reduction programs, planning capital expenditures, and supporting new product design.

In my current job as an Industrial Engineer and Cost Reduction Coordinator, I have implemented the new manufacturing concept known as continuous process flow cells and have functioned as the "in-house expert" in training my associates in this area. While managing a $700,000 cost reduction program, I investigate and implement cost reductions through alternative materials and manufacturing processes as well as design modifications. I am involved on a daily basis in on-the-floor problem solving, costing of component processing, tooling and gaging, and capital equipment acquisitions. I have had extensive experience in project management.

Prior to graduating with my B.S. degree in Industrial Engineering, I worked my way through college in jobs which I was involved in producing computer-aided drawings and participating in new product design. Although I worked my way through college, financing 80% of my education, I excelled academically and received the Outstanding Senior Award.

I am knowledgeable of numerous popular software and drafting packages. I offer a proven ability to rapidly master new software and adapt it for specific purposes and environments.

Single and willing to relocate, I can provide outstanding personal and professional references. I am highly regarded by my current employer, Ingersoll-Rand, and have been credited with making numerous contributions to the company through solving problems, cutting costs, determining needed capital equipment, and implementing new processes. I am making this inquiry to your company in confidence because I feel there might be a fit between your needs and my versatile areas of expertise.

I hope you will call or write me soon to suggest a time convenient for us to meet and discuss your current and future needs and how I might serve them. Thank you in advance for your time.

Sincerely yours,

Douglas Atkinson

Alternate last paragraph:
I hope you will welcome my call soon to arrange a brief meeting at your convenience to discuss your current and future needs and how I might serve them. Thank you in advance for your time.

DOUGLAS ATKINSON

1110½ Hay Street, Fayetteville, NC 28305   •   preppub@aol.com   •   (910) 483-6611

OBJECTIVE

To add value to an organization that can use an accomplished young industrial engineer who offers specialized know-how in coordinating cost reductions, experience in both manufacturing and process engineering, proven skills in project management, and extensive interaction with product design, quality control, vendor relations, and capital expenditures.

EDUCATION

Bachelor of Science (B.S.) degree, Industrial Engineering Major with a concentration in manufacturing, East Carolina University, Greenville, NC, 2000.
- Achieved a 3.5 GPA (3.8 in my major); inducted into Epsilon Pi Tau Honorary Fraternity.
- Received **Outstanding Senior Award** in manufacturing concentration.
- Worked throughout college and financed 80% of my education.

Associate of Applied Science (A.A.S.) degree, Mechanical Engineering and Design Technology Major, Richmond Community College, Hamlet, NC, 1996; achieved 3.7 GPA.

From 2000-present, completed business minor at St. Andrews Presbyterian College and have participated in continuing education sponsored by Ingersoll-Rand, Ford Motor Company, and the George Group in these and other areas:

ISO 9000 Internal Auditing	Root Cause Analysis
Total Quality Management	Value Engineering/Value Analysis
Continuous Flow Manufacturing	Synchronous Manufacturing

TECHNICAL KNOWLEDGE

Software: Quattro Pro, Freelance, Microsoft Word, Excel and PageMaker
Drafting: VERSACAD, CADCAM, Cascade, Intergraph, Unigraphics
Machining: Knowledge of machining processes and tooling and gaging equipment; some experience programming CNC equipment.

CERTIFICATIONS

Certified Manufacturing Technologist; Certified ISO 9000 Internal Auditor

EXPERIENCE

INDUSTRIAL ENGINEER/COST REDUCTION COORDINATOR. Ingersoll-Rand Co., Southern Pines, NC (2002-present). Responsible for the processing of machined components from raw material to finished product while also coordinating a $700,000 annual cost reduction program; investigate and implement cost reductions by exploring the possibility of alternative materials, other manufacturing processes, and design modifications.
- Involved on a daily basis in on-the-floor problem solving, costing of component processing, tooling and gaging, and capital equipment acquisitions.
- Implemented and coordinated continuous process flow cells, a new concept in the manufacturing area; completed extensive training and trained my associates.
- Performed cost justifications and complete equipment installs for capital equipment acquisitions totaling half a million dollars.
- Continuously interact with new product teams, problem-solving groups, purchasing specialists, vendors, as well as manufacturing and quality control personnel.
- Evaluated ergonomic equipment in assembly environment to reduce operator fatigue.

ASSOCIATE MANUFACTURING ENGINEER. [Temporary contract position]. Rockwell International, Maxton, NC (2001). Coordinated project workloads, designed assembly tooling, and established data bases for tracking and calibration of gaging used in the shop; gained experience related to self-directed work teams, facilities layout, and routing procedures.
- Identified equipment needed and assisted in capital acquisition of that equipment.

Other experience:
DESIGNER. For the *Precision Controls Division of Dana Corporation*, (1996-99), produced computer-aided drawings and actively participated in new product design while interacting with engineering and manufacturing.
- Was part of the team that introduced the first microprocessor controlled cruise control.

DEPARTMENT ASSISTANT. On a part-time work scholarship, produced drawings on VERSACAD computer-aided drafting system for Richmond Community College.

AFFILIATIONS

Society of Manufacturing Engineers, Sandhills Division; National Association of Industrial Technology; Epsilon Pi Tau International Honorary Fraternity for Education in Technology.

INDUSTRIAL

Date

Exact Name of Person
Title or Position
Name of Company
Address (no., street)
Address (city, state, zip)

Industrial Management and Quality Control

Dear Sir or Madam:

I would appreciate an opportunity to talk with you soon about how I could benefit the PWC through my education, knowledge, and supervisory skills. I am especially interested in receiving your consideration for the positions of Laboratory Supervisor and Chemist.

You will see by my enclosed resume that I have a B.S. degree in Biology and a B.S. in Business Administration along with additional graduate-level course work at The University of North Carolina at Chapel Hill. This UNC-CH program is in the area of medical education development and allows students an opportunity to complete a concentrated course showing them the academic, physical and mental stresses of medical school. I earned certification for completing this program two different summers.

My versatile background includes acting as a coordinator for Fayetteville Technical Community College where I helped administer a program for PWC employees from a three-state area in the pipe and water meter distribution course. This program which I have been involved in since 1999 on a part-time basis, instructs students on the American Waste Water Association (AWWA) standards and procedures. I am also a Technical Instructor for the Industrial Maintenance program at FTCC which leads to certification in areas including lift truck operation, safety in the work place, math and measurements, and blueprint reading.

In addition to the experience and education mentioned above, I also offer well-developed supervisory skills refined as a military officer. After several years in the field of transportation operations, I requested and was accepted for the field of supply management. My military experience allowed me opportunities to build a reputation as a talented developer of comprehensive raining plans as well as a successful manager of human, material, and fiscal resources.

I offer a well-rounded background directly related to PWC operations along with the ability to quickly master new ideas and procedures. I feel that through my versatility and ability to adapt to new things I could quickly become a valuable asset to your organization. I hope you will welcome my call soon to arrange a brief meeting at your convenience to discuss your current and future needs and how I might serve them. Thank you in advance for your time.

Sincerely yours,

Terry Brand

Industrial Management and Quality Control

TERRY BRAND

1110½ Hay Street, Fayetteville, NC 28305   •   preppub@aol.com   •   (910) 483-6611

OBJECTIVE

To offer a versatile background which includes experience in the areas of developing training programs and instructing technical subjects as well as managing supply and transportation operations while becoming known for my versatility and intellectual abilities.

EDUCATION

B.S., Biology, Fayetteville State University, NC.
B.S., Business Administration, Appalachian State University, Boone, NC.
Completed graduate-level medical education development programs, The University of North Carolina at Chapel Hill (UNC-CH), 2003 and 1998; emphasis was on gross anatomy, histology, biochemistry, physiology, and dental lab operations while ensuring participants were subjected to the mental, physical, and intellectual stresses of medical school.

TRAINING

Completed extensive training programs for military executives with an emphasis on the refinement of managerial and supervisory skills as well as specific programs in the areas of transportation, supply, and civil affairs management.

EXPERIENCE

TECHNICAL INSTRUCTOR. Fayetteville Technical Community College (FTCC), Fayetteville, NC (2000-present). Am applying my communication and technical skills as a coordinator for the American Waste Water Association (AWWA) pipe and water meter distribution courses which are given to PWC employees from a three-state area.
- Provided instruction in the Industrial Maintenance program which included lift truck operation, safety, math and measurements, and blueprint reading.
- Was selected to teach courses jointly sponsored by FTCC and the Women's Center of Fayetteville: taught construction, basic math/measurements, and blueprint reading courses in the Women in Construction class (2000).
- Provided the guidance for a successful class project in which a 24 by 48-foot freestanding shelter was built and renovations made to the Farmer's Market.

QUALITY CONTROL SUPERVISOR. Hancock Turf, Inc., Stedman, NC (2000-01). Ensured the quality of work performed in projects at Ft. Bragg, NC: saw that Simmons Army Airfield and Knox Street landscaping projects were properly completed including compliance work reference, material quality/quality, and safety data sheets as well as calculating costs and implementing blueprints.

FULL-TIME STUDENT. Fayetteville and Chapel Hill, NC (1995-99). Learned to manage my time for maximum results while completing a B.S. in Biology from Fayetteville State University, UNC courses in a pre-dental program, working part-time in a family mobile home and house rental business, and earning recognition as the Honor Graduate of an Army Reserve training program.

SUPPLY OPERATIONS MANAGER. National Guard, various locations (1987-1994). Was selected for attendance at numerous management training programs in the transportation and supply fields while also completing college course work in pre-dentistry and pre-pharmacy programs.

Highlights of other experience: Applied a variety of skills and abilities while handling such full- and part-time jobs as maintaining rental units for a family property management company, volunteering at the VA Hospital dental clinic, and totally rebuilding a mobile home which had been destroyed by fire.
As a U.S. Army Officer, handled the training and administrative support for a 25-person supply center supporting a National Guard unit.
- Developed and implemented training programs in areas including maintenance, personnel, logistics, and workplace safety.
- Planned and prepared all aspects of training as well as overseeing security for a large-scale supply support organization.
- As General Manager of a 160-person organization, directed personnel operating and maintaining a fleet of 61 5-ton tractors and 5,000-gal. tanker-trailers as well as support equipment and supplies.
- Gained experience in managerial roles in the transportation field while earning numerous awards and letters of commendation for my professionalism and dedication.

PERSONAL

Am a versatile and adaptable professional who can quickly learn new procedures, equipment, and operational methods. Excellent references on request.

INDUSTRIAL

Date

Exact Name of Person
Title or Position
Name of Company
Address (number and street)
Address (city, state, and ZIP)

Industrial Purchasing

Dear Exact Name of Person: (or Dear Sir or Madam if answering a blind ad.)

I would appreciate an opportunity to talk with you soon about how I could contribute to your organization through my extensive background in purchasing production parts and services for a manufacturing firm.

You will see from my enclosed resume that I have been with Goodyear Consumer Products, Inc., in Fayetteville, NC, for several years. Although I enjoy this position and have advanced with the company through the years, the company is undergoing a major reorganization and moving most administrative functions out of Fayetteville.

After starting with Goodyear as a Departmental Secretary, I moved up to an Expediter's position and became a Buyer Trainee. Through the years my responsibilities have increased until earlier in 2002 I was placed in charge of MRO buying in addition to my other responsibilities. I have consistently reduced costs while gaining a strong background in this specialized field.

I believe that you would find me to be an enthusiastic and outgoing professional who can offer strong organizational abilities and attention to detail.

I hope you will welcome my call soon to arrange a brief meeting at your convenience to discuss your current and future needs and how I might serve them. Thank you in advance for your time.

Sincerely yours,

Shawn Hardwick

Alternate last paragraph:
I hope you will call or write me soon to suggest a time convenient for us to meet and discuss your current and future needs and how I might serve them. Thank you in advance for your time.

SHAWN HARDWICK

1110½ Hay Street, Fayetteville, NC 28305   •   preppub@aol.com   •   (910) 483-6611

OBJECTIVE   To offer an extensive background in purchasing for a major manufacturer to an organization that can use a positive and enthusiastic professional known for attention to detail and expertise in buying production parts and services.

EXPERIENCE   **MATERIALS BUYER.** Goodyear Consumer Products, Inc., Fayetteville, NC (1986-present). Advanced as a materials buyer with this manufacturer of consumer electrical products and have seen many changes in product lines and areas of emphasis for production.

- Received a letter of recommendation from the company president in recognition of my accomplishments and contributions including my ability to continually reduce costs, January 2003.
- Was placed in charge of overseeing MRO (Maintenance, Repair, and Operating) purchasing contracts for plant services including lawn care and cleaning in addition to fasteners and printing responsibilities, March 2002.
- Selected for corporate training, completed a course in blueprint reading and technical measurements, 2002.
- In 1996, became the buyer for additional types of commodities including labels and instruction books.
- In 1991, changed to commodity buying which included purchasing all electrical and electronic parts, fasteners, screw machine, and imported parts including finished goods.
- Was handpicked for a task force which developed a new line of ceiling fans: the project was successfully completed ahead of schedule and within corporate budget guidelines and restrictions.
- Selected to receive buyer training after a short period as an Expediter, set up a complete system and did the expediting for two buyers and the materials manager.
- In my first assignment as a Materials Buyer for one specific product — ceiling fans — which included all steel, fasteners, die castings, semiconductors, and injection molded parts.
- Wrote the standard operating procedures (SOP) guidelines which were used by all purchasing department personnel from 1991 to 2002.

Highlights of previous experience: Refined skills as a Clerk/Typist and Secretary for a Human Relations/Equal Opportunity Office and the Director of Personnel and Community Affairs for an Army post in Germany.
- Earned several letters and certificates of commendation and a Sustained Performance Award in recognition of professionalism and accomplishments as a government employee.

Became familiar with the functions of a purchasing office as a Departmental Secretary, Goodyear Industries, Inc., Fayetteville, NC.

Gained experience in jobs as a Office Clerk/Claims Handler/Dispatcher for a trucking company and Real Estate Salesperson.

EDUCATION   Associate's degree in **Industrial Management Technology,** Fayetteville Technical Community College, NC.
Completed 60 credit hours in **Personnel Management** through a correspondence course.
Attended Bohecker's Business College, Ravenna, OH: received training in the field of executive secretarial duties.

PERSONAL   Active in church activities, have served as vice president and secretary of the women's organization and served on the finance committee. Am a friendly and enthusiastic individual.

INDUSTRIAL

Exact Name of Person
Title or Position
Name of Company
Address (number and street)
Address (city, state, and ZIP)

Manufacturing Productivity, Training, and Quality Control

Dear Exact Name of Person: (or Dear Sir or Madam if answering a blind ad.)

I would appreciate an opportunity to talk with you soon about how I could benefit your organization through my outstanding work ethic and persistence in striving for high standards of professionalism and productivity in everything I attempt.

You will see by my enclosed resume that I excel in developing and running training programs which produced qualified and effective employees. I am a quick learner who easily absorbs new methods and procedures and then can take that information and present it to others clearly and concisely. In my present job as a Training Specialist and Team Leader for Eaton Corporation, I have been very effective in helping put together a team of dedicated workers who are achieving high levels of productivity for this manufacturer.

In every position I have held, training and instructing others was at least a part of my responsibilities, and in each case I applied my leadership and knowledge to increase productivity and efficiency. Having worked in a nuclear power plant as a decontamination specialist, built a successful day care center from the ground up, and managed a multifaceted food service program among other roles, I have demonstrated that I am adaptable and versatile. My strongest abilities are in building teams, providing quality training, and motivating others to excel and maximize their own individual talents. I possess sound judgment and problem-solving skills along with a reputation as an articulate public speaker and training specialist.

I hope you will welcome my call soon to arrange a brief meeting at your convenience to discuss your current and future needs and how I might serve them. Thank you in advance for your time.

Sincerely yours,

Barbara Barragan

Alternated last paragraph:
I hope you will call or write me soon to suggest a time convenient for us to meet and discuss your current and future needs and how I might serve them. Thank you in advance for your time.

Manufacturing Productivity, Training, and Quality Control
BARBARA BARRAGAN

1110½ Hay Street, Fayetteville, NC 28305 • preppub@aol.com • (910) 483-6611

OBJECTIVE

To contribute to an organization that can benefit from my skills in organizing, supervising, and training others to achieve outstanding results and increased productivity/profitability while assuring the highest standards of safety and quality control.

EXPERIENCE

TEAM LEADER/TRAINING SPECIALIST. Eaton Corporation, Sierra Vista, AZ (2003-present). Selected to train and develop a team of skilled employees from the start-up of a new manufacturer, maintain certification in the operation of nine different pieces of production machinery and met production goals.
- Screened and selected new employees; personally trained more than 50 people.
- Increased productivity 40% through numerous suggestions which were accepted.
- Oversaw the Continuous Improvement (CI) program which targets methods of increasing productivity and presented weekly CI training classes.
- Counseled personnel on the ways to be effective and productive team members and how to provide technical support services to other departments.
- Excelled in communicating with other team leaders, shift supervisors, and staff members so that my team always had the supplies and equipment to do the job.
- Handled scheduling for vacations and overtime and kept attendance records.
- Completed detailed technical work including entering calibration data into a computer data base, reviewing data on Excel spreadsheets, and assigning ID numbers to gauges.

DECONTAMINATION SPECIALIST and **APPRENTICE PIPE FITTER.** Fluor Daniel, Inc., Shearon Harris Nuclear Power Plant, Apex, NC (2000-03). Handled a wide range of activities including maintaining safety standards, cleaning controlled spills, disposing of radioactive waste, operating forklifts, and preparing parts and equipment for use by pipe fitters.
- Conducted informative training sessions as a member of the Safety Committee and ensured employees were aware of applicable NRC (Nuclear Regulatory Commission) and OSHA (Occupational Safety and Health Agency) regulations.
- Taught myself to be constantly aware and communicate with others on ways to work smartly while limiting exposure to radioactive materials.

NURSE'S ASSISTANT. Forest Hill Rest Home, Fayetteville, NC (1999-00). Was respected for my unselfishness in giving one-on-one care to patients, actions which had a favorable impact on the mental health of patients.
- Ensured the safety and well being of 40 patients while seeing that treatments were given and any emergencies that came up were handled promptly.

ASSISTANT MANAGER. AAFES, Germany (1998-99). Supervised over 100 employees in a food service program which supported three food court restaurants and two schools while taking care of functions including coordinating vendor activities, processing payroll, scheduling, and maintaining employee records.
- Developed a cleaning schedule accepted for use in all five facilities resulted in a 100% pass rate for all health and safety inspections.
- Oversaw a project to build a pizza restaurant from the construction phase, to screening and hiring employees, to running an orientation program which earned the praise of the District Manager as the best and most thorough he had seen.

OWNER/MANAGER. Black's Day Care, Germany (1995-98). Set up a day care center which consistently had a waiting list and was licensed to provide care for up to 30 children: developed and typed all documentation, forms, and contracts used in the business.

EDUCATION & TRAINING

Completed extensive college and corporate training in areas including:

decontamination	team dynamics	hazardous materials handling
radwaste evolutions	lift truck operation	radioactive material shipment
nuclear fuel programs	confined space	Total Quality Management (TQM)
respiratory protection	firewatch duties	competitive manufacturing
chemical control	spill control	environmental health safety
decontamination/frisking for deconners		team effectiveness

Was certified as a Nurse's Aide, Saint Francis School of Nursing, Peoria, IL.

PERSONAL

Quickly absorb and apply new information and procedures. Skilled public speaker and instructor.

LAW ENFORCEMENT

Date

Mr. Jack Smith
Personnel Officer
City of Red Springs
P.O. Box 249
Red Springs, NC 28353

Deputy Sheriff   Dear Mr. Smith:

Enclosed please find a copy of my resume. I would appreciate your consideration for the position of Identification Officer with the Red Springs Police Department.

I do meet the qualifications for this position based on my experience as a crime scene investigator with the Wake County Sheriff's Department in Raleigh, NC. My background includes almost three years in investigation, collection and interpretation of fingerprints, photography, and other technical police work.

I completed the Basic Law Enforcement Training Program in 2001 after earning an A.A.S. degree in **Criminal Justice-Protective Services Technology** from Wake County Technical Community College. As detailed on my enclosed resume, I have also received specialized training in such specific areas as crime scene preservation, infectious control and handling of hazardous materials, reporting procedures, and law enforcement photography.

With a reputation as a thorough, detail-oriented young professional, I feel that I offer the training and experience your department needs to fill this important position. I hope you will call or write me soon to suggest a time convenient for us to meet and discuss your current and future needs and how I might serve them. Thank you in advance for your time.

Sincerely yours,

Christopher Love

CHRISTOPHER LOVE

1110½ Hay Street, Fayetteville, NC 28305 • preppub@aol.com • (910) 483-6611

OBJECTIVE	To offer a reputation as a confident, articulate, and detail-oriented law enforcement professional with special emphasis in the areas of crime scene investigation and the technical aspects of police work.

EXPERIENCE

DEPUTY SHERIFF and **CRIME SCENE TECHNICIAN.** The Wake County Sheriff's Department, Raleigh, NC (2001-present). Rapidly earned a reputation as a self-motivated professional who could be counted on to ensure that crime scene evidence was thoroughly collected, investigated, and documented according to regulations and so that the chain of custody remained intact.

- Have a 100% conviction rate for the few occasions when my cases have gone to trial and have proven myself a reliable and credible witness — however, the bulk of my cases are settled by plea bargains and never go to trial.
- Received a Letter of Commendation for single-handedly locating and detaining two suspects upon responding to an attempted armed robbery.
- Responded to the full range of crimes: burglary, felony larceny, recovered stolen vehicles, armed robbery, sexual assaults, and child abuse as well as shootings, stabbings, homicides, officer-involved shootings, suicides, and auto or fire fatalities.
- Provided support by processing crime scenes for all of the separate police departments in Cumberland County and handled a wide range of duties including the following:
  processed the scene to *collect and preserve* latent prints
  photographed the scene for preservation and evidence which could not be removed
  prepared sketches and diagrams
  collected items of evidence to be submitted to the SBI lab for processing
  prepared evidence for use in court and *testified* when required
  responded to identification calls from other agencies
  performed clerical tasks dealing with reports, evidence, and identification
  maintained detailed files and ensured the proper control of records
  researched files for suspects
  arrested suspects at the crime scene and held them until the investigation was complete or until relieved
- Earned special praise from Cape Fear Valley Medical Center personnel as one of several deputies who fingerprinted and photographed large numbers of children "with patience and calm" despite long lines at a community EMS awareness program.
- Was promoted to Corporal early in 2003.

Highlights of other experience: Learned to contribute to team efforts and take responsibility for my own work as an Electrician's Apprentice installing/maintaining residential systems.

**EDUCATION,
TRAINING
&
CERTIFICATIONS**

Completed the 500-hour Basic Law Enforcement Training (BLET) leading to certification, Raleigh, NC, 2001.
- Excelled in studies which included weapons, self-defense, civil law, and criminal law.

Earned an Associate of Applied Science (A.A.S.) degree in **Criminal Justice-Protective Services Technology**, Wake County Technical Community College (WCTCC), NC, 1998.
- Maintained a 3.5 GPA.

Completed WCTCC and department-sponsored specialized training related to crime scene preservation, juvenile laws, dealing with victims and witnesses, domestic violence, patrol techniques and OSHA standards, reporting procedures, involuntary commitment, use of force, pursuit driving, infectious control and the handling of hazardous materials; also completed Polaroid-sponsored training in law enforcement photography.

**TECHNICAL
EXPERTISE**

Through training and experience, offer special skills and knowledge of the following:
- Am experienced with 35mm and instant cameras.
- Use different powders and chemicals to develop latent fingerprints: graphic powder, magnetic powder, "super-glue," and iodine fuming.
- Am experienced in using plaster casting to make tire and shoe impressions.
- Offer state certification with the .45 caliber and .380 caliber Sig Sauer pistols.
- Am thoroughly familiar with the proper techniques used in the collection and preservation of physical evidence and in maintaining the chain of custody.
- Have gained experience with autopsy and post-mortem examination procedures.
- Offer basic computer knowledge with Word, Powerpoint, and QuarkXpress.

LAW ENFORCEMENT

Date

Exact Name of Person
Title or Position
Name of Company
Address (no., street)
Address (city, state, zip)

Police Officer

Dear Exact Name of Person: (or Dear Sir or Madam if answering a blind ad.)

I would appreciate an opportunity to talk with you soon about how I could contribute to your organization through my practical experience in law enforcement. As you will see from my resume, I offer a record of exceptional performance during 9 1/2 years with the Milwaukee (Wisconsin) Police Department.

During my years of service as a Police Officer in this city of approximately 750,000 people, I earned the respect of my superiors, peers, and members of the community for my dedication to excellence in every aspect of my responsibilities. I was often singled out for difficult and sensitive assignments in recognition of my exceptional communication skills and ability to deal with any situation through my fair but firm manner. During one eight-month period in 1999-00, I worked as an Undercover Narcotics Enforcement Officer, and I participated in activities which resulted in closing 25 inner-city drug houses.

I have demonstrated that I work well under pressure, can follow directions from superiors and official guidelines, and also use my own common sense and intelligence to take charge and make decisions. Additionally I offer excellent public relations abilities and understand the importance of maintaining a strong community presence.

I left the law enforcement field to try to reach another of my career goals and completed rigorous training to become a U.S. Army warrant officer aviator. Literally tens of thousands of applications are received each year and only 750 of the most highly qualified applicants are chosen for this training program. I am very proud to have completed this training and earned a position as a helicopter pilot and military officer.

I feel that through my success in these demanding roles, I have proven my adaptability and versatility. Both professions require a person to think on his feet and handle crisis situations on a daily basis. I feel that I offer a unique mix of abilities which could make me a valuable addition to an organization such as yours.

I hope you will welcome my call soon to arrange a brief meeting at your convenience to discuss your current and future needs and how I might serve them. Thank you in advance for your time.

Sincerely yours,

Angela Coppedge

Alternate last paragraph:
I hope you will call or write me soon to suggest a time convenient for us to meet and discuss your current and future needs and how I might serve them. Thank you in advance for your time.

ANGELA COPPEDGE

1110½ Hay Street, Fayetteville, NC 28305 • preppub@aol.com • (910) 483-6611

OBJECTIVE

To offer my exceptional communication and motivational skills to an organization that can use a mature professional who has excelled in the demanding fields of law enforcement and aviation through demonstrated intellectual skills and an aggressive, enthusiastic personality.

EXPERIENCE

AVIATOR/TRAINING PILOT and **OPERATIONS MANAGER.** U.S. Army, Ft. Bragg, NC (2002-present). Am excelling as a professional aviator operating a million-dollar aircraft: plan, coordinate, and carry out assigned missions as the senior member of an air crew operating under an 18-hour notice as art of the rapid deployment forces.

- Chosen to train and supervise a 16-person Nuclear/Biological/Chemical (NBC) defense team; provided specialized proficiency training to a 45-person company, earning commendable — the highest possible — ratings in two consecutive inspections.
- Oversee the physical security for $20 million worth of equipment.
- Placed third in a 9mm team pistol competition.

Served with distinction as a Police Officer known for my common sense approach and high moral values. Was effective in relating to people from diverse ethnic and cultural backgrounds by taking charge when the situation demanded, Milwaukee, WI:
POLICE OFFICER. (1996-02). Often singled out for highly sensitive and particularly demanding jobs, handled a range of activities including accident and crime investigations, enforcement of state and local laws, domestic dispute response and intervention, and "first responder" for first aid and emergency situations.

- Applied my public speaking skills while giving testimony in criminal and traffic court.
- Received special recognition for saving the life of a man whose clothing caught fire in his yard — smothered the flames and treated him for shock until the ambulance arrived.
- Contributed to the police department's public image while coaching neighborhood youth in Police Athletic League competition.

UNDERCOVER NARCOTICS ENFORCEMENT OFFICER. (1999-00). Handpicked for this sensitive assignment, spent approximately eight months on teams which executed search warrants resulting in the shut down of more than 25 inner-city drug houses.

- Received training in specialized techniques which included "sting" operations, the use of personal listening devices (wires), undercover narcotics purchases, and surveillance.
- Developed cases through informants and received additional training in chemical testing from the state's crime lab.

POLICE AIDE. (1992-96). After placing first from among 300 applicants, at age 17 was accepted for this position which gave me the opportunity to learn about the daily routines and inner workings of the department.

- Gained experience in areas such as fingerprinting, maintaining records, assisting in booking, and in-processing prisoners.
- Provided administrative assistance during medical exams for applicants and by maintaining medical records for applicants being processed into the department.
- Conducted warrant queries for street officers and maintained files of criminal warrants.

EDUCATION & TRAINING

B.S., Criminal Justice, Mount Senario College, Ladysmith, WI, 2001.

- Graduated *magna cum laude* with a 3.89 GPA: refined my time-management skills attending college full-time while holding a demanding job as a police officer.

Completed more than 4,800 hours of advanced programs including flight training and warrant officer professional development schools as well as law enforcement courses in training and evaluation techniques, narcotics identification, and radar speed detection.

LICENSES & SPECIAL SKILLS

FAA Commercial Pilot license, rotorcraft helicopter/ instrument helicopter, 2003.
"Law Enforcement Officer" certification, Wisconsin Law Enforcement Standards Board, 1996.
Am an experienced field training officer and undercover narcotics agent familiar with surveillance, search warrants, sting operations, and undercover purchases from suspects.
Qualified as an Expert with the M-16 rifle and 9mm pistol.

PERSONAL

Honed public speaking skills on award-winning high school debate and forensics teams.

MANAGEMENT

Exact Name of Person
Title or Position
Name of Company
Address (no., street)
Address (city, state, zip)

Automobile Dealership Office Operations

Dear Exact Name of Person: (or Dear Sir or Madam if answering a blind ad.)

I would appreciate an opportunity to talk with you soon about how I could contribute to your organization through my well-rounded experience related to automobile dealership business office and support department operations.

In my position as the Business Manager for Sanford Honda — Isuzu in Raleigh, NC, I became adept at handling the details which ensured that everything was done correctly and on time in order to complete sales and deliver the vehicle to the customer. Some of my main areas of responsibility included running credit checks, negotiating loan agreements, seeing that sales personnel complete proper documentation, and selling warranties and additional products.

As you will see from my resume, prior experience included jobs which called for strong sales and customer service skills as well as a base of knowledge in all phases automobile dealership operations.

With a degree in Marketing (concentrating in Retail Business), I have earned a reputation as a dependable and honest professional. I enjoy the challenge of learning new methods and procedures. Known for a high degree of self motivation, I offer a strong ability to motivate others through my enthusiasm and dedication. I can provide excellent personal and professional references.

I hope you will welcome my call soon to arrange a brief meeting at your convenience to discuss your current and future needs and how I might serve them. Thank you in advanced for your time.

Sincerely yours,

Willa Clark

Alternate last paragraph:
I hope you will call or write me soon to suggest a time convenient for us to meet and discuss your current and future needs and how I might serve them. Thank you in advance for your time.

Automobile Dealership Office Operations

WILLA CLARK

1110½ Hay Street, Fayetteville, NC 28305 • preppub@aol.com • (910) 483-6611

OBJECTIVE
To offer my experience as a professional with a broad base of knowledge of automobile dealerships and of what must be done to ensure the smooth operation of the business department and supporting areas in order to make the greatest impact on the bottom line.

EXPERIENCE
BUSINESS MANAGER. Sanford Honda — Isuzu, Raleigh, NC (2002-03). In a busy dealership, oversaw a wide range of behind-the-scenes activities which guaranteed support for the sales force as well as completion of contracts as soon as possible after automobiles were sold.
- Handled sales support functions ranging from running credit checks, to assisting the sales personnel in completing documents necessary for bank approval and ultimate vehicle delivery, to completing all paperwork needed to get contract cashed.
- Used my communication skills and knowledge to negotiate with lending institutions, find the best rates, and secure loan approval.
- Dealt closely with customers while selling them additional services such as extended warranties, credit life insurance, A & H, and security systems.
- Prepared documentation in case of warranty cancellations; researched problems and saw that corrections were made.

Advanced to a position of increased responsibility based on my accomplishments and performance with Patrick Ford, Inc., Fayetteville, NC:
BUSINESS MANAGER. (2000-02). Advanced to this position after displaying an aptitude for quickly learning new aspects of dealership support operations.
- Gained experience in daily activities ranging from running credit checks, to assisting the sales personnel in document preparation, negotiating with lending institutions, selling extended warranties and other services, and preparing regular reports.

GENERAL OFFICE CLERK. (1998-00). Was cross trained in a wide range of areas including cashier for the parts and service departments, service dispatcher, and receptionist as well as assisting with warranty claims processing and inventory control.
- Adapted to every area of operations quickly and easily and became known for my willingness to take on new responsibilities.

SALES ASSOCIATE. The Closet/Maurice's, Fayetteville, NC (1999-00). Consistently set sales records for these popular clothing stores which have different types of clientele: helped customers make decisions on styles and colors as well as on accessories to complement the items they selected.
- Placed on the "Shining Star" list for six consecutive months for having the top volume of sales.
- Gained additional experience in inventory control and stocking.

CASHIER/CLERK. Lafayette Ford, Fayetteville, NC (1997-98). Became familiar with the background support needed to keep an automobile dealership running smoothly while learning to prepare bank deposits, stock car parts, provide customer service in the service area and parts department, and file records.

Highlights of other experience: Gained sales and customer experience in a jewelry store and fast food restaurant.

EDUCATION & TRAINING
Associate's degree in Marketing, South Central Technical Community College, St. Elmo's Ridge, NV, 2000. Completed corporate training seminars on the following topics: Ford Motor Company's leasing programs and a Heritage Insurance program on management techniques.

PROFESSIONAL AFFILIATION
Hold membership in the Ford ESP Professional Sales Guild — maintained a warranty penetration rate above 50% and passed an examination.

PERSONAL
Am a very hard-working individual with a reputation for dependability, honesty, and integrity. Am very well organized and detail oriented. Enjoy a challenge.

MANAGEMENT

Exact Name of Person
Title or Position
Name of Company
Address (number and street)
Address (city, state, and ZIP)

Business Management   Dear Exact Name of Person: (or Dear Sir or Madam if answering a blind ad.)

I would appreciate an opportunity to talk with you soon about how I could contribute to your organization through my experience in financial management as well as through my skills in the areas of personnel and operations management along with my strong customer service orientation.

You will see from my enclosed resume that I offer an in-depth knowledge of finance and business. My most recent job was as Controller and General Manager of a real estate rental company for approximately eight years. During this time I substantially reduced the company's debt load, virtually eliminated the amount of uncollectibles, and increased occupancy rates to a consistently high 95%. Through my diplomatic but assertive managerial style, I brought this business out of debt and transformed it into a viable operation.

During a successful career in the U.S. Army, I advanced to hold increasingly more responsible managerial positions in the fields of finance, budgeting, and pay administration as well as in personnel administration. I gained skills and refined a natural aptitude for analyzing, controlling, and resolving problems while earning a reputation as a versatile and adaptable professional.

With an associate's degree in Banking and Finance, I feel that I offer the dedication to excellence that would make me a valuable asset to an organization that can use a mature individual with the ability to get along with others in supervisory roles.

I hope you will welcome my call soon to arrange a brief meeting at your convenience to discuss your current and future needs and how I might serve them. Thank you in advance for your time.

Sincerely yours,

Roger Rose

Alternate last paragraph:
I hope you will call or write me soon to suggest a time convenient for us to meet and discuss your current and future needs and how I might serve them. Thank you in advance for your time.

Optional sentence that can go as the second sentence in last paragraph:
I would be happy to discuss the details of my salary history with you in person.

ROGER ROSE

1110½ Hay Street, Fayetteville, NC 28305 • preppub@aol.com • (910) 483-6611

OBJECTIVE

To offer a track record of success in managerial roles with organizations requiring knowledge of finance, personnel, and administrative functions along with a reputation for analytical skills and attention to detail as well as a strong customer service orientation.

EXPERIENCE

FINANCE AND GENERAL MANAGER. Rentals Incorporated, Raleigh, NC (1996-03). Brought about major improvements in several important functional areas while handling multiple roles as a financial manager, partner, and operations manager for a company with 160 rental units.

- Reduced the organization's debts more than $20,000 within less than a year through the application of my knowledge and prior experience in business management and finance.
- Almost totally eliminated uncollectibles while reducing them to under 1%.
- Prepared advertising materials which resulted in improved occupancy levels and consistently maintained 95% fill rates on leased units.
- Took charge of all aspects of finance and business administration ranging from maintaining books, to processing all accounting data, to accounts receivable and payable.
- Prepared and managed the budget and reconciled bank accounts.
- Represented the company through heavy contact with the public while showing prospective residents various units available for lease or rent.
- Resolved a wide range of customer service as well as budget and fee problems.

GENERAL MANAGER. The Novelty and Games Company, Buies Creek, NC (1993-96). Applied my knowledge of business and finance to build this company from a concept into a viable organization.

- Dealt with all aspects of establishing and successfully operating a small business: prepared and managed budgets, made bank deposits, and reconciled bank accounts as well as maintaining accounts receivable and payable ledgers.
- Controlled inventory from ordering supplies and merchandise to setting prices.

Highlights of earlier experience: Gained and refined knowledge of personnel management and finance/pay activities during a career with the U.S. Army, locations worldwide.

- As the Manager of a program studying the need for changes to the personnel structure of the Army, processed information and resolved problems, researched possible changes to determine their impact, and contributed input used in budget preparation.
- As a Senior Personnel Management Supervisor, directed the activities of up to 40 specialists engaged in processing promotions, reclassifications, transfers, and performance reports.
- As a Finance Section Manager, updated personnel's finance records and verified information before entering it into computers; maintained ledgers, cash books, and all related accounting records.
- As the Chief of Military Pay and Travel, processed pay activities for personnel in 11 states and four overseas areas.
- As Manager of a Personnel Actions Section, processed military personnel and their family members who were going overseas; made arrangements for transportation to overseas assignments; provided information and briefings on customs, laws, and conditions in overseas areas.
- As a Retirement Counselor, oversaw activities in a center which processed personnel upon their separation from the military service; briefed retirees on their benefits, entitlements, and rights.

EDUCATION & TRAINING

A.S. degree in **Banking** and **Finance,** Fayetteville Technical Community College, NC.
Completed numerous courses in finance, management, and personnel administration sponsored by the U.S. Army.

PERSONAL

Am known for my dedication and insistence on seeing any job through to completion. Have a high level of initiative. Enjoy public relations and customer service activities.

Date

Exact Name of Person
Title or Position
Name of Company
Address (number and street)
Address (city, state, and ZIP)

Child Care Center Management

Dear Sir or Madam:

I am writing to express my interest in the job you recently advertised for a Director of Child Care Services.

As you will see from my resume, I am a proven performer in the child care services field. Since 1992, I have enjoyed a track record of increasing advancement with Quality Day Care Centers, which operates more than 2000 facilities nationwide. In my current position as a center director which I have held since 1993, I have reduced staff turnover, increased profits, and led our 200-child center to win numerous awards for excellence. In the evenings during 2001 and 2002, I was a college instructor and taught classes for up to 25 day care providers. As the company needs have required, I have filled in as an Interim District Manager and I frequently travel in my current job to train new center directors throughout the South. The center which I manage is considered a model within the company of what a quality day care center should be.

In addition to the college teaching I have described, my educational background includes the Child Care Associate (CDA) Certificate, which is the equivalent of an associate's degree. I have also completed more than two years of other college-level coursework including one year of coursework in Elementary Education at Pembroke State University as well as numerous professional workshops and seminars.

I feel certain you would find me in person to be a congenial individual who relates well to staff, employees, parents, regulators, and children. I have a genuine love for the day care field and am proud of the contributions I have made to the early childhood years of thousands of children.

I hope you will write or call me soon to suggest a time when we might meet to discuss your current and future needs and how I might serve them. Thank you in advance for your time.

Yours sincerely,

Clarice Stoeckley

Child Care Center Management

CLARICE STOECKLEY

1110½ Hay Street, Fayetteville, NC 28305 • preppub@aol.com • (910) 483-6611

OBJECTIVE

To offer my creativity, enthusiasm, and love for the field of child care and development combined with my experience in managing day care facilities and training day care providers.

CERTIFICATE

Received Child Development Associate (CDA), May 2003; this is the equivalent of an Associate's degree in Child Care Services.

EXPERIENCE

HAVE EXCELLED IN POSITIONS OF INCREASING RESPONSIBILITY WITH QUALITY DAY CARE CENTERS, VARIOUS LOCATIONS.

DIRECTOR. Charlotte, NC (1993-present). For this nationwide chain with 2000 centers all over the U.S., have increased profits and enrollment since taking over center; in addition to managing total operations of the center and providing quality day care for up to 200 children, travel frequently in order to train new center directors throughout the state.

- Received **"Manager's Excellence Award"** for four quarters.

- Have further enhanced problem-solving, motivational and management abilities which is evidenced by a low turn-over in staff.

- Manage total center operation, providing care/education for up to 185 children.

- Hire, train, manage, and evaluate up to 20 staff members and ensure their continued training and development.

- Ensure that facility and daily activities meet or exceed state regulations.

- Plan and prepare for annual relicensing evaluation.

- Collect and process $9,150 weekly while handling accounts payable and receivable, payroll and other supplies; oversee maintenance activities.

- As a **COLLEGE INSTRUCTOR** with Fayetteville Technical Community College in the evenings from 2001-02, taught courses including "Day Care Discipline" and "Directing a Day Care Center" to classes of up to 25 day care professionals.

INTERIM DISTRICT MANAGER. Charleston, SC (1998). Interviewed, selected, and monitored new center directors; assisted District Manager in training new staff and center directors in Charleston, Greenville, Fayetteville, Charlotte, Wilmington.
- Set up marketing fairs locally and in Wilmington, NC; monitored Child Care Assistants and accounts for centers in Charlotte and Fayetteville, NC.

DIRECTOR. Lumberton, NC (1992-93). Center showed an increase in enrollment in only six months; responsibilities similar to current duties.

Other experience:
TEACHER'S AIDE. The Sinclair Elementary School, Charlotte, NC. (1987-91). Assisted a Third Grade Teacher in all areas of classroom instruction. Successfully organized a Teacher's Assistant Association for the City School System.
PRE-SCHOOL AIDE. American Creative School, Charlotte, NC (1986-87). Taught a class of four-year-olds.
TEACHER'S AIDE. Heywood Elementary School, Charlotte, NC (1985). Assisted a Second Grade Teacher in all areas of classroom instruction.

EDUCATION

Completed Elementary Education coursework, Pembroke State University, Pembroke, NC (1983-84).

AFFILIATIONS & CERTIFICATION

Member, North Carolina Day Care Association, Charlotte Jaycees
Certified in CPR and First Aid.

MANAGEMENT

Mr. Tom Fineagan
Greystone Funeral Home
3512 Buloxi Boulevard
New Orleans, LA 87503

**Funeral Home
Operations**

Dear Mr. Fineagan:

I would appreciate an opportunity to talk with you about how I could contribute to your organization through my extensive experience in the death care industry.

At 43 years of age, I have been in the funeral service industry for more than 25 years and offer expertise in every facet of the business, including pre-need sales and arrangement, funeral direction, as well as embalming and embalming management. I have utilized my business degree well in our industry; through the years I have devised and implemented numerous techniques and systems which have improved efficiency and profitability while maintaining quality service and absolute customer satisfaction. I have applied my business background also while managing and maintaining $1.5 million worth of property through a family trust and over the past eight years increased annual income more than 100%.

Considered an expert in embalming and restorative procedures, I have enjoyed sharing my knowledge with the many young students whom I have trained over the years. I am also known as a leading citizen in my community and have established an excellent personal and professional reputation, a fact which has generated much business through the years. I genuinely enjoy working with the public, and I am skilled at earning the trust and confidence of people from all races, religions, and backgrounds.

If you need a truly versatile professional who is skilled at every functional area related to mortuary science and funeral direction, I hope you will contact me to suggest a time when we might meet to discuss your needs and how I might serve them. Thank you for your time.

Sincerely,

Frank Davidson

Funeral Home Operations

FRANK DAVIDSON

1110½ Hay Street, Fayetteville, NC 28305 • preppub@aol.com • (910) 483-6611

OBJECTIVE

To contribute to an organization that can use a versatile and knowledgeable professional who is experienced in all aspects of the death care industry including pre-need sales and arrangement, funeral direction, as well as embalming and embalming management.

EDUCATION

Received **Diploma in Mortuary Science**, Cincinnati, OH, 1982.
Associate's **Degree in Business**, MaComber College, MaComber, LA, 1979.

LICENSE

Am a **Licensed Funeral Director**; became a Florida Funeral Service Licensee in 1982 and am required to obtain five hours of continuing professional education annually.
Am National Board Certified.

AFFILIATIONS

Have been active in my community; following are highlights of my involvements:
- Member, Nursing Home Advisory Board
- Member, Parks and Recreation Board
- Member, Administrative Board, Wilson United Methodist Church
- Master of Masonic Lodge, Shriner
- Past member, West Ft. Lauderdale Rotary Club

EXPERIENCE

FUNERAL DIRECTOR and **EMBALMER**. Wesleyan Funeral Service Crematory, Ft. Lauderdale, FL (2002-03). Used my extensive experience in funeral directing and embalming to enhance the overall profitability and efficiency of funerals; introduced several new techniques which simplified funeral arrangements.
- Applied my expert knowledge of the laws and requirements related to funeral home administration and State Board licensing.
- Refined the skills of junior personnel by sharing with them the many secrets and shortcuts in embalming and restorative work which I have learned in my 20 years of experience.
- Have a reputation as an outstanding communicator who easily establishes rapport with people from every race and background, and am very knowledgeable with regard to discussing and tailoring funeral needs to specific religious beliefs.
- Gained my first experience with cremation; learned how to operate a crematory and process cremated remains.

FUNERAL DIRECTOR and **EMBALMER**. Best Funeral Home, Ft. Lauderdale, FL (1988-01). Excelled in handling the full range of activities involved in the selling, conducting, and pre-need arranging of funerals.
- Was responsible for the overall preparation of bodies, and became known for my expertise in embalming and restorative procedures.
- Played a key role in supervising the maintenance of the extensive building and grounds.
- Took pleasure in training many students working at this funeral home through the years.
- Wrote the policy training manual related to OSHA, EPA, and other similar standards and regulations.
- Helped design and plan a new preparation room as well as numerous improvements to the physical plant and grounds.
- Maintained outstanding relationships with law enforcement officials, the media, and with a wide variety of community, state, and local organizations and officials.
- Promoted a strong relationship between the death care industry and the public; became known for my compassionate style in dealing with families.

ASSISTANT MANAGER. Piedmont Funeral Home, Lexington, NC (1982-87). Excelled in my first job in the funeral industry; moved up through the ranks to assume responsibilities in all phases of funeral home operations including shift leader and assistant manager.

PERSONAL

Can provide outstanding personal and professional references. Genuinely enjoy working with the public. Am a talented organizer, motivator, communicator, and manager.

Date

Exact Name of Person
Title or Position
Name of Company
Address (no., street)
Address (city, state, zip)

Maintenance Management

Dear Exact Name of Person: (or Dear Sir or Madam if answering a blind ad.)

I would appreciate an opportunity to talk with you soon about how I could contribute to your organization through my experience and skills. I am especially interested in the position of Maintenance Technician and feel that I offer strong electronics skills and a reputation as a fast learner which would make me a valuable asset to your organization.

As you will see from my resume, my technical skills include using my knowledge of drafting while planning security systems for residential, industrial, and commercial customers. My additional experience includes time spent as a cellular phone, VCR, and mobile radio technician. During approximately three years with Southeast Security Systems, I routinely worked with blueprints, schematics, plans, and electrical drawings while making decisions in order to develop the best plan for each customer.

I feel that my "track record" of rapid promotion and selection for special training are indications of my talents. I have often been singled out by customers to receive their thanks for "a job well done" while earning their trust and confidence for my professionalism and emphasis on customer service.

I hope you will welcome my call soon to arrange a brief meeting at your convenience to discuss your current and future needs and how I might serve them. Thank you in advance for your time.

Sincerely yours,

Lenwood Temm

Alternate last paragraph:
I hope you will call or write me soon to suggest a time convenient for us to meet and discuss your current and future needs and how I might serve them. Thank you in advance for your time.

LENWOOD TEMM

1110½ Hay Street, Fayetteville, NC 28305   •   preppub@aol.com   •   (910) 483-6611

OBJECTIVE

To offer my excellent technical electronics skills to an organization that is in need of a self-motivated young professional who possesses a reputation for reliability, attention to detail, and the ability to relate to and get along well with others.

**EDUCATION,
TRAINING
&
CERTIFICATIONS**

Studied electronics, computer science, and drafting at Fayetteville Technical Community College, Fayetteville, NC, and Central Carolina Community College in Sanford, NC.

Received training in digital technology, computers, customer service, and drafting, including corporate-sponsored programs leading to manufacturer's certification in technical repair of a number of major transmitting equipment brands including:

Motorola	Uniden	Audiovox	Mitsubishi N.E.C.

Licensed by North Carolina Private Protective Services (alarms).

**SPECIAL
SKILLS**

Through training and experience, am familiar with drafting equipment including:

drafting table	French curve	compass	protractor
T-square	triangles	scales	templates

Use standard and specialized test equipment including oscilloscopes, multimeters, spectrum analyzers, cell site simulators, and tone generators.

EXPERIENCE

PRIVATE CONTRACTOR. Raleigh, NC (2003-present). Successfully earned contracts to repair camera equipment and install locking systems and am becoming familiar with the government contracting process at Pope AFB and Ft. Bragg.

OPERATIONS MANAGER. Southeast Security Systems, Fayetteville, NC (2000-03). Handled a wide range of day-to-day activities ranging from sales, to drafting requirements, to customer service, to record keeping while leading the company to achieve a higher volume of business than it had in its previous 18 years of operation.
- Refined my knowledge of drafting by drawing plans used to explain to the customer how the security system, its access controls, and closed circuit TV all tied together.
- Sold industrial, commercial, and residential alarm systems valued as high as $50,000.
- Inspected blueprints, schematics, and electrical drawings used to develop systems.
- Completed a major project setting up an access control system for Purolator.
- Gained extensive computer experience since each system was computer controlled.
- Installed, programmed, repaired, and maintained systems; managed the maintenance contracts for all security systems at Ft. Bragg, the world's largest U.S. military base.
- Maintained customer files, acted as liaison with the monitoring company, ordered equipment, and controlled a $10,000 inventory of parts and equipment.

ELECTRONICS TECHNICIAN and **INSTALLER.** Cellular One, Fayetteville, NC (1998-00). Hired to explain to customers how cellular phones worked and to install them, was soon selected to receive special training and earned manufacturer's certification as a technician.
- Achieved the highest number of monthly installations and the lowest vehicle damage rate of Cellular One employees nationwide!
- Operated sophisticated equipment including a $25,000 cell site simulator.
- Learned to deal with manufacturer's representatives while handling warranty work.
- Read schematics and applied my technical electronics skills to repair phones.
- Was often singled out by customers to receive praise for my dedication, professionalism, and determination to provide excellent customer service.

MOBILE RADIO TECHNICIAN. Certified Communications, Fayetteville, NC (1997-98). Rapidly earned promotion from installing equipment to becoming a technician involved in repairing transmitting equipment, pagers, and restaurant drive-through systems.
- Became skilled in reading blueprints and schematics.

PERSONAL

Have a strong interest in science and technology — was the overall winner of the Harnett County Science Fair while in high school. Am a team player who gets along with others.

MANAGEMENT

Date

Exact Name of Person
Title or Position
Name of Company
Address (no., street)
Address (city, state, zip)

Manufacturing Management

Dear Exact Name of Person: (or Dear Sir or Madam if answering a blind ad.)

I would appreciate an opportunity to talk with you soon about how I could contribute to your organization through my strong management and communication skills as well as my leadership ability and organizational know-how.

As you will see from my resume, since 2001 I have been involved in a management trainee program with Burlington Industries and have advanced into a supervisory position in less time than any management trainee in my plant. Although I am considered within Burlington to be on the "fast track" and am being groomed for rapid promotion into corporate management, I have a great desire to put down roots in the South Carolina area, where both my wife and I are from. As you will also see from my resume, I graduated from VMI and was elected to serve on the Honor Court in my senior year.

While working at Burlington, I have had an opportunity to demonstrate my supervisory ability and have managed people in various jobs within the plant. I am widely respected for my knack for solving stubborn technical problems, and I have recently improved the speed and efficiency of a particular yarn for a major customer through taking a new approach to an old problem.

You would find me in person to be a dedicated and hard-working individual who prides myself on giving my best effort to my employer. I believe I could become a valuable asset to your organization, and it would be my desire to make a difference to your strategic posture and operating efficiency. I can provide outstanding personal and professional references upon request.

I hope you will welcome my call soon to arrange a brief meeting at your convenience to discuss your current and future needs and how I might serve them. Thank you in advance for your time.

Sincerely yours,

Rick Nunez

Alternate last paragraph:
I hope you will call or write me soon to suggest a time convenient for us to meet and discuss your current and future needs and how I might serve them. Thank you in advance for your time.

RICK NUNEZ

1110½ Hay Street, Fayetteville, NC 28305   •   preppub@aol.com   •   (910) 483-6611

OBJECTIVE
To contribute to an organization that can use a resourceful young professional who offers a proven ability to troubleshoot and solve problems in industrial environments along with exceptionally strong communication skills, leadership ability, and organizational know-how.

EDUCATION
Earned B.A. degree in **Economics and Business**, Virginia Military Institute, Lexington, VA, 2001.
• Was elected by my peers in my senior year to serve on the **Honor Court**, the judicial body which administers the VMI Honor System.

EXECUTIVE TRAINING
During 2002 and 2003, completed several months of technical and professional training sponsored by Burlington Industries and North Carolina State University in these areas:

Spun yarn manufacturing   Industrial engineering
Production management   Quantitative analysis
Employee supervision   Systematic decision making

COMPUTER SKILLS
Am proficient in the use of personal computers using software including the following:

Word   Excel
FORMTOOL   PageMaker

Am thoroughly knowledgeable of Uster Sliverdata, an on-line production and quality monitoring system in spinning production.

EXPERIENCE
PRODUCTION MANAGER and **MANAGEMENT TRAINEE**. Burlington Industries, St. Pauls, NC (2001-present). Was specially recruited for this management trainee position by Burlington Industries, and am being groomed for rapid promotion to key corporate management positions; while excelling in Burlington's rigorous management trainee program, advanced to a supervisory position more rapidly than any trainee in my plant.
• Through the formal training program, have gained knowledge about every phase of the manufacturing process.
• Acquired "hands-on" experience in a variety of supervisory jobs throughout the plant as the regular and off-shift manager of operational areas ranging from raw material coordination to finished product distribution.
• Supervised between 10 and 35 employees in nearly every aspect of plant operation.
• On my own initiative, combined what I learned in formal training with my natural creativity in devising a way of improving speed and efficiency of a particular yarn for a major customer.
• Have been commended for my ability to rapidly master complex technical concepts and for my ability to apply my training in solving stubborn production problems.
• Have become not only well versed in the details of production management but also knowledgeable about the "big picture" of the textile industry and sister industries in the global market.

SUPPLY MANAGER/MILITARY OFFICER. U.S. Army, Ft. Lee, VA (2001). After graduating from VMI, where I participated in the ROTC program, was commissioned as a second lieutenant, and then completed a six-month course pertaining to these and other areas:

supply management   service operations management
subsistence ordering   petroleum supply management

• Became knowledgeable about the "nuts and bolts" of the supply process, from the procurement process to the disposal of environmentally hazardous materials.

TECHNICAL ASSISTANT. Ivy Hill Golf Club, Forest, VA (Summers, 1998-01). Learned supervisory skills at an early age while supervising three adults in performing daily maintenance on a championship golf course.

PERSONAL
Am respected within Burlington Industries for my hard-working nature and my drive to succeed. Have been told that I am on Burlington's "fast track" and have a bright future in the company. Feel confident in my ability to transfer my management skills, creative problem-solving ability, and technical training to any industry.

MANAGEMENT

Date

Exact Name of Person
Title or Position
Name of Company
Address (no., street)
Address (city, state, zip)

Office Management

Dear Exact Name of Person: (or Dear Sir or Madam if answering a blind ad.)

I would appreciate an opportunity to talk with you soon about how I could contribute to your organization through my versatile skills related to medical office operations and financial services, as well as through my proven sales ability, initiative, and creativity oriented toward improving the "bottom line."

As you will see from my resume, most recently I played a key role in the startup of a new orthopedics practice. While developing office systems and office procedures "from scratch," including designing all forms, I used and trained other employees to use UNIX software and made valuable suggestions which the UNIX vendor applied to refine and upgrade the system. Skilled in bookkeeping and insurance claims administration, I have filed insurance claims and performed ICD-9 and CPT-4 coding. I also handled accounts payable/receivable and payroll and acted as Credit Manager. In my previous job at Scotland Memorial Hospital I was rapidly promoted to coordinate business office systems and supervised a large staff while acting as the "internal expert" on the computer system and software problems.

In earlier experience in the banking field, I was involved in loan administration, supervised teller transactions, and managed credit card accounts. I am skilled in dealing with the public.

I am confident you would find me in person to be a poised communicator and dynamic personality who enjoys solving technical and business problems. I have been told that I am a "natural" for sales, although I personally believe that the ability to sell a product has a lot to do with the salesperson's product knowledge. A fast learner with the ability to rapidly master new areas of knowledge, I am always eager to learn new things and accept new challenges.

I hope you will welcome my call soon to arrange a brief meeting at your convenience to discuss your current and future needs and how I might serve them. Thank you in advance for your time.

Sincerely yours,

Rosalind Rulnick

Alternate last paragraph:
I hope you will call or write me soon to suggest a time convenient for us to meet and discuss your current and future needs and how I might best serve them. Thank you in advance for your time.

ROSALIND RULNICK

1110½ Hay Street, Fayetteville, NC 28305   •   preppub@aol.com   •   (910) 483-6611

OBJECTIVE   To add value to a company that can use a creative professional and dynamic communicator who offers proficiency with computer software, expertise in managing offices and developing business systems, as well as knowledge of the medical and financial fields.

EXPERIENCE   **OFFICE MANAGER.** Gravelley & Associates, Chapel Hill, NC (1996-03). Worked with UNIX software and made numerous suggestions which the UNIX vendor used to upgrade and refine the system; supervised six clerical employees in medical office operations and trained the entire staff in the operation of the computer system.
- *Business development*: Joined this practice during its initial setup and played a key role in helping it become a profitable operation; developed office systems and internal procedures "from scratch" including designing all forms.
- *Insurance claims administration*: Filed insurance claims and performed ICD-9 and CPT-4 coding.
- *Customer service*: Acted as Patient Accounts Representative and Receptionist.
- *Accounting/bookkeeping*: Handled accounts payable/receivable and payroll and acted as Credit Manager.
- *Written communication*: Composed reports, memos, and correspondence.

BUSINESS OFFICE SYSTEM COORDINATOR. UNC Memorial Hospital, Chapel Hill, NC (1986-96). Began with this hospital as a **Patient Account Representative** and was promoted to coordinate all systems in the business office; earned a reputation as a creative problem-solver who could develop efficient and simple new procedures and work flows.
- *Office systems coordination*: Supervised a large staff composed of insurance clerks, file room clerks, mail room personnel, cashiers, and switchboard operators; worked closely with the business manager to interview, hire, and train employees.
- *Customer service*: Supervised four people while overseeing the process of interviewing patients, determining sources of financial aid, collecting past due accounts, and filing insurance claims.
- *Computer consulting*: Acted as the internal expert/consultant on the operations of the computer system used to maintain patient information; performed keying and batching and continuously found innovative new ways of managing data.

PERSONAL BANKER. Cape Fear Bank & Trust Company, Raleigh, NC (1978-86). Began with this financial institution as a Sales Finance Secretary and earned rapid promotions in succession to Assistant to Installment Loan Manager; Senior Teller; and Personal Banker.
- *Loan administration*: Approved loan applications, conducted credit history investigations, sold and opened new accounts, and became skilled in solving a wide range of banking problems on behalf of customers.
- *Teller transactions*: Ordered currency and coin from the Federal Reserve, sold financial services, balanced vault and teller windows, trained tellers.
- *Credit card accounts*: Managed Ready Reserve and Master Charge Accounts and computed terms for payment.

EDUCATION   Elon College, North Carolina, 1977-78.

PERSONAL   Outstanding personal and professional references on request. Am an adaptable team player who works well under pressure. Am a creative person who welcomes new learning opportunities. Single. Will cheerfully relocate.

Date

Exact Name of Person
Title or Position
Name of Company
Address (number and street)
Address (city, state, and ZIP)

**Store Management,
Automotive Industry**

Dear Exact Name of Person: (or Dear Sir or Madam if answering a blind ad.)

I would appreciate an opportunity to talk with you soon about how I could benefit your organization through my outstanding abilities gained in a multifunctional business where I oversaw activities ranging from training and supervision, to development of merchandising and promotional activities, to directing sales and customer service activities, to handling administrative and fiscal operations.

As the Store Manager of a Southern Auto location which had $2.5 million in sales its last fiscal year, I have become very efficient at managing my time while dealing with three different operational areas — parts, tires and service, and automotive accessories. This store averages from 1,500 to 1,700 transactions a week with average weekly sales in the $40-60,000 range. In my five years as Store Manager I have achieved consistently high levels of productivity, sales, and customer satisfaction.

As you will see from my enclosed resume, before joining Southern Auto I earned rapid advancement with Quality Auto Parts. In my five years with this organization I was promoted to Store Manager after starting as a part-time sales person and then becoming a Merchandiser, a Parts Specialist, and Assistant Manager. As Store Manager I was involved in making decisions concerning merchandising, computer operations and fiscal control, inventory control, and public relations as well as internal employee counseling and supervision.

I am a very dedicated hard-working professional who can be counted on to find ways to ensure customer satisfaction and productivity while always impacting favorably on the organization's bottom line.

I hope you will welcome my call soon to arrange a brief meeting at your convenience to discuss your current and future needs and how I might serve them. Thank you in advance for your time.

Sincerely yours,

Eugene Lobato

Alternate last paragraph:
I hope you will call or write me soon to suggest a time convenient for us to meet and discuss your current and future needs and how I might serve them. Thank you in advance for your time.

EUGENE LOBATO

1110½ Hay Street, Fayetteville, NC 28305 • preppub@aol.com • (910) 483-6611

OBJECTIVE

To benefit an organization in need of an experienced manager with a strong background in inventory control/ parts ordering, merchandising and sales, public relations, and fiscal operations along with specialized knowledge of the automotive parts business.

EXPERIENCE

STORE MANAGER. Southern Auto, Atlanta, GA (2000-present). Direct and oversee all phases of daily operations in an established store with 28 employees and with average weekly sales of from $40,000 to $60,000; motivate employees to achieve high levels of productivity, sales, and customer satisfaction.
- Played an important role in the success of a location with $2.5 million in annual sales and from 1,500 to 1,700 transactions a week.
- Received an Award of Excellence as an Auto Parts Specialist in recognition of my professionalism and knowledge of the inventory control aspect of the business (June 2003).
- Received a Customer Service Award Pin recognizing my exceptional customer relations.
- Earned certification in tires and parts in recognition of my expertise in providing customer service in these areas (June 2003).
- Was chosen to attend a corporate training program for store managers in 2002.
- Participated in setting up and running a job fair booth in order to recruit management trainees for Southern Auto at technical colleges throughout the southeast (summer 2004).
- Carried out interesting sales merchandising and promotional activities which helped to increase sales of additional services once customers entered the store.
- Became skilled in time management while overseeing the operation of distinctly different areas within one location — parts, tires and service, and automotive accessories.
- Contributed to successful customer relations efforts by monitoring employee performance and guiding them in the development of their sales and service skills.
- Handled administrative details such as scheduling, making bank deposits, taking care of personnel paperwork, and preparing various types of reports.
- Arranged for new employee training and directed work flow throughout the business while also making recommendations on performance evaluations and selection.
- Saw that security and safety policies were followed, inventory levels controlled, and documentation prepared properly in order to eliminate loss and internal theft.

STORE MANAGER. Quality Auto Parts, Macon, GA (1995-00). Earned rapid promotion with this business and was placed in charge of overseeing all aspects of store operations from personnel, to sales, to inventory control.
- Advanced from a part-time sales position to Merchandiser, then to Parts Specialist and Assistant Manager, and in 1999 was promoted to Store Manager.
- Became familiar with management unique to the automotive parts industry involving public relations, computer operations/fiscal controls, and parts and inventory control.
- Supervised as many as 14 employees in a location which averaged from $15,000 to $18,000 in sales a week.

EDUCATION

Completed one semester of Business Administration, Methodist College, Fayetteville, NC.
Studied Electronic Engineering and Business Management, Fayetteville Technical Community College, NC.

TRAINING

Was selected for corporate-sponsored training including:
"Introduction to Management" — a part of the Southern Auto Management School
Technical Electronic Ignition Course — Wells Manufacturing Corp.

CERTIFICATIONS

Received ASE (Automotive Service Excellence) certification as a Parts Specialist and Western Auto certification as a Master Tire Specialist and Parts Specialist.

PERSONAL

Am a well-rounded professional with excellent communication skills in all areas — dealing with the public and with employees. Have a pleasant and friendly personality.

MANANGEMENT

Date

Exact Name of Person
Title or Position
Name of Company
Address (no., street)
Address (city, state, zip)

**Store Management,
Grocery Industry**

Dear Exact Name of Person: (or Dear Sir or Madam if answering a blind ad.)

Can you use a hard-working professional who offers a track record of promotion based on accomplishments in increasing sales, boosting productivity, improving morale, reducing costs, lowering employee turnover, improving merchandising, and strengthening customer service?

As you will see when you look over my enclosed resume, I gained expertise in most aspects of retailing and business management while excelling in a history of promotion with the Winn-Dixie Corporation at locations in North Carolina and Georgia. I can say proudly, but without boasting, that I have increased sales in every job I have ever held, from department manager to store co-manager. In my most recent job with Winn-Dixie I was promoted from co-manager of a $135,000 weekly store to co-manage a store with weekly revenues of $285,000. In three separate jobs as a Department Manager, I either doubled or tripled weekly sales by implementing new training programs coupled with prudent inventory ordering and control techniques.

I offer a strong working knowledge of computers and cash registers, and I have utilized computerized inventory ordering and control systems. I believe I offer a talent, refined by experience, for retailing and operations management. I can provide excellent personal and professional references, and I offer a reputation as a tactful and sensitive communicator who is skilled at solving customer, employee, and vendor problems.

I hope you will welcome my call next week when I try to arrange a brief meeting at your convenience to discuss your needs and goals and how I might help you fulfill them. Thank you in advance for your time.

Sincerely,

Walter King

Alternate last paragraph:
I hope you will call or write me soon to suggest a time when we might meet to discuss your needs and goals and how I might serve them. Thank you in advance for your time.

WALTER KING

1110½ Hay Street, Fayetteville, NC 28305 • preppub@aol.com • (910) 483-6611

OBJECTIVE

To contribute to the profitability and growth of a company that can use a skilled manager who offers a track record of accomplished results related to increasing sales, reducing employee turnover, boosting productivity, cutting costs, and improving merchandising.

EXPERIENCE

DEPARTMENT MANAGER. Kroger Sav-On, Spring Lake, NC (2002-03). While supervising a three-person produce department, instituted changes in ordering, buying, stocking, and merchandising that led to a $2,000 weekly increase in sales and made my department the second most profitable of its kind within the chain.

- Became skilled in adjusting buying patterns according to the local area's supply and demand patterns; earned a reputation as an astute planner.
- Maintained extensive contact with local customers and local vendors.

EXCELLED IN THE FOLLOWING PATTERN OF PROMOTION AND ADVANCEMENT WITHIN THE WINN-DIXIE CORPORATION, Atlanta, GA, and Fayetteville, NC (1988-01).
STORE CO-MANAGER. Atlanta, GA (2000-01). Shared management responsibilities of a 100-employee store; was credited with increasing store sales and developing an internal working environment that reduced friction between labor and management, resulting in lower employee turnover, better morale, and higher productivity.

- Was promoted to co-manager of this store grossing $285,000 weekly after excelling as the co-manager of a store grossing $135,000 weekly in another Atlanta location.
- Personally oversaw all aspects of customer relations, employee relations, and vendor relations; became known for my sensitive and tactful communication style.
- Hired, trained, and scheduled all employees who worked at this store.
- Carefully monitored all planning, ordering, receiving, stocking, displaying, and rotation.
- Monitored cashiering, bookkeeping, and payroll administration.

STORE CO-MANAGER. Atlanta, GA (1999-00). Was promoted to the job above after solving numerous inventory control problems caused by customer and employee theft at this 60-person store; was selected for this job because of my proven ability to troubleshoot internal problems.

ASSISTANT MANAGER. Atlanta, GA (1999). Oversaw these areas in a 60-person store:

cashiering	budgeting and bookkeeping
receiving and stocking	organizing and training a crew

- In a store with few operational problems, developed and implemented a more in-depth training program which improved employee skills and strengthened customer service.

DEPARTMENT MANAGER. Stone Mountain, GA (1998-99). Took over the management of a four-person dairy/frozen food department and increased sales from $14,000 weekly to $45,000 weekly in just six months; hired and trained new employees.

- From hands-on experience, learned the sensitivity of sales to proper display.

DEPARTMENT MANAGER. Alpharetta, GA (1998). Became skilled in inventory control in a small department while managing a four-person dairy/frozen food department; gained valuable mechanical knowledge of refrigeration techniques and became skilled in ordering "the right amount at the right time" in order to avoid both stock out and spoilage.

DEPARTMENT MANAGER. Raleigh, NC (1996-98). Shouldered a heavy workload at this fast-growing Raleigh Winn-Dixie; more than doubled weekly sales from $9,000 to $19,000 while managing a four-person department.

Other Winn-Dixie experience: At Winn-Dixie in both Fayetteville and Raleigh, NC, was trained in all areas including grocery, dairy, seafood, deli, frozen foods, produce, cashiering, and bookkeeping.

TRAINING

Graduated from Southview High School in Fayetteville; have completed numerous training courses sponsored by Winn-Dixie related to management, supervision, and retailing.

PERSONAL

Believe I offer a knack, refined by experience, for retailing and operations management. Offer a strong working knowledge of computers and cash registers. Have utilized the MSI ordering system. Can provide excellent personal and professional references.

MEDICAL

Date

Exact Name of Person
Title or Position
Name of Company
Address (no., street)
Address (city, state, zip)

Dental Assistant

Dear Exact Name of Person: (or Dear Sir or Madam if answering a blind ad.)

I would appreciate an opportunity to talk with you soon about how I could contribute to your organization through my experience as a skilled dental assistant.

As you will see from my resume, I am an experienced Chairside Dental Assistant who also offers the ability to function, as needed, as a front office receptionist. I am experienced at assisting in all phases of general dentistry including prosthodontics, endodontics, surgical removal of impacted third molars, pediatrics, and amalgam and composite fillings. In addition to my Certification in Dental Radiation, I completed extensive coursework in dental radiation while excelling in my 7-month Dental Assistant Certification Program.

In addition to my experience and formal training leading to my certifications, I have completed extensive professional development coursework through Blatchford Seminars which included Dynamo Workshop, Top Gun Workshop, and Integrity Selling. Those courses taught proven concepts related to maximizing profitability, improving management care, and refining customer relations skills. I always enjoy learning new skills and techniques related to both dentistry and office operations.

If you can use a dedicated and highly motivated hard worker who would surely be an asset to your dental practice, I hope you will call or write me to suggest a time when we could meet to discuss your needs. I can provide outstanding personal and professional references.

Sincerely yours,

Amanda Zier

Dental Assistant

AMANDA ZIER

1110½ Hay Street, Fayetteville, NC 28305   •   preppub@aol.com   •   (910) 483-6611

OBJECTIVE

I want to contribute to an organization that can use a skilled dental assistant with excellent office and secretarial skills who offers experience related to dental radiation, laboratory procedures, as well as restorative and cosmetic dentistry.

EXPERIENCE

CHAIRSIDE DENTAL ASSISTANT. Dr. James Kitwell, D.D.S., Charlotte, NC (2003-present). Assist Dr. Kitwell in all phases of general dentistry including prosthodontics, surgical removal of impacted third molars, pediatrics, and amalgam and composite fillings; chart and maintain patient records; expose and develop dental radiographs; and apply sealants.

CHAIRSIDE DENTAL ASSISTANT. Dr. James B. Williams, D.D.S., and Dr. Ellis Davidson, D.D.S., Charlotte, NC (2000-02). Assisted Dr. Ellefson in all phases of general dentistry including the areas mentioned in the job above as well as endodontics, prosthodontics, utilization of nitrous oxygen, and application of sealants.
*   Attended numerous professional development seminars designed to improve communication and customer service skills, increase management care knowledge, and teach proven concepts related to maximizing profitability.

DENTAL ASSISTANT. Dr. Douglas E. Harrison, Captain, USAF, and Dr. Deborah Bennett, Lt. Col., Rhein-Main Dental Clinic, Germany (1999). Assisted two doctors in all phases of general dentistry including preparing new patient documentation and evaluations of diet, dental habits, and vital signs; assisted in crown and bridge work, prosthetics, endodontics, surgical removal of impacted third molars, non-surgical periodontal therapy, intravenous sedation, pediatrics, as well as restorative and cosmetic dentistry.

DENTAL ASSISTANT. Dr. Marileth Coria, D.D.S., San Bernardino Dental Group, San Bernardino, CA (1997-98). Worked primarily for Dr. Marileth Coria while also assisting other doctors in this 10-doctor dental practice.
*   Gained extensive experience in all aspects of dental hygiene.
*   Assisted in procedures of amalgam, bonding restorations, non-surgical periodontal therapy, prophylaxis, and application of sealants.
*   Charted and maintained patients' records; exposed and developed dental radiographs.
*   Was complimented on my tactful and courteous style in working with patients and peers.

Other experience:
RECEPTIONIST/SECRETARY. At Harris Department Store in Redlands, CA, worked in sales and inventory control while also coordinating with buyers.
QUALITY CONTROL TECHNICIAN. For a company in Cape Cod, MA, that manufactured computer disks, worked in quality control and final production.
SECRETARY. At a hardware/lumber company, utilized my secretarial skills while also handling some collections and sales.

EDUCATION

Certification as a Dental Assistant, Norton Dental Clinic, Norton Air Force Base, San Bernardino, CA, March 1997.
*   Excelled in a 7-month program that included extensive coursework in dental radiation.
Certification in Dental Radiation, Redlands Adult School, Redlands, CA, Jan. 1997.
Certification in Secretarial Science, Silay Institute, Silay City, Philippines, 1988.
Recertification in Adult CPR by American Red Cross, Fayetteville, NC, 2002.
Completed extensive professional development courses through "Blatchford Seminars," Atlanta, GA, 2002 and Charlotte, NC, 2002; courses included Dynamo Workshop, Top Gun Workshop, and Integrity Selling.

PERSONAL

Am known for a cheerful disposition and excellent communication skills. Am a highly self-motivated individual and try to remain knowledgeable of latest developments in the field of dentistry. Enjoy learning new techniques and procedures. Outstanding references.

MEDICAL

TERRI ALLIGOOD

1110½ Hay Street, Fayetteville, NC 28305   •   preppub@aol.com   •   (910) 483-6611

OBJECTIVE

To offer my strong background in health care management to an organization that can use a mature professional known for high degrees of self motivation as well as analytical and problem-solving abilities which enhance practical nursing and patient care skills.

EXPERIENCE

Advanced in administrative roles with Comprehensive Home Health Care, Atlanta, GA:
REGIONAL DIRECTOR. (2000-present). Oversee operational areas including patient management, regulatory affairs, corporate planning and development, and financial management of six branch offices and a work station.

- Coordinated each office's accounts receivable issues and concerns while working with the accounts receivable supervisor.
- Assisted in the development of and then managed Quality Assurance and Risk Management programs as well as policy and programs in all operating areas.
- Ensured compliance with applicable federal, state, and local laws, regulations, and rules.
- Provided and coordinated staff development in such a way that personnel matters were handled promptly and fairly.
- Ensured that staff loads were equitable and adequate staff available for care.
- Participated in public relations efforts by preparing for and arranging for news releases, TV and radio public service announcements as well as for staff members to make presentations and arrange for displays and exhibits.
- Managed the western region which included Fayetteville, Lumberton, Elizabethtown, Durham, and Greensboro, NC, and Bennettsville, SC.

ASSISTANT ADMINISTRATOR and **DIRECTOR OF PROFESSIONAL SERVICES (DPS).** (1997-00). Continued to function as DPS after earning a promotion to assist the administrator in overseeing activities in each branch office and ensuring that staff members received adequate training and supervision.

DIRECTOR OF PROFESSIONAL SERVICES. (1993-97). Held responsibility for managing both clinical and operational activities in the Fayetteville branch office.

HOME HEALTH NURSE and **HOSPITAL COORDINATOR.** (1992-93). Provided home health care to patients as well as keeping primary care staff informed of the disposition of their patients when they received hospital care; received updates from hospital staff on our patients and developed contacts with their physicians.

HOME HEALTH NURSE. Cape Fear Valley Medical Center, Fayetteville, NC (1991-92). Hired during a period when the agency was awaiting a Certificate of Need, worked in various departments to gain exposure in areas including: discharge planning, patient education, short-stay surgery, rehabilitation, staff development, employee health, radiation therapy, the IV Team, and infection control.

- Participated in a team approach while working with disabled patients and providing emotional and physical support through the rehabilitation process.
- As back-up Discharge Planning Nurse, processed home health referrals and made contacts with support agencies while assessing applicant needs.
- Gained expertise in the area of patient education while instructing patients and family members in diabetes, cardiovascular disease, decubiti, skin care, and ostomy care.
- As back-up Stroke Team Coordinator, assessed patients with neurological deficits associated with CVAs and spinal cord or head injuries while working closely with specialists in physical therapy, occupational therapy, speech pathology, and social services.
- Assisted in the operating and recovery rooms for the short-stay surgery center.
- As back-up Infection Control Nurse, performed surveillance of documented hospital infections and assisted in logging culture reports and compiling statistics.
- Assisted in CPR training needed for hospital personnel to recertify their skills.
- Scheduled and conducted employee health screenings including following up on any abnormal laboratory reports and conducting health counseling on hypertension, nutrition, and exercise.
- Oriented new oncology patients in radiation therapy procedures, possible side effects, treatment regimens, nutrition, and medications.
- Worked with the IV Team to maintain skills and obtain IV Therapy certification.

OFFICE NURSE. Dr. Thomas Woodworth, M.D., Fayetteville, NC (1990-91). Completed general nursing care involving patient assessment and education, the administration of medications and immunizations, phlebotomy, and performing urinalysis, hematocrits, and EKGs.

- Gained experience in medical office clerical activities including filing patient records, scheduling appointments, bookkeeping, typing, and filing Medicare and BCBS claims.

STAFF REGISTERED NURSE. North Carolina Baptist Hospital, Winston-Salem, NC (1988-90). Provided total nursing care for surgical urology and other general medical/surgical patients including making regular assessments of each patient's physical and mental condition and recording information in their charts.

- Implemented treatment plans and dispensed prescribed medications as well as followed day-to-day concerns, complaints, and needs of each patient.
- Handled Charge Nurse duties.

STAFF REGISTERED NURSE. Moore Memorial Hospital, Pinehurst, NC (1988). Ensured that general medical/surgical patients received total nursing care; assessed physical and mental health and recorded information on patient charts; implemented treatment plans; followed day-to-day concerns and needs of each patient under my care.

OFFICE CLERK and **NURSING ASSISTANT.** Dr. James G. Macaulay, West End, NC (1987-88). Assisted office nurses as well as taking care of filing, scheduling, bookkeeping, making deposits, and typing.

EDUCATION

Bachelor of Science in Nursing degree, Fayetteville State University, Fayetteville, NC, 2002.
- Maintained a 3.9 GPA and placed on the Chancellor's List in 2002 and 2001.
Associate's degree in Nursing, Sandhills Community College, Carthage, NC, 1988.
- Graduated with honors.

CERTIFICATIONS

Received Home Health Nurse certification from the American Nurse's Credentialing Center, October 2002.
Licensed to practice nursing as a Registered Nurse in the state of North Carolina, certification number 75075 issued by the NC Board of Nursing, 1988.
Licensed to practice nursing as a Registered Nurse in the state of South Carolina, license number R00056475 issued by the State Board of Nursing for South Carolina, 2001.

PROFESSIONAL AFFILIATIONS

American Nurse's Association, 1998
North Carolina Association for Home Care Intermediary Relations Committee, 1997-99
North Carolina Association for Home Care Ethics Subcommittee, 1999-00
North Carolina Association for Home Care Provider Services Committee, 2001-03

AWARDS

Award for Academic Excellence in Nursing, May 2002
Award for Academic Excellence, April 2002
North Carolina "Great 100 Nurses," October 2000
Hanni Schultz Memorial Award for Academic Excellence, May 1988

PERSONAL

Am results oriented. Have an enthusiastic, caring manner which makes others comfortable. Feel that I offer a well-rounded background of clinical and managerial skills.

MEDICAL

Date

Sally Kennedy
Personnel Department
Tampa Medical Center
1638 Thousand Flower Drive
Tampa, FL 86703

Laboratory Clerk

Dear Ms. Kennedy:

I would appreciate the opportunity to talk with you soon about how I could contribute to Tampa Medical Center through my strong interest in applying for the position of Laboratory Clerk. I feel that I offer the experience and education which would qualify me for this position.

Enclosed you will find a copy of my resume which covers in detail my training, education, and experience. Through my background in business administration and several jobs in office settings, I offer knowledge of filing, computer operations, customer service, and recordkeeping which would make me a valuable asset to an office where detail is critical.

My certifications as a Nursing Assistant include Levels 1 and 2 in Florida and Level 1 in North Carolina. I am certified in CPR, first aid, AIDS education, home health, and hospice operations and earned a Certificate of Merit for maintaining a GPA of 93 or above.

I am very adaptable with a reputation as a compassionate, hard-working individual with a talent for dealing with difficult situations and stressful conditions professionally and efficiently.

I hope you will call or write me soon to suggest a time convenient for us to meet and discuss your current and future needs and how I might serve them. Thank you in advance for your time.

Sincerely yours,

Tabitha Wise

TABITHA WISE

1110½ Hay Street, Fayetteville, NC 28305   •   preppub@aol.com   •   (910) 483-6611

OBJECTIVE

To offer my experience related to office operations and administration along with my education and know-how in the medical field to an organization in need of a hard-working, dedicated professional with strong communication, troubleshooting, and problem-solving skills.

EDUCATION & TRAINING

Completed a refresher program for recertification as a Nursing Assistant, Charlotte Technical Community College, NC, 2003: course work included CPR and first aid.
Attended Levels 1 and 2 of a three-month Nursing Assistant training program, Medical & Dental Careers, Tampa, FL, 1998.
- Gained knowledge of AIDS education, first aid, CPR, and hospice operations.
Completed 1-1/2 years of Business Administration course work at Charlotte Technical Community College, Charlotte, NC.
- Studied subjects including typing, filing, computerized accounting, business law, and the use of various standard office machines.
Completed additional training in how to interact with hospice patients; causes, stages, and isolation techniques for AIDS patients; and one-on-one care for home health aides.

CERTIFICATION

Hold NC and FL registry certification as a CNA

EXPERIENCE

BOOKKEEPER, OFFICE MANAGER, and **OWNER/OPERATOR.** The Helping Hand, Charlotte, NC (2003-present). Handle all aspects of operating a small residential cleaning service: schedule appointments, clean, and maintain applicable records and files.

NURSING ASSISTANT. Charlotte Medical Center, Charlotte, NC (2003). Applied both my office operations skills and medical knowledge while taking care of a wide range of daily activities from admitting and discharging procedures, to taking vital signs, to bathing and feeding patients.
- Gained experience in maintaining medical records by entering information such as blood pressure, temperature, and symptoms into patients' charts.

ADMINISTRATIVE ASSISTANT. Quality Paint and Glass, Charlotte, NC (2001-02). Displayed a helpful, pleasant manner as the public's first contact with this auto glass specialist company: answered phones and greeted customers in person.
- Remained cheerful and professional while handling any customer complaints.
- Gained experience in office activities such as accepting and processing payments, filing, making appointments, ordering parts, and processing paperwork for insurance claims.

COLLECTIONS CLERK. Abundant Finance, St. Pauls, NC (1999-00). Refined my troubleshooting and problem-solving skills in a job which required the ability to deal with customers who were frequently mad and often rude while doing what was needed to satisfy both the customer and company management.

NURSING ASSISTANT. Wallingford's Rest Home, Tampa, FL (1998). Was known for my willingness to work long, physically demanding hours in order to improve the quality of life for people who required 24-hour care.

ASSISTANT MANAGER. Circle K, Tampa, FL (1997-98). Displayed my adaptability while dealing with the public in a 24-hour gas station/convenience store setting which called for strong customer service and time management skills.
- Prepared detailed paperwork including reports at the end of each shift and bank deposits as well as inventory forms and stock reorder forms.

GENERAL OFFICE CLERK. Walley's Service Co., Tampa, FL (1994-97). Handled office and customer service activities such as alternate dispatcher, appointment clerk, and records clerk.

PERSONAL

Am very people oriented and have been cited for my contributions to youth activities such as acting as den leader for a Boy Scout troop and as a major supporter of a t-ball team.

MEDICAL

Exact Name of Person
Title or Position
Name of Company
Address (no., street)
Address (city, state, zip)

Medical Lab Technician

Dear Exact Name of Person: (or Dear Sir or Madam if answering a blind ad.)

I would appreciate an opportunity to talk with you soon about how I could contribute to your organization through my expertise as a medical laboratory technician/technologist along with my proven ability to train, motivate, supervise, and develop others. As an Indiana native, I shall be relocating back home upon completing my military service.

As you will see from my resume, most recently I have excelled in working at two jobs simultaneously while also going to school at night to earn a second bachelor's degree — a Bachelor of Science degree in Medical Lab Technology. As a Medical Lab Technician with a civilian major medical center, I perform quantitative and qualitative tests on blood and body fluids while working in all lab sections. In my other job, I am excelling as an Instructor/Writer while developing lesson plans and instructing more than 300 students annually in laboratory procedures. I take great pride in the fact that I have trained some of the world's finest medics, and I have redesigned lesson plans for teaching bacteriology, blood bank, parasitology, and mycology.

Previously I worked as a Medical Lab Technician at a forensic toxicology drug testing laboratory, where I also acted as supervisor of 10 people performing specimen testing.

I can provide outstanding personal and professional references, and I offer a reputation for unquestioned integrity. While serving my country in the U.S. Army, I received a medal for my role in a covert operation with the C.I.D., during which I was offered a bribe for "fixing" a specimen of a cocaine user. I am known for attention to detail, honesty, and reliability.

I hope you will welcome my call soon to arrange a brief meeting at your convenience to discuss your current and future needs and how I might serve them. Thank you in advance for your time.

Sincerely yours,

Jose Mandonado

Alternate last paragraph:
I hope you will call or write me soon to suggest a time convenient for us to meet and discuss your current and future needs and how I might serve them. Thank you in advance for your time.

JOSE MANDONADO

1110½ Hay Street, Fayetteville, NC 28305　　•　　preppub@aol.com　　•　　(910) 483-6611

OBJECTIVE

To benefit an organization that can use an experienced medical lab technician/technologist with skills related to chemical pathology, forensic toxicology, and other areas along with proven supervisory, communication, instructional, research, and problem-solving abilities.

LICENSES & CERTIFICATIONS

Medical Laboratory Technician, American Society of Clinical Pathologists
Medical Laboratory Technician, American Medical Technologists
Eligible for ASCP Certification as a Medical Technologist

EDUCATION

Bachelor of Science, Biology and Psychology, University of the State of New York, 2003.
Bachelor of Health Science in Medical Lab Technology, Campbell University, Buies Creek, NC, 2003.
More than one year of training at Academy of Health Sciences in advanced laboratory skills.
Completed training sponsored by Society of Armed Forces Medical Lab Scientists.

EXPERIENCE

For the past two years, have been working at two jobs — one military, one civilian — while also going to college full time in the evenings; offer strong time management skills:
INSTRUCTOR/WRITER. U.S. Army Special Warfare Center, Ft. Bragg, NC (2000-present). Have earned a reputation as an outstanding communicator while instructing more than 300 students annually in laboratory procedures and in techniques for maintaining medical standards established by physicians and veterinarians.

- Developed and refined lesson plans; redesigned and rewrote bacteriology, blood bank, parasitology, and mycology lessons in a new, more user-friendly format.
- Taught laboratory subjects including hematology, urinalysis, bacteriology, blood bank, parasitology, mycology, and serology.

MEDICAL LAB TECHNICIAN. Cape Fear Valley Medical Center, Fayetteville, NC (2000-present). At one of the largest medical centers in the southeast, performed quantitative and qualitative tests on blood and body fluids in the stat lab and in these other lab sections:

chemistry	hematology	urinalysis
coagulation	blood bank	microbiology

MEDICAL LAB TECHNICIAN and **SUPERVISOR.** Forensic Toxicology Drug Testing Laboratory, Ft. Meade, MD (1996-99). While excelling as a Medical Lab Technician, acted as supervisor of 10 military and civilian personnel involved in specimen processing, and was responsible for the legal chain of custody on all specimens as well as the processing of specimens for further testing.

- Also functioned as a *Radio Immuno Assay Technician*, monitoring quality control and assurance; produced controls and standards, performed calibration of pipettes, and prepared statistical calculations.
- Developed expertise in performing *extractions*, including chemical extractions of specimens for final analysis in GC/MS.
- Played a key role in rewriting the Standard Operating Procedures Manual.
- Received an Army Achievement Medal for a covert operation I performed with the C.I.D.; refused to accept a bribe for "fixing" a specimen for a cocaine user.
- Received two other medals during this time period, one for being named *Soldier of the Quarter* and the other for exceptionally meritorious service.

SECURITY SQUAD LEADER. Pine Knob Music Theatre, Clarkston, MI (1995). Refined my ability to stay calm during crises while supervising security patrols during concerts.

EQUIPMENT EXPERTISE

Proficient in the operation and general maintenance of the following:

Kodak Ektachem 700 & 850, DT 60	**Abbott** TDX, FLX, ADX, IMX
Coulter STKR, STKS, MAXM **MLA** 1000, 800	**Rapimat** Auto UA Machine
BACTEC Bacti-Alert for Blood Culture	**Baxter** microscan

PERSONAL

Can provide strong personal and professional references upon request. Take pride that I have trained some of the best medics in the world. Have **Top Secret security clearance.**

MEDICAL

September 12, 2003

Ms. Gini Bowling
Britthaven of Chapel Hill
1716 Legion Road
Chapel Hill, NC 27514

**Nursing Home
Administrator**

Dear Ms. Bowling:

With the enclosed resume, I would like to formally introduce myself to you and acquaint you with the considerable skills and experience I have to offer Britthaven of Chapel Hill.

A Licensed Nursing Home Administrator (L.N.H.A), I also hold an Associate of Science degree in Banking and Finance. Prior to obtaining my L.N.H.A., I excelled in the banking field and was selected by The First National Bank of Leesport as its first-ever Customer Service Representative. In that position, I gained valuable skills in the "nuts and bolts" of marketing and promotion that have been enormously useful to me in medical administration.

In one job as administrator of a long-term care facility, I led this operation to show a profit for the first time in four years while also increasing the census from 90% to 95%. In other administrative positions in medical facilities, I solved a variety of staffing problems while improving public relations, boosting profits, reducing aging receivables, and writing policies/procedures to ensure compliance with government guidelines.

I can provide outstanding personal and professional references, and I can assure you that I offer a proven ability to communicate with people at all levels. I enjoy the challenges of solving problems within nursing home environments, and I look forward to learning how my background could be of use to Britthaven of Chapel Hill.

Yours sincerely,

Lucy Atherton, L.N.H.A.

Nursing Home Administrator

LUCY ATHERTON, L.N.H.A.

1110½ Hay Street, Fayetteville, NC 28305   •   preppub@aol.com   •   (910) 483-6611

OBJECTIVE

I want to contribute to an organization that can use a skilled administrator who offers proven skills related to hiring and training employees, managing service operations, performing bookkeeping, providing customer service, and overseeing public relations and marketing.

EXPERIENCE

PHLEBOTOMIST and **BOOKKEEPER.** Fayetteville, NC (2003-present). Am excelling in two jobs simultaneously: as a **phlebotomist** with Alpha Therapeutic Corporation, am involved in the overall plasmapheresis process; as a **bookkeeper** with Spell & Spell Builders, perform office duties and prepare spreadsheets using Microsoft Excel.

ADMINISTRATOR. Elizabethtown Nursing Center, Elizabethtown, NC (2002-03). Through my management skills and problem-solving skills, played a key role in "turning around" an 84-bed nursing facility that was experiencing numerous internal difficulties; just 12 days after I was hired, the facility received its provisional license and, six months later, regained its licensure status.
* Recruited, hired, and trained department heads.

ADMINISTRATOR. Autumn Care of Raeford, Raeford, NC (2001-02). Led this 70-bed long-term care facility to show a profit for the first time in four years while also increasing the census from 90% to 95%; reduced aged receivables to 22% of total receivables.
* Planned, organized, and directed all administrative functions and monitored conformance to guidelines promulgated by regulatory agencies.
* Within one month, hired and trained four new department heads and worked with them to dramatically improve the quality of services provided.

ADMINISTRATOR. The North Carolina Cancer Institute, Inc., Lumberton, NC (1999-01). Took over the management of an organization that was experiencing a variety of staffing problems; stabilized and restored confidence in the staff while improving public relations, increasing the census, and boosting profits.
* Planned, organized, and directed administration for this 56-bed long-term facility.
* Improved the performance of this facility in all operational areas evaluated by federal and state regulatory agencies.
* Implemented OBRA guidelines and wrote policies and procedures that conformed with government regulations.

BOOKKEEPER. Bethesda Health Care Facility, Fayetteville, NC (1998-99). Completed a Nursing Home Administration Course while being trained in Medicare/Medicaid; performed bookkeeping while maintaining medical records and residents' charts.

HEAD CUSTOMER SERVICE REPRESENTATIVE and **PUBLIC RELATIONS COORDINATOR.** The First National Bank of Leesport, Leesport, PA (1985-98). Began as a teller and eventually was selected as the bank's first Customer Service Representative, a newly created position; was commended for my creativity and technical skill in improving the bank's public relations posture, represented the bank as a member of the Board of Governors of the American Institute of Banking, and was selected "A.I.B.-er of the Year" based on my accomplishments.
Banking: Projected a positive image that cemented the bank's relationships.
Promotions/Public Relations: Wrote and developed advertising for radio and newspaper; designed billboard displays; developed and delivered slide presentations; was the driving force behind the establishment of a new newsletter.
Sales: Became skilled in cross selling services, providing financial advice, opening new accounts, as well as marketing and promoting financial products.

**EDUCATION
&
TRAINING**

Associate of Science degree, Banking and Finance, Alvernia College, Reading, PA, 1997.
Completed 50-week Administrator-in-Training Course and a Medical Terminology Course.
Licensed **Nursing Home Administrator (L.N.H.A.)** and CPR certified.
Completed courses in finance, customer service, word processing, and management.

PERSONAL

Can provide outstanding personal and professional references. Possess strong people skills and communicate well at all levels. Offer proven leadership ability. Will relocate.

MEDICAL

Exact Name of Person
Title or Position
Name of Company
Address (no., street)
Address (city, state, zip)

**Licensed Practical
Nurse (LPN)**

Dear Exact Name of Person: (or Dear Sir or Madam if answering a blind ad.)

I would appreciate an opportunity to talk with you soon about how I could contribute to your organization through my extensive medical experience in pediatric, surgical, nursing home, and private duty nursing environments as well as my strong management skills.

I am in the early planning stages of moving to the Pinehurst area, where I can be nearer to my aging parents and, hopefully, work for Moore Regional County Hospital. It is my genuine desire to become a part of your team, and I believe I offer versatile skills in many areas that could benefit you. Although I am not available for a full-time position until the fall, I would be willing to accept part-time weekend work or work on a per diem basis immediately.

As you will see from my resume, I currently am employed as an LPN and Office Manager at Raeford Road Children's Clinic, a new clinic which I played a major role in opening "from scratch." During my employment at Cape Fear Pediatrics, I became acquainted with the pediatrician for whom I now work, and he recruited me to assist him in opening his new clinic. Out of loyalty to the clinic, I would not wish to leave Dr. Matthews until he completes the kindergarten checkups through August. I can provide outstanding references from Dr. Matthews as well as from all other previous employers.

You would certainly find me in person to be a congenial and down-to-earth professional who relates well to children, co-workers, adult patients, and medical professionals. In my current position as LPN and Office Manager, I ordered the computers and medical equipment for the office, and I routinely use and train others to use Microsoft Word, Excel and Medisoft. I also have worked with CLIA officials and supervise CLIA compliance of our lab. Although I am experienced in numerous medical areas and would cheerfully work in your area of greatest need, I feel I am ideally suited to pediatrics and I truly enjoy working with children.

I hope you will welcome my call soon to arrange a brief meeting at your convenience to discuss your current and future needs and how I might serve them. Thank you in advance for your time.

Sincerely yours,

Grace Young

GRACE YOUNG

1110½ Hay Street, Fayetteville, NC 28305 • preppub@aol.com • (910) 483-6611

OBJECTIVE To benefit an organization through my versatile medical experience in pediatric, surgical, nursing home, and private duty nursing environments as well as my strong management and administrative skills.

LICENSE Licensed Practical Nurse, Certificate # 050856, May 7, 2003

EXPERIENCE **LICENSED PRACTICAL NURSE** and **OFFICE MANAGER.** Raeford Road Children's Clinic, Raeford, NC (2003-present). While employed at Fayetteville Pediatrics, met pediatrician Foster Matthews and was subsequently recruited by him to help him open this new children's clinic.
- Have played a key role in opening this clinic, and now manage a five-person staff while performing all duties of an LPN.
- Selected and ordered office computers; routinely utilize Microsoft Word, Excel and Medisoft.
- Handle all finances including the doctor's taxes, accounts payable and receivable, and insurance claims.
- Work with CLIA officials and supervise CLIA compliance of the lab; have attended several CLIA seminars.

NURSING DEPARTMENT SUPERVISOR and **CNA II.** Cape Fear Pediatrics, Fayetteville, NC (2001-02). Handled both administrative and clinical duties for this busy pediatrics office including CBC's, performing lab work, and giving immunizations.

MEDICAL TECHNICIAN. Fayetteville Plastic Surgery Specialists, P.A., Fayetteville, NC (1996-00). As Medical Technician, scheduled surgeries with Cape Fear Valley, Highsmith-Rainey, and Fayetteville Ambulatory Surgery Center; in-office procedures included setting up rooms for surgery, assisting in surgery, and providing post-operative care.
- Attended OSHA certification program and became responsible for meeting the requirements for OSHA regulations.
- Arranged for meetings between doctors and other experts.
- Handled insurance for patients requiring surgery or other medical procedures.
- Maintained and ordered inventory of supplies and medications.
- Ensured the cleanliness of all rooms and sterilization of surgical instruments.

CERTIFIED NURSING ASSISTANT. Medical Personnel Pool, Fayetteville, NC (1995-96). Monitored patients during in-home care while providing service as a private duty nurse at Cape Fear Valley Medical Center and Highsmith-Rainey Memorial Hospital.

CENTRAL SUPPLY TECHNICIAN. Fairbanks Memorial Hospital, Fairbanks, AK (1992-94). While supplying the operating room, developed the ability to run and maintain the equipment used for operating room procedures, including sterilizing with the ethylene oxide and the steam sterilizer, and using aerators.
- Gained knowledge of incubators used to test the sterility of the instruments and checking for positive spores; set up operating room with instruments for several procedures.

Highlights of earlier experience: Have worked extensively with nursing homes as a CNA.

SPECIAL Offer office skills in typing, filing, scheduling, inventory control, and medical transcription.
SKILLS Familiar with several types of computers and software including Microsoft Word, Excel and Medisoft.

EDUCATION Have attended numerous management seminars, 2001-present.
Licensed Practical Nurse (LPN) Graduate, Tri-Smith College, Fayetteville, NC (Dec 2002).
CNA I and CNA II, Tri-Smith College, Fayetteville, NC (June 2002).
Studied Nursing at University of Fairbanks, Fairbanks, AK (1991-93).
Studied Nursing at Mount Wauchsett Community College, Gardner, MA (1984-88).
CNA, Sacred Heart Nursing Home, Plattsburgh, NY (1986).

PERSONAL Am a careful listener and empathetic professional committed to quality patient care.

MEDICAL

Date

Exact Name of Person
Title or Position
Name of Company
Address (number and street)
Address (city, state, and ZIP)

Medical Marketing

Dear Exact Name of Person: (or Sir or Madam if answering a blind ad.)

Can you use an energetic, creative, and articulate professional who offers a degree in Marketing combined with approximately seven years of experience in the Health Care Systems field?

You will see from my enclosed resume that I have advanced to positions in project implementation and training with SAIC in San Diego, CA, a corporation which provides support personnel to military medical facilities throughout the country. I train people in all aspects of the functions of Radiology, Clinical, and Managed Health Care Program Systems as well as activating sites and providing implementation assistance to end users of the systems.

I am effective as a troubleshooter and a specialist in customer service due to my ability to make others comfortable around me. In the course of my job, I have earned the respect and confidence of everyone I have come into contact with from hospital administrators, to vendors, to my students. I am adept at taking the latest technical information and presenting it to users in one-on-one, small group, and large group settings.

I am confident that through my education in Marketing, experience in dealing with people, and diplomatic, positive personality I am capable of making important contributions to your organization and would relocate according to employer's needs.

I hope you will welcome my call soon to arrange a brief meeting to discuss your current and future needs and how I might serve them. Thank you in advance for your time.

Sincerely,

Zandra Zepp

Alternate last paragraph:
I hope you will call or write me soon to suggest a time convenient for us to meet and discuss your current and future needs and how I might serve them. Thank you in advance for your time.

ZANDRA ZEPP

1110½ Hay Street, Fayetteville, NC 28305   •   preppub@aol.com   •   (910) 483-6611

OBJECTIVE To combine my education in marketing with my knowledge of medical systems operations and applications to an organization in need of a bright, enthusiastic young professional who excels in dealing with people, defusing difficult situations, and solving problems.

EXPERIENCE *Have become known as a diplomatic and involved professional while advancing in the following track record of accomplishments and knowledge with SAIC, San Diego, CA:*
MEDICAL SYSTEMS OPERATIONS TRAINING SPECIALIST. (2002-present). Currently involved in training military personnel as an Implementation Specialist, ensure that end users of radiology, clinical, and managed care program systems are properly trained and knowledgeable of the equipment and its operation.
- Implemented a 2003 four-month project at Womack Army Hospital, Ft. Bragg, NC, in which I trained hundreds of medical personnel and earned praise from site personnel for my ability to solve problems and issues.
- Handled all aspects of site activation including ensuring equipment deployment and set up, training users, overseeing and assisting in file and table building, and troubleshooting during the actual activation.
- Provided implementation assistance at three radiology sites and three clinical sites as well as training personnel at these six locations.
- Directly managed all aspects of a Ft. Carson, CO, radiology site project including training 60 people and guiding the site throughout the activation on my own.
- Was cited for my ability to quickly learn and absorb new concepts and information and then pass that knowledge on to others.
- Recognized for my knack for dealing with people others find hard to work with and for ensuring high levels of customer satisfaction, worked closely with people ranging from project officers, to hospital executives, to co-workers, to students, to vendors.

TRAINING ADMINISTRATOR. (2000-02). Coordinated more than 100 classes while displaying my diplomacy as the point-of-contact for numerous vendors, contractors, and customers.
- Coordinated several ethics briefing classes, each attended by more than 100 people.
- Coordinated with instructors for classes as well as prepared course materials for a Relational Database Systems class and several Introduction to C/C++ classes which included desktop publishing of two large manuals.
- Learned budget procedures, then successfully tracked and justified budgets to executives within a training group headquarters: provided five groups with budget support.
- Supervised and trained the department's Database Administrator, Training Specialist, and a staff of temporary secretaries and word processors.
- Handled the details of locating materials, coordinating with vendors for outside instructors, setting up a schedule, and overseeing two successful MUMPS classes — a 12-15 class program developed in-house to upgrade the skills of programmers.

TRAINING ASSISTANT. (1999-00). Was selected for this role as a training specialist for technical classes for creators of health-related systems.
- Gained experience in applying effective teaching methods and learned proper procedures for setting up, organizing, and conducting informative classes.
- Utilized my computer skills while developing and desktop publishing a manual which is still in use and has been much lauded.

EDUCATION & TRAINING Earned a B.A. degree in Marketing, National University, San Diego, CA, 2002.
Attended corporate-sponsored training programs emphasizing supervisory skills and conflict management.

AFFILIATION Have been a member of the American Marketing Association since 2002.

PERSONAL Am skilled in seeing the big picture and quickly able to find solutions to problems and issues.

MEDICAL

Exact Name of Person
Title or Position
Name of Company
Address (no., street)
Address (city, state, zip)

Nutritionist and Medical Marketing Representative

Dear Exact Name of Person: (or Dear Sir or Madam if answering a blind ad.)

I would appreciate an opportunity to talk with you soon about how I could contribute to your organization through my extensive experience in medical sales and marketing, medical billing, and nutritional consulting.

Fluent in English and Spanish, I hold an undergraduate degree in Nutrition and Dietetics **cum laude**, and I have worked as a full-time Nutritionist and Marketing Consultant for both the Beech-Nut and Quaker Oats Companies. In those jobs, I visited hospitals, doctors, health centers, and supermarkets to promote products and conduct special marketing events. I am a skilled public speaker and have coordinated numerous conferences and publicity activities.

I have also excelled in sales and sales management positions with a major pharmaceutical company. I began with the company in 1994 as a Medical Marketing Representative and progressed rapidly into sales management responsibilities which involved training up to eight medical sales professionals. With my naturally outgoing personality and extensive background in the sciences and nutrition, I became one of the company's most valuable employees and most visible spokespersons.

You will see from my resume that I am a hard worker. While excelling in my full-time positions mentioned above, I worked part-time during the evenings and on the weekends for nearly ten years handling all medical billing for a six-doctor medical practice. I had a fully equipped office in my home, and I am very experienced in utilizing Microsoft Word and medical billing software including Medifast.

You would find me to be a personable and well-educated individual who relates well to people and who adapts easily to new organizational environments. I can provide excellent personal and professional references.

I hope you will call me soon to suggest a time when we might meet to discuss your current and future needs and how I might serve them. Thank you in advance for you time.

Sincerely yours,

Soraya Zahran, LDN

Alternate last paragraph:
I hope you will welcome my call soon to arrange a brief meeting at your convenience to discuss your current and future needs and how I might serve them. Thank you in advance for your time.

Nutritionist and Medical Marketing Representative

SORAYA ZAHRAN, LDN

1110½ Hay Street, Fayetteville, NC 28305 • preppub@aol.com • (910) 483-6611

OBJECTIVE
To contribute to an organization that can use an experienced young professional who offers an education as a dietitian along with experience in medical marketing and administration.

EDUCATION
Bachelor of Science in Nutrition and Dietetics, **cum laude**, University of Puerto Rico, 1991.
Completed graduate-level internship in Dietetics, 1991-92.

EXPERIENCE
DIRECTOR OF BILLING. Northern Internal Medicine Group, Puerto Rico (1995-03). In this part-time job which I performed in my home during the evenings and on weekends, was in charge of all medical billing related to private insurance and Medicare for a medical practice with six doctors including cardiologists and family practice physicians.

NUTRITIONIST & MARKETING CONSULTANT. Quaker Oats Company, Puerto Rico (1997-00). As the company's internal nutritionist, coordinated visits to hospitals and health centers in order to present lectures on nutrition, dietetics, and other subjects; explained the benefits of Quaker products in the outpatient setting.
- Trained sales professionals and suppliers regarding product knowledge.
- Marketed Quaker products through visits to doctors' and nutritionists' offices.
- Coordinated and participated in conventions in order to promote products.
- Trained and supervised outside publicists in developing marketing materials.
- Participated in a television program in which recipes which used our products were prepared and nutritional tips were provided to the audience.
- Developed and presented educational lectures in different settings.

MEDICAL MARKETING REPRESENTATIVE/ASSISTANT MANAGER. Sterling Products, Intl., Puerto Rico (1994-97). For a major pharmaceutical company, marketed medical and pharmaceutical products to public and private hospitals; began with the company as a Medical Sales Representative and then progressed into sales management responsibilities.
- Became one of the company's most productive sales professionals as well as a highly visible and trusted spokesperson respected for my extensive expertise related to over-the-counter drugs.
- Developed special events at medical conventions to promote the company's products; coordinated all special publicity and promotional activities.
- Trained company as well as customer personnel on new products.
- Visited prospective new clients to present products; was known as a skillful negotiator with the ability to close the sale.
- Supervised up to eight medical sales representatives.
- Visited doctors, hospitals, and pharmacies in order to promote the company's products.

NUTRITIONIST/MARKETING CONSULTANT. Beech-Nut Nutrition Corporation, Puerto Rico (1993-94). As a Nutritionist, visited hospitals, health centers, doctors' offices, and supermarkets in order to explain the advantages of Beech-Nut products.
- Promoted products for babies, infants and expectant mothers.
- Designed special promotions with supermarkets and stores which generated extensive publicity and sales.
- Marketed products and trained sales/marketing sales professionals for the company in both Puerto Rico and the Dominican Republic.

CHIEF OF DIETETIC SERVICES. Hospital Gubern, Puerto Rico (1992-93). Supervised a department with 12 employees, and oversaw the training and scheduling of all employees.
- Performed nutritional assessments of hospital patients; provided dietary instructions to patients being discharged.
- Purchased nutritional products and food and integrated products into the hospital menu.

COMPUTERS, LANGUAGES
Extremely computer literate and skilled in using Word, Excel and Medifast for medical billing.
Fluent in both English and Spanish.

PERSONAL
Social Security number 581-21-0710. Extremely self-motivated individual who adapts easily.

MEDICAL

Administrator
Duke Medical Center
P.O. Box 449
Durham, NC 28395

Office Management   Dear Sir or Madam:

I would appreciate an opportunity to talk with you soon about how I could contribute to your organization through my experience in the medical field as well as my clerical, accounting, and office management skills.

As you will see from my resume, I currently handle accounting and data entry for a company which has recently computerized its operations while experiencing a 20% growth in patient volume. I am skilled at accounts receivable/payable, billing/collections, insurance liaison, data entry, and customer service within a medical environment.

In previous jobs I excelled in a field dominated by fire and rescue professionals. I started out as a Fire Dispatch Operator for the City of Raleigh and was promoted to Telecommunications Supervisor of Wake County's Emergency Operation Center based on strong work performance and professional recommendations. A hard-working and highly motivated individual, I am always seeking to refine my skills and knowledge. I am certified as an Emergency Medical Technician and trained to provide CPR and other medical support.

You would find me to be a dedicated person who would pride myself on contributing to your goals and objectives. I can provide outstanding personal and professional references.

I hope you will call or write me soon to suggest a time convenient for us to meet and discuss your current and future needs and how I might best serve them. Thank you in advance for your time.

Sincerely yours,

Katie Eubanks

Office Management

KATIE EUBANKS

1110½ Hay Street, Fayetteville, NC 28305　•　preppub@aol.com　•　(910) 483-6611

OBJECTIVE　To contribute to an organization that can use a well organized young professional who offers outstanding clerical/secretarial skills, extensive data entry experience, along with an expert understanding of medical terminology.

EXPERIENCE　**ACCOUNTS REPRESENTATIVE.** U.S. Health Services, Raleigh, NC (2003-present). Learned to balance accounts totaling $120,000 monthly while also mastering computerized accounting procedures as the company expanded to a new automated accounting and billing system; continuously increased my efficiency as patient volume increased rapidly by 20%.
- *Accounts receivable:* Receive and post payments to patients' accounts.
- *Accounts payable:* Prepare a wide range of bills for companies and individuals.
- *Billing/collections:* Bill more than 150 patients monthly; follow up on past due accounts.
- *Insurance billing:* Prepare paperwork for Medicare, Medicaid, and commercial companies for insurance billing purposes.
- *Data entry:* Perform data entry for 150 accounts which require three entries weekly.
- *Customer service/public relations:* Have earned a reputation as a hard-working professional with a cheerful disposition and a helpful attitude toward the public.

TELECOMMUNICATIONS SUPERVISOR III. Wake County Emergency Operation Center, Raleigh, NC (1997-03). Was promoted to this job because of my excellent performance in the job below; was commended for remaining calm in emergencies and for my ability to soothe people in stressful situations while supervising the Emergency Operation Center.
- At a time when the emergency dispatch field was dominated by fire and rescue professionals, became a respected supervisor because of my significant contributions to the city/county at a time when they were enhancing their 911 system.
- Continuously monitored electronic telecommunications equipment.
- Maintained detailed dispatch records for all emergency response.

FIRE DISPATCH OPERATOR. City of Raleigh Fire Department, NC (1991-97). Learned to operate complex communications equipment and acquired transcriptionist skills while monitoring multi-channel fire and rescue dispatch equipment.
- Maintained public records, reports, and documents.
- Made decisions about appropriate equipment to dispatch to emergencies.
- Received a Letter of Congratulations from the Chief of Police and was promoted.

INSURANCE CLERK. Mid-South Insurance Company, Fayetteville, NC (1991-97). While operating a wide range of office equipment and learning internal operations of an insurance company, determined correct charges for patients' premiums and distributed correct insurance policies to both companies and individuals.

AVIATION MAINTENANCE ADMINISTRATOR. U.S. Navy, Sicily (1988-89). Earned a reputation as a disciplined, hard-working professional while completing discrepancy reports on naval aircraft, typing and distributing various reports, and making determinations about scheduling aircraft inspections.

EDUCATION　Completed Supervisory School, Fayetteville Technical Community College (FTCC), NC, 1996.
Studied Computer Programming, FTCC, 1993-94.
Certified Emergency Medical Technician; completed Basic Life Support studies, FTCC, 1993.

SKILLS　*Medical equipment:* Skilled in oxygen setup and knowledgeable of equipment used to record vital signs; operate traction equipment.
Medical skills: Can provide basic life support, CPR, airway management, splinting, bandaging, hemorrhage control, and shock management.

CERTIFICATIONS　Certified as an EMT and in CPR, State of North Carolina, since 1993.

PERSONAL　Am a highly motivated person who strives to make a contribution in my job.

MEDICAL

Date

Exact Name of Person
Title or Position
Name of Company
Address (no., street)
Address (city, state, zip)

Registered Nurse

Dear Exact Name of Person: (or Dear Sir or Madam if answering a blind ad.)

I would appreciate an opportunity to talk with you soon about how I could contribute to your organization as an R.N. through my strong combination of nursing experience, leadership skills, and caring attitude.

For approximately eight years I have excelled in direct patient care at two major area hospitals, most recently as a Surgical Intensive Care Unit (SICU) Staff Nurse at Tar Heel Medical Center. Prior to this job I was a Charge Nurse at Moore Regional County Hospital where I sharpened my skills related to direct patient care and staff supervision while becoming known for my skill in communicating with patients and their families as well as other medical professionals.

With an associate's degree in Nursing from Sandhills Technical Community College, I offer general office skills in addition to my nursing experience. I am confident I could contribute to your organization through my strong analytical and decision-making skills as well as my cheerful disposition, flexible attitude, and ability to rapidly master new tasks.

I hope you will welcome my call soon to arrange a brief meeting at your convenience to discuss your current and future needs and how I might serve them. Thank you in advance for your time.

Sincerely yours,

Deborah Lynn Griffin

Alternate last paragraph:
I hope you will call or write me soon to suggest a time convenient for us to meet and discuss your current and future needs and how I might serve them. Thank you in advance for your time.

DEBORAH LYNN GRIFFIN

1110½ Hay Street, Fayetteville, NC 28305 • preppub@aol.com • (910) 483-6611

OBJECTIVE
To offer my experience as an R.N. as well as my leadership, analytical abilities, and time management skills to an organization that can use a compassionate and caring professional whose first priority is always the needs of the patient.

LICENSES
A Licensed R.N., hold licenses or certifications in the following specialities and areas:
Advanced Pediatric Life Support (PALS)
Advanced Cardiac Life Support (ACLS)
Basic Cardiac Life Support (BCLS)

TRAINING
Completed in-house training programs at Moore Regional County Hospital, Moore County, NC, in subjects including the following:
hemodynamic monitoring (1999)
basic and 12-lead EKG interpretation and procedures (1998)

EDUCATION
Associate's degree in **Nursing,** Sandhills Technical Community College, NC, 1996.

SKILLS
Offer skills related to equipment and functional areas including the following:
IV pumps	cardiac monitoring
feeding pumps	pulse oximeters
venodynes/SCDs	PCA/CADD pumps
Pyxis	EKG interpretation
venipuncture	emergency response

Operate computers using Microsoft Word and Access and office equipment including fax machines and copiers.

EXPERIENCE
REGISTERED NURSE. Tar Heel Medical Center, Piedmont, NC (2003-present). As a Staff Nurse in a Surgical Intensive Care Unit (SICU), provide direct patient care for one or two critically ill patients requiring constant attention.
• Provided rapid response to "Code Blue" emergency situations.

REGISTERED NURSE. Moore Regional County Hospital, Moore County, NC (1997-03). Gained experience and honed my skills in the areas of direct patient care, staff supervision and education, and communication with family members as well as other medical professionals.
• Used my time management skills and judgment to make decisions on which staff member to place in charge of which patient depending on how acute their condition was and the nurse's specific strong points and experience level.
• Was selected to apply my leadership skills and knowledge as the preceptor for new staff members and for category II procedures.
• Managed emergency code calls both within the unit and in other units.
• Became skilled in procedures including titrating critical drips such as lidocaine, dopamine, and tridel.
• Learned a great deal about caring for patients on mechanical ventilation.
• Was recognized as having excellent familiarity with hospital equipment including IV pumps, cardiac monitors, and speciality beds.
• Learned to interpret basic and 12-lead EKGs.
• Earned a reputation as an expert in venipuncture, monitoring A-lines, CVP, and Swan-Ganz catheters.

PERSONAL
Am known as a "good listener" who offers compassion and a true concern for what is best for the patient. Have a reputation for being assertive with well-developed decision-making skills. Quickly learn to use new equipment and adapt to change.

MISCELLANEOUS TECHNICAL

Date

Exact Name of Person
Title or Position
Name of Company
Address (no., street)
Address (city, state, zip)

**Electrical Installer
and Industrial Mechanic**

Dear Exact Name of Person: (or Dear Sir or Madam if answering a blind ad.)

I would appreciate an opportunity to talk with you soon about how I could contribute to your organization through my expertise as an Industrial Plant Mechanic and Electrician (Commercial or Residential). I am in the process of relocating to Rhode Island where my wife is already living, and I would be delighted to make myself available for a personal interview at your convenience. I hold certifications as an Industrial Mechanic, Electrical Installer, and Electrical Systems Maintenance Specialist.

As you will see from my resume, since 2003 I have excelled in a job as an Electrician with the VA Medical Center where I maintain and repair all electrical systems and equipment as well as a wide range of medical equipment, appliances, and telephone and computer cable systems.

In a prior job as an Industrial Mechanic with Tar Heel Poultry, I supervised eight maintenance personnel on the second and third shift while performing as the only electrician on both shifts. I maintained all electrical systems throughout the plant and was responsible for the entire production line.

I can assure you that you would find me in person to be a congenial individual with excellent communication and interpersonal skills as well as highly refined troubleshooting and problem-solving abilities. I can provide outstanding personal and professional references. I hope you will write or call me soon to suggest a time when we could meet in person to discuss your current and future needs and how I might serve them. Thank you in advance for your time.

Sincerely yours,

Eric Pascal

Electrical Installer and Industrial Mechanic

ERIC PASCAL

1110½ Hay Street, Fayetteville, NC 28305 • preppub@aol.com • (910) 483-6611

OBJECTIVE

I am in the process of relocating to Rhode Island to join my wife, and I am seeking employment with an organization that can use an Industrial Plant Mechanic or Electrician (Commercial or Residential) who can provide outstanding personal and professional references.

CERTIFICATIONS

Industrial Mechanic
Electrical Installer and Electrical Systems Maintenance

SKILLS

Experienced industrial plant maintenance mechanic with the ability to work within general instructions or guidelines while installing, maintaining, and repairing a variety of electrical machinery, systems, circuits, equipment and controls including:

lighting systems	gauges and valves
actuators and motor controls	switches and breakers
paging systems	office and medical equipment
pumps, generators, and boilers	uninterrupted power supply
gear boxes and motor control centers	
high temperature heating and cooking equipment	central air conditioning systems

- Interpret and use blueprints, wiring diagrams, engineering drawings, and building plans.
- Excellent working knowledge of the NEC.
- Am a licensed **Trencher Operator** (Ditch Witch) and **Forklift Operator**.
- Skilled in performing appliance repair.
- Proficient in **welding:** Oxyacetylene, arc, heliarc, stainless and carbon steel, aluminum.

EXPERIENCE

ELECTRICIAN. VA Medical Center, Raleigh, NC (2003-present). Maintain and repair all electrical systems and equipment throughout the Center including building service systems, i.e., 250 KW and 600 KW generators, lighting, ventilating and environmental systems, engineering services equipment, kitchen, canteen and laundry equipment.

- Also maintain medical equipment including electric motors, lighting, infrared systems, hydraulic systems, air and fluid pumps, medical air and vacuum systems.
- Maintain and repaired office equipment and small appliances used throughout the facility.
- Installed and altered telephone and computer cable systems.

ELECTRICIAN. Cape Fear Feed Products, Raleigh, NC (2002). Was responsible for maintenance, repair, installation, troubleshooting, and alteration on electrical systems, machinery, motors, and circuits throughout compound of Cape Fear Feed Products Company.

- Followed blueprints and wiring diagrams of starter controls and light circuits; replaced or repaired damaged electrical systems.
- Installed light sockets and power supply systems, switches, outlet boxes indoor and outdoor.
- Measured, cut, threaded, bent, and assembled/installed rigid conduit and armored cable non-metallic cable which connected to various out motors/panel boxes.
- Performed all work in a strict safety-conscious manner and in accordance with the National Electric Code.

INDUSTRIAL MECHANIC/ELECTRICIAN (SUPERVISOR). Tar Heel Poultry, Apex, NC (2001-02). Supervised eight maintenance personnel on the second and third shift while performing as the only electrician on both shifts; maintained all electrical systems throughout the plant and was responsible for the entire production line.

- Maintained and replaced valves, pumps, gauges.
- Inspected, maintained, and repaired electric motors and motor control centers on trolley lines, electric forklift trucks, and tow motors, including the drive gear boxes.
- Fabricated and welded machinery and parts.

EDUCATION

Raleigh Technical Community College, Raleigh, NC:
Electrical Installation and Maintenance (76 hours), 2001
Industrial Mechanics (70 hours), 2000

- Excelled academically and was named to President's List, 1999-01.

MISCELLANEOUS TECHNICAL

Date

Exact Name of Person
Title or Position
Name of Company
Address (no., street)
Address (city, state, zip)

**Electronics Repair
Maintenance**

Dear Exact Name of Person: (or Dear Sir or Madam if answering a blind ad.)

I would appreciate an opportunity to talk with you soon about how I could contribute to your organization through my excellent technical electronics skills as well as through my reputation as a knowledgeable and effective troubleshooter.

As you will see from my enclosed resume, through training and experience I have earned a reputation for my technical expertise related to electronics troubleshooting, repair, and maintenance. My experience covers several areas in the electronics field such as television, residential security alarms, and telephone switching operations.

My TV and security system experience has been gained since leaving the U.S. Army in 2000. While serving my country in the military, I earned advancement to supervisory roles and was often called on to diagnose difficult problems. After the war in the Middle East, I was placed in charge of seeing to the details of re-establishing communication services for my unit at Ft. Hood, TX, a major military facility.

I hope you will welcome my call soon to arrange a brief meeting at your convenience to discuss your current and future needs and how I might serve them. Thank you in advance for your time.

Sincerely yours,

Richard Psaki

Alternate last paragraph:
I hope you will call or write me soon to suggest a time convenient for us to meet and discuss your current and future needs and how I might serve them. Thank you in advance for your time.

RICHARD PSAKI

1110½ Hay Street, Fayetteville, NC 28305　　•　　preppub@aol.com　　•　　(910) 483-6611

OBJECTIVE	To offer excellent technical electronics skills and troubleshooting abilities to an organization that can use a hard worker with a reputation for initiative, ambition, and drive to succeed.
TRAINING	Excelled in U.S. Army-sponsored technical and leadership development courses including: 　　Mobile Subscriber Equipment (MSE) and maintenance supervisor's courses, 1998 　　professional leadership development school, 1997 　　principles of electronics and solid state equipment, 40 hours, 1995 　　SB3614A communication equipment/NET equipment, 80 hours, 1995 　　Completed four semester hours of solid state electronics and three semester hours of electric circuits, Central Texas College, Germany, 1995.
CERTIFICATIONS & SPECIAL SKILLS	Have held the Security Systems License, State Bureau of Investigations, Private Protective Services. Use standard and specialized test equipment; offer expertise in the following areas and with the following equipment:

troubleshooting relays	electronic schematics	oscilloscopes
computer-aided troubleshooting	electronic board repairs	multimeters
troubleshooting and repair of DC power supplies		
diagnosing defective automatic telephone switchboards		
current-voltage relationships in component soldering		
transistor and operational amperes and solid-state logic		
performing diagnostic tests on basic AC and DC circuits		
subscriber dial-tone multiple-frequency, dial pulse, and hand-cranked systems		

EXPERIENCE	**APPRENTICE ELECTRICIAN.** Roberts' Electrical Contractors, Ft. Bragg, NC (2002-03). Completed inside wiring jobs including installing switches, lights, and outlets for new living quarters housing thousands of military soldiers at the largest U.S. military base in the world. **MASTER CONTROL OPERATOR.** Channel 62 TV, Fayetteville, NC (2002). Gained experience in activities ranging from airing TV programs according to prepared program logs, to conducting minor maintenance on tapes and recorders, to following procedures for powering up the station's transmitter, to assisting the chief engineer. 　•　Provided support in day-to-day functional areas such as office administration and applying my technical knowledge while tuning receivers to receive satellite broadcasts. **SECURITY SYSTEM INSTALLER.** Ace Security, Fayetteville, NC (2000-02). Became familiar with several types of security alarm products while installing them in private residences: inspected the home to determine how and where to install the particular system, completed the installation, programmed the system, and tested for errors. 　•　Became thoroughly skilled in all phases of installation including pulling wires under foundations or through attics, wiring equipment, setting up control panel wiring, hard wiring up to 18 separate zones, troubleshooting, and repairing system failures. *Received training and polished my skills in the electronics field, U.S. Army:* **TELEPHONE MAINTENANCE SHOP SUPERVISOR.** Ft. Hood, TX (1998-00). Selected to supervise five specialists, provided technical guidance for telephone equipment repair and maintenance while handling administrative details such as scheduling and the preparation of forms and records. 　•　Applied my knowledge and organizational expertise by coordinating arrangements for re-establishing service to my unit at this major military base following the Middle East war. **TELEPHONE MAINTENANCE SPECIALIST.** Germany (1995-97). Earned a reputation as a talented troubleshooter and was often called on to solve unique problems found in a wide range of equipment; performed diagnostic tests on basic AC and DC circuits in order to diagnose defective automatic telephone switchboard operations.
PERSONAL	Have been officially cited for displaying strong moral character. Offer a positive attitude.

MISCELLANEOUS TECHNICAL

Date

Exact Name of Person
Title or Position
Name of Company
Address (no., street)
Address (city, state, zip)

Mechanic   Dear Exact Name of Person: (or Dear Sir or Madam if answering a blind ad.)

I would appreciate an opportunity to talk with you soon about how I could contribute to your organization through my experience in troubleshooting hydraulic, mechanical, pneumatic, electrical, and computer control problems in industrial equipment.

As you will see from my resume, I have solved a wide variety of stubborn technical problems while working as a Mechanic at The DuPont Corporation. On my own initiative I have invented new sources of power supplies and created circuit boards when the company was threatened with expensive downtime caused by waiting for needed components to arrive.

I am skilled in working with formal quality control systems including Statistical Process Control (SPC) and Total Quality Process (TQP). Whether working individually on my own initiative, or as part of a team, or with manufacturers/vendors of equipment used by the company, I am always committed to helping the company achieve quality results at minimum cost.

I hope we will have an opportunity to meet in person so I can demonstrate that I am someone who could add value to your company and contribute to your strategic goals and objectives. I can provide outstanding personal and professional references.

Yours sincerely,

Malcolm Ellington

Alternate last paragraph:
I hope you will call or write me soon to suggest a time convenient for us to meet and discuss your current and future needs and how I might serve them. Thank you in advance for your time.

MALCOLM ELLINGTON

1110½ Hay Street, Fayetteville, NC 28305 • preppub@aol.com • (910) 483-6611

OBJECTIVE

To contribute to an organization that can use a resourceful professional who offers a proven ability to solve stubborn technical problems while troubleshooting problems in hydraulic, electrical, pneumatic, and computer control equipment.

EXPERIENCE

MECHANIC. The DuPont Corporation, Fayetteville, NC (2003-present). Have made valuable contributions to this company through my mechanical knowledge, and have solved numerous quality problems through my individual initiative as well as through my participation on the Corrective Action Team (CAT).

- Became skilled in formal quality control systems including Statistical Process Control and Total Quality Process (TQP).

- Refined my expertise in using equipment including the following:

drill presses	cutting torches	I.D. micrometers
grinders	band saws	metals breaks
alignment jigs	dynamometers	pipe benders
torque tools	hydraulic presses	honing and boring equipment
dial calipers	lap and die sets	depth micrometers

- Performed troubleshooting of hydraulic, mechanical, pneumatic, electrical, and computer control equipment; performed some programming of microcontrollers.

- Worked on equipment manufactured by Globe, Auto-Matic, Micro Posie, Gould, Hoffoman, Alliance, and Ransburge; worked on Allen Bradley programmable controllers, field winders, armature winders, and armature balancers.

- Consulted with vendors about equipment quality problems; recommended remedies.

- Replaced electronic modules and circuit boards costing between $600 and $2500 with boards that I created "from scratch" without a print.

- On one occasion when the company had experienced two days of downtime waiting for a power supply for the magnet systems, I analyzed the problem and invented a homemade power supply in my hobby shop that is still being used by the company three years later.

- On another occasion eliminated a two-week wait for a tester circuit board by making a drawing, building a board, and installing it in only four hours.

MANAGER TRAINEE. Radio Shack, Fayetteville, NC (2002-03). Opened and closed the store, made bank deposits, handled sales, and prepared payroll.

MAINTENANCE TECHNICIAN. Southeastern Foam, Fayetteville, NC (1999-01). Controlled repair of equipment and oversaw the second shift while assuring continuous boiler room service including the fire eye flame systems; became knowledgeable of plastic and expandable polystyrene control and set up.

MAINTENANCE SPECIALIST. Kelly's Cleaners, Clinton, NC (1998-00). Maintained dry cleaning equipment in a part-time job while in college.

EDUCATION

Completed two years of college studying history/political science, Fayetteville State University, Fayetteville, NC. At Fayetteville Technical Institute, studied radio communications, industrial and electrical technology, and advanced shop skills focusing on blueprint reading and the use of tool including calipers and micrometers. In correspondence courses, studied wire systems for industry, tv repair, and electronics.

PERSONAL

Can provide outstanding personal and professional references upon request.

Date

The Charlotte News
P.O. Box 9875
Charlotte, NC 28547

Plumbing   Dear Sir or Madam:

With the enclosed resume, I am responding to your ad for Chemical Plant Technicians. I am in the process of relocating to the Charlotte area to be near my aging parents, and I can make myself available for a personal meeting at your convenience.

As you will see from my resume, I offer the strong mechanical aptitude you are seeking and, in fact, have earned a reputation for being "able to fix anything." I credit my mechanical know-how to starting work at a young age. From the time I was 16 years old, I worked in a plumbing business as a plumber's helper and, even though I worked part-time every day after school, I managed my time well enough to graduate from high school as an Honor Graduate and as president of the Vocational Industrial Clubs of America (VICA) for two years.

After high school, I continued to work as a plumber and in 2001 I was promoted to manage the plumbing supply business where I began working as a youth. When I took over as manager, the business had profitability problems. I have transformed it into a very profitable operation while instituting inventory controls, reorganizing accounts payable/receivable, and altering purchasing policies and procedures. I am currently designing and implementing a safety program to assure absolute compliance with OSHA standards. Through my management experience, I have acquired excellent customer service skills.

Although I am highly regarded by my current employer, I have the goal of becoming a maintenance foreman in a large industrial plant one day, and I am positive I have the mechanical knowledge, natural intellect, and management ability to advance into such a position.

If you can use a talented and versatile young professional such as myself, please call me at home and I would be delighted to meet with you during one of my frequent trips to Charlotte. I can provide exceptionally strong personal and professional references, and I am seeking a company where I can make a long-term commitment. Thank you in advance for your time in considering my resume for employment with your company.

Sincerely yours,

Paul Jones

PAUL JONES

1110½ Hay Street, Fayetteville, NC 28305   •   preppub@aol.com   •   (910) 483-6611

OBJECTIVE   To offer my extensive experience in all aspects of plumbing installation, repair, and operations management along with my skill in reading and fabricating from sketches and prints.

LICENSES & CERTIFICATIONS   Completed the Plumbing Code Level #3 course, and am preparing to sit for the state exam in order to become a licensed plumber.
Certified in backflow prevention testing and repair, certification #020-G; certified by Public Works Commission in 1997 and recertified in 1999 and 2001.

EDUCATION   In February 2003, made a perfect score on both the math and reading assessment portions of the General Manufacturing Certification Program, Fayetteville Technical Community College.
Graduated as an **Honor Graduate** from Douglas Byrd Senior High School, Fayetteville, NC, 1995; achieved a 3.8 GPA on a 4.0 scale.
* Through my excellent planning and time management skills, was able to excel academically and socially as a leader even though I held a part-time job as a plumber's helper from the time I was sixteen and throughout high school.
* Was elected president of Vocational Industrial Clubs of America (VICA) for two years.
* In both 1994 and 1995, was named **Student of the Year** in Industrial Cooperative Training.

SPECIAL SKILLS
* Am mechanically resourceful and creative, and can repair or install just about anything.
* Skilled in all types of plumbing repairs and new installation.
* Proficient in cutting and threading steel pipes and fitting the same.
* Experienced in managing accounts receivable/payable, purchasing, and sales.
* Skilled in operation of equipment including generators, electric drain cleaning machines, electric pipe threaders and cuttings, tamping machines, jack hammers, chipping hammers, flaring tools, and propane and acetylene torches.

EXPERIENCE   **PLUMBER.** Cumberland County Schools, Fayetteville, NC (2003-present). Perform plumbing repairs for schools and administrative buildings throughout the Cumberland County School System.
* Install boilers and install/repair heat and return lines for boilers and heating systems.
* Install commercial dishwashers and kitchen equipment in cafeterias.

MANAGER. Cason's Plumbing Supply Company, Inc., Fayetteville, NC (2001-03). Was promoted to manage the company after excelling as a plumber's helper and then plumber; upon taking over the management of this plumbing supply business, transformed it from an unprofitable operation into one that made substantial profit.
* After analyzing procedures and practices, instituted new inventory controls that eliminated waste and loss, and also dramatically altered purchasing policies/procedures.
* Reorganized the accounts payable and receivable departments.
* Demonstrated my belief that a manager must have a cheerful attitude about doing any job in the business, and was always willing to tackle weekend or night plumbing repair jobs to meet customer needs in addition to my regular management responsibilities.
* Designed and implemented a safety program to assure absolute compliance with all OSHA standards; gained valuable knowledge of OSHA and other regulations.

PLUMBER. Cason's Plumbing Company, Inc., Fayetteville, NC (1993-00). Began working after school as a plumber's helper when I was 16 years old, and slowly became skilled in every aspect of the plumbing trade for commercial and residential properties.
* Performed commercial and residential rough-in, top out, and setting out of plumbing fixtures in new homes and buildings.
* Repaired plumbing in offices, schools, restaurants, apartments, and homes.
* Installed and repaired water and drain lines in new construction; installed galvanized airlines and black steel gas and steam lines.

PERSONAL   Have a desire to eventually become a maintenance foreman or leadman in a large industrial plant. Known for my knack for being able to fix anything! Am single; would relocate.

MISCELLANEOUS TECHNICAL

Date

Exact Name of Person
Title or Position
Name of Company
Address (no., street)
Address (city, state, zip)

**Plumbing, Heating,
and Refrigeration**

Dear Exact Name of Person: (or Dear Sir or Madam if answering a blind ad.)

I would appreciate an opportunity to talk with you soon about how I could contribute to the growth and profitability of your organization.

As you can see from the enclosed resume, I have a high level of expertise related to plumbing, heating, and refrigeration, including my extensive personnel and operations management experience.

Regarded within the industry as an innovator and leader, I have developed the ability to "build a team" of highly motivated and productive employees. I believe you would find me personally to be a warm professional who enjoys sharing my "wealth" of experience with other managers.

I hope you will call or write me soon to suggest a time convenient for us to meet and discuss your current and future needs and how I might best serve them. Thank you in advance for your consideration.

Sincerely yours,

Ernest Walker

Plumbing, Heating, and Refrigeration

ERNEST WALKER

1110½ Hay Street, Fayetteville, NC 28305 • preppub@aol.com • (910) 483-6611

OBJECTIVE

To contribute to corporate growth/profitability through my expertise related to plumbing and heating, including my superior product knowledge and personnel management experience.

EXPERIENCE

OPERATIONS MANAGER. *Purdue Chickens, Raeford, NC (2001-03). Because of my "track record" of accomplishments in cutting costs and improving morale, was promoted well ahead of my peers in the following positions:*

MAINTENANCE MANAGER. Directed all personnel matters, shift operations, and equipment maintenance.
- Reorganized the maintenance department and reconfigured the pay scale, saving the plant $1,500 a week in labor costs.
- Reduced maintenance costs by 30%.
- Earned a reputation as a "top notch" supervisor of 54 employees.
- Dramatically "turned around" employee attitude through improvements to the working environment, for example, painting and cleaning up.

REFRIGERATION MANAGER. Monitored all factors affecting the profitability of my department, including labor efficiency, machine maintenance, and costs.
- Supervised and coordinated activities of eight technicians.
- Ensured quality control and that all USDA requirements were met.
- Saved the plant $20,000 by constructing a refrigerator door for one-third of the amount one could be purchased.
- Demonstrated such a clear head for efficiency and cost-effectiveness that I advanced to Maintenance Manager after just six months.

REFRIGERATION TECHNICIAN. Excelled in assignments covering all aspects of refrigeration maintenance and repair.
- Gained valuable expertise regarding ammonia compressor units.
- Qualified for a rapid promotion to Refrigeration Manager after only 30 days on the job.

GENERAL MANAGER. Raleigh Plumbing and Heating, Raleigh, NC (1973-00). Over a 27-year period, developed a successful plumbing and heating contract business, employing 24 people.
- *Finances*: Managed pricing and bidding/estimating jobs.
- *Customer service*: Established a loyal clientele of satisfied residential and commercial customers, including hospitals (Cape Fear Valley Medical Center), shopping centers (Harris Teeters), and professional offices.
- *Cost management*: Lowered operating costs of jobs by 15%.
- *Employee relations*: Boosted productivity by starting an employees' benefit program.
- *Sales and profitability*: Maintained continuous growth and profitability through my expert sales and purchasing techniques, increasing volume of business from $300,000 to $1 million.

CERTIFICATIONS

Completed CFC Certification, Sandhills Community College, Pinehurst, NC, September 2003.
Hold plumbing/heating licensures in the state of North Carolina: Class 1 P, H1, H3.

EDUCATION

Attended refrigeration courses at Cape Fear Technical Institute, Cape Fear, NC, 1976.
Have completed several training courses throughout my career to stay current with changes in the industry and the latest equipment.

COMMUNITY COMMITMENT

A native of the Sandhills, have served my community in the following ways:
Elected Deacon of the First Baptist Church of Raeford, 1991.
First as a Member (1991-1992) and as President (1994-2000) of the Band Boosters, raised more than $200,000 dollars for Hoke and Moore county school systems.
Received a **Volunteer Award** for fundraising efforts from NC Governor James Martin in 1994.

PERSONAL

Enjoy the challenge of motivating a team of employees who are determined to make a profit while serving satisfied customers. Subscribe to high standards of loyalty and honesty.

MISCELLANEOUS TECHNICAL

Date

Sprint
14111 State Street
Chapel Hill, NC 27514

**Telecommunications
Repair**

Dear Sir or Madam:

With the enclosed resume describing my considerable technical skills and knowledge, I would like to formally initiate the process of being considered for employment with your company.

As you will see, I am a skilled young technician with the proven ability to excel in any responsibility I take on, whether technical repair and troubleshooting or administrative. In my current job I install telephone lines while also installing and servicing a wide variety of other equipment including security systems, closed circuit camera systems, and fire alarm systems. On my own initiative, I have received informal training in roadside line location using the pipe horn, cable hound, and other line locating instruments.

I am very familiar with Sprint and with your reputation for quality performance. I feel certain I could contribute to your high standards through my reputation as a hard worker as well as through my strong technical skills.

I can provide outstanding personal and professional references at the appropriate time, and I am single and will cheerfully relocate according to your needs. I offer an outstanding reputation as a safety-conscious individual with a commitment to Total Quality results.

I hope you will write or call me soon to suggest a time when we might meet to discuss your current and future needs and how I might serve them. Thank you in advance for your time.

Sincerely yours,

Ervin Williams

ERVIN WILLIAMS

1110½ Hay Street, Fayetteville, NC 28305　•　preppub@aol.com　•　(910) 483-6611

OBJECTIVE

To contribute to an organization that can use a hard-working young professional with extensive skills related to telecommunications repair and installation along with outstanding technical troubleshooting and problem-solving skills.

EXPERIENCE

SECURITY SYSTEMS INSTALLATION TECHNICIAN. SuperSafe Security Systems, Inc., Charlotte, NC (2001-03). For this company which does business all over the eastern part of North Carolina, have become a valuable technician and am highly respected for my skill in installing telecommunications, cable television equipment, and security systems.
- Joined the company immediately after graduating from high school.
- Install telephone lines and prewire houses for telephones.
- Handle the installation of cable television in new developments; add second cable and telephone lines in existing dwellings.
- For 90% of the Wendys and Hardees in eastern NC, install and service equipment including closed circuit tv.
- Am involved in the hands-on training of two junior technicians.
- Have become skilled in the service and design related to fire alarm systems and camera systems.
- Have become proficient in handling daily paperwork dealing with working procedures, start and finishing time, work site address, materials used, and any matters related to safety and inventory control.

ELECTRICAL MOTOR MAINTENANCE TECHNICIAN. Slot Machines, Inc., Charlotte, NC (1999-00). In my junior and senior years of high school, worked in an after-school job and handled a wide variety of technical repair and management responsibilities.
- Rebuilt and repaired motors which powered remote control cars used on slot car tracks; held this job after school.
- Opened the store in the afternoon after school and managed the office until the operating manager arrived.
- Refined my customer relations and customer service skills working with the public.

LICENSES

Security Systems License, State Bureau of Investigations, Private Protective Services
Am a licensed and bonded technician

EDUCATION

Graduated from Myers Park Senior High School, Charlotte, NC, 2001.
Completed Technical Advisory Training, Charlotte, NC, 2001-03; this is essentially an apprenticeship program with an emphasis on on-the-job training.
Completed Security System/Telecom and Cable Training, Charlotte, NC, 2001-03; learned how to put together a telecom.

OTHER SKILLS & KNOWLEDGE

- In early 2002, became familiar with roadside line location using the pipe horn, cable hound, and other line locating instruments through training.
- Am skilled in crawling under homes and in attics to perform repair work.
- Proficient in using a wide variety of tools; own a large tools inventory.

PERSONAL

Single (never been married) with no children. In excellent health, will relocate and travel as needed. Can provide excellent personal and professional references.

OTHER MISCELLANEOUS

Date

Exact Name of Person
Title or Position
Name of Company
Address (no., street)
Address (city, state, zip)

**Communications--
Writing, Television,
Photography**

Dear Exact Name of Person: (or Dear Sir or Madam if answering a blind ad.)

I would appreciate an opportunity to talk with you soon about how I could contribute to your organization through my creativity and wide ranging skills in the field of corporate communications and graphics/visual arts.

As you will see from my resume, I hold an M.S. degree in Communications Education and a B.A. degree in Communications/Mass Media. In addition to my formal education, I am by nature a "hands-on" creative individual who has demonstrated an ability to master a wide variety of technical tools and media ranging from computer software and television equipment to woodworking utensils and automotive tools. In most of the jobs I have held, I have been selected to supervise my co-workers during the absence of the manager, so I offer a proven ability to train, motivate, and supervise others.

Experienced in all phases of educational/training program design and development, I am skilled in corporate/instructional video design and production. I am also knowledgeable of all aspects of television writing and production and have won awards in national photography contests.

You would find me in person to be a congenial individual who rapidly masters new technical skills. I can provide outstanding personal and professional references upon request.

I hope you will welcome my call soon to arrange a brief meeting at your convenience to discuss your current and future needs and how I might serve them. Thank you in advance for your time.

Sincerely yours,

Stacy Lampros

Alternate last paragraph:
I hope you will call or write me soon to suggest a time convenient for us to meet and discuss your current and future needs and how I might serve them. Thank you in advance for your time.

Communications--Writing, Television, Photography

STACY LAMPROS

1110½ Hay Street, Fayetteville, NC 28305 • preppub@aol.com • (910) 483-6611

OBJECTIVE

To contribute to an organization that can use a creative "hands-on" professional with versatile skills related to writing, television production, and photography along with expertise in using automotive, wood working, and many other kinds of tools and equipment.

EDUCATION

Master of Science (M.S.) degree in Communications Education, Ithaca College, Ithaca, NY, 2000; excelled academically with a **3.8 GPA.**
Bachelor of Arts (B.A.) degree in Communications/Mass Media, State University of New York, Plattsburgh, NY, 1992.
Associate of Arts (A.A.) degree in Liberal Arts, Broome Community College, NY, 1989.

HONORS, PROFICIENCIES

- Have won awards in worldwide **photography** contests.
- Am skilled in corporate/instructional **video design and instruction.**
- Knowledgeable of all aspects of **television writing and production.**
- Experienced in all phases of educational/**training program design** and development.

EXPERIENCE

DESIGN CONSULTANT. Self employed, Germany and U.S. (1998-present). Design and coordinate the building of custom-made furniture.

LIBRARY TECHNICIAN/PUBLICIST. U.S. Library System in Stuttgart, Germany (2002-03). Wrote and designed publicity materials marketing books, upcoming events, and programs while applying my expertise in creating original art and graphics, utilizing clip-art, and performing cut-out and paste-up.
- Handled publicity and public relations for a wide range of events.
- Supervised up to three employees and performed all duties at the circulation desk.

PRINTER/ENGRAVER, TOOL & PARTS SPECIALIST, WOODWORKING INSTRUCTOR. The Arts and Crafts Center, Pope Air Force Base, NC (1999-02).
Was known for my willingness to do any job while working at the Automobile Hobby Shop.
- *Inventory control*: Controlled an extensive inventory of automotive tools and issued correct tools to customers; inspected tools upon their return and performed minor repairs.
- *Finance*: Accounted for daily receipts and made bank deposits.
- *Technical duties*: Changed oil filters and air filters; checked fluid levels; checked and corrected air pressure in tires; changed and rotated tires; vacuumed cars; checked/charged batteries; performed maintenance on the automatic car wash and refilled wax, soap, and water; operated forklift and pickup truck.
- *Merchandising and sales*: Supervised store design and promotional displays.
Worked briefly at the Arts & Crafts Center's Award Plaque & T-Shirt Shop.
- *Custom printing and engraving*: Handled custom printing and engraving of plaques and T-shirts; utilized a wide range of art utensils as well as paper, metal, and glass cutters and operated machines including the heat press, letter machine printer, engraving machine, and heat and press machine.
Provided instruction to individuals and groups on woodworking techniques.
- Coordinated the first annual "Arts and Crafts Christmas Fair" at Pope AFB; made crafts to sell, arranged for prizes, selected craft participants, and handled publicity.

PRODUCER/WRITER & EDUCATIONAL TRAINING SPECIALIST. Department of Wildlife, Seattle, WA (1997-99). Worked on a special project which involved creating an educational training program called Project Wild which teachers used to teach children the basic concepts of wildlife ecology.
- Wrote, produced, and created an audio-visual slide program.

TELEVISION OPERATIONS ENGINEER. KXLY Television, Spokane, WA (1995-97). Acted as both Master Control Operator, Video Tape Operator, and Remote Broadcast Operations Engineer in this job which required me to have an FCC Radio Operators License.
- Produced mini-documentaries concerning wildlife for the Washington State Game Department; developed pre-production ideas and transformed them into outlines, scripts, continuity, storyboards, and graphics.

PERSONAL

Offer a proven ability to apply my education and technical knowledge to profit an organization.

OTHER MISCELLANEOUS

Date

Exact Name of Person
Title or Position
Name of Company
Address (no., street)
Address (city, state, zip)

Interior Designer

Dear Exact Name of Person: (or Dear Sir or Madam if answering a blind ad.)

I would appreciate an opportunity to talk with you soon about how I could contribute to your organization through my education and experience in interior design.

As you will see from my resume, I am presently the Acting Interior Designer for the UNC Hospital in Chapel Hill where I oversee repair, renovation, and construction projects throughout the Hospital system. Originally accepted for a 200-hour internship, I found myself in a position where my supervisor was absent half of the time and I was training myself. I took over when she left and am currently holding this job on an interim basis.

This opportunity has given me the chance to prove myself at a level not usually enjoyed by a young person at this stage of her career. I have taken on a wide range of projects throughout the facilities while becoming skilled at budget analysis, preparing specifications, ordering products to be used in various projects, and overseeing the actual renovations and repairs.

While in college I was an instrumental player in efforts to gain FIDER (Foundation for Interior Design Education Research) accreditation for my school and was a member of the first class to graduate with this accreditation in place.

I am a customer service-oriented good listener known for my ability to handle pressure and deadlines. Through my creativity and knowledge, I have a great deal to offer to an organization that can use a detail-oriented and mature young professional.

I hope you will welcome my call soon to arrange a brief meeting to discuss your current and future needs and how I might serve them. Thank you in advance for your time.

Sincerely,

Joanna Woldstad

Alternated last paragraph:
I hope you will call or write me soon to suggest a time convenient for us to meet and discuss your current and future needs and how I might serve them. Thank you in advance for your time.

Interior Designer

JOANNA WOLDSTAD

1110½ Hay Street, Fayetteville, NC 28305 • preppub@aol.com • (910) 483-6611

OBJECTIVE

To offer creativity and knowledge of residential and industrial interior design to an organization that can use a detail-oriented communicator who thrives on deadlines and challenges.

EXPERIENCE

INTERIOR DESIGNER. UNC Hospitals, Chapel Hill, NC (2003-present). Oversee the details of coordinating repair and construction projects as well as facility enhancements throughout the university hospital facilities.

- Hired for a 200-hour internship, stepped into the designer's job when it was unexpectedly left vacant and became involved in working with the department supervisor to restructure the position and eliminate problems which had existed for some time.
- Assisted in restructuring the facility enhancement portion of the budget ($450,000) including combining corrected figures into a concise report for the hospital administrators.
- Handled operational areas ranging from ordering products to overseeing installation and repair.
- Consulted with physicians, nurses, and other involved staff members to get their input into design projects for areas which directly affected them.
- Participated in meetings in preparation for design competition at IIDA, the International Institution of Designers of America.
- Oversaw a wide variety of projects throughout the hospital including:
  burn center: wall coverings, lockers, and seating for the staff locker rooms
  food and nutrition lounge: seating specs and color scheme determination
  pediatric house staff lounge: flooring specs and budget analysis
  pulmonary unit: artwork specs and installation, budget analysis for seating in treatment areas, and finish selections for seating
  gynecology unit: site inspections, specs, budget analysis, and procurement for window treatments
  design department storage unit: inventoried all items and prepared inventory binder
  patient education offices: site analysis, space planning, and budget analysis
  ICU waiting area: rearranged furniture to maximize space and convenience
  cardiac catheterization unit: completed specs and procured wallpaper
  ambulatory center: completed specs and procured wall and floor coverings
  pediatric waiting room: specs and budget analysis for seating renovations, provided assistance with artwork donation collection and installation
  imaging department: specs, budget, and procurement of flooring
  radiology waiting: procurement of pre-specified furniture
  hematology-blood lab: site inspection for finishes on upcoming renovations

INTERIOR DESIGN ASSISTANT and **SALES ASSOCIATE.** Now & Then Designs, Greenville, NC (2000-02). Became familiar with all aspects of the business while helping in a variety of capacities from assisting clients and guests, creating displays as well as keeping them updated and fresh looking, assisting with office operations, and learning about the various suppliers the company used and the best sources for whatever decorating needs were to be met.

- "Sold" myself and my potential to management through the creative idea of working free for two weeks and proving myself so that I was soon offered a permanent position.
- Learned about color, arrangement, and space planning while assisting designers in selecting fabric, wallpaper, window treatments, carpet, and all other aspects of design.
- Refined my communication skills and became adept at understanding what a client wanted so that those needs could be communicated in turn to a decorator.
- Utilized my creativity while designing ads and helping with advertising sales projects.
- Organized the filing system and assisted other staff members in using computers.

EDUCATION

Earned a B.A. degree in Interior Design, East Carolina University, Greenville, 2003.

- Was instrumental as a member of the class which completed all the preliminary work resulting in gaining the program FIDER (Foundation for Interior Design Education Research) accreditation; this degree program is the model for the university's future.
- Coordinated formal and social events as well as serving on the standards board which helped promote a positive image for Sigma Sigma Sigma sorority.

AFFILIATIONS

Hold membership in ASID, American Society of Interior Design; was selected for membership in NKBA (the National Kitchen and Bath Association) after judging a competition.

OTHER MISCELLANEOUS: Massage Therapist

MICHELLE NAPOLI

1110½ Hay Street, Fayetteville, NC 28305 • preppub@aol.com • (910) 483-6611

OBJECTIVE

To contribute through knowledge of the medical value of massage and physical therapy while also applying skills in patient care and general office operations as well as a reputation as an enthusiastic and energetic quick learner experienced in the medical field.

EDUCATION

Completed the following professional educational programs:
Massage Therapy: Seminar Network International, Lake Worth, FL, 2002
Medical Lab Assistant: Los Medanos College, Pittsburg, CA, 1997
Travel Agent: Garber Travel, Boston, MA, 1991

CERTIFICATION IN MASSAGE THERAPY

Earned certification as a **Massage Therapist** upon completion of a 600-hour program and an additional 28 hours of continuing education credit from the NISA-Basic course in "Neuromuscular Integration and Structural Alignment."

EXPERIENCE

ADMINISTRATIVE ASSISTANT and **PHLEBOTOMIST.** St. Mary's Hospital, West Palm Beach, FL (2000-03). Gained experience in supervising an office staff while earning a reputation as a fast worker and very caring professional who was especially effective in dealing with pediatric, neonatal, and pediatric oncology patients while drawing blood.

- Became familiar with standard office equipment including multi-line phones as well as fax and copy machines while running the department office during frequent absences of a busy office manager.
- Learned to communicate with and put patients at ease while drawing blood: displayed a competent, concerned attitude dealing with post-trauma and post-surgical patients.
- Completed additional training programs in "Reiki energy work" and HIV awareness.
- Refined time management skills while meeting the demands of this full-time job, attending massage therapy school, and working part-time as a **PHLEBOTOMIST** for the JFK Medical Center in Atlantis, FL, performing early-morning blood draws.

PHLEBOTOMIST. John Muir Medical Center, Walnut Creek, CA (1998-00). Became adept at rapidly and efficiently drawing blood as part of a trauma team working under constantly stressful conditions; learned techniques for drawing blood from babies.

PHLEBOTOMIST. Pathology Institute, Berkeley, CA (1997-98). Gained a strong base of knowledge in drawing blood from all types of patients on morning rounds, some exposure to specimen processing, and how to communicate and deal with patients.

CUSTOMER SERVICE REPRESENTATIVE. Bank of America, Concord, CA (1996-97). Helped bank customers with any type of problem which occurred with their accounts from obtaining balances, to placing stop payments, to finding lost deposits while becoming skilled in using computers to do research.

- Polished my listening skills and ability to deal with people who were upset or angry and to find a way to solve the problems as quickly as possible.

CUSTOMER SERVICE SPECIALIST. Chemlawn Service Corp., Concord, CA (1996). Responded to customer calls and entered data into computer records while finding ways to solve problems and prepare correspondence related to how problems were to be resolved.

SALES REPRESENTATIVE. NEA Enterprises, Walnut Creek, CA (1994-96). For a wholesaler, handled every aspect of sales from making cold calls on potential customers, to taking orders, to processing orders, to filing and typing documents, to following up on completed sales to ensure customer satisfaction.

Highlights of earlier experience: Was recognized as "top seller" within three months of joining a travel agency and became familiar with using computers to maintain data and track reservations and prices with hotels, car rental agencies, and airlines.

PERSONAL

Operate ten-key adding machines by touch; am familiar with using telex machines and CRTs for data entry. Have a pleasing and friendly personality and can get along with anyone!

LYNNETT UNDERWOOD

1110½ Hay Street, Fayetteville, NC 28305 • preppub@aol.com • (910) 483-6611

OBJECTIVE

I want to contribute to the public relations image and activities of an organization that can use an experienced young news reporter who offers an excellent understanding of the media and how companies can maximize media relations.

EDUCATION

Bachelor of Science degree in English with a minor in Biology, N.C. State University, Raleigh, NC; 1996-98.
• Staff writer for *The Technician*, NC State University.
Studied English, Atlantic Christian College, Wilson, NC; 1994-96.
• Copywriter for *The Pineknot*, Atlantic Christian College Annual.

SKILLS

• Offer the ability to prepare publicity materials and press kits.
• Knowledgeable of how to write press releases, public service announcements, as well as feature, news, and sports articles for publication and broadcast.
• Knowledgeable of environmental issues and trends.
• Familiar with the Associated Press (AP) News Desk and the AP data base.
• Have earned a reputation as a creative professional with a knack for making complex issues understandable to the public.
• Skilled in video, writing, and production.

EXPERIENCE

ASSISTANT NEWS DIRECTOR. Tar Heel Broadcasting, Raleigh, NC (2003-present). Was promoted to this job after excelling as a reporter, and am in charge of making assignments for a three-person staff in the news room of this radio station; handled numerous administrative responsibilities related to maintaining the news room's productivity and efficiency.
• As a **Reporter**, cover local government and other issues.
• Am respected for my skills in identifying, researching, and developing interesting stories.
• Have learned how to manage a news operation.
• Have covered a wide variety of environmental issues.

REPORTER. Tar Heel Broadcasting, Raleigh, NC (1999-03). Sharpened my creative writing skills and interpersonal/interviewing abilities in building news beats.
• Covered county/community issues, and developed stories about education and environmental issues for use in regular newscasts; generated much public awareness/discussion based on stories I produced on saving natural resources and a proposal for a new incinerator.
• Anchored and occasionally produced special reports on a wide range of issues of local interest.

REPORTER/NEWS DIRECTOR. WCEC-AM, Rocky Mount, NC (1998-99). Was solely responsible for local news production and anchoring.
• Through my hard work and initiative, greatly strengthened this station's coverage of local government issues, educational matters, and spot news events.
• Was commended for my soothing voice and professional manner of delivering the news.

NEWS ASSISTANT and **PUBLIC AFFAIRS PRODUCER**. WTRG-FM, Raleigh, NC (1997-98). Developed and produced stories of local interest to morning news casts.
• Originated the concept for and produced a weekly public affairs show focusing on issues in the station's city of license (Rocky Mount).

PERSONAL

Offer excellent interpersonal skills which have helped me build solid working relationships with government officials, politicians, business people, and citizens. Have developed an easygoing style of interviewing people.

OTHER MISCELLANEOUS

Date

Exact Name of Person
Title or Position
Name of Company
Address (no., street)
Address (city, state, zip)

Nutritional Consulting

Dear Exact Name of Person: (or Dear Sir or Madam if answering a blind ad.)

I am writing in response to your ad in the *Los Angeles Times*. I am planning to relocate to the Los Angeles area and am sending you a copy of my resume so that you can assist me in my search for a challenging and rewarding position in this area.

As you will see from my resume, since early in 1997 I have been successful in a management position with the nationally known Nutrition for Life organization. Despite the fact that this corporation has declared bankruptcy and more than 800 locations have had to close, I have been able to not only keep my Raleigh, NC, locations open but have increased sales. In 1999, I edged out some tough competition to earn the respected "Manager of the Year Award" from among approximately 1,600 other professionals.

My degree is in Psychology and Sociology and I offer additional experience as a Social Worker. After demonstrating that I could handle a case load of 120-150 clients and consistently complete my cases ahead of schedule, I was promoted to Eligibility Specialist in the Department of Social Services.

I have managed a staff of up to 25 and all aspects of operations in a facility which reached the $900,000 level in annual sales and serviced as many as 300 clients a week.

I am an enthusiastic, energetic, and well-organized professional. I offer a talent for getting the most from employees and finding effective ways to keep things running smoothly and productively — even under very unsettled circumstances.

I hope you will welcome my call soon to discuss how you might be able to help me in my job search in your area. Thank you in advance for your time.

Sincerely yours,

Veronica Wagner

VERONICA WAGNER

1110½ Hay Street, Fayetteville, NC 28305 • preppub@aol.com • (910) 483-6611

OBJECTIVE

To offer my superior communication and motivational skills to an organization that can use an experienced management professional who has demonstrated a bottom-line orientation and a talent for selling concepts and services through an enthusiastic and energetic style.

EXPERIENCE

GENERAL MANAGER and **SALES AND CUSTOMER RELATIONS ADVISOR**. The Matthews Group (Nutrition for Life), Raleigh and Goldsboro, NC (1997-present). Continue to set sales records and steadily increase the customer base despite the fact that the parent corporation declared bankruptcy in 2002 and more than 800 locations nationwide have been forced to close.

- Singled out as "Manager of the Year for 1999" from among 1,600 qualified professionals nationwide, displayed knowledge of every aspect of Nutrition for Life operations.
- Increased sales by more than 50% during reorganization following a corporate takeover.
- Handled a wide range of functional activities ranging from setting sales and service goals, to developing business plans, to recruiting/training/supervising employees.
- Oversaw daily operational areas including financial management, inventory control, and customer follow up procedures.
- Handpicked for my effectiveness in running the Raleigh site, was selected to open the Goldsboro location and hold the position of interim area manager.
- During a two-month period prior to opening the Goldsboro center, hired and trained personnel and set up their operation.
- Applied my knowledge of marketing techniques while developing campaigns which used successful clients in radio ads and placed "lead boxes" throughout the city.
- Supervised up to 25 employees in a facility which saw from 250 to 300 clients a week and made $900,000 in its peak years before corporate reorganization.
- Maintained a $500,000 to $600,000 level with approximately 140 clients a week and about 12 employees in 2003.
- Through personal attention and rapport with clients, built a strong customer base which continues to generate about four new clients a week.

ELIGIBILITY SPECIALIST. Department of Social Services, Raleigh, NC (1995-96). Through my ability to communicate effectively with others and quickly establish rapport, was effective in working closely with agency clients to assess their needs and using established guidelines to determine their eligibility for various types of aid.

- Was promoted after managing a case load of from 120 to 150 clients and displaying my ability to organize and deal with a heavy schedule by always completing my cases on schedule and pitching in to help other social workers with theirs.
- Investigated approximately 60 cases a month through a combination of office and home visits to obtain information to determine eligibility for aid.

EDUCATION

B.S., Psychology and Sociology, University of Wisconsin, River Falls, WI, 1993.

- Earned recognition in "Who's Who Among American College Students" on the recommendation of Sociology Department faculty members.
- Maintained a 3.8 GPA and was one of the top two students in my graduating class.
- Received "Special Honors" and "Highest Academic Honors" upon my graduation.
- Founded and then served as president of the university's Sociology Club; planned and coordinated a wide range of campus activities for the Student Activities Committee.
- Completed independent study in Europe on the use of alternative medicines.
- Served as a volunteer counselor at a domestic abuse house.

COMPUTER SKILLS

Utilize Microsoft Word, Excel and Access for record keeping and data control.

PERSONAL

Am an energetic and enthusiastic individual with a flair for handling human, material, and fiscal resources. Contribute to my community through my church's Social Ministries Committee which is very active in assisting the homeless and disadvantaged.

OTHER MISCELLANEOUS

Date

Exact Name of Person
Title or Position
Name of Company
Address (no., street)
Address (city, state, zip)

Paralegal

Dear Sir or Madam:

Can you use a hard-working young professional who has excelled as a paralegal and legal secretary?

I recently moved to Fayetteville to join my husband, a military professional who expects to be stationed here for several more years. I can provide outstanding personal and professional references from previous employers who would describe me, I am certain, as a cheerful and adaptable office professional who can be counted on to meet tight deadlines and produce quality work under pressure.

In my most recent job I worked with a 15-person staff of attorneys, paralegals, and secretaries with the Department of Transportation in Florida. Since the department's primary mission was to continue building Florida's network of roads and superhighways, we dealt routinely with contractors who were in the field valuing real estate that the Transportation Department might want to buy. I used the dictaphone routinely and worked with several popular software programs while also functioning as an executive secretary, organizing and scheduling meetings among the contractors and legal staff.

You would find me to be an intelligent person who is good at problem solving in office environments. In my paralegal studies, I excelled academically, too, and achieved a 3.9 GPA on a 4.0 scale.

I hope you will call or write me soon to suggest a time convenient for us to meet and discuss your current and future needs and how I might serve them. Thank you in advance for your time.

Sincerely yours,

Rolanda Llaneta

ROLANDA LLANETA

1110½ Hay Street, Fayetteville, NC 28305   •   preppub@aol.com   •   (910) 483-6611

OBJECTIVE   To contribute to an organization that can use a poised young professional who offers specialized training and experience as a paralegal and legal receptionist.

EDUCATION   **Associate of Paralegal** degree, Tampa College, FL, 2001.
- Excelled academically with a 3.9 GPA based on a 4.0 scale.

Fields of study included the following:

Civil Litigation	Legal Research I & II
Legal Document Writing	Torts
Real Estate	Criminal Law
Legal Vocabulary	Business Law
Computer Applications	Accounting I, II, and III
Eminent Domain	

COMPUTERS
- Familiar with Microsoft Word and Excel
- Offer proven ability to rapidly master interoffice software packages
- Experienced in using E-Mail

EXPERIENCE   **PARALEGAL SPECIALIST**. State of Florida Department of Transportation, Tampa, FL (2002-03). Earned a reputation as a cheerful worker who readily adapted to new working environments as needed while working within a department which was primarily concerned with the mission of building roads throughout Florida; interfaced regularly with contractors who were "in the field" valuing properties that the department might want to purchase in order to continue Florida's highway transportation system.
- Worked with a 15-person staff of attorneys, paralegals, and secretaries.
- Routinely utilized software including Microsoft Word, Excel, CICS, and Samas.
- Developed expertise in the area of preparing legal documents.
- Prepared expert witness contracts as well as discovery requests, orders, and letters.
- For several months, was assigned to operate a busy three-line switchboard and became known for my telephone etiquette.
- Used the dictaphone on a daily basis in the process of transcribing communication of attorneys.
- Functioned frequently in the capacity of an **Executive Secretary** as I organized and scheduled meetings among attorneys and contractors so they could meet face-to-face over matters of land valuation.

SALES ASSISTANT. Thom McAn, Tampa, FL (2002-03). Became skilled in working with customers in a retail environment while assisting people with shoe selection; was entrusted with the responsibility of opening and closing the store.
- Won the respect of management because of my attention to detail when handling financial transactions and accounting for cash.
- Helped the store cement its relationships with previous customers through my warm personality and customer service skills.

WAITRESS/HOSTESS. Pizza Hut, Tampa, FL (1999-02). Was rapidly promoted to greater responsibility related to handling cash and receipts in this popular "fast-food" restaurant.

PERSONAL   Known as a conscientious, professional young person who excels in dealing with people.

OTHER MISCELLANEOUS

Date

Exact Name of Person
Title or Position
Name of Company
Address (number and street)
Address (city, state, and ZIP)

Travel Consultant

Dear Exact Name of Person: (or Sir or Madam if answering a blind ad.)

I would appreciate an opportunity to talk with you soon about how I could contribute to your organization through my experience in the travel industry and my reputation as a gracious individual with excellent customer service and problem-solving skills.

As a Travel Consultant in Charlotte NC, I have built a diverse clientele through my knowledge and my ability to courteously deal with people. Since graduating in 2000 from the Lucas Travel School in Raleigh, NC, I have continued to attend regular annual training in the use of the SABRE system as well as programs to familiarize individuals with the nearly limitless travel options and opportunities.

I have an aptitude for easily learning new computer programs and am familiar with Apollo and System One as well as SABRE. As you will see from my enclosed resume, I am familiar with all aspects of arranging transportation by air, land, and sea including the details of arranging business travel, cruises, and trips to popular vacation destinations throughout the world.

You would find me in person to be a congenial and poised person who is accustomed to dealing with people and developing travel plans to suit their style and tastes. In my experience, a satisfied customer nearly always returns for repeat business, and I am proud of the track record of satisfied customers I have established. Although I am highly regarded in my current job and am regarded as a valuable asset to the business, I would like to join a travel agency which is aggressive in its orientation to be the best in town. I am a high-powered, highly motivated individual and am confident I would have much to offer an organization that is determined to be the travel agency of choice in our city.

I hope you will welcome my call soon to arrange a brief meeting to discuss your current and future needs and how I might serve them. Thank you in advance for your time.

Sincerely,

Betty Watkins

Alternate last paragraph:
I hope you will call or write me soon to suggest a time convenient for us to meet and discuss your current and future needs and how I might serve them. Thank you in advance for your time.

Travel Consultant

BETTY WATKINS

1110½ Hay Street, Fayetteville, NC 28305 • preppub@aol.com • (910) 483-6611

OBJECTIVE

To benefit an organization that can use my expertise related to the travel industry, computer skills, and strong customer service orientation as well as my reputation as a thorough and helpful professional with a common sense approach to problem solving.

EXPERIENCE

TRAVEL CONSULTANT. Travel Coordinators, Charlotte, NC (2003-present). Apply my thorough knowledge of travel destinations and attention to detail while planning trips to all geographical areas of the world for a clientele consisting of corporate clients and vacationers; personally book between $8,000 to $20,000 worth of business a week.
- Expanded on my awareness of how different each client's needs are when leaving their home base for business travel and of how to deal with the details of providing personalized service.
- Became more adept at "reading" people and recommending travel options that satisfied their particular tastes and style.
- Handled all aspects of arrangements from air, land, and sea travel, to Amtrak scheduling, to group tours by bus.

TRAVEL CONSULTANT. Tar Heel Travel, Pinehurst, NC (2001-03). Ensured that the needs of travelers were taken care of in every detail: arranged plane flights, ground transportation, and lodging for worldwide travelers usually working within tight time schedules and meeting strict deadlines.
- Became increasingly more familiar with the cruise business and refined my ability to sell any type of travel services a client might need.

TRAVEL CONSULTANT. Quality Travel, Pinehurst, NC (2000-01). Learned the travel business in this high-volume agency; refined my skills in attending to the minute details of keeping busy business people satisfied with their flight scheduling and lodging as they traveled throughout the world.
- Became known as a fast learner who could quickly master new procedures and methods while ensuring that clients were satisfied.

RESTAURANT MANAGER. The Corner Restaurant, Pinehurst, NC (1992-00). Refined customer service skills which were easily transferable and valuable in the travel industry while handling dual roles of providing managerial skills and providing customer service as a waitress in this busy restaurant.
- Applied a variety of skills while taking care of day-to-day operations including scheduling wait personnel and cooks as well as controlling inventories of supplies.

TRAINING

Graduated from Lucas Travel School, Raleigh, NC, 2000.
- Attended the 16-week program which covered all aspects of travel theory.
Completed one year of general studies and an introduction to the travel industry, Cape Fear Technical Community College, Pinehurst, NC.
Attend regular additional training programs including the following:
SABRE — intensive computer training sponsored by American Airlines
Seminars, trade shows, and hands-on training

COMPUTERS

Am familiar with industry-specific software programs including:
SABRE   Apollo System One

PERSONAL

Am a well-organized individual who is highly self motivated. Enjoy seeing new parts of the world and meeting people. Have traveled widely throughout the U.S. and Caribbean.

Date

Exact Name of Person
Title or Position
Name of Company
Address (no., street)
Address (city, state, zip)

**Customer Service
and Sales**

Dear Exact Name of Person: (or Dear Sir or Madam if answering a blind ad.)

I would appreciate an opportunity to talk with you soon about how I could contribute to your organization through my versatile experience in serving customers, managing projects, and coordinating a wide range of activities.

As you will see from my resume, I have received rapid promotions and performance-based awards in every job I have ever held. I can provide outstanding personal and professional references which will attest to my strong problem-solving and customer service skills as well as my friendly disposition, professional style, and high personal standards.

In my most recent job with the Holiday Inn Hotel, I was commended for exemplifying the hotel's "Yes I Can" motto through my strong customer service abilities. In a previous job I won a prestigious medal and was rapidly promoted to manage four of my peers involved in property management and leasing activities. Although I am known for my outgoing personality and ability to work well with people at all levels, I am a very detail-oriented person and believe that "attention to detail" is an essential ingredient in providing exceptional customer service. You will see from my resume that I have excelled in a job as a Budget/Investment Analyst. In one job for the City of Jackson in Mississippi, I made investment decisions for the city while also coordinating the research and decision making as well as the compilation and publication of the city's 1999 Budget Book.

You would find me in person to be someone who is comfortable walking into new situations and who enjoys a new challenge. I am positive that I could quickly become an asset to your organization.

I hope you will call or write me soon to suggest a time convenient for us to meet and discuss your current and future needs and how I might serve them. Thank you in advance for you time.

Sincerely yours,

Joanna Tyndall

Alternate last paragraph:
I hope you will welcome my call soon to arrange a brief meeting at your convenience to discuss your current and future needs and how I might serve them. Thank you in advance for your time.

JOANNA TYNDALL

1110½ Hay Street, Fayetteville, NC 28305   •   preppub@aol.com   •   (910) 483-6611

OBJECTIVE

To benefit an organization that can use a versatile and dynamic young professional with exceptional organizational, management, customer service, and public relations skills along with a reputation as a creative opportunity finder and problem solver.

EDUCATION

Bachelor of Arts (B.A.) degree, Jackson State University, Jackson, MS, 1998.
- Was elected *Miss Jackson State University School Ambassador*, 1997-98.
- Was Faculty Editor, Jackson State University Yearbook.

Excelled in graduate courses in Human Relations, University of Oklahoma, 2002.

PUBLICATIONS & AWARDS

Researched, compiled, and directed the publication of a financial publication for the City of Jackson which contained the 1999 city budget.

Have received awards and honors in every job I have ever held including two "Working Friendly" awards, a Spirit of America award, Army Commendation medals, and a Certificate of Appreciation from the Mayor of Jackson's office.

COMPUTERS

Proficient with Microsoft Word, Excel, PageMaker and dBase III+; familiar with Enable and Windows applications.
- Taught myself several software packages; offer proven ability to master new programs.

EXPERIENCE

CUSTOMER SERVICE REPRESENTATIVE. Holiday Inn Hotel, Atlanta, GA (2003). Functioned as a Reservationist while planning, scheduling, and managing a variety of customer service activities which I always performed with a "Yes I Can" attitude.
- Was commended for my poise working in an environment in which last-minute changes and capacity/ staffing problems were constant challenges.
- Coordinated business packages and VIP arrangements; worked on a daily basis with travel agents and other hospitality industry professionals.
- On a daily basis, compiled an occupancy report as well as a ten-day forecast.

HOUSING MANAGEMENT ASSISTANT. Housing Services Branch, Germany (2001-03). Received a prestigious medal recognizing my exceptional performance in handling a difficult transportation management project, and was quickly promoted to Lead Housing Counselor, which put me in the position of training and managing four customer service counterparts.
- Conducted group and individual briefings of Americans relocating to and from this German community.
- Negotiated with local property owners, worked with managers of temporary lodgings, and arranged long-term leasing; monitored waiting lists for housing.
- Coordinated maintenance and other matters with the Facilities Management Branch.
- Prepared reports related to lost or damaged property; coordinated with commercial transportation companies involved in relocating personal property.

BUDGET ASSISTANT. U.S. Army Contracting Command, Germany (2001). Was responsible for requesting and consolidating budget input data for supplies, equipment, and other contractual services for 15 regional contracting offices throughout Germany, the Netherlands, and the United Kingdom.
- Worked alongside budget analysts in consolidating budget estimates covering projected annual operating expenses for submission to higher authorities; reconciled detailed obligation reports and labor cost reports.

BUDGET/INVESTMENT ANALYST II. City of Jackson, Jackson, MS (1999-00). Supervised the work of a Budget/Investment Analyst I while personally formulating, analyzing, and controlling numerous departmental annual budgets, including operating and revenue-sharing budgets; prepared budgets after analyzing historical expenditures and projecting future needs.
- Negotiated interest rates with savings and loan institutions in order to invest idle city funds in interest-bearing securities.
- Prepared and filed tax returns for all city funds; prepared detailed reports and data tables for use in budget hearings; prepared the 1999 City Budget Book for publication.

PERSONAL

Can provide exceptionally strong personal and professional references. Will travel.

SALES

Exact Name of Person
Title or Position
Name of Company
Address (no., street)
Address (city, state, zip)

Industrial Sales   Dear Sir or Madam:

Can you use an experienced sales professional with a history of success in training others and setting sales records while applying my knowledge of inventory control and record keeping in the process of establishing new accounts and building repeat business? I would especially enjoy discussing with you how I might serve your needs in the east/middle Tennessee or north Georgia areas. My extended family is located in those parts of the country, and I have many contacts and acquaintances throughout that region.

Since 1990, I have been a record-setting representative for Greystone, Inc., in Pinehurst, NC. After winning recognition as the top producer for 1997, 1996, 1994, and 1992, I have reached the $1.5 million in annual sales level for fiscal 2003. I regularly service approximately 60 accounts in an area which covers not only Fayetteville, but also Raleigh-Cary, Pinehurst and Southern Pines, and as far west as Albemarle.

Prior experience includes dealing with both the general public and building contractors with Lowe's, selling heating and air-conditioning supplies and equipment, and managing outside sales for another refrigeration supply business. I am skilled at conducting sales meetings and coordinating awards programs.

I hope you will welcome my call soon to arrange a brief meeting at your convenience to discuss your current and future needs and how I might serve them. Thank you in advance for your time.

Sincerely yours,

Claude Ingersoll

CLAUDE INGERSOLL

1110½ Hay Street, Fayetteville, NC 28305   •   preppub@aol.com   •   (910) 483-6611

OBJECTIVE

To contribute to an organization that is in need of an experienced sales professional who, in addition to a well-honed sense of salesmanship, offers knowledge related to sales management, inventory control, report preparation, and training others.

EXPERIENCE

REGIONAL SALES REPRESENTATIVE. Greystone, Inc., Pinehurst, NC (1990-present). Consistently among the region's top producers, have a sales volume of over $1.5 million for fiscal year 2003 for this home-comfort products company.
- Was honored as the region's top sales professional in 1997, 1996, 1994, and 1992.
- Excelled in earning the respect and trust of professionals in the building and electrical industries through my skills in every phase of making contact, demonstrating products, and closing the sale.
- Demonstrated excellent planning skills by researching a company's needs and requirements prior to my initial call.
- Serviced approximately 60 accounts in an area ranging from Albemarle, to Sanford, to Cary and Raleigh, to Fayetteville, to Southern Pines and Pinehurst.
- Used my abilities as a communicator and my product knowledge to conduct sales meetings where employees learned effective techniques for selling the company's product line.
- Spend a great deal of my time calling on the end users of my company's products to ensure *their* satisfaction with our products.
- Became involved in the design and installation of display systems while selling to lighting showrooms, electrical wholesales, building supply stores, and plumbing wholesalers.

Highlights of prior experience in the sales field, Raleigh, NC:
<u>Lowe's</u>. Further developed my salesmanship abilities and knowledge of customer relations while dealing with both building contractors and the general public.
- Gained experience in stocking, inventory control, and computer operations.
<u>Merritt-Holland</u>. Sold heating and air conditioning equipment to customers throughout the eastern part of North Carolina.
- Was selected to oversee the details of coordinating special awards such as trips for high-volume sales personnel.
- Managed a wide range of advertising programs including newspaper, radio, and yellow pages advertising.
- Applied my organizational skills to arrange and coordinate dealer sales meetings.
<u>Longley Supply Co.</u>. Established a sales territory which included Lumberton, Hamlet, and Laurinburg as well as Fayetteville: sold heating and air-conditioning equipment and supplies.
- Handled the details of arranging and then hosting dealer conventions.
<u>W.L. Smith Refrigeration Supply</u>. As the Outside Sales Manager, was in charge of pricing and inventory control for five stores.
- Conducted regular monthly inventories and rotated stock between the stores.

EDUCATION & TRAINING

Attended courses in professional sales techniques, stress management, and positive self-suggestions as well as a 10-week Dale Carnegie course in human relations.
Studied heating and air-conditioning at Fayetteville Technical Community College, NC.

PERSONAL

Am a results-oriented professional. Offer a high degree of expertise in the qualities that add up to "salesmanship." Am skilled in establishing and maintaining effective relations.

SALES

Mr. Dick Vanderhoost
Regional Personnel Manager
Rocket Auto Regional Office
2670 Canada Avenue
Charlotte, NC 28229

Retailing Auto Parts Dear Mr. Vanderhoost:

With the enclosed resume, I would like to make formal application for the position of Service Manager for the Southern Avenue superstore.

As you will see from my resume, I have been a loyal and hard-working employee of Rocket Auto since 2000, when I began as a Cashier. I was promoted to Lead Cashier, then to Parts Specialist, and then to my current job of Tire Specialist. I have won the Employee of the Month award on 10 separate occasions and have also received the Customer Service Excellence award.

My professional goal is to stay with Rocket Auto and further grow into positions of responsibility as I have done in the past. I am working to become a store manager eventually and then to train as a district manager. I am totally confident that I could excel in those positions as well as in the position of Service Manager, which I am now seeking.

I would appreciate your keeping confidential my direct approach to you about the job of Service Manager. Although my supervisor is submitting my resume to the District Manager, my supervisor also suggested that I let you know of my strong interest in the job. I also wanted to acquaint you with the fact that I sincerely wish to make a career out of my employment with Rocket Auto, and I am confident that I offer the management ability, sales skills, and knowledge of the industry and company that would make me a valuable Service Manager at this time.

Please consider me for the job of Service Manager in the Southern Avenue superstore.

Yours sincerely,

Ernestine Weimann

ERNESTINE WEIMANN

1110½ Hay Street, Fayetteville, NC 28305 • preppub@aol.com • (910) 483-6611

OBJECTIVE

As a loyal and hard-working employee of Rocket Auto, I wish to place my name in application for the position of Service Manager of the Service Shop; my long-range goal is to become store president of one of Rocket Auto's stores and then to advance to district manager.

EXPERIENCE

Have advanced in this history of promotion within Rocket Auto, Charlotte, NC (2000-present).
TIRE SPECIALIST. (2002-present). Have received *Employee of the Month* award on three separate occasions because of my demonstrated ability to satisfy customers while assuring that the company's goals for profitability and productivity are always achieved or exceeded.

- *Sales*: While selling tires, am skilled at add-on sales of items including shocks, alignments, brakes, front-end parts, and struts.
- *Paperwork*: Am known for my accuracy and attention to detail in preparing service orders for shops; keep service log up-to-date.
- *Costing and estimating*: Prepare estimates for customers and explain the need for other services.
- *Inventory control and ordering*: Acquire parts for service personnel; handle outside purchase orders and vendor deliveries.
- *Employee training*: Have trained and developed several new employees.
- *Customer service and communication*: Have acquired a knack for really *listening* to customers and have reduced potential problems by keeping customers well informed.

PARTS SPECIALIST. (2002). Received the **Customer Service Excellence** award and the **Employee of the Month** award while carefully researching customer needs and identifying needed parts.

- Learned importance of "doing things right the first time" while gaining technical knowledge and research skills to diagnose customer needs.
- Returned defective items to distribution center for credit; handled exchanges/outside purchase orders; recommended service/add-on sales.

LEAD CASHIER. (2001). Learned valuable inventory control techniques which I used to reduce overstock on slow-moving items and to increase stock on fast-moving items in order to increase sales and customer satisfaction; received **Employee of the Month** award three times.

- Was involved in planogram merchandising while also handling floor sales.
- Opened new personal and commercial accounts; trained new employees.

CASHIER. (2000). Received **Employee of the Month** award three times,

Other experience:
CASHIER. Quick Food Mart, Charlotte, NC (1999). Became known for honesty and accuracy in handling cash while balancing registers daily as well as reading gas pumps, restocking store, opening/closing store, handling charge accounts, training new personnel, and performing light maintenance such as repairing refrigeration units and food warmers.

EXPLOSIVES ASSEMBLER. Grove Industries, Newton, IL (1997-98). Reduced company costs by setting up a computerized inventory control system while also involved in the assembly, test firing, storage, inventory, shipping, receiving, and materiel handling of explosives; on my own initiative, reduced safety hazards by creating safer shipping methods.

EDUCATION

Studied Industrial Maintenance, Central Carolina Community College, Sanford, NC, 1997-98; maintained *Dean's List* throughout college.
Completed several Rocket Auto training courses related to upgrading sales.
Was named to "Who's Who Among American High School Students" and published several short stories and poems in high school magazines.

PERSONAL

Am known for my attention to detail and willingness to learn new tasks and activities. Can always be counted on for strong sales performance. Can operate and perform limited troubleshooting of the TRI-AD parts/tire computer. Have a cheerful, professional attitude.

SALES

Date

Exact Name of Person
Title or Position
Name of Company
Address (no., street)
Address (city, state, zip)

Retail Management

Dear Exact Name of Person: (or Dear Sir or Madam if answering a blind ad.)

I would appreciate an opportunity to talk with you soon about how I could contribute to your organization through my purchasing, financial management, and inventory control experience, along with my excellent public relations and writing skills.

As you will see from my resume, I excelled in the business administration program at Fayetteville State University, graduating cum laude. My coursework emphasized personnel, financial, and production management in addition to business policy and strategic planning.

You would find me to be an organized, results-oriented professional who works well with others and who also has a special knack for working with numbers. I sincerely enjoy contributing to my employer's bottom line."

I hope you will welcome my call soon to arrange a brief meeting at your convenience to discuss your current and future needs and how I might serve them. Thank you in advance for your consideration.

Sincerely yours,

Larry Bass

Alternate last paragraph:
I hope you will call or write me soon to suggest a time convenient for us to meet and discuss your current and future needs and how I might best serve them. Thank you in advance for your time.

LARRY BASS

1110½ Hay Street, Fayetteville, NC 28305 • preppub@aol.com • (910) 483-6611

OBJECTIVE

To benefit an organization through my purchasing, financial management, and inventory experience, along with my excellent communication and organizational skills.

EDUCATION

B.S. in Business Administration/Finance, Mercer University, Mercer, GA, 2003.
- Completed a rigorous degree program in 3 1/2 years with a 3.33 GPA, graduating *cum laude*.
- Awarded a **Certificate of Achievement** for maintaining an exceptional standard of scholarship.

EXPERIENCE

ASSISTANT STORE MANAGER. Waldenbooks, Atlanta, GA (1998-2000). In this fast-paced position, conducted day-to-day financial transactions and supervised up to 10 employees at one of the nation's largest retail booksellers.

- Responsible for store operations, including loss prevention, in-store audits, cash handling and reconciliation.
- Assisted with setup and opening of new stores.
- Developed an effective style in dealing fairly and patiently with the public in both sales and customer relations.
- Acquired skills in marketing, merchandising displays, and personnel administration.
- Gained professional poise while learning to use my time effectively.

MERCHANDISE MANAGER. Dress to the Nines, Fayetteville, NC (1998). Played a key role in the setup and opening of this popular retail clothing store.

- Gained valuable "hands-on" experience in business administration, cash flow, and inventory control management.
- Supervised up to eight employees in planning and executing daily operations.
- Acquired skills in clothing merchandising and marketing.

RETAIL MANAGER. Paper Peddler, Burlington, VT (1995-1997). Supervised day staff and managed inventory while developing a loyal clientele for this retail business.
- Assisted management in most facets of branch operation.
- Applied my creative design skills in developing decorations for both individual customers and business promotions.
- Gained valuable skills in buying, ordering, and merchandising store product.

MANAGER'S AIDE. Shed House, South Burlington, VT (1995). With little or no supervision, handled numerous details in the daily operations of this retail business.
- Supervised and managed a small staff of 3 to 4 people.
- Learned how to handle cash transactions quickly and accurately.
- Responsible for daily bank deposits and drawer reconciliations.

Highlights of other experience:
- Tutor, Pine Ridge School, Williston, VT (1994). Created and used lesson plans to teach three dyslexic children.
- Special events volunteer, Chittenden County United Way, Burlington, VT (1997). Developed my public relations and communication skills during the planning and coordinating of special events.

COMPUTERS

Have experience with Microsoft Word and Excel software programs.

PERSONAL

Am a self-directed innovative thinker with high personal and professional standards. Work well under pressure and enjoy working closely with others to achieve a common goal.

SALES

Exact Name of Person
Title or Position
Name of Company
Address (no., street)
Address (city, state, zip)

Retail Sales and Management

Dear Sir or Madam:

I would appreciate an opportunity to talk with you soon about how I could contribute to your organization through my exceptionally strong "track record" in management and sales.

As you will see from my resume, I have been promoted rapidly in every job I have ever held because of my proven leadership ability and willingness to assume responsibility. A self starter and fast learner, I have excelled most recently in retail management and was promoted to Sales Area Manager by the Army & Air Force Exchange Service after beginning as a stocker and advancing rapidly to reorder associate. As Sales Area Manager I supervised a department of 13 employees and became skilled in hiring and interviewing.

I believe that my exceptionally strong management "track record" is due to a combination of natural ability, excellent training which I received from my employers, and a "hard-charging" personality that thrives on a fast pace. I offer a talent for training and motivating people, and experience has taught me how to handle "problem" employees and how to motivate marginal workers. I guarantee you can trust me to produce outstanding results with little or no supervision.

I hope you will welcome my call soon to arrange a brief meeting at your convenience to discuss your current and future needs and how I might serve them. Thank you in advance for your time.

Sincerely yours,

Patricia Cresswell

PATRICIA CRESSWELL

1110½ Hay Street, Fayetteville, NC 28305 • preppub@aol.com • (910) 483-6611

OBJECTIVE

To offer my proven management, organizational, and sales skills to an organization that can use a fast learner and hard worker who thrives on serving customers and solving problems in a fast-paced, competitive environment in which I am handling lots of responsibility.

EDUCATION

Completed extensive executive development training sponsored by Army & Air Force Exchange Service (AAFES) in these and other areas:

- Managing a department of employees
- Ordering/reordering merchandise throughout the U.S.
- Using the AAFES computer system for retail sales, accounting, and control
- Was selected to attend specialized OSHA training for supervisors

EXPERIENCE

SALES AREA MANAGER. Army & Air Force Exchange Service (AAFES), Germany (2001-03). Began with AAFES as a stocker and after two months was promoted to reorder associate; after less than ten months in that job was selected as Sales Area Manager, a position usually reserved for someone with much more experience.

- Received a cash bonus and Excellence Awards for superior performance, 2003.
- Was recommended through a formal letter from my supervisor for selection as Sales and Merchandise Manager because of my trustworthiness, ability to motivate a team, and willingness to tackle any responsibility.
- Supervised a department of 13 employees and learned how to adopt a neutral attitude with "problem" employees; became skilled in hiring and interviewing.
- Acquired considerable skills related to merchandise ordering, reordering, shipping, and markdowns.
- Was commended on my flair for creating eye-catching displays.
- Learned valuable techniques for maximizing the turnover of seasonal merchandise.
- Continuously assured correct merchandise pricing and stocking; set planograms.
- Gained extensive experience with retail hard lines.

ASSISTANT MANAGER. Biscuit Kitchen, Fayetteville, NC (2000). Learned "the ropes" of managing a fast food service business.

STORE MANAGER. The Pantry, Inc., Sanford, NC (2000). Always exceeded sales and inventory turnover goals, and earned a bonus with every paycheck I received from this company; handled the responsibility for making daily deposits of up to $8,000.

- Learned to do every job in this store including cashiering, ordering merchandise, controlling inventory, cleaning the store, hiring/firing/training employees, closing the store, and completing extensive paperwork.

ASSISTANT MANAGER. The Pantry, Inc., Sanford, NC (1997-98). Was groomed for eventual store management, and became knowledgeable about every job in this convenience store.

- Acted as cashier and made deposits; learned to order inventory and stock shelves; prepared planograms; trained and scheduled employees; handled all the paper work required of shift managers; was responsible for vendor check-ins; sold gas; handled customer relations.

COMPUTERS

Rapidly master new software and have used numerous AAFES programs to check mail, assess inventory levels in the warehouse, and to determine location of products in route to their final destination.

PERSONAL

Sincerely thrive on a fast pace and work well under deadlines and pressures. Enjoy applying my talent for organizing and training people. Am a self starter and can be trusted to do an outstanding job with little or no supervision. Am skilled at producing team results.

SALES

Mr. Paul Zorbatsky
Supervisor
Smith and Douglas
3716 National Drive, Suite 101
Raleigh, NC 27612

Sales and Customer Service

Dear Mr. Zorbatsky:

As you requested per our phone conversation, I am sending my resume as my formal indication of interest in a sales position with Smith and Douglas.

Can you use a dynamic and hard-working sales professional who has excelled in solving problems, finding new business opportunities, developing new markets, and outperforming my peers in sales production and customer service?

As you will see from my resume, I began my working career as a bookkeeper but rapidly saw that my sales and management skills were not being utilized. After I went into the banking industry, I led the branches where I worked to win "Branch of the Year" and similar honors while I received the highest company awards including **Top Salesperson** and **Customer Service Representative of the Year.**

Because of my outstanding reputation, I was recently recruited by a bank president to handle the highly visible job of raising start-up capital for a proposed new bank. In that role, I have become the trusted confidante of the president in all matters, and while working to sell stock, I have also taken on the responsibility of selecting the software program the new bank will use.

You would, I am sure, find me to be a congenial and intelligent individual who offers a proven ability to mingle with people at all organizational levels. A naturally outgoing person, I always take a hands-on approach to community involvement, and I headed up a very successful United Way campaign for State Bank. I know it takes great teamwork to succeed in business, and although I offer proven leadership ability, I pride myself on being a team player and have always emphasized teamwork when I have managed others. I can provide outstanding personal and professional references.

I hope you will welcome my call again soon to arrange a brief meeting at your convenience to discuss your current and future needs and how I might serve them. Thank you in advance for your time.

Sincerely yours,

Winona Vannatter

WINONA VANNATTER

1110½ Hay Street, Fayetteville, NC 28305   •   preppub@aol.com   •   (910) 483-6611

OBJECTIVE

I want to contribute to the success and growth of an organization that can use a vibrant and enthusiastic professional who offers a proven ability to excel in sales and customer service while solving difficult problems and discovering new business opportunities.

EXPERIENCE

SALES REPRESENTATIVE/EXECUTIVE ASSISTANT. Tar Heel Bank & Trust (proposed), Raleigh, NC (2003-present). Because of my outstanding reputation and exceptional results at State Bank, was specially recruited by the President for a highly visible job of raising start-up capital for a proposed new bank.

- Worked with the directors of the bank and followed up on their leads for stock sales.
- Was also placed in charge of analyzing available software packages and recommending the right software for the new bank.
- Played a key role in recruiting, interviewing, hiring, and training employees.
- As the trusted "right arm" of the bank president, displayed an ability to keep confidences and to choose my words carefully in public when marketing this new financial institution.

CUSTOMER SERVICE REPRESENTATIVE & HEAD TELLER. Cardinal Bank, Raleigh, NC (1999-03). Rapidly advanced to handle greater and greater responsibilities while playing a major role in leading our branch to win the "Prime 50" campaign for bottom-line results and to be singled out for recruiting more new customers than any other branch; became known for my aggressive and strategic sales instincts.

- As the Customer Service Representative, trained and managed up to five employees on the teller line.
- Was placed in charge of all bank audits because of my keen attention to detail and thorough understanding of bank operations.
- Was selected to be in charge of the vault at the branch.
- Used a management style that emphasized teamwork, sales spirit, and customer service.

CUSTOMER SERVICE REPRESENTATIVE/TELLER. Barclays Bank, Raleigh, NC (1997-99). Won the bank's award for **Top Salesperson** and was named **Customer Service Representative of the Year** based on my selling the most products for the year out of all the Barclay's Bank branches in NC; also won the Top Commissions award every month for product sales, and was the major reason why we won the "Branch of the Year" award.

- Handled all cash transactions as teller.
- Was the individual at the branch in charge of selling the high-ticket services to customers while also shouldering the responsibility for resolving difficult customer problems.

CUSTOMER SERVICE REPRESENTATIVE/TELLER. Southern National Bank, Raleigh, NC (1993-97). While handling all cash transactions and being responsible for the vault, excelled in product sales; lead my branch to win the 1996 award for most product sales within the entire region through my personal sales production.

- Because of my analytical and problem-solving abilities, was recruited to help balance and repair the ATM machines at night and on weekends.

Other experience: **BOOKKEEPER.** Managed other employees and was responsible for opening/closing the store while performing all duties of a bookkeeper; balanced ledgers, prepared payroll, handled all cash transactions, and managed accounts payable and receivable.

EDUCATION

Completed courses in accounting and banking at Cape Fear Technical Community College after graduating from Seventy First High School.

Excelled in numerous college-level management development programs and technical seminars sponsored by the banks above; gained valuable knowledge from seminars including "Keeping the Customer," "Dealing with the Problem Customer," "Cross Selling Products," and other areas.

PERSONAL

Am very physically fit and am quite disciplined about my exercise program. Have run in several 10K runs. Have volunteered my time to tutor children within the school system. Have a knack for mastering new software quickly and am very computer proficient.

SALES

Exact Name of Person
Title or Position
Name of Company
Address (number and street)
Address (city, state, and ZIP)

Sales Management

Dear Exact Name of Person: (or Dear Sir or Madam if answering a blind ad.)

Can you use a top-notch sales professional who offers exceptional communication and marketing skills which have resulted in increasing territory profitability?

Currently the District Sales Manager for the New York City-based McAllister News Company, Inc., since 2003 I have consistently increased sales and currently handle a territory with $2 million in sales annually. While selling and distributing magazines to wholesalers throughout both North and South Carolina, I have used my analytical skills and "industry instincts" to determine trends and make changes which increased sales. Because the publishing/wholesaling business is in such a state of flux, with larger companies buying up the smaller ones, I have become accustomed to the need for flexibility and resourcefulness.

As you will see from my enclosed resume, I am a versatile professional who can easily adapt to selling different types of products or services. I am highly effective in developing new sources and expanding a territory for increased sales and profits. Known for my warm sense of humor, I can provide outstanding references.

I hope you will welcome my call soon to arrange a brief meeting at your convenience to discuss your current and future needs and how I might serve them. Thank you in advance for your time.

Sincerely yours,

Preston Blum

Alternate last paragraph:
I hope you will call or write me soon to suggest a time convenient for us to meet and discuss your current and future needs and how I might serve them. Thank you in advance for your time.

PRESTON BLUM

1110½ Hay Street, Fayetteville, NC 28305 • preppub@aol.com • (910) 483-6611

OBJECTIVE

To offer my top-quality communication and marketing skills to an organization that can use an accomplished sales professional with sales management experience who offers a track record of increasing territory profitability.

EXPERIENCE

DISTRICT SALES MANAGER. McAllister News Company, Inc., New York, NY (2003-present). Sell and distribute magazines to wholesalers in North and South Carolina while consistently increasing sales in this territory which now has a volume of over $2 million annually.
- Analyze sales information from retail chains; create strategic plans and continuously monitor/modify distribution efforts to maximize sales.
- Have increased sales by at least 5% every year at a time when the industry was experiencing much turbulence, with larger wholesalers buying smaller ones with the result that buyer names and faces were constantly changing.
- Am extremely knowledgeable of the channels of distribution and industry structure related to magazine/book publishing and wholesaling; am highly respected for the strong negotiating and customer service skills I use to compete for shelf space in this competitive industry with tight margins.

SALES REPRESENTATIVE. Southeastern Concrete, Fayetteville, NC (2002). Demonstrated my ability to rapidly excel in the sale of industrial products; while selling concrete, checked building permits for leads and contacted contractors, concrete finishers, and other members of the building public to arrange delivery of the product.

SALES REPRESENTATIVE. Systel Business Equipment Company, Fayetteville, NC (2000-01). Cold-called businesses and non-profit organizations to evaluate the need for copier equipment and deliver proposals for services.
- Was honored as "*Salesman of the Month*" for six out of 12 months.
- Negotiated selling prices, lease agreements, and maintenance contracts.
- Maintained accurate records of customers' equipment in order to be able to offer them upgraded equipment.

CREW LEADER/TRUCK DRIVER. Trucking Movers, Durham, NC (1997-99). Negotiated contract and insurance agreements for moving household and personal property and goods; conducted thorough inventory of household items before packing and moving items to both short and long distances.

GENERAL MANAGER. Shear Honesty, Southern Pines, NC (1992-95). Started "from scratch" and then managed a hair salon business and became skilled in purchasing supplies and in obtaining the best prices for materials through resourceful buying and skillful negotiating.
- Managed all operational areas of this thriving business including bookkeeping, payroll, merchandising, and hiring/training.

EDUCATION

Earned an **A.A. degree in English**, Sandhills Community College, Southern Pines, NC.
- Graduated *with honors*.

PERSONAL

Have earned the respect of both my peers and upper-level management for my outstanding sales and marketing skills. Enjoy developing territories and providing top-quality service. Am known for my warm sense of humor.

SALES: Sales and Management

MARGARET ANDERSON

1110½ Hay Street, Fayetteville, NC 28305 • preppub@aol.com • (910) 483-6611

OBJECTIVE

I want to contribute to an organization that can use my management and organizational skills along with my reputation as a resourceful self starter with strong entrepreneurial instincts combined with an aggressive sales attitude.

EDUCATION

Received Supervision Certificate, Pic N Pay Stores, 2002; am currently in District Manager's Training Program, 2003.
Have attended numerous seminars and training programs related to managing nearly every area of retail operations.
Studied Business and Accounting, Campbell University, Buies Creek, NC, 1998.
Received a Diploma in college preparatory coursework, Johnston High School, Austin, TX, 1996; was an honors student.

EXPERIENCE

CLUSTER MANAGER DEVELOPER. Pic N Pay Shoes, Rome, GA (2001-present). Have rapidly advanced with this company, and am now being groomed for promotion to District Manager.

- Travel with the District Manager or alone to document store visits, oversee special projects, and observe/audit special areas of concern.
- Oversee the operations of three stores in addition to my responsibilities for training managers in 15 different stores; have met or exceeded quarterly sales goals two out of four times and received the "Above and Beyond Duty Award" for 2002.
- Train and develop managers for placement in stores within 10 weeks; empower managers to successfully operate stores with little supervision.
- Coordinate training guidelines and follow up on training provided in order to assure compliance of 15 managers in 15 individual stores.
- Performed troubleshooting in 26 locations and have excelled in correcting problems related to shrinkage, staffing, and general store operations.
- On my own initiative, designed a Training Recap for the entire district which has greatly facilitated the proper development of staff.

ASSISTANT CO-MANAGER. Merry Go Round, Fayetteville and Raleigh, NC (1999-01). Recruited, hired, and trained new associates in an extensive three-day program; assigned duties to a 27-person staff while directing the fast pace of sales activities.

- Performed a wide range of administrative duties which included making deposits, preparing weekly and monthly paperwork, administering payroll, conducting performance and salary reviews, controlling inventory, organizing and leading store meetings, overseeing assets, and communicating store policies.
- Received 1999 award for "Best performance in a new position."
- In 2000, exceeded 1999 sales by 33%.

ASSISTANT MANAGER & COLLECTIONS MANAGER. All American TV & Stereo, Fayetteville, NC (1998). Performed light accounting while handling the responsibility of approving or denying credit applications; developed financial contracts, started allotments, checked references and established client applications.

- Prepared and distributed collections letters; ran credit checks and handled all areas of collections including CBI and TRW.
- Developed numerous new forms and documents which became valuable parts of the company's credit and collections systems.
- Achieved seven days of taking in $10,000 and consistently beat the previous year's sales records on a daily basis.

SALES PACESETTER. The Limited, Fayetteville, NC (1996-98). Began as a Sales Associate and was promoted to Pacesetter and trained for the Assistant Manager Position; set sales pace for this store which became upgraded to a superstore because of its 1997 sales increases.

- Was #4 sales associate in entire nation in sales volume and was #2 in our store's classification volume; was honored with various gifts and awards including a trip to Vail, CO.

PERSONAL

Am skilled in using aggressive sales tactics and pride myself on achieving ambitious sales goals. Known for my ability to motivate, train, and develop others. Am a strategic thinker with the ability to see "the big picture."

ROLF WATTS
1110½ Hay Street, Fayetteville, NC 28305   •   preppub@aol.com   •   (910) 483-6611

OBJECTIVE

To contribute to an organization that can use a hard-working young professional who offers exceptionally strong sales and customer relations skills along with proven abilities related to managing operations, boosting profitability, controlling inventory, directing shipping and receiving, and solving a wide range of problems related to product quality and service.

EXPERIENCE

SALES REPRESENTATIVE, WARRANTY MANAGER, & SHIPPING MANAGER. Breakway Supply, Charlotte, NC (2001-present). Began with this company as a salesman and supply/equipment delivery person, and have become a respected part of the company's management team while advancing to handle a wide range of responsibilities.

- **On-time delivery:** As a Delivery Person, single-handedly performed work normally handled by two people, and became known for my strong time management skills.

- **Shipping and receiving:** As Shipping and Receiving Manager, prepared a daily Back Order Report and Order Hangout Report and checked those reports against current inventory; created invoices and then packaged merchandise for shipping by UPS and other carriers; filled out bills of lading and palletized items.

- **Inside sales:** As a Counter Sales Representative, was in contact with dozens of customers daily face-to-face and by telephone; was respected by customers for my expert ability to match up parts from air conditioning, heating, and refrigeration units as well as major appliances and mechanical devices by utilizing my expert ability to use microfiche machines, technical data books, and knowledge gained from past experience.

- **Outside sales:** Have excelled as an Outside Sales Representative; on my own initiative, prospected for customers and set up 12-14 sales calls per day which tremendously increased company sales; have personally serviced the company's most valuable contracts at Ft. Bragg.

- **Bottom-line orientation:** Have become known as the company's most effective problem solver in difficult customer relations situations; have learned the art of satisfying the customer without harming the company's bottom line; through my effective style of sales and customer service, have greatly increased overall company sales.

- **Vendor relations/warranty management:** In 2003, took over management of the company's complex warranty programs; now oversee warranties provided by more than 900 vendors and personally established the company's internal procedures for warranty management; am now considered an expert in obtaining credit for in-warranty merchandise and carefully monitor the warranty program to assure satisfaction of all parties.

- **Inventory control:** Continuously control inventory and oversee purchasing of stock; installed new inventory control procedures that minimized inventory investment costs.

SALESMAN. Southern Appliance Parts, Charlotte, NC (2000-01). Learned the nuts and bolts of the appliance parts business while becoming an expert in using microfiche to cross reference parts to determine their potential for utilization in various products.

ASSISTANT MANAGER. Wendys, Fayetteville, NC (2000). Was groomed for management; excelled in dealing with the public and fellow employees while ordering inventory, overseeing maintenance and sanitation, and scheduling employees on all shifts.

Other experience: Began work at 16 at A & P Grocery Store; became Frozen Food Manager.

PERSONAL

Completed training related to motors and ventilation and HVAC controls; completed the Dale Carnegie course in public speaking and sales. Am a notary public.

Date

Exact Name of Person
Title or Position
Name of Company
Address (number and street)
Address (city, state, and ZIP)

Sales or Sales Management

Dear Exact Name of Person: (or Sir or Madam if answering a blind ad.)

Can you use an enthusiastic, results-oriented sales professional who offers outstanding communication skills, a talent for reading people, and a reputation for determination and persistence in reaching goals?

With a proven background of success in sales, I have displayed my versatility while selling and marketing a wide variety of products and services including residential real estate and land, new and used automobiles, and financial products/investment services. In one job I trained and supervised a successful team of mutual fund and insurance sales agents. Most recently as an Independent Real Estate Broker, I achieved the $3 million mark in sales for 2003. While excelling in all aspects of the business, I have used my experience and knowledge to create marketing strategies and tools which reached large audiences and generated much business.

Earlier experience gave me an opportunity to refine my sales and communication abilities as well as gain familiarity with business management including finance and collections, inventory control, personnel administration, and customer service. Prior to owning and managing a business which bought, reconditioned, and marketed automobiles, I was one of Raleigh Buick's most successful sales professionals, earning the distinction of being "Salesman of the Month" for 13 consecutive months and "Salesman of the Year."

If you can use a seasoned professional with the ability to solve tough business problems, maximize profitability, and increase market share under highly competitive conditions, I would enjoy an opportunity to meet with you to discuss your needs and how I might serve them. Known for my resourcefulness, I can provide outstanding personal and professional references.

I hope you will welcome my call soon to arrange a brief meeting at your convenience. Thank you in advance for your time.

Sincerely,

Keith Toomey

Alternate last paragraph:
I hope you will call or write me soon to suggest a time convenient for us to meet and discuss your current and future needs and how I might serve them. Thank you in advance for your time.

KEITH TOOMEY

1110½ Hay Street, Fayetteville, NC 28305 • preppub@aol.com • (910) 483-6611

OBJECTIVE

To offer a track record of success in sales and managerial roles where outstanding communication skills and the ability to close the sale were key factors in building a reputation as a highly motivated professional oriented toward achieving maximum bottom-line results.

EXPERIENCE

INDEPENDENT REAL ESTATE BROKER. Quality Real Estate, Inc., Myrtle Beach, SC (2002-present). Reached the $3 million personal sales level for 2003 while providing a range of experience which has played a key role in boosting overall sales and profitability of a thriving agency in this highly competitive market.

- Have become known for my strong interpersonal and communication skills while coordinating with potential buyers, lending institutions, construction professionals, sellers, and others.
- Negotiate all aspects of financial transactions; deal with mortgage company representatives to arrange financing and with attorneys to handle real estate closings.
- Utilize my expert marketing abilities while creating sales strategies and preparing direct mail materials which capture the interest of prospective clients and generate new business.
- Routinely make presentations to other agents and buyers.
- Have become skilled in all aspects of property evaluation and am skilled in comparing newly available homes with those having comparable features.

SALES AND MARKETING REPRESENTATIVE. Self-employed, Fayetteville, NC (1996-02). Trained and then supervised the efforts of as many as 12 agents while also personally marketing and selling mutual funds and insurance.
- Refined my abilities in a competitive field and excelled in developing sales and marketing techniques which resulted in increased sales.

Highlights of earlier experience: Gained versatile experience in sales, inventory control, and customer service in jobs including the following:
FINANCE AND OPERATIONS MANAGER: Became highly effective in handling finances, marketing, and sales as the owner of a business with six sales professionals, a title clerk, a bookkeeper, and 12 employees in the body shop (Gene's Auto Shop, Fayetteville, NC).
- Learned small business management while handling sales, finances, and collections.
- Created marketing and advertising plans and products which were highly effective.

SALES REPRESENTATIVE: For a major automobile dealer, consistently placed in the top three of 22 sales professionals (Raleigh Buick, Raleigh, NC).
- Was "Salesman of the Month" for 13 consecutive months and named "Salesman of the Year."

FIELD SALES MANAGER: Became the youngest person in the company's history to hold this position after only a year with this national company (Fuller Brush Company, Plattsburgh, NY, and Phoenix, AZ).
- Became skilled in earning the confidence of potential customers and achieved a highly successful rate of positive responses from four out of each five people I approached: increased the amount of sales per customer.

STORE MANAGER/SUPPORT SERVICE SPECIALIST: Gained business management experience and learned to handle inventory control and funds (U.S. Navy).

TRAINING

Completed corporate training programs in areas such as real estate law, brokerage, finance, and securities as well as life, accident, and health insurance.
Am licensed as a real estate salesman, broker, and life/accident/health insurance agent.

PERSONAL

Am known for my ability to see "the big picture" while managing the details. Offer a proven ability to develop strategic plans that maximize profitability and market share in competitive environments. Am a results-oriented, persistent individual who can be counted on to finish any project on time and within budget. Can provide outstanding references.

SALES

Exact Name of Person
Title or Position
Name of Company
Address (no., street)
Address (city, state, zip)

Agricultural and Industrial

Dear Exact Name of Person: (or Dear Sir or Madam if answering a blind ad.)

I would appreciate an opportunity to show you soon in person that I am the young, energetic, dynamic salesperson you are looking for.

As you can see from my resume, I am a proven professional with a demonstrated ability to "prospect" and produce sales. Under my direction, The Tobacco Warehouse was able to maintain a sales volume of $3.5 million despite a depressed agricultural economy. As a salesman and warehouse supervisor with Industrial Agricultural Cooperative, I increased sales from $500,000 to $1.5 million in two years. I have earned a reputation for my dedication and hard work in addition to a sincere concern for the customers I serve.

I feel certain you would find me to be a well-organized, reliable professional with a genuine customer service orientation. I pride myself on my ability to make "cold calls" and relate to people at all levels of any organization, from the mail clerk to the president. I can provide excellent personal and professional references.

I hope you will welcome my call soon to arrange a brief meeting at your convenience to discuss your current and future needs and how I might serve them. Thank you in advance for your time.

Sincerely yours,

Larry McPhail

Alternate last paragraph:
I hope you will call or write me soon to suggest a time convenient for us to meet and discuss your current and future needs and how I might best serve them. Thank you in advance for your time.

Sales --Agricultural and Industrial

LARRY MCPHAIL

1110½ Hay Street, Fayetteville, NC 28305 • preppub@aol.com • (910) 483-6611

OBJECTIVE

To offer my leadership, problem-solving ability, and public relations skills to an organization that can use a hard-working young professional who is known for unquestioned integrity, unflagging enthusiasm, and tireless dedication to excel.

EXPERIENCE

SALES MANAGER. The Agricultural Market, Inc., Marietta, GA (2003-present). Applied my financial expertise and excellent public relations/communication skills to contribute to the "bottom line" of this agricultural chemical and fertilizer manufacturer.

- Performed "cold calls" within a 30-mile sales territory; established and maintained approximately 175-200 accounts with dealers and individual customers.
- Ensured timely delivery of products and services.
- Billed customers and collected on delinquent accounts.
- Supervised three employees in administration/distribution.

SALES SUPERVISOR. The Tobacco Warehouse, Bunnlevel, NC (2000-2003). Built "from scratch" this successful tobacco sales and distribution center with sales totaling $3.5 million even though the agricultural economy was at a low point.

- As co-owner, managed all administrative and financial aspects of operations.
- Hired, supervised, and trained 12 employees, including floor workers, secretaries, and bookkeepers.
- Developed and maintained a loyal customer network of local farmers.
- Organized and conducted auctions to sell the product to tobacco companies.

SALESMAN and **WAREHOUSE SUPERVISOR**. Industrial Agricultural Cooperative, Dunn, NC (1996-2000). Excelled in a variety of roles because of my versatile management skills.

- Was accountable for warehouse inventory; determined product line and ordered fertilizers and agricultural chemicals.
- Performed collections and made bank deposits.
- Astutely managed finances and purchasing, meeting the company's budget goals each year.
- Through exceptional customer service to approximately 200 accounts, was able to increase sales from $500,000 to $1.5 million in two years.

SALESMAN. Best Seed Co., North Carolina (2000). As a "sideline" to my other sales positions, applied my top-notch customer service skills to introduce this company's cotton seed line to 12 distributors throughout the state.

SPECIALIZED TRAINING

Attend 36 hours of instruction on pesticides each year at North Carolina State University, Raleigh, NC to maintain North Carolina Dealers Association (NCDA) license.

PERSONAL

Am a hard worker with a high energy level. Enjoy the challenge of motivating a team of employees while contributing to my organization's "bottom line" and serving customers.

SALES

Mr. James Brown
Regional Sales Manager
Excalibur Company

Sales and Distribution Management

Dear Mr. Brown:

Upon the strong recommendation of Ann Williams with Pate Derby Company, I am faxing you my resume.

As you will see, I have an outstanding track record in producing sales and profit for Frito-Lay Company, where I have worked since 1989. I believe my fine personal reputation as well as my extensive knowledge of convenience store operations in TX could be of value to the Excalibur Company, and I would enjoy an opportunity to speak with you in confidence about employment opportunities.

At the appropriate time, I can provide exceptionally strong personal and professional references, including from Frito-Lay Company, but I would appreciate your not contacting Frito-Lay until after we have a chance to talk.

I pride myself on high standards of loyalty and integrity, and I am well known within my industry for delivering on whatever promises I make.

Please let me know if you would be interested in discussing the possibility of putting my talents, knowledge, sales skills, contacts, and background to use. In advance I send warm holiday greetings and best wishes for the new year.

Sincerely,

Joe Vieira

Sales and Distribution Management

JOE VIEIRA

1110½ Hay Street, Fayetteville, NC 28305 • preppub@aol.com • (910) 483-6611

OBJECTIVE

To benefit an organization that can use a loyal and dedicated sales professional who offers versatile skills in sales management, extensive knowledge of convenience store operations in Texas, as well as a "track record" of achievement in maximizing sales and profit.

TRAINING

Have excelled in extensive executive development course work sponsored by Frito-Lay Company and previous employers; areas studied included merchandising, advertising, budgeting, buying, marketing, sales, inventory control, quality control, shrinkage control, and human resources administration.
Was born and raised in Austin, TX, and graduated from Austin High School.

EXPERIENCE

DISTRICT SALES MANAGER. Frito-Lay Company, Austin, TX (1989-present). Began with this company as a warehouseman and was rapidly promoted to route sales representative; then advanced quickly into management: was named supervisor of five sales representatives and in 1991 was promoted to District Sales Manager.

- From 1991-96, built the existing territory from five to 22 routes; the parent company then divided up the huge territory I had created and I was named Regional Sales Manager of the Year in 1996.

- Currently supervise 10 sales representatives and two spare reps.

- Plan and administer a budget of $2 million annually.

- In 2003, doubled projected profit for my territory; exceeded the sales budget by 20%.

- In 2003, was named National District Manager of the Year as well as Regional District Manager of the Year.

- Accomplished an historical sales record within Frito-Lay of $124,000 net sales for one week, and was the first and only district manager to ever exceed quarterly sales of $1 million.

- Am completely familiar with convenience store operations in TX, having made headquarters calls and presentations to buyers and owners.

- Offer extensive knowledge of the chain convenience stores such as Quik Stop, Scotchman, and Short Stops.

Other experience:
- As a manager for a shoe division, opened three stores and trained the managers, assistant managers, and other personnel.
- As an insurance salesman, was named Top Salesman for the year for the eastern Texas region.

REFERENCES

Outstanding personal and professional references available upon request.

PERSONAL

Believe in the pursuit of excellence in all areas of life, and have become skilled in motivating employees to give their best effort. Have excellent contacts throughout Texas.

SALES

Exact Name of Person
Title or Position
Name of Company
Address (number and street)
Address (city, state, and ZIP)

Sales of Automotive Supplies

Dear Exact Name of Person: (or Dear Sir or Madam if answering a blind as.)

I would appreciate an opportunity to talk with you soon about how I could contribute to your organization through my sales experience with both wholesale and retail automotive parts suppliers with an emphasis on providing strong customer service support.

From my enclosed resume you will gain a sense of my accomplishments, skills, and abilities. After joining the EverReady Signal Automotive Aftermarket team as a Service Representative in 1998, I earned a 2001 promotion to Account Sales Representative. While providing eight automotive warehouses scattered throughout North Carolina with high-quality support, I increased my 2003 sales figures 8% over the 2002 figures for this territory. As part of an eight-person team working in the three-state area of North and South Carolina and Virginia, I contributed to an $11 million record in sales for fiscal 2003 and was singled out by my peers as the team's "Most Valuable Player" for both 2002 and 2001.

In addition to experience as a Parts Manager and Service Writer, I earned ASE certification in seven areas (suspension and steering, heating and air conditioning, engine repair, electrical systems, engine performance, brakes, and parts specialist) and attended the antilock brake clinic and school. I am very proud of achieving this Automotive Service Excellence certification in very difficult testing, a rare accomplishment for someone who is not involved on a daily basis in car and light truck repair.

With strong mechanical abilities and technical skills, I offer a proven understanding of the aftermarket business and can relate to people at all levels — from the small garage owner/operator, to service center managers, to mechanics, to warehouse distributors and retail sales personnel.

Accustomed to travel, I feel that my approximately 15 years in the vehicle service and automotive aftermarket industries would be of value to an organization in need of a dependable and knowledgeable professional with outstanding sales and marketing skills. During this time I have seen many changes in the industry and have kept up with the latest trends and most efficient methods of transacting business.

I hope you will welcome my call soon to arrange a brief meeting at your convenience to discuss your current and future needs and how I might serve them. Thank you in advance for your time.

Sincerely yours,

Howard Higgins

Alternate last paragraph:
I hope you will call or write me soon to suggest a time convenient for us to meet and discuss your current and future needs and how I might serve them. Thank you in advance for your time.

HOWARD HIGGINS

1110½ Hay Street, Fayetteville, NC 28305   •   preppub@aol.com   •   (910) 483-6611

OBJECTIVE

To apply my sales and service experience to an organization that can use a dedicated and loyal hard worker who has earned a reputation as a talented sales professional with strong technical and mechanical skills as well as a genuine customer-service orientation.

EXPERIENCE

Set numerous sales records, earned promotion on the basis of my accomplishments, and gained considerable knowledge in this track record with the EverReady Automotive Aftermarket sales team based in Raleigh, NC:
ACCOUNT SALES REPRESENTATIVE. (2001-03). Excelled in providing quality sales support to eight automotive warehouse distributors who handled Fram, Autolite, and Bendix parts within the state of North Carolina and as a member of an eight-person team which enjoyed $11 million in sales during the most recent fiscal year.

- Increased 2003 sales an impressive 8% over 2002 sales while supporting such major accounts as United Automotive in Winston-Salem and AEA in Greensboro.
- Was singled out as "Most Valuable Player" in the region in both 2002 and 2001.
- Contributed to the success of a team which called on a total of 55 warehouses in the three-state region of North Carolina, South Carolina, and Virginia; the team's major accounts included the following:
  Dixie Tool — Columbia, SC   U.C.I. — Goldsboro, NC
  P.D.I. — Roanoke, VA   Tidewater Battery — Norfolk, VA
  C.R.W. — Charlotte, NC   U.C.I. — Richmond, VA
- Performed product changeovers while selling to and servicing customers in the field.
- Gained additional experience in running promotional programs designed to increase sales and in organizing technical clinics for mechanics throughout the territory.
- Learned to deal with the general public by representing the parts dealers at trade shows and auto races throughout the southeast.
- Became very effective in dealing with people at all levels while making frequent visits to small independently owned garages and installers as well as the larger service centers.

SERVICE REPRESENTATIVE. (1998-01). Traveled extensively throughout the southern and midwestern states as a member of a team of specialists involved in major product line changeovers as well as providing the merchandising and store display support to large warehouses as requested.

- Became familiar with the sales activities required to provide warehousers with the support they needed and was promoted on the basis of my accomplishments in this role.

PARTS MANAGER and **SERVICE WRITER.** H & L Auto Parts and Service, Raleigh, NC (1992-98). Supervised three people in a 10-bay service center with 20 employees: handled the purchase and resale of automotive and light truck parts to customers and company mechanics.

- Was persistent in locating sources for hard-to-find, custom, and high-performance parts.
- Advised customers on what repairs were needed on their vehicles and coordinated the arrangements for scheduling and making the repairs.
- Gained in-depth knowledge of automotive and light truck troubleshooting and mechanical repairs along with the operating aspects of running the auto parts section.

TRAINING, CERTIFICATIONS, & SPECIAL SKILLS

Earned certificate in **Electrical Installation & Maintenance,** Sampson Technical Community College, NC.
Received ASE (Automotive Service Excellence) certification after completing very difficult technical training despite not being involved on a regular basis with mechanical work:
  suspension and steering   brakes
  engine repair   heating and air conditioning
  electrical systems   parts specialist
  antilock brake school and clinic   engine performance
Attended additional corporate-sponsored training courses emphasizing the areas of sales skills and understanding the automotive aftermarket; excelled in the Total Quality Leadership School.
Offer computer knowledge and experience in using Microsoft Word, and Excel.
Am experienced in the use of various automotive repair test equipment including basic Sun diagnostic machine features and engine building tools.

SALES

Exact Name of Person
Title or Position
Name of Company
Address (number and street)
Address (city, state, and ZIP)

Sales of Business Equipment

Dear Exact Name of Person: (or Sir or Madam if answering a blind ad.)

Can you use a highly motivated young professional who has excelled in academic, sales, and management responsibilities?

When you look at my enclosed resume, you will see that I am a conscientious young professional who possesses the ability to succeed in any task I take on. After graduating with a B.S. in Microbiology, I was aggressively recruited for the sales team of a company which markets office equipment and business products. Within a few months, I had distinguished myself as the Number One Sales Representative among my peers and was promoted to a job which involved higher sales quotas and more sophisticated products.

I pride myself on my ability to motivate others, including customers. In one of the many jobs I held during college to finance my college education, I managed a staff of food and beverage professionals and played a key role in motivating them to achieve a 30% increase in sales. In a retail sales job at the LSU Union Bookstore, I was named Employee of the Month twice and gained the confidence of managers and store buyers because of my common sense, creativity, and reliable work habits.

My communication skills are highly refined, and I believe they are the key to my ability to establish and maintain effective business relationships. I have learned, too, that time management skills are essential to success in sales.

If you can use a poised and self-confident young professional with the desire to contribute to your profitability and market share, I would enjoy an opportunity to meet with you in person to discuss your needs and how I might serve them. I hope you will welcome my call next week to check your schedule and see if my track record of accomplishments and proven potential to excel are of interest to you. Willing to travel according to employer's needs, I can provide excellent personal and professional references.

Sincerely,

Tamara Zysk

Sales of Business Equipment

TAMARA ZYSK
1110½ Hay Street, Fayetteville, NC 28305 • preppub@aol.com • (910) 483-6611

OBJECTIVE   I want to contribute to an organization that can use a highly motivated young professional who offers a proven ability to handle challenging sales and management responsibilities while utilizing my creative problem-solving approach, organizational and time management abilities, as well as my highly effective communication and consulting skills.

EDUCATION   **Bachelor of Science in Microbiology**, Louisiana State University, Baton Rouge, Louisiana, May 2002.
* Excelled academically; was the recipient of a Board of Supervisor's Four-Year Scholarship and was named to the Dean's List.

EXPERIENCE   **SALES REPRESENTATIVE/ACCOUNT EXECUTIVE.** Innovative Office Systems, Inc. (an ALCO Standard Company), Baton Rouge, LA (2002-03). Immediately after graduating from college, was recruited by this company because of my strong sales potential, excellent communication skills, and highly professional style.
* Quickly distinguished myself as a Facsimile Sales Representative: exceeded my sales quotas in Dec 02, Jan 03, and Feb 03 and was promoted to Copier Representative, a position which involved more challenging quotas which I always met or exceeded.
* Prospected for new accounts; became very successful in applying proven techniques of cold calling.
* Serviced existing accounts and cemented the loyalty of existing accounts by providing expert consulting and problem solving related to their business needs.
* Wrote and presented proposals which consisted of highly technical pricing data as well as equipment leasing and service information; became skilled in explaining highly technical data in easy-to-understand terms.
* Conducted highly professional demonstrations on Sharp and Canon copiers, Panasonic facsimiles, and associated software; after the sale, trained users.
* Created and implemented effective marketing strategies, including business mailers, which generated a large volume of new business after my persistent and thorough follow-up.
* Have become very skilled in setting high sales goals and then developing appropriate plans and schedules for consistently achieving or exceeding the targets.
* Have learned how to deal with all types of accounts, ranging from local and state government accounts to large corporate clients.

Earned 90% of my college living expenses by working part-time at these and other jobs while excelling academically in a demanding undergraduate curriculum:
FOOD AND BEVERAGE MANAGER. TGI Friday's, Baton Rouge, LA (1999-02). Managed nine bartenders and scheduled/supervised food and beverage employees at this popular restaurant.
* Was responsible for ordering and maintaining the bar stock.
* Instilled in employees the need to ensure customer satisfaction by always presenting a professional image and a commitment to quality service.
* Played a key role in increasing bar sales by 30% within a few months of my assuming responsibility for supervising the bartending staff.

SALES REPRESENTATIVE. LSU Union Bookstore, Baton Rouge, LA (1997-99). Was named "Employee of the Month" in Jan 98 and April 99 because of my sales volume and personal attitude; assumed increasing responsibility for store operations, and was consulted by the store buyer in store merchandising decisions.
* Helped establish a new stocking facility (store room).
* Played a key role in improving store appearance through my creative suggestions as well as my skill in implementing creative visual merchandising ideas.

LIFEGUARD. Bocage Racquet Club and Ramada Hotel, Baton Rouge, LA (summers of 98, 99, and 00). Assured the safety of large numbers of people in congested areas and became the trusted friend of many families who invited me into their homes to care for their children.

PERSONAL   Can provide exceptional personal and professional references. Will travel as needed.

SOCIAL WORK

Exact Name of Person
Title or Position
Name of Company
Address (no., street)
Address (city, state, zip)

Crisis Intervention   Dear Exact Name of Person: (or Dear Sir or Madam if answering a blind ad.)

I would appreciate an opportunity to talk with you soon about how I could contribute to your organization through my experience and education in the areas of social work and human services along with my reputation for maturity and dedication.

Having earned my B.S. in Social Work and Psychology, I am attending a graduate program leading to a Master of Social Work (MSW) degree with a concentration in clinical social work. While attending North Carolina State College in Raleigh, NC, I completed an internship with the Wake County Department of Social Services (DSS). This internship led to positions within the department, as you will see from my resume.

Among my major personal strengths are my enthusiasm, knowledge of available resources, ability to quickly and easily establish rapport with clients, and my determination to exhaust all available resources in order to do everything possible to help my clients.

In my current position as a Social Worker in the Family and Children's Services of the Wake County DSS, I am involved in crisis intervention and in resolving problems which place families at risk for abuse. Through my experience as an intern as well as in both temporary and permanent positions, I have gained experience in developing care plans with both short- and long-term goals, interviewing and assessing client needs, and locating resources from other community agencies.

I believe that through my enthusiasm, motivational abilities, empathy, and compassion for others I can make valuable contributions to an organization that seeks a professional with these qualities.

I hope you will welcome my call soon to arrange a brief meeting at your convenience to discuss your current and future needs and how I might serve them. Thank you in advance for your time.

Sincerely yours,

Joselyn Lytton

Alternate last paragraph:
I hope you will call or write me soon to suggest a time convenient for us to meet and discuss your current and future needs and how I might serve them. Thank you in advance for your time.

JOSELYN LYTTON

1110½ Hay Street, Fayetteville, NC 28305   •   preppub@aol.com   •   (910) 483-6611

OBJECTIVE

To offer my reputation as a compassionate, dedicated, and enthusiastic young professional to an organization that can use my education and experience related to social work and human services and my willingness to go the extra mile for my clients.

EDUCATION

Attend a graduate program leading to Master of Social Work (M.S.W.) degree, North Carolina State University, Raleigh, NC.
B.S., Social Work and Psychology, Methodist College, Fayetteville, NC, 2002.
- Earned a 3.2 GPA while completing specialized course work including the following:
  abnormal psychology   social psychology   psychological statistics
  juvenile delinquency   social policies and analysis   working with groups
  human developmental psychology   social change
- Held offices and earned honors including:
  was elected as president of the Social Work Club
  volunteered to serve as vice president of Psi Chi Psychology Club
  served as president of Sigma Omega Chi Honor Society
  was honored with the "Outstanding Social Work Student Award"
Attended St. Mary's College, Raleigh, NC.

EXPERIENCE

CRISIS INTERVENTION SOCIAL WORKER. Wake County Department of Social Services (DSS), Raleigh, NC (2002-03). Learned how to locate and maximize community resources in ways that would make the most of benefits for clients while making determinations on potential clients' eligibility for financial assistance from federal, state, and local programs.
- Became skilled in assessing needs within the family as well as external factors that could lead to a family being considered at high risk for abuse.
- Gained experience in crisis intervention and in finding ways to defuse problems.
- Learned to read between the lines while interviewing and assessing client needs.

SOCIAL WORKER. Wake County DSS, Raleigh, NC (2002). For the Wake County JOBS (Job Opportunities and Basic Skills) program, assisted in the process of completing initial assessments of potential clients for the program which enabled participants to obtain an education and/or training for a career.
- Helped clients by developing case plans which included short-term and long-term goals.
- Ensured participants in the program received support in areas such as transportation, child care, tuition assistance, and educational tools; this support ensured clients were able to complete the program and find jobs which allowed them to be independent.
- Made home visits which gave the clients emotional and motivational assistance and also gave me the opportunity to see if community resources were being taken advantage of.

SOCIAL WORK INTERN. North Carolina State University, Raleigh, NC (2001-02). Gained the respect of my superiors at the Wake County DSS for my maturity and dedication to providing clients with a high quality of concerned services.
- Displayed organizational and written communication skills while developing and editing a 100-page resource manual for patients at a free health care clinic.
- Contributed to the community by seeing that information about this new one-of-a-kind clinic and other area resources for services were made available.
- Used my research skills while compiling information from numerous sources into one easy-to-use manual.
- Analyzed statistical data collected from confidential questionnaires: the resulting data was very useful to staff members because it gave them insight into how the clients really felt about the department's programs and services.

Volunteer experience: Cared for the terminally ill in a hospice home; administered and monitored patients' emotional, mental, and physical condition.

PERSONAL

Am very persistent — will not give up until I am sure I have exhausted every possible source of assistance for my client. Have earned a reputation for my enthusiasm and energy.

SOCIAL WORK

Date

Personnel Director
Sanford Department of Social Services
130 Carbonton Road
Sanford, NC 27330

Family Advocacy

Dear Sir or Madam:

I am responding to your advertisement in the newspaper for a Social Worker II. I am enclosing a resume along with the completed State Application for Employment PD-107.

I was quite excited when I read the ad in the newspaper because I offer all the skills and abilities you seek. Fluent in Spanish, I have counseled clients in both languages while providing case management services to individuals with a wide range of problems and impairments.

In my most recent job as a social worker, I served as the "subject matter expert" on family advocacy issues at a military community in Panama, and I developed the Safe Shelter and Foster Home Programs now used in that community.

What my resume does not reveal is my affable nature and warm personality that is well suited to the social services field, which I truly enjoy. Although my chosen profession is one in which case workers encounter tragic and sad human realities on a daily basis, I am confident of my ability, refined through experience, to help anyone improve his or her situation.

I am an experienced social services professional who would enjoy contributing to your needs and goals, and I hope you will favorably review my application and call me to set up an interview at your convenience. Thank you in advance for your time.

Sincerely yours,

Monica Carter

MONICA CARTER

1110½ Hay Street, Fayetteville, NC 28305   •   preppub@aol.com   •   (910) 483-6611

OBJECTIVE

To contribute to an organization that can use a skilled social worker who is fluent in Spanish and who offers extensive education as well as "hands-on" experience in handling problems including child abuse, mental illness, and family violence as well as the wide range of problems associated with poverty, illiteracy, and joblessness.

EXPERIENCE

FAMILY ADVOCACY SPECIALIST. U.S. Army Family Support Division, Panama (2000-03). Played a key role in implementing and coordinating the Atlantic Family Advocacy Program (FAP) at this military community in Panama; performed assessments of clients in crisis situations involving child or spouse abuse, and made appropriate referrals to military and civilian agencies.

- Both in Spanish and English, counseled clients on a short-term basis.
- Conducted surveys to identify deficiencies in services for abused spouses or children.
- Implemented an innovative community education program which included training programs for soldiers which publicized information and grounds for reporting suspected abuse.
- Trained military police, social services representatives, youth services staff, social services volunteers, as well as personnel in other organizations and agencies in the procedures for identifying and referring suspected child abuse.
- Served as the "subject matter expert" on family advocacy issues as a member of the Family Advocacy Case Management Team.
- Developed the Safe Shelter & Foster Home Programs now used in this community.

EDUCATION SPECIALIST. U.S. Army, Ft. Bragg, NC (1998-00). At the world's largest U.S. military base, worked as Training Coordinator in the Child Development Services Branch; advised and trained those providing day care to preschoolers on age appropriate activities, and assured that centers/homes were arranged to enhance the physical, emotional, social, and cognitive development of children.

- Completed extensive assessments on each home or center module regularly.
- Planned training modules which were used as instructional guides for caregivers.
- Completed assessments/screenings of children identified as having problems such as development delay or behavioral difficulty.
- Gained valuable insight into the factors that cause stress in caregiving and counseled workers about how to anticipate, avoid, and cope with such problems.
- Provided both individual training as well as group sessions.
- Became skilled in enhancing day care provided in small homes and large centers.

PRESCHOOL TEACHER. Tot Town Development Center, Ft. Benning, GA (1996-97). Enjoyed the opportunity to work with small children in this private day care facility.

SCHOOL SOCIAL WORKER. Panamanian Institute of Special Habilitation, Colon, Panama (1987-94). Worked with nearly every kind of social services problem while counseling individuals and families; dealt with problems associated with unhappy marriages, unwed parenthood, and financial difficulties as well as problems related to caring for the ill and handicapped.

- Developed programs appropriate for mentally retarded and Down Syndrome children.
- Created educational materials and provided instruction related to first aid, sex education, nutrition, home management and home economics, and other areas.
- Became extensively involved in delinquency prevention; counseled juveniles.
- Worked closely with doctors to serve mentally and emotionally disturbed patients.

EDUCATION & TRAINING

Bachelor of Science (B.S.) degree, University of Panama, 1991.
Completed extensive professional development training related to family advocacy, parent effectiveness, substance abuse, children's services, and programming services for the mentally and physically impaired.

PERSONAL

Am considered an experienced public speaker and have also completed extensive training related to preparing and delivering briefings. Truly enjoy the social services field.

SOCIAL WORK

Date

Exact Name of Person
Title or Position
Name of Company
Address (no., street)
Address (city, state, zip)

Family Resources

Dear Exact Name of Person: (or Dear Sir or Madam if answering a blind ad.)

I would enjoy an opportunity to meet with you in person to discuss with you the ways in which I could become a valuable part of your team in the mental health and human services area. I am writing in response to your ad for Habilitation Specialist II.

You will see from my resume that, since graduating with my B.S. degree from Texas A & M University, I have worked in preventive medicine, coordinated treatment for the mentally retarded and physically disabled, provided crisis intervention services to children up to young adults, and developed "from scratch" a program providing services to at-risk families.

I am proud of the fact that I have made valuable contributions to every organization I have served. Even in my internship with the U.S. Army Medical Department, I became the department's first intern to receive an Army Achievement Award as a result of my efforts in research and program development. Most recently, I played a key role in developing a new program serving at-risk military families, and I taught a highly popular parenting class entitled "Parenting with Love and Logic." In a prior job I worked in a short-term, inpatient crisis intervention hospital for children and won the highly respected "I Make A Difference" award in my first quarter of employment based on a secret election by peers and patients. A Qualified Mental Retardation Professional (QMRP), I have also coordinated programs for the mentally retarded and physically disabled.

You would find me in person to be a caring and enthusiastic young professional who genuinely thrives on the challenge of helping others. I can provide exceptionally strong personal and professional references.

I hope you will write or call me soon to suggest a time when we might meet to discuss your current and future needs and how I might serve them. Thank you in advance for your time.

Sincerely yours,

Norma Zanders

NORMA ZANDERS

1110½ Hay Street, Fayetteville, NC 28305   •   preppub@aol.com   •   (910) 483-6611

OBJECTIVE

To benefit an organization that can use a human services and mental health professional who has earned a reputation as an innovative, compassionate hard worker while serving the needs of at-risk families, performing crisis intervention for children up through young adults, and coordinating programs for the physically disabled and mentally handicapped.

EDUCATION

B.S., *Community Health Education*, Texas A & M University, College Station, TX, 1997.
Achieved the professional status of Qualified Mental Retardation Professional (QMRP).

EXPERIENCE

FAMILY RESOURCE SPECIALIST. Army Community Service (ACS), Germany (2001-03). In an essentially "entrepreneurial" role after being hired for one of two newly created positions, utilized my resourcefulness and enthusiasm in establishing a network throughout the community; developed a clientele of "at-risk" military families and eventually provided support services and education for over 100 families while personally handling a normal caseload of 20 families at any one time.
- Effective at earning the trust and respect of others, in numerous situations was the only professional in the community who could gain access to a home when problems arose.
- Made home visits to families at risk for spouse abuse or child neglect/abuse for the Family Advocacy Program; prepared home studies for prospective adoptive parents.
- Represented families' interests as an "expert" on the Family Advocacy Case Management Team; was a member of the Community Early Childhood Intervention Board.
- Taught a highly effective parenting class entitled *"Parenting with Love and Logic,"* as well as classes designed to teach household management skills, self-esteem and coping principles, and orientation classes.

MENTAL HEALTH ASSISTANT. Northridge Hospital, Columbus, GA (2000). In a short-term, inpatient crisis intervention hospital for children up through very young adults, provided one-on-one care to children and adolescents while organizing activities and schedules for non-medical tasks and guiding informal group sessions.
- Was highly respected for my skills: in my first quarter of employment, was nominated for and won the "I Make a Difference Award" in a secret ballot by peers and patients.

TREATMENT COORDINATOR. Jefferson Rehabilitation Center, Watertown, NY (1998-00). For a client load of 21 mentally retarded/physically disabled adults, developed, oversaw, and evaluated personal programs which would increase their level of independence.
- Coordinated with and instructed professionals at each client's residence, day treatment program, and sheltered workshop in order to bring every stage together for a successful total program.
- Became a **Qualified Mental Retardation Professional (QMRP).**
- Trained as an investigator, was selected to serve on the Special Review Committee which reviewed and made decisions on cases.
- Directly impacted on the life of one woman who moved to the least restrictive living quarters available, happily held a job in the community as a dishwasher, and was able to go downtown alone after years in a physically restrictive home and sheltered workshop.
- Simultaneously volunteered as a **Children's Facilitator** with the city's Office of Mental Health: gained my first exposure to abused children and parents who were resistant to counseling while attending court-mandated programs.

PREVENTIVE MEDICINE INTERN. U.S. Army Medical Department, Ft. Drum, NY (1997). Excelled in an internship created especially for me, and then became the department's first intern to be awarded an Army Achievement Award as a result of my initiative and accomplishments in research and program development.
- Interviewed 20 preventive medicine professionals, created slides and a script, presented the results to the department chief, and produced a comprehensive tool for the Community Health Nursing Department which is still being utilized.

PERSONAL

Use computers with MS Word, Excel, and PowerPoint for word processing, record keeping, and preparing reports. Am CPR and First Aid certified.

SOCIAL WORK

Date

Larry Bailey
Clinton Department of Social Services
1216 Sunset Avenue
Clinton, NC 28328-3822

Social Worker   Mr. Bailey:

I would appreciate an opportunity to talk with you soon about how I could contribute to the Department of Social Services as a field service representative for migrant workers.

As you will see from my resume, I currently work for the Department of Social Services and am involved in screening low-income families with dependent children to assess their needs for basic services and resources while counseling them and helping them set priorities. In 2001-02, I was involved in hiring 60 people to help distribute goods and services to victims of Hurricane Andrew, and I gained experience in working with the vast network of agencies and organizations that join hands to help people in such emergencies. I received special recognition for my leadership during that disaster from Dade County.

In prior work experience I have worked with abused and neglected children at the Children's Hospital in Miami, and I have spent much time helping people in rest homes.

Fluent in Spanish, I feel certain I could be a valuable asset to DSS as a field service representative to migrant workers. Although I am just 25 years old, I have been told many times that I am "mature beyond my years" in terms of having common sense, and I do feel I am very effective in assuring that public funds are used for legitimate needs. I am very knowledgeable of the internal workings of the Department of Social Services.

I hope you will call or write me soon to suggest a time convenient for us to meet and discuss your current and future needs and how I might serve them. Thank you in advance for your time.

Sincerely yours,

Sheila Bigford

SHEILA BIGFORD

1110½ Hay Street, Fayetteville, NC 28305 • preppub@aol.com • (910) 483-6611

OBJECTIVE   To contribute to society as a poised young social worker.

EDUCATION   **B.A. degree in Sociology with a minor in Psychology**, Florida International University, Miami, FL, 2003.
- Received three special acknowledgements for my work in helping students in other clubs and organizations in my role as a Student Government Fiscal Assistant.

A.A. degree in Psychology, Miami Dade Community College, Miami, FL, 1999.

LANGUAGES   Fluently speak Spanish and understand Italian.

EXPERIENCE   **SOCIAL WORKER.** Department of Social Services, Fayetteville, NC (2003-present). Screen low-income families with dependent children in order to assess their needs for electricity, rent, and the resources to pay other essential bills; counsel clients and help them set priorities.
- Prepare paperwork to obtain federal funds or government money for verified needs.
- Have learned to work tactfully and delicately with people in serious financial situations; have become skilled at counseling people who don't want to be told what to do.
- Believe strongly in the value of working with other social workers to share ideas and to gain insight into the proper approaches to a client's problem.

DAY CARE INTERN. Children's Hospital, Miami, FL (2002-03). In this hospital environment, gained insight into the many ways in which children are physically battered, emotionally mistreated, mentally abused, or neglected; also learned about the variety of programs and services which are available to provide intervention and problem solving for abusive parents and their children.
- Gained experience in placing children in foster care.
- Refined my ability to deal with abusive personalities and help some of them begin the path to recovery.

SITE COORDINATOR. Metro Dade, Miami, FL (2001-02). Handled the responsibility of hiring 60 people to help distribute goods and services to victims of Hurricane Andrew.
- Gained insight into how numerous relief agencies, social service agencies, and religious organizations work together in crisis; worked closely with the Salvation Army, Red Cross, and FIMA to provide medical aid, money, trailer homes, other support.
- Used my counseling skills while helping people cope with the loss of loved ones and material assets; counseled people who were suddenly homeless or who were suicidal.
- Saw firsthand that finding satisfactory employment is often the key to regaining self esteem, and was instrumental in helping many people find jobs.
- Received special recognition from Dade County for the leadership and organizational skills I provided during this natural disaster; also received a special award from the U.S. Army for my service and contributions.

SENIOR SECRETARY. Walter A. Spock & Associates, Miami, FL (1999-01). Rapidly became a valuable and versatile worker in this small office; operated computers, answered phones, handled filing, assisted in maintaining accounting entries, and became involved in both sales and financing.
- Was repeatedly told by my boss that I was his "right arm."

PERSONAL   Have been told on many occasions that I am mature "beyond my years."

SOCIAL WORK: Social Work

VICTORIA ZUBROD

1110½ Hay Street, Fayetteville, NC 28305 • preppub@aol.com • (910) 483-6611

OBJECTIVE	To obtain a permanent position in the mental health field that utilizes my educational background, organizational and program management skills, and planning abilities.
EDUCATION	**Master of Education in Counseling**, Reed College, Portland, OR, 2003. • Graduated *magna cum laude*. **Bachelor of Arts in Psychology**, University of California, Los Angeles, CA, 2001.
EXPERIENCE	**INDIVIDUAL AND FAMILY COUNSELING INTERN.** The Center for Individual and Family Therapy, Portland, OR (2002-03). Provided age and situationally appropriate counseling for individuals in a variety of age groups ranging from young children to middle-age adults, acted as a co-leader for therapy groups for sexually abused girls, and provided marital therapy.

* Helped develop the curriculum for two counseling groups — the four-year-olds and the nine to 12-year-old group of sexually abused females — including reorganizing guidelines in such a way that future leaders would have a foundation for additional groups.
* Provided a buffer between sexually and/or physically abused children and their parents during supervised visitations scheduled after gaining the childrens' trust.
* Led groups so that each member was given an opportunity for individual growth.
* Staffed the front desk on rotation for intake and referrals.

COUNSELING INTERN. Los Angeles School District, WA (2001). Assisted the counseling staff at Wiley Middle School in the implementation of in-school counseling under the sponsorship of "Second Step — Seattle Committee for Children," a violence intervention program.

* Participated in support activities including facilitation of violence intervention classes, attendance at parent conferences, and individual or group meetings with students.
* Experienced first hand the positive effects of an early intervention initiative which taught the students alternatives and solutions to potentially dangerous situations.

CAMP COUNSELOR. Portland Parks and Recreation, Portland, WA (summer 2000). For the city's special programs summer camp, provided support for physically and mentally handicapped children in overnight as well as day-camp settings.

* Supervised a wide range of areas including assistance with general hygiene, dressing, and meals as well as evening and overnight activities.
* Planned and conducted outdoor group activities for as many as 11 children of varying abilities and temperaments.

FACILITY ASSISTANT. L'Arche Limited International, Kent, England (1998-99). As assistant to the facility manager, provided support to mentally disabled home residents as well as supervising five staff members in an intense work environment.

* Challenged residents to take the maximum responsibility for decisions such as daily life skills, money management, and social interaction.
* Provided the least restrictive possible assistance to residents to allow them to integrate into mainstream society.
* Participated in and led team meetings to assess residents' progress and future goals.
* Was known for my style of respecting each client for his/her unique qualities.

Highlights of other experience: Enjoyed working with young people and encouraging them to set and maintain high personal goals and standards.

* Coached high school long-distance runners with an emphasis on personal improvement and team involvement (spring 2001) as well as teaching a variety of sports to elementary and middle school youth for the YMCA (2001).

TRAINING & PROFESSIONAL AFFILIATIONS	Attended training programs in subjects including marital therapy emphasizing integrative research and practice as well as a health forum which provided valuable information on intervention techniques and treatment facilities for eating disorders. Member, American Counseling Association

DORIS DERBY

1110½ Hay Street, Fayetteville, NC 28305 • preppub@aol.com • (910) 483-6611

OBJECTIVE

I want to contribute to an organization that can use an experienced social worker with excellent supervisory and program management skills along with a reputation as a creative, caring, and compassionate individual.

EDUCATION

B.S.S.W. degree in Social Work, University of Maryland, 2000.
- Made the Dean's List 1995, 1996, 1997, 1998, 1999, and 2000.

Completed 38 hours of graduate study in Social Work, East Carolina University, Greenville, NC, 2002-03.

Have completed numerous seminars and courses which included the North Carolina School for Alcohol and Drug Studies, UNC, Wilmington, 2002:

Reality Therapy (30 hours)	Healing the Whole Person (two hours)
Rational Behavior Therapy (six hours)	Ethical Dilemmas (three hours)
Case Coordination Techniques (three hours)	Counseling minority populations (1 hour)
Adolescent Counseling/Crisis Intervention (three hours)	

- In 2000, completed the Alcohol and Drug Prevention Program (120 hours)
- In 1999, completed Family Counseling/Working with Families in Crisis (30 hours)
- In 1998, completed Working with Families and Couples (30 hours)

AFFILIATIONS

- National Association of Social Work
- American Association of Counseling Development

EXPERIENCE

SOCIAL WORKER/SUBSTANCE ABUSE COUNSELOR II. Sandhills Mental Health Center, West End, NC (2001-02). Performed intake and assessment to include gathering collateral information from school, family, and social agencies; was responsible for case management and client advocacy as well as for resource development and outreach.

- Prepared treatment planning based on client needs as presented by client and client family and support system.
- Maintained records to meet Medicare, private insurance, and managed health care criteria.
- Facilitated group sessions for clients and conducted individual counseling on a weekly or bi-weekly basis for client case loads.
- Developed and conducted classes to educate community, school, and court support systems concerning drug awareness and community services.
- Acted as community school and court liaison to advocate clients' progress and needs.

DRUG & ALCOHOL ABUSE SPECIALIST. Department of Psychiatry, Alcohol & Drug Resident Treatment Facility, Nuernberg USAH MEDDAC, Germany (1996-01). Received an Army Commendation Award for my exceptional performance in this job in a 40-bed facility; assessed patients upon admission to determine appropriate course of treatment while supervising three people.

- Gathered information from sources including family and client support system.
- Presented case histories in multi-disciplinary staffing environment.
- Prepared and maintained patient records to conform with quality assurance standards and applicable regulations.
- Served as a primary counselor to over 100 patients and family members; facilitated primary patient and couples groups which consisted of 10-12 people and 5-6 couples; facilitated AA training groups in order to familiarize patients with Alcoholics Anonymous self-help program; facilitated a women's group consisting of 10-12 women once a week in which women worked through abuse, rape, and incest issues.
- Trained and supervised counselors Europe-wide through the Alcoholism Training Program to familiarize them with the disease concept of alcoholism and family dynamics.
- Coordinated Family portion of the treatment program; coordinated and supervised classes which taught family dynamics and led discussion groups of family members.
- Researched, designed, and instructed classes for patients on topics including forgiveness, assertiveness, and relapse process; conducted classes for colleagues on recognizing personality disorders and diagnosing Axis II disorders according to DSM III-R; served as a subject matter expert on incest, rape, and abuse issues.

PERSONAL

Received a Certificate of Appreciation for my efforts in Alcoholism Education from the Girl Scouts of America and from the LIFE Group. Was named Volunteer of the Quarter, Family Services Center at McClellan AFB. Can provide excellent references upon request.

SPORTS

Date

Exact Name of Person
Title or Position
Name of Company
Address (no., street)
Address (city, state, zip)

Football Coach

Dear Exact Name of Person: (or Dear Sir or Madam if answering a blind ad.)

I would appreciate an opportunity to talk with you soon about how I could contribute to your organization through my background as a successful coach and athletic director who offers 13 years of experience as a head coach and six as an athletic director.

As you will see from my resume, the bulk of my experience is in coaching football and I am now at 71st Senior High School in Fayetteville, NC, a 4A school which has averaged 10 wins a year for the past two seasons in a conference recognized as the toughest and most competitive in the state. In fact, in my two years here, I have guided the team to an impressive current streak of scoring in double figures for the past 21 games, a fact recently publicized by the High School Football PREP News. Earlier I led the football team at Chester (SC) High School, the state's smallest 4A school which had not been to a playoff since 1970, to four consecutive playoff seasons.

A versatile professional, I have also excelled in coaching track, basketball, wrestling, and golf. I am confident that I can build any sports program into a successful one while guiding young people to prosper academically and grow in character through athletics. My track record will show that I am not only a talented coach and administrator, but also an enthusiastic, intelligent, and motivated professional who handles pressure well. I am extremely effective in molding groups of young people into productive, winning teams. For example, when I became the youngest 4A Head Coach in North Carolina at Cape Fear High School in Fayetteville, in 1993, I quickly produced a team with the most conference wins in the school's history.

I can provide a school system with a winning coach who is also an excellent teacher, administrator, and communicator. I will cheerfully relocate, and I can provide outstanding personal and professional references from all previous employers.

I hope you will call or write me soon to suggest a time convenient for us to meet and discuss your current and future needs and how I might serve them. Thank you in advance for your time.

Sincerely yours,

Daniel Boisvert

DANIEL BOISVERT

1110½ Hay Street, Fayetteville, NC 28305 • preppub@aol.com • (910) 483-6611

OBJECTIVE
To offer my positive and results-oriented leadership style, along with my experience in building and coaching winning teams, to an ambitious high school that can use an enthusiastic and intelligent professional with a reputation for the highest work and personal ethics.

EXPERIENCE
Offer a track record of success which includes 20 years of coaching with 13 years as a head coach and six as an athletic director with an emphasis on the high school level:
OFFENSIVE COORDINATOR and **PHYSICAL EDUCATION TEACHER.** 71st Senior High School, Fayetteville, NC (2003-present). Was hired as offensive coordinator for a football team which has built an impressive record of wins in a conference recognized as the toughest and most competitive in the state.
- Averaged 10 wins a year over the past two seasons while building teams that work well under pressure.
- Contributed intelligence, leadership, and knowledge of the game of football as a member of a coaching staff which has been effective in winning "the big games."
- In my two years here, have guided the team to an impressive current streak of scoring in double figures for the last 21 games, a fact recently publicized by the *High School Football PREP News*.
- Displayed versatility as coach of the golf team; taught PE to 10th-12th grade students.

HEAD FOOTBALL COACH and **ATHLETIC DIRECTOR.** Lumberton Senior High School, Lumberton, NC (2000-02). Provided the management and guidance for a project in which three high schools combined and then coached the football program and directed all other sports for the consolidated school.
- Polished my communication skills as an elementary physical education teacher, but after the 2002-03 school year returned to my first love of coaching.

HEAD FOOTBALL COACH and **ATHLETIC DIRECTOR.** Chester High School, SC (1996-00). Led the state's smallest 4A school to four consecutive winning seasons in the state's toughest league; acted as administrator of the school's total athletic program.
- Coached four consecutive teams to state-level playoffs and record-setting years including the first time the school had reached the state playoffs since 1970.
- Supervised 20 coaches and administered a $75,000 athletic budget.
- Taught weight training and physical fitness to participants in all athletic programs.

HEAD FOOTBALL COACH. Cape Fear High School, Fayetteville, NC (1993-96). Joined this organization as the youngest 4A high school head coach in the state and led the team to break several school records; supervised and trained an eight-person staff.
- Faced with a previous 1-9 record, turned the program around and in 1993 produced a team with the most conference wins in the school's history.
- Guided the 1995 team to the best overall record in the school's 18-year history.
- Scored in every game over a three-year period covering 30 games while playing against teams in the state's "Top 10" as the smallest 4A school in the state.

HEAD FOOTBALL COACH and **INSTRUCTOR.** Farmville Central High School, Farmville, NC (1990-93). Obtained my Master of Education degree in Physical Education while teaching classes and coaching three sports — football, wrestling, and track — at this 3A school.
- After two years of hard work, developed an 0-7 junior varsity football team into an 8-4 varsity playoff team. Coached track and wrestling teams to become conference champions.

Highlights of other experience: Worked 11 summers as a **SWIMMING INSTRUCTOR, POOL MANAGER, SWIM TEAM COACH,** and **LIFEGUARD.** While serving an apprenticeship as a **COACH** and **INSTRUCTOR** for Lumberton High School (Lumberton, NC), learned to motivate young people to excel athletically, academically, and personally; was Assistant Football Coach, J.V. Basketball Coach, and Track Coach.

EDUCATION/ PROFESSIONAL DEVELOPMENT
M.Ed. degree, East Carolina University, Greenville, NC, 1993.
B.S., Physical Education, Pembroke State University, NC, 1988.
Attend summer clinics every year sponsored by the state coaches association.

FOOTBALL COACHING EXPERTISE & ACHIEVEMENTS
In my coaching career, have gained experience in these areas:

offensive and defensive coordination	formulation of game plans
special team coordination	fundamentals in all positions

Was "MVP" of my high school football team and won a Merit Scholarship to the University of North Carolina.

Date

Mr. David Geer
East West Partners
190 Finley Golf Club Road
Chapel Hill, NC 27514

Golf Pro   Dear Mr. Geer:

With the enclosed resume, I am formally indicating my interest in the Head Golf Professional position at The Governor's Club in Chapel Hill.

In my current job as the Head Golf Professional at The Foxfire Resort and Country Club in Pinehurst, NC, I have improved every aspect of the golf program at this esteemed country club. Although I am quite happy in my current situation and am appreciated for the significant improvements I have made in every area of the golf program, it has always been my goal to become associated one day with a prestigious club such as The Governor's Club. I am aware of the high-profile clientele you serve, and I feel certain I could add value to your operation and enhance the superior climate for which you already are known.

At Foxfire Resort and Country Club, I have resourcefully found new ways to save money every year while making sure customers are satisfied with all "the little things" that can drive members crazy if they're not perfect! By those "little things" I include things such as the variety and quality of golf shop inventory, the tournament program, golf instruction, golf cart operation and bag storage, driving range administration, as well as the operation of starters and rangers. I have taken golf instruction to a new level and, while supervising seven employees, I have continually developed the instructional abilities of my assistants.

I have completed PGA Business School I, II, and III, have served on the PGA Oral Interview Committee, and was invited by fellow PGA Professionals to act as instructor for the Triangle Junior Golf League. In my previous job at The Country Club of North Carolina, I gained extensive experience in organizing and managing an extensive tournament schedule including The Southern Amateur Tournament, National Amputee Tournament, and the U.S. Senior Golf Association Tournament.

You would find me in person to be a congenial individual who prides myself on my ability to relate well to anyone. I believe strongly in the ability of golf to teach and refine virtues including honesty, fairness, courtesy, responsibility, determination, and discipline. I can provide outstanding personal and professional references.

I hope you will write or call me to suggest a time when we might meet in confidence to discuss your current and future needs and how I might serve them. Thank you in advance for your time.

Sincerely yours,

Charles Gebhardt

CHARLES GEBHARDT

1110½ Hay Street, Fayetteville, NC 28305   •   preppub@aol.com   •   (910) 483-6611

OBJECTIVE   To benefit an organization that can use a respected golf professional who offers experience in financial management, proven skills in teaching and training, as well as an intense commitment to the highest standards of excellence in both personal and professional areas.

EXPERIENCE   **HEAD GOLF PROFESSIONAL.** Foxfire Resort and Country Club, Pinehurst, NC (2001-present). Have earned a reputation as an enthusiastic and hard-working professional who has improved every aspect of the golf program at this prestigious country club.

- **Golf shop sales and service**: Improved customer service, accounting practices, and the quality of merchandise; boosted sales from $155,000 to $177,000 in my first year, to $223,000 in my second year, and to more than $230,000 in the third year.
- **Financial administration**: Resourcefully found new ways to decrease expenses while improving services; proposed a 2002 budget that is $21,000 less than the 2001 budget and have already reduced expenses by $6,000 in 2003.
- **Tournament program**: Hosted the 2003 North Carolina Amateur Tournament and generally increased the club's level of interest in competition.
- **Golf instruction**: Continually developed the instructional abilities of my assistants and improved the golf game of every student I taught.
- **Starters and rangers**: Improved course scheduling, developed new approaches to helping members find games, and ensured a reasonable pace on busy days.
- **Junior Golf Program**: Exposed juniors to the great virtues golf can teach — honesty, fairness, courtesy, responsibility, determination, and discipline.
- **Golf cart operation and bag storage**: Improved maintenance, repairs, and customer satisfaction with all aspects of these operations.
- **Driving range**: Developed an attractive range membership plan.
- **Employee supervision**: Supervised seven employees; am known for my fairness.

ASSISTANT GOLF PROFESSIONAL. The Country Club of North Carolina, Pinehurst, NC (1998-01). Supervised nine bag storage and cart operation personnel while managing accounts receivable/payable, inventory control, and merchandising.

- Organized and managed an extensive tournament schedule which included The Southern Amateur Tournament, National Amputee Tournament, and U.S. Senior Golf Association Tournament.
- Taught clinics and provided private instruction to men, women, and juniors.

FIRST ASSISTANT PROFESSIONAL. Chapel Hill Country Club, Chapel Hill, NC (1995-98). Managed part-time cart staff and pro shop staff; planned budgets for cart staff and operation costs for the driving range; and handled accounts receivable/payable, inventory control, and merchandise selection.

- Organized Men's and Ladies' Clinics as well as a week-long Junior Golf Camp.

FIRST ASSISTANT PROFESSIONAL. Foxfire Resort and Country Club, Pinehurst, NC (1993-95). Began as Second Assistant Professional in 1993 and was promoted to First Assistant Professional in less than a year; learned the "nuts and bolts" of golf program management.

- As First Assistant, taught 30% of private lessons; was responsible for the tournament schedule for men and women.

EDUCATION   Completed **PGA Business School I, II, and** III, Nashville, TN, and Atlanta, GA, 1993, 1994, and 2001. Completed workshops focused on business planning for the golf professional, techniques for outclassing the competition, improving the appearance of the club scoreboard, food and beverage principles, wage and hour laws, and computer software.

HONORS
- Invited by fellow PGA Professionals to be an instructor, Triangle Junior Golf League, 1996.
- Appointed member, PGA Oral Interview Committee, 1997.

PERSONAL   Enjoy hunting, fishing, and spending time with my family when not at work. Am known as a powerful motivator and communicator who knows how to develop people to their fullest.

SPORTS

Date

Exact Name of Person
Title or Position
Name of Company
Address (no., street)
Address (city, state, zip)

Tennis Pro   Dear Exact Name of Person: (or Dear Sir or Madam if answering a blind ad.)

I would appreciate an opportunity to talk with you soon about how I could contribute to your organization through my outstanding personal reputation and technical expertise as a Director/ Head Tennis Pro.

Although I am highly regarded in my current job as Head Pro for the New World Country Club, where I have been since 1997, I am attracted to your organization because of its fine reputation and feel I have much to offer you. As you will see from my resume, I have excelled as a Tennis Pro at Van Der Meer Tennis University, Tennis Coach at a tennis academy, and Head Pro at a sports center and country club before coming to New World Country Club as Head Pro. In 2002 I became one of only four people in North Carolina certified as a USPTR National Tester, and I have conducted USPTR coaches' workshops for persons wanting to be certified or to upgrade their certification.

So much of what I could offer an already-outstanding program such as yours is my creativity, I believe, since I know you have an excellent staff. I believe that the main way to keep the membership involved and the tennis professionals motivated is by developing new programs, and I have combined my tennis skills and creativity in developing highly successful programs for adults and juniors while also utilizing my public relations and media skills to develop new community awareness of and involvement in tennis.

I would appreciate your keeping my interest in your club confidential at this point, but if you have any idea that you could use a talented tennis pro who could take your program to new levels of excellence, I would appreciate your contacting me.

Sincerely yours,

Clifton Newman

Alternate last paragraph:
I hope you will welcome my call soon to arrange a brief meeting at your convenience to discuss your current and future needs and how I might serve them. Thank you in advance for your time.

CLIFTON NEWMAN

1110½ Hay Street, Fayetteville, NC 28305   •   preppub@aol.com   •   (910) 483-6611

OBJECTIVE

I want to contribute to an organization that can use a well-trained tennis professional who offers expert teaching and motivational skills, along with the proven ability to develop, manage, and promote new programs.

CERTIFICATION

Am a USPTR **National Tester**, one of only four in North Carolina (since October 2002).
Am certified by the Professional Tennis Registry of the U.S.A. as a **Tennis Professional**, the highest of three ratings (rated August 1998).

EXPERIENCE

HEAD TENNIS PRO. New World Country Club Charlotte, NC (1997-present). At this 2700-member club, dramatically increased tennis participation; manage classes, tournaments, maintenance, and a full-service pro shop, while supervising a staff of four and administering a $65,000 facility budget.
- Was awarded a Local Excellence Training (LET) Program, which has trained youngsters from throughout North Carolina.
- Ran two very successful USTA tournaments (KCC Junior Invitational and KCC Men's Invitational), which drew players from all over the southeast.
- Developed the Adult Team Tennis Interclub Program, the most successful adult program at KCC to date; formed three USTA adult league teams.
- Have participated in the Teams Across America Program sponsored by USPTA.
- Have developed several community programs to boost tennis popularity, including work with school programs (Super Saturdays — a kindergarten through third-grade program).
- Have conducted USPTR coaches' workshops for persons wanting to be certified or to upgrade their certification.
- Participated in an internship program with students from an area college.
- Led over 75 players of all ages to compete in their first tournaments.
- Totally re-created the juniors' program; organized and implemented the Rick Martin Tennis Academy, a highly successful program I developed.
- Gave the entire tennis area an exciting "new look": rebuilt the clay courts and redesigned the pro shop and surrounding areas.

TENNIS PROFESSIONAL. Pinehurst Country Club, Fayetteville, NC (1996-97). Increased participation in the club's juniors' program to an all-time high.
- Conceived and developed the Clifton Newman Tennis Academy which trained over 80 young tennis players from all over the southeastern U.S.
- Managed a juniors' tournament which included nationally ranked players.

TENNIS COACH. James Johnson Tennis Academy, Atlanta, GA (1995-96). Taught daily classes and weekend clinics for junior, college, and pro-tour tennis players; traveled to ATP and WTA tours as a professional coach.
- While traveling on the National Junior Circuit, worked with top-ranking junior players including the #1 ranked J.J. Jackson.

HEAD TENNIS PRO. The Sports Center, Raleigh, NC (1994-95). While managing the total tennis program at this 1,000-person club, developed a juniors' program with 30 participants who ranked in the state.
- Increased adult participation; was USTA Schools' Program Coordinator.
- Maintained soft courts; supervised two assistants; managed annual budget.
- Taught classes, ran tournaments, and worked with schools and Special Olympics.

TENNIS PRO. Van Der Meer Tennis University, Hilton Head, SC (1994). Had the opportunity to work with world-class players at this famous tennis university/resort while working as a clinician and in the pro shop.

EDUCATION/ TRAINING

Achieved USTA Sport Science Level I certification, with training in bio-mechanics, nutrition, fitness, and other areas; will complete Sport Science Level II training by April 2003.
Attended several Elite Coaches training programs conducted by the USTA and USPTR.
Attended numerous professional development workshops at the Annual Tennis Symposium, 1996-present.
Was awarded a scholarship to **Van Der Meer Tennis University**, Sweet Briar College, VA, 1993.

PROFESSIONAL AFFILIATIONS

Am a member of the following professional organizations/associations:
United States Professional Tennis Registry (USPTR), United States Professional Tennis Association (USPTA), U.S. Tennis Association (USTA), North Carolina Association of Tennis Professionals, and Prince Pro Team.

TEACHING & EDUCATIONAL ADMINISTRATION
MYRNA MACIAS
1110½ Hay Street, Fayetteville, NC 28305   •   preppub@aol.com   •   (910) 483-6611

OBJECTIVE

To offer a background of achievements in developing innovative and exciting new programs, providing a fair and confident leadership style, and displaying an enthusiastic and open personality to a school system that can use an articulate and talented administrator.

EXPERIENCE

Have become known as a creative thinker, effective writer and speaker, and respected administrator with the school system which serves the children of the nation's largest military base worldwide, Ft. Bragg, NC:
PRINCIPAL. The Casey School (2002-present). For a 400-student pre-kindergarten through fourth grade facility, am implementing change in a school which had the same principal for 30 years.

- Provided strong leadership and kept the school operating smoothly in the midst of a fluid situation in which half of the staff will change at the end of the 2002-03 school year due to redistricting and the opening of a new school.
- Quickly earned the respect and trust of community members in an environment where support was strong for change and progress.
- Have excelled in dealing with budget procedures including keeping within government guidelines for average daily members and per pupil cost.

PRINCIPAL. Baker School (1994-02). Developed a number of creative, fun, and interesting programs which helped the school earn a reputation for being "on the cutting edge" with a very real spirit of team work and growth as teachers and staff learned to work together.

- Used a variety of resources and materials to prepare and write programs for staff development activities while focusing on providing staff members with information and the opportunity to earn CEU (continuing education units) credit and to assist them in advancing toward highly original and progressive styles of teaching.
- Played a significant role in developing sources for additional funding by researching and writing grants which resulted in funds for computers, math and science programs, reading programs, and a writing center.
- Provided the vision and leadership which kept a 450-500 student pre-kindergarten through fourth grade school a place where children enjoyed learning while using the most up-to-date aids and facilities possible.
- Was honored by Phi Delta Kappa Professional Education Fraternity for my continuing commitment to excellence in education (January 2002).

PRINCIPAL. Findley School (1991-94). Began the planning and development of long-range goals for curriculum and staff development changes and improvements while refining my abilities in areas ranging from instructional leader, to administrator and manager, to public relations representative in an elementary school which reached its highest level of enrollment of more than 600 students in 1991.

- Refined a different type of skill such as how to be diplomatic yet compassionate while learning to take on the human resource management aspects of school administration and change from the mind set of assistant principal to the senior leadership role.

ASSISTANT PRINCIPAL. Findley School (1989-91). Learned to be a catalyst for change and progress while supervising the kindergarten teachers and custodial staff in a school with approximately 650 students; took on additional responsibilities as a staff development planner, test coordinator, observer/evaluator, and co-administrator.

- Became very adept at finding solutions to problems and heading off potential problems so that they did not escalate during a period of change and reconfiguration (from a first through sixth grade school to a kindergarten through fourth grade facility).
- Led efforts to bring about needed changes in curriculum, professional development, and procedural issues while helping move the school toward an integrated approach which emphasized process-based teaching.

Gained experience as a classroom teacher/program administrator, Panama Canal Zone:
TEACHER. Made and implemented suggestions which resulted in improving the effectiveness of teachers in the pre-kindergarten/kindergarten program which included from 25 to 30 children in each morning and afternoon session; learned how to work with ESL (English as a Second Language) students.

DIRECTOR. After beginning as a teacher for the four-year-old class, was soon promoted to handle the responsibilities of managing the administrative, financial, and operational aspects of educating up to 150 children; learned the importance of providing a varied but integrated program of instruction so that young children could learn and grow.

Highlights of earlier experience: Taught 25 students in a self-contained first grade classroom and prepared lesson plans for subject matter including reading, math, science, health, social studies, art, writing, handwriting, spelling, and physical education.
- Promoted self esteem and encouraged children to relate and work together while learning how to balance personal concern and professionalism.

EDUCATION

Have completed 36 hours in an Ed.D. degree program in Education Administration, South Carolina State University, Orangeburg, SC; in conjunction with this program, attended a Summer Institute at Cornell University, NY.
Master's degree in Education Administration, Campbell University, Buies Creek, NC.
B.S. in Elementary Education, Southern Nazarene University, Bethany, OK.

TRAINING

Continually attend training programs, courses, and seminars to expand my knowledge and learn new skills including the following:

higher-level thinking skills	creative leadership
Junior Great Books leadership	Hands-on Science workshop
technology in NC schools conference	science conference
National Elementary Principal's Conference	multi-age teaching
portfolio development	Apple computer training
NC Effective Teacher training	Teacher Performance Appraisal Training
Performance-Based Assessment	Cooperative Discipline

managing instructional time and student behavior
Harry Wong Conference — supporting new teachers
CAI lab — operating a computer assisted instruction lab

PROGRAMMING EXPERTISE

Applied my creativity and implementational skills in developing a wide range of programs:
Wellness Program — addressed all aspects of physical wellness from nutrition and food preparation, to skin care, to dancing and aerobics — one offshoot was "Heart to Heart Walk with Mrs. Macias" weekly walks and using strider poles for a full-body workout.
Publishing Center — motivated students to write a book and publish it — wrote the grant and used funds from the Officers' Wives Club (OWC) to fund the program.
Reading Is Fundamental (RIF) — received funds which allowed the program to distribute free books three times a year (funds were provided through grants from Hallmark, Nestle's, and other major corporations as well as the OWC).
Running Start (an offshoot of RIF created for first graders) — wrote a grant and received funds from Chrysler Corp.
- Was flown to Washington, DC, to attend a "think-tank" session at the Smithsonian Institute with 11 other Running Start coordinators from across the nation.

Lights, Cameras, Kids Program — started as a summer school project, became an after-school program in which children were involved in writing and producing videos.
PAFA Honor's Banquet — established an annual event to honor children who received Presidential Academic Fitness Awards.
Young Astronauts Program — provided a scholarship to NASA Space Camp for a fourth grader and received a visit from an astronaut because of participation and interest.
For Love of Reading — began the school year with special events such as story tellers or a hot air balloon and contest and ended the year with a recognition program.

PERSONAL

Have often been described as decisive, fair, energetic, and supportive. Have a talent for bringing out the best in others. Use SEMS/400 Procurement Management System on an IBM AS-400 for ordering through the Department of Defense contracting process. Am familiar with Microsoft Word, Excel, Access and QuarkXpress software programs.

TEACHING & EDUCATIONAL ADMINISTRATION

Date

Exact Name of Person
Title or Position
Name of Company
Address (no., street)
Address (city, state, zip)

Secretary in School System

Dear Exact Name of Person: (or Dear Sir or Madam if answering a blind ad.)

I would appreciate an opportunity to talk with you soon about how I could contribute to your organization through my experience in payroll administration and accounts payable administration within the unique environment of a school system.

As you will see from my resume, I have excelled since 1996 in working for the Bladen County School System in Bladenboro. From 1996-03 I administered payroll for 130 employees involved in plant operations and facilities maintenance, and I was also asked to handle a wide variety of other duties because of my excellent computer operations skills and background in purchasing and quality control. Highly proficient in computer operations, I am extremely knowledgeable of software including Microsoft Word, Excel, Powerpoint, Network Electronic Mail, Multi-Mate spreadsheets. A quick learner, I offer a proven ability to rapidly master new programs.

Most recently I was promoted to Energy Accounts Specialist and currently am in charge of authorizing payment of all utility bills for all schools in Bladen County. As part of this job I manage a fuel oil program, coordinate with vendors, and maintain an extensive database for all school locations while cheerfully assisting with other projects as needed.

Before joining the Bladen County School System in 1996, I excelled in a track record of promotion with a Fortune 500 Company, where I was involved in quality control and materials ordering/control.

You would, I am sure, find me in person to be a congenial professional who prides myself on my ability to work well with people at all levels.

I hope you will call or write me soon to suggest a time when we might meet to discuss your current and future needs and how I might serve them. Thank you in advance for you time.

Sincerely yours,

Christina Zwaga

Alternate last paragraph:
I hope you will welcome my call soon to arrange a brief meeting at your convenience to discuss your current and future needs and how I might serve them. Thank you in advance for your time.

CHRISTINA ZWAGA

1110½ Hay Street, Fayetteville, NC 28305   •   preppub@aol.com   •   (910) 483-6611

OBJECTIVE

To contribute to an organization that can use my excellent skills in office administration and computer operations as well as my specialized expertise in payroll administration, accounts payable, purchasing, inventory control and quality control, and customer service.

EDUCATION

Completed 48 credit hours in Business Administration, Fayetteville Technical Community College, and 12 credit hours in Business Administration, Campbell University.
• Excelled in these college courses at night while working full-time in demanding jobs.
Graduated from Seventy-First Senior High School, Fayetteville, NC

TECHNICAL SKILLS

• Offer the ability to expertly operate every kind of office machinery; am a notary public
• Operate word processors including IBM, Zenith, and Wang Mini Computers
• Proficient in using 10-key machine
• Knowledgeable of computerized purchasing, sales, shipping and inventory control
• Extremely knowledgeable of Microsoft Word, Excel, Powerpoint, Network Electronic Mail, Multi-Mate spreadsheets
• Skilled in technical library maintenance
• Expert in the operation of various telephone switchboards

EXPERIENCE

Have excelled in the following track record of advancement with the Bladen County School System, Bladenboro, NC, 1996-present:
ENERGY ACCOUNTS SPECIALIST. (2003-present). Was recently promoted to this job in which I authorize payment of every utility bill for all the schools in Bladen County including gas and electric bills.
• Manage a fuel oil program including reporting, ordering, transfers, and compliance with statutory requirements on Underground Storage Tanks (USTs) including Tier II report forms.
• Monitor the cost of fuel oil and make projections based on current market conditions and past price history.
• Receive and review utility bills for accuracy using data entry techniques; solve problems in the case of questionable bills.
• Maintain telephone equipment database for all school locations; order equipment.
• Review telephone bills for accuracy and process using data entry.
• Maintain utility vendor files and energy reports.
• Maintain safety database to include Employee and Student Accident Records and Safety Training Records.
• Maintain fire drill reports and emergency weather list.
• Cheerfully assist with other duties as needed, including special project research, newsletters, and publications.

PAYROLL ADMINISTRATOR/SECRETARY III. (1996-03). Administered payroll for 130 employees involved in plant operations and facilities maintenance.
• Established and maintained personnel files and set up new employees on payroll; logged all days which employees used as sick leave, annual leave, and no-pay days, and keyed absences into the Kronos payroll system.
• Prepared weekly punch detail reports, month ending reports, end-of-payroll reports, and a payroll schedule.
• Abide by state regulations with regard to Workman's Compensation.
• Oversee the work order system including assigning the job to the proper department, assisting schools with problems, and closing work order when job was complete.
• Produced daily reports for the department foreman.
• Maintained certifications for the State Inspections Department in reference to the operation of all boilers; issued work orders for the inspections and also issued work orders for new boilers, pressure vessels, water tanks, air rec, cast irons, and fire tubes.

PERSONAL

Can provide outstanding letters of recommendation. Am known for my positive attitude and willingness to help other co-workers. Dependable hard worker who produces quality work.

TEACHING & EDUCATIONAL ADMINISTRATION

Date

Exact Name of Person
Title or Position
Name of Company
Address (no., street)
Address (city, state, zip)

Teaching   Dear Exact Name of Person: (or Dear Sir or Madam if answering a blind ad.)

I would appreciate an opportunity to talk with you soon about how I could contribute to your organization through my experience and education as well as through my strong belief in the importance of maintaining and improving the quality of education in our public schools.

As you will see from my resume, I am an educator with a great deal of experience in curriculum development, program coordination, and administration. With a B.A. in English and History, I earned my master's degree in Educational Administration. Having spent approximately 20 years as an educator, I am known as a persuasive and informative speaker who offers outstanding leadership and motivational skills.

By always taking part in any professional development opportunities that come my way, I feel that I am continuing to grow as a professional educator and as a person. As the School Advisory Council Chairman for two years at Ramstein American High School (Ramstein, Germany), I feel that I was effective in keeping the group on task and discussions controlled and productive.

I am at a point in my career where I am ready to step over to the administrative side of the educational process. While staying in the public schools, I feel that I am ready and qualified to move to a position as an associate principal. Because my experience has covered elementary and secondary schools and students ranging from the learning disabled to the talented and gifted, I feel I am capable of success at either the elementary or secondary school level.

I believe I can bring creativity, maturity, talent, and experience which will enrich your school and help make it one where children grow, learn, and prosper.

I hope you will welcome my call soon to arrange a brief meeting at your convenience to discuss your current and future needs and how I might serve them. Thank you in advance for your time.

Sincerely yours,

Edith Horne

Alternate last paragraph:
I hope you will call or write me soon to suggest a time convenient for us to meet and discuss your current and future needs and how I might serve them. Thank you in advance for your time.

EDITH HORNE

1110½ Hay Street, Fayetteville, NC 28305 • preppub@aol.com • (910) 483-6611

OBJECTIVE

To offer my background of dedication to excellence and progress in education to a school system that can use a creative administrator known for outstanding communication, motivational, and leadership abilities.

EDUCATION & CERTIFICATIONS

M.Ed., Educational Administration, University of North Carolina at Charlotte.
B.A., English and History, University of North Carolina at Charlotte.
Hold certifications from the states of NC, NJ, and PA in the following areas:

administration	junior college	academically gifted	reading
world history	social studies	language arts	English

EXPERIENCE

CLASSROOM INSTRUCTOR. Albritton Junior High School, Ft. Bragg, NC (2002-present). Motivate and instruct Advanced Placement (AP) reading classes as well as teaching regular seventh grade reading and social studies classes.

- Contributed leadership to the Cultural Awareness and Young Authors committees.
- Was nominated for membership in Phi Delta Kappa professional education fraternity.
- Selected for my effective communication skills, delivered a presentation on Department of Defense Schools at the Fourth National Conference on Creating the Quality School, sponsored by the University of Oklahoma, Oklahoma City, April 2003.

HIGH SCHOOL TEACHER. Ramstein American High School, Ramstein Air Force Base, Germany (1997-02). As the mentor for several student activities and special programs, provided advice and guidance as well as classroom instruction in subjects including Honors English, world history, contemporary issues, and general English.

- Elected for two terms as School Advisory Council Chairman, earned the principal's respect for keeping meetings productive and discussions open and to the point.
- Coordinated the Young Authors and Sketches literary magazine programs and acted as faculty advisor for the writing club.
- Supervised student teachers from Colorado State and Morehead (KY) State Universities.
- Chosen for my diplomatic manner and ability to relate to others, participated in the administration of Russian and Lithuanian school exchanges.
- Was selected to participate in professional programs including three courses at the Konrad Adenauer Institute, a writing workshop sponsored by the University of California at Berkeley, and staff development programs on teaching and expectations.

LANGUAGE ARTS TEACHER. Charles E. Lewis Middle School, Blackwood, NJ (1993-96). Applied my knowledge while developing special projects for the enrichment of the curricula and as a seventh grade teacher for approximately 120 students each day.

- Revised the language arts curricula in order to address district objectives and standards.
- Developed materials accepted for use by the University of Pennsylvania's Literacy Network.

DEPARTMENT CHAIRPERSON and **EDUCATOR.** Massey Hill Junior High School, Fayetteville, NC (1989-93). Honored as the 1992-93 "Teacher of the Year," supervised and motivated members of the Social Studies and English departments while involved in planning and conducting seventh and eighth grade language arts and social studies classes.

- Designed and conducted in-service writing instruction for the faculty at two area junior high schools.
- Analyzed curricula and created courses which updated faculty effectiveness.
- Established a positive structure to minimize time spent on discipline. Coached school's forensics team.
- Represented the school at social studies conventions and the 1991 NC Writing Project.

Highlights of earlier experience: Refined my motivational, instructional, administrative, and leadership abilities in positions including Learning Disabilities Teacher, Educational Consultant, and Classroom Teacher.

- Worked in a variety of situations with students ranging from the academically gifted, to learning disabled, to those for whom English is a second language.
- Honored as "Favorite Teacher" for three consecutive years, coordinated a school travel program which enriched students by exposing them to European cultures.

PERSONAL

Hold memberships in the Overseas Education Association and Cross Creek Reading Council. A creative and dependable professional, I thrive on motivating others to exceed their expectations. Am very flexible.

TEACHING & EDUCATIONAL ADMINISTRATION

MARGOT WERKHEISER

1110½ Hay Street, Fayetteville, NC 28305 • preppub@aol.com • (910) 483-6611

OBJECTIVE

To offer my biological technical, research, and teaching skills to an organization that can benefit from my strong interest in scientific laboratory technology, my inventory and financial management skills, and my excellent communication and people skills.

EDUCATION & TRAINING

Have completed 30 graduate level credit hours in Biology, Botany, and Biotechnology, University of California at Los Angeles, LA, CA.

Earned an B.A. degree in Biology, University of California at Los Angeles.

Additional course work in computer applications and keyboarding at Los Angeles Technical Community College and Physical Science at Los Angeles State University, CA.

Attended professional development courses and workshops including the following:

40-hour, three graduate credit biotechnology workshops, various college campuses —
PCR and Forensic DNA, 2003
Biotechnology II, 2002
Introduction to Biotechnology, 2001
CA Vegetation, 1999, and Field Investigations of the Geology of CA, 1998
Teaching Advanced Placement Biology for the Secondary Teacher, 1990

Education courses required for CA teaching certification
Selected topics in physical science education

EXPERIENCE

SCIENCE DEPARTMENT CHAIRMAN and **BIOLOGICAL SCIENCES INSTRUCTOR.** The Los Angeles Academy, Los Angeles, CA (1989-03). For this private college preparatory school, held dual roles as an instructor for high school-level biological science courses and administrator of the science department which covered the upper level classes for the seventh through 12th grades.

- Played an important role in the design and planning for building a $1.4 million science wing.
- Accomplished the improvement of a sound science curriculum including development of a new course in ecology and a sequential program of science courses for the seventh through 12th grade level.
- Contributed many other ideas which had a positive impact on the school including policies on absenteeism, athletic eligibility, and discipline.
- Provided inventory control management for lab and scientific equipment including coordinating the use of audio-visual aids.
- Developed and managed the department's annual budget.
- Supervised and evaluated the performance of all members of the science teaching staff.
- Represented the department as liaison with the administration.

LAB RESEARCH TECHNICIAN. Stanford University Medical Center, Stanford, CA (1974). Performed procedures and experiments for a gastroenterologist who was involved in investigating nutrient transport systems in the small intestine.

- Learned research techniques using lab animals: diet management, giving injections, humanely sacrificing, excising and preparing tissue for experimentation, performing nutrient transport experiments, and assaying for results.

LAB RESEARCH TECHNICIAN. Stanford University Medical Center, Stanford, CA (1970-74). Learned and refined basic research skills helping carry out research experiments designed to investigate treatments for gout by and under the direction of the Chief of Medicine.

- Participated in projects in tissue preparation, enzyme purification, and analyzing enzyme pathways using spectrophotometric assay and radioisotope (14C) labeling.
- Carried out experiments, collected data, and prepared data and notes for articles for scientific publications such as the Journal of the American Medical Association (JAMA).
- Worked closely with postdoctoral fellows, assisting them in the development of technical research skills and use of equipment.
- Learned laboratory management which included prioritizing schedules, equipment use, and supplies for postdoctoral fellows.
- Learned value of experimental repeatability, accuracy, and observation objectivity.

Highlights of earlier experience: As a K-3 (kindergarten-third grade) Teacher and Substitute Teacher, gained skills related to lesson plan development, teaching subjects other than my main field of science, and learning to work with children of all socioeconomic levels.

TECHNICAL KNOWLEDGE

Am proficient with the following biological research and teaching skills, techniques, and areas of education with specific areas of knowledge gained as a Lab Research Technician and then applied as a science teacher at the secondary education level:

- **plant and animal microscopy** — wet and dry mount slide preparation, cell differentiation, organelle differentiation, tissue differentiation, and microbiological differentiation

- **microbiology** — slide preparation, sterile techniques, liquid and agar media preparations, liquid and agar growth procedures, and cell lysis procedures

- **biochemistry** — cell fractionation, enzyme extraction, enzyme purification via ultracentrifugation and column chromatography, enzyme processes via spectrophotometric assays, and radioisotope tracing

- **spectrophotometry** — pigment analysis and enzyme processes

- **chromatography** — column and paper

- **balances** — analytical, pan, and digital

- **basic biological lab equipment and procedures**

Gained teaching applications of the following areas in workshops sponsored by the California Biotechnology Center, Palo Altos, CA, and given at various state university campuses by specialists in each specific area from that particular campus:

- **biotechnology** — restriction enzyme digest, transformation, polymerase chain reaction, hybridization, jel electrophoresis, and DNA extraction

COMMUNITY INVOLVEMENT

Have a strong history of involvement in civic and church activities:

The Junior League of Los Angeles (1984-present)
- Collated and tested recipes, published, and marketed *The California Collection* cookbook — $50,000 was raised in two years through sales of this publication.
- Played a major role in raising $30,000 for community development projects as Properties Chairman of the Spring Follies Fair.

The Los Angeles Lutheran Church (1974-present)
- Served on the stewardship committee, the Altar Guild, and Project Good Shepherd.
- Taught Sunday School and was Youth Director for the Episcopal Young Churchmen.

The Los Angeles Academy (2000-02)
- Participated in a capital campaign which raised $1.4 million for construction of a science wing.

PERSONAL

Possess well-developed laboratory, planning, and organizational skills. Offer a strong work ethic and am known for my dedication as well as my persistence in achieving excellence.

TRADE ASSOCIATION EXECUTIVE

Date

TO: Search Committee
FROM: John Mertz

Director   RE: Position of Executive Vice President, National Association of the Self Employed

In response to the urging of someone familiar with your search for an executive vice president for the National Association of the Self Employed, I am sending you a resume which summarizes my background. I offer a unique combination of knowledge, experience, and abilities which I believe would ideally suit the requirements of the National Association of the Self Employed.

Health industry expertise

You will see from my resume that I offer expertise related to health insurance and underwriting. In my current job I have sought out and negotiated contracts with major insurance companies to provide insurance for the organization. On a $1 million budget, I have developed insurance programs which generated $2 million in net income based on $32 million in premiums. These highly regarded programs which I developed have brought 6,000 new members into the organization.

Proven executive ability

I offer proven executive ability. I have earned a reputation as someone who has not only strategic vision and imagination but also the tenacity and persistence to follow through on the "nitty-gritty" details of implementing new projects, programs, and concepts. I know how to delegate, and I know how to "micro manage," and I am skilled at tailoring my management style to particular circumstances while always shouldering full responsibility and accountability for results. My current job has involved the responsibility of recruiting, training, and continuously developing a national sales force of brokers throughout the U.S. which broke with the tradition of passive mail solicitation and led to dramatic growth in sales and profitability. With a strong "bottom-line" orientation, I have streamlined headquarters staff and reduced central office expenses to save at least half a million dollars while continuously supervising the association's five regional offices in the recruitment and training of more than 1,200 insurance agents nationally.

Extension association experience

You will also see from my resume that I am accustomed to "getting things done" within the unique environment of a trade/membership association. I am well known for my ability to attract and retain a cohesive and productive staff, and I am also respected for my exceptional skills in relating to, inspiring, and supporting key volunteer members. A skilled communicator, I have made countless appearances and speeches.

I am aware of the requirements defined by the research committee, and I would enjoy the opportunity to discuss this position further with the Executive Committee. I feel certain I could contribute significantly to the growth and financial health of the National Association of the Self Employed as its Executive Vice President. Thank you for your time and consideration.

JOHN MERTZ

1110½ Hay Street, Fayetteville, NC 28305　•　preppub@aol.com　•　(910) 483-6611

OBJECTIVE

To contribute to the growth and financial health of an organization that needs a savvy, creative executive with expert knowledge of the health insurance/underwriting industry along with a proven ability to innovate, manage, motivate, coordinate, communicate, and troubleshoot within the unique environment of a membership association.

EXPERIENCE

DIRECTOR, MEMBERS' INSURANCE. B'nai B'rith, Washington, DC (1999-present). Have excelled in originating insurance programs for the members of B'nai B'rith: developed highly regarded insurance programs which brought 6,000 new members into the organization while producing millions of dollars in net income.

- Sought out and negotiated contracts with major insurance companies to provide insurance for the organization.

- On a $1 million operating budget, developed insurance programs which generated $2 million in net income based on $32 million in premium.

- Recruited, trained, and continuously developed a national sales force of B'nai B'rith brokers throughout the U.S. which first, arrested declining sales that were the result of passive mail solicitations and second, dramatically boosted sales and profitability.

- Streamlined headquarters staff and reduced central office expenses, resulting in a $500,000 savings; developed annual programs of work and budgets.

- Supervise five regional offices in the recruitment and training of more than 1,200 insurance agents nationally.

- Closely monitor government affairs related to health insurance; maintain excellent relationships with governmental regulatory bodies and state departments of insurance.

- Maintain liaison with association personnel in charge of operations, legislation, education, public relations, and communications as well as with the executive committee.

- Am known for my extraordinary ability to attract, develop, and retain a cohesive and productive staff and for my talent in motivating and inspiring key volunteer leadership.

Other experience:
NATIONAL MEMBERSHIP FIELD DIRECTOR. B'nai B'rith, Washington, DC. Was promoted to this position after excelling as **Membership Director for Mid-western and Western U.S. and Canada**; formulated and implemented national membership programs and campaigns that led to the development of new units in the U.S. and Canada.

VICE PRESIDENT OF MARKETING. SETCO, Inc., Los Angeles, CA. Developed marketing programs for manufacturing and marketing companies owned by conglomerate.

LIFE AND HEALTH INSURANCE BROKER. Universal Insurance Agency, Chicago, IL. Was a property and casualty underwriter as well as a life and health insurance broker.

EDUCATION
&
TRAINING

Hold a Bachelor of Arts (B.A.) degree, Drake University, Des Moines, IA.
Complete yearly 15 hours of continuing education to maintain Life and Health Insurance Broker's License.
Took numerous courses to comply with life and health insurance industry requirements.

PERSONAL

Have given numerous speeches and made hundreds of personal appearances. Am known for my ability to ensure optimum utilization of personnel. Offer a reputation for integrity.

TRANSPORTATION

Date

Exact Name of Person
Title or Position
Name of Company
Address (No., street)
Address (city, state, zip)

**Freight
Coordination**

Dear Exact Name of Person: (or Dear Sir or Madam if answering a blind ad.)

I would appreciate an opportunity to talk with you soon about how I could contribute to your organization through my experience in all aspects of traffic and transportation management. I offer extensive knowledge of LTL, TL, Intermodal, rate negotiations, pool shipments, and cost analysis to determine the most economical method of shipping.

As you will see from my resume, I am currently site freight coordinator for a Fortune 500 company, and I have continuously found new ways to reduce costs and improve efficiency while managing all inbound and outbound shipping. On my own initiative, I have recovered $10,000 in claims annually while saving the company at least 40% of a $10 million LTL budget. In addition to continuous cost cutting, I have installed a new bar code system in the finished goods shipping area and have also installed a new wrapping system.

In previous jobs supervising terminal operations, I have opened up new terminals, closed down existing operations which were unprofitable, and gained hands-on experience in increasing efficiency in every terminal area.

With a reputation as a savvy negotiator, I can provide excellent personal and professional references. I am held in high regard by my current employer.

I hope you will call or write me soon to suggest a time convenient for us to meet and discuss your current and future needs and how I might serve them. Thank you in advance for you time.

Sincerely yours,

Pedro Palacios

Alternate last paragraph:
I hope you will welcome my call soon to arrange a brief meeting at your convenience to discuss your current and future needs and how I might serve them. Thank you in advance for your time.

PEDRO PALACIOS

1110½ Hay Street, Fayetteville, NC 28305 • preppub@aol.com • (910) 483-6611

OBJECTIVE

To contribute to an organization that can use a skilled traffic management professional who offers a proven ability to reduce costs, install new systems, optimize scheduling, negotiate rates, anticipate difficulties, solve problems, and keep customers happy.

EXPERIENCE

SITE FREIGHT COORDINATOR. DuPont Corporation, Wilmington, DE (2003-present). For this Fortune 500 company, have continuously found new ways to cut costs and improve service while managing all inbound transportation as well as outbound shipping totaling in excess of one million dollars in finished goods daily; supervise ten people.

- Saved the company at least 40% of a $10 million LTL budget by resourcefully combining my technical knowledge with my creative cost-cutting skills.
- Recovered $10,000 annually in claims; prepare all cargo claims documents for corporate office and oversee all procedures for proper claims documentation.
- Installed a bar code system in Finished Goods Shipping, and also installed a new wrapping system.
- Reduced overtime by 90% while simultaneously cross-training some employees and improving overall morale.
- Became familiar with Total Quality Processes while analyzing transit times to ensure consistent and timely Just In Time delivery schedules.
- Am a member of the B & D corporate committee for North American rate negotiations; negotiate rates with various carriers on special moves.
- Justify capital appropriation requests for funding special projects; audit all freight bills and process them for payment.
- Prepare all documents for export shipments to Canada; also advise about the shipment of hazardous materials and maintain proper documentation placards and labels.
- Coordinate all site printing of product information and warranty cards.
- Am responsible for site switcher and equipment such as leased trailers.
- Have earned a reputation as a savvy negotiator with an ability to predict future variables that will affect traffic costs.

SUPERVISOR. International Freightways, Inc., Atlanta, GA (2000-02). Supervised up to 12 drivers while managing second-shift operations and controlling inbound and outbound freight at this terminal operation.
- Increased efficiency in every operational area; improved the load factor, reduced dock hours, and ensured more timely deliveries.

INVENTORY SPECIALIST. La-Z-Boy East, Inc., Florence, SC (1998-00). Learned the assembly process of this name-brand furniture manufacturer while managing replenishment of subassemblies for daily production.

Highlights of other experience:
- As Terminal Manager for Spartan Express, opened a new terminal in South Carolina; determined the pricing structure, handled sales, and then managed this new operation which enjoyed rapid growth.
- Gained experience in closing down a terminal determined to be in a poor location.
- As Operations Manager for a break bulk operation, supervised up to 12 people in a dock center while managing the sorting/segregating of shipments from origin to destination.

EDUCATION

Studied business management and liberal arts, Ohio State and LaSalle University.
Completed extensive executive development courses in the field of transportation and traffic management sponsored by University of Toledo, Texas Technical University, and other academic institutions as well as corporate-sponsored courses.

PERSONAL

Can provide outstanding personal and professional references. Will relocate.

TRANSPORTATION

John Bailey
Quality Shipping
4250 Jonestown Road SE
Atlanta, GA 30315

Terminal Management　　　Dear Mr. Bailey:

I would appreciate an opportunity to talk with you soon about how I could benefit Quality Shipping as a Branch Terminal Manager/Account Manager through my strong background in the transportation industry.

Known for my expertise in increasing sales and revenue while reducing costs, you will see by my enclosed resume that I have in-depth experience gained while working for the regional carrier McDonald Transportation. In my 14 years with this company I advanced to hold management roles after beginning in a ground-floor position as a Driver and Freight Handler. I am also a skilled accounts representative and enjoy the challenge of selling transportation services. I have become very adept at selling transportation services based mostly on quality and service rather than on price.

Throughout my career with McDonald Transportation I consistently made changes which resulted in increased sales and revenue while reducing costs and eliminating unnecessary expenses. For instance, in my most recent position as Branch Terminal Manager at the Raleigh, NC, terminal I was credited with bringing about a 35% increase in sales and revenue, a 15% reduction in operating costs, and an increase in on-time rates from 89% to a near-perfect 98%.

Selected to attend corporate training courses in quality management, sales, and front-line supervisory techniques, I was appointed to Quality Improvement Teams beginning in 1998 and was elected as team chairman for 2002.

I am certain that you would find in me a talented manager who communicates effectively with others at all levels and is experienced in making sound decisions under pressure. With an excellent reputation within the transportation industry, I am a flexible and versatile individual who would consider serving your needs in a variety of capacities and functional areas. I can provide very strong references.

I hope you will welcome my call soon to arrange a brief meeting at your convenience to discuss your current and future needs and how I might serve them. Thank you in advance for your time.

Sincerely yours,

William Velasquez

WILLIAM VELASQUEZ

1110½ Hay Street, Fayetteville, NC 28305   •   preppub@aol.com   •   (910) 483-6611

OBJECTIVE   To offer my reputation as a thoroughly knowledgeable professional with special abilities related to terminal operations, sales, quality management, and customer service gained while advancing to increasingly higher managerial levels within the trucking industry.

QUALITY
MANAGEMENT   Appointed to Quality Improvement Teams in Georgia, North Carolina, and South Carolina (1998-03), was elected as chairman in 2002. Believe in total quality results, top to bottom.

EXPERIENCE   *Built a track record of promotion while becoming known for my expertise in increasing sales and reducing operational costs with McDonald Transportation, an interstate trucking company operating predominately in the southeastern U.S.:*
BRANCH TERMINAL MANAGER. Raleigh, NC (2000-03). Continued to find ways to increase revenue and efficiency while managing all aspects of daily terminal operations ranging from staffing and training, to managing a sales territory, to supervising the terminal's account manager.
- Displayed a talent for introducing changes which increased annual sales/revenue 35%.
- Brought about a 15% reduction in operating costs while increasing on-time delivery rates to an almost-perfect 98% rate from the previous 89%.

TERMINAL MANAGER. Greensboro, NC (1998-00). Reduced operating costs 10% over a two-year period while directing total terminal operations including staffing and training employees in every section of the business; supervised two account managers.
- Increased annual sales and revenue 30% each year.

ACCOUNT MANAGER and BRANCH TERMINAL MANAGER. Baxley, GA (1997-98). Wore "two hats" as a combination Account Manager and Branch Terminal Manager; earned rapid promotion because of my success in sales as well as in hiring/supervising 15 people.
- During only nine months in this job, made improvements resulting in a 30% growth in sales and revenue as well as an 18% decrease in operating costs.

SALES REPRESENTATIVE. Miami, FL (1996-97). Refined sales and customer service skills as the account manager for approximately 50% of the customer base for a company which provides sales and service within 80-100 miles of each local terminal.
- Maintained a strong repeat customer base while bringing about a 41% increase in sales,

DISPATCHER/OPERATIONS MANAGER. Orlando, FL (1993-96). Learned to remain in control under pressure and constant deadlines while scheduling deliveries and pick ups and dispatching trucks throughout the area.
- Applied my problem-solving skills by decreasing the number of missed pick ups 70%, thereby increasing customer satisfaction and boosting the bottom line.

SHIPPING SUPERVISOR. Orlando, FL (1991-93). Supervised ten dock workers; established truck routes and ensured that shipments were on time and handled with no errors or damage.
- Improved procedures so that the number of damage claims was greatly reduced while also reorganizing routes so that work loads increased and costs decreased.

DRIVER and FREIGHT HANDLER. Orlando, FL (1989-91). Hired as a dock worker and driver, learned the trucking industry from the ground up; quickly gained the notice of management and began to advance within the company.
- Loaded and unloaded trucks with no damage and made all deliveries on time, error free.

TRAINING   Was selected to attend numerous corporate-sponsored professional development programs and seminars related to these and other areas:

    Front-line supervisory practices   Sales and closing techniques
    Breaking down work processes   Making quality improvements

PERSONAL   Offer an outstanding reputation within the transportation industry and can provide excellent references. Am skilled in competing based on quality and service, not just on price.

PART THREE:

Students and College Graduates

STUDENT

Exact Name of Person
Title or Position
Name of Company
Address (no., street)
Address (city, state, zip)

**Facing College
Graduation, Seeking
Sales Position**

Dear Exact Name of Person: (or Dear Sir or Madam if answering a blind ad.)

Can you use a dynamic and highly motivated young professional who offers a track record of outstanding sales and managerial results based on hard work, enthusiasm, and persistence?

As you will see from the resume I am enclosing, I worked full-time while earning my B.S. degree at East Carolina University. In every job I have held — ranging from warehouse co-manager, to shift supervisor, to painter — I have prided myself on doing every task to the best of my ability.

I feel my highly motivated nature and enthusiastic personality are especially suited to sales situations, and you will also see from my resume that I have excelled in selling both life and health insurance products as well as pest control services. In one job as an Insurance Salesman for Bankers Life & Casualty, I was in charge of a territory including Greenville, NC, and surrounding counties and I rapidly became skilled at prospecting for customers, telemarketing, overcoming objections, and closing the sale. I excelled in that and other jobs while attending college full time.

I offer a mature understanding of what it takes to succeed in sales, and I am aware that discipline, patience, and persistence are critical. I believe I demonstrated those qualities at a young age when I achieved the Eagle rank in Boy Scouts, an accomplishment which few attain.

I hope you will welcome my call soon to determine if there is a time when we could meet in person so that I could show you that I am a highly motivated, ambitious person who could become a valuable part of your team. Thank you in advance for your time.

Sincerely yours,

Jack Wolford

Facing College Graduation, Seeking Sales Position

JACK WOLFORD

1110½ Hay Street, Fayetteville, NC 28305 • preppub@aol.com • (910) 483-6611

OBJECTIVE

I want to contribute to an organization that can use a dynamic and results-oriented young professional who offers proven sales, marketing, and communication skills along with an enthusiastic and highly motivated nature that always persists until a job is done in an excellent manner.

HONORS

- Achieved Eagle Scout rank in 1995; this is the highest award in Boy Scouts and is attained by only 2% of those who join Scouts.
- Elected President, Vocational Industrial Clubs of America (DECA), in high school.
- Elected Vice President, Pi Kappa Phi Fraternity, in college.
- Elected Philanthropy Chairman for Pi Kappa Phi Fraternity.

EDUCATION

B.S. degree, Community Services, East Carolina University, Greenville, NC, 2003.
- Worked full-time in the jobs described below in order to finance my college education.
Graduated from Southview Senior High School in Fayetteville, NC, 1996.

LICENSES

Licensed in NC to sell Life and Health Insurance.
Licensed pest controller in NC.

EXPERIENCE

PAINTER. ABLE Custom Paint, Greenville, NC (2000-02). Worked full time in this job while putting myself through college; was known for my professional attitude and expert workmanship on both industrial and residential sites.
- Frequently provided leadership to inexperienced crews.

SHIFT SUPERVISOR. H.P.R.G., Inc., Greenville, NC (1999-00). While financing my college education, worked up to 15 hours a day at a local pool hall/bar within walking distance from my college campus; handled management responsibilities including supervising waitresses on the shift, overseeing the serving of alcohol within strict legal guidelines, and accounting for all money made on my shift.

SALES REPRESENTATIVE. Orkin Pest Control, Fayetteville, NC (1999). After obtaining my pest control license, excelled in selling pest control services based on the professional inspections I conducted.
- Gained experience in selling a service and in communicating the technical details of pesticides and chemicals in language which the general public could understand.
- Rapidly became one of the company's most productive sales representatives.
- Demonstrated my ability to step into an industry with which I was unfamiliar and quickly transform myself into a valuable employee.

INSURANCE SALESMAN. Bankers Life & Casualty Company, Fayetteville, NC (1997-98). After studying for and obtaining my Life and Health Insurance License, quickly became one of the company's top sales performers.
- Was in charge of a territory including Greenville, NC, and surrounding counties.
- Learned valuable techniques in selling financial services and in explaining abstract concepts to people.
- Refined my skills in prospecting for customers, telemarketing, overcoming objections and closing the sale as well as in servicing customers.
- Demonstrated my ability to handle rejection and displayed the discipline, patience, and persistence that is critical for success in sales.

CO-MANAGER, WAREHOUSE. American Carpets, Fayetteville, NC (1995-97). Managed forklift operators and other personnel in this busy warehouse, and was involved in every job related to smooth warehouse operation.

Other experience: For an automobile dealership and a carwash, detailed cars in high school.
Have volunteered my time to such organizations as the Greenville Community Shelter, The Harbors Outpatient Treatment Facility, and the Boys and Girls Club.
- Completed college internship at Walter B. Jones Drug and Alcohol Abuse Treatment Center.

PERSONAL

Excel at dealing with people on the telephone and in person. Am skilled at building rapport with people of all backgrounds. Believe that my enthusiastic nature is a valuable asset in sales situations.

STUDENT

Exact Name of Person
Title or Position
Name of Company
Address (no., street)
Address (city, state, zip)

**Seeking First Job
After College**

Dear Exact Name of Person: (or Dear Sir or Madam if answering a blind ad.)

I would appreciate an opportunity to talk with you soon about how I could contribute to your organization through my proven abilities related to customer service, sales, management, and finance.

In the process of completing my B.S. degree in Economics with concentrations in Banking and Finance, I worked during the summers and Christmas seasons and held part-time jobs throughout the school year. While juggling those part-time jobs with a rigorous academic curriculum, I also found time to become a respected campus leader and was elected Treasurer of my residence hall in my junior year and President in my senior year. Although I am just 21 years old, I have been told often that I am "mature beyond my years." I am known for my responsible and hard-working nature.

Last summer as an Assistant to a Financial Analyst with Merrill Lynch, I gained exposure to the operations of the stock market and acquired hands-on experience in working with customers of various financial services and financial instruments. I obtained my current job as Customer Service Representative with Blockbuster Video because the company created a position for me in Fayetteville when I moved from Burlington, where I had become a valued employee and was a major contributor to achieving the fourth highest Christmas sales volume of all stores in the chain. I have been encouraged by both Merrill Lynch and Blockbuster to seek employment there after college graduation, and I feel certain I could become a valued part of your organization within a short period of time, too.

You would find me in person to be an outgoing individual who prides myself on my ability to remain poised in all customer service situations. I can provide outstanding personal and professional references, and I would cheerfully relocate and travel extensively according to your needs.

I hope you will call or write me soon to suggest a time convenient for us to meet and discuss your current and future needs and how I might serve them. Thank you in advance for you time.

Sincerely yours,

Daryl Urbanowicz

Alternate last paragraph:
I hope you will welcome my call soon to arrange a brief meeting at your convenience to discuss your current and future needs and how I might serve them. Thank you in advance for your time.

Seeking First Job After College

DARYL URBANOWICZ

1110½ Hay Street, Fayetteville, NC 28305   •   preppub@aol.com   •   (910) 483-6611

OBJECTIVE

To contribute to an organization that can use a hard-working young professional who offers proven leadership ability and management potential along with a congenial personality, outstanding communication skills, and an ability to relate well to anyone.

EDUCATION

Bachelor of Science (B.S.) degree with a major in **Economics** and concentrations in **Banking** and **Finance**, Fayetteville State University (a campus of the University of North Carolina), Fayetteville, NC, 2003.
- Worked part-time during the school year as well as every summer and Christmas season in order to finance my education; became a highly valued employee of every organization in which I worked and can provide outstanding references from all of them.
- Was a popular and respected campus leader; was elected **President** of my residence hall, Bryant Hall, in my senior year and **Treasurer** of Bryant Hall in my junior year.
- Was an active member of the Economics/Finance Club and the Illusions Modeling Club.

COMPUTERS

Familiar with Microsoft Word and Excel; knowledgeable of PageMaker.
- Offer an ability to rapidly master new software and operating systems.

EXPERIENCE

CUSTOMER SERVICE REPRESENTATIVE. Blockbuster Video, Burlington and Fayetteville, NC (April 2001-present). Worked in the Burlington Blockbuster Store part-time while going to college and was commended for playing a key role in helping the Burlington store achieve the fourth highest sales volume in the chain during the 2001 Christmas season; when I transferred to FSU to complete my degree in economics, Blockbuster Video persuaded me to stay with the company and found a similar spot for me in Fayetteville.
- Am responsible for handling thousands of dollars daily; handle transactions utilizing computer-assisted cash registers.
- Train new personnel hired by the company.
- Earned a reputation as a polite and gracious individual while assisting dozens of people daily in video selection.
- Have been told I have a bright future in management with Blockbuster Corporation; have been encouraged to enter the company's management trainee program after college.

RESIDENCE MANAGER. Bryant Hall at Fayetteville State University, Fayetteville, NC (2002-present). In a part-time job simultaneous with the one above, work closely with the dorm director to ensure the efficient administration of this residence hall housing 400 students.
- Supervise the conduct and activities of students living the dorm, and pride myself on setting an example for them in terms of my own morals and actions.
- Solved a wide range of maintenance and administrative problems while also counseling students with financial matters and personal problems ranging from depression and loneliness to poor academic performance and insufficient motivation.
- Acquired experience in mentoring others, most of whom were older than I am.

CREDIT ANALYST. Vanguard Cellular Systems, Greensboro, NC (Christmas 2002). At this cellular phone company, determined credit ratings for prospective customers and made decisions about whether or not deposits were required before cellular lines were established.

ASSISTANT TO FINANCIAL ANALYST. Merrill Lynch, Fayetteville, NC (Summer 2002). Was the "right arm" of a financial analyst with this worldwide investment company; prepared documents designed to persuade potential clients to transact business with Merrill Lynch, and also processed and filed accounts of current customers.
- Gained insight into how selling and customer service occur within a brokerage firm.
- Scored very high on a mock test administered by my supervisor to test my knowledge of stock market issues and facts.
- Was commended for my hard work and financial aptitude, and was encouraged to seek employment with Merrill Lynch upon college graduation.

PERSONAL

Am skilled at remaining calm and courteous in all customer service situations. Can provide outstanding personal/professional references. Will relocate according to employer need.

STUDENT

Date

Exact Name of Person
Title or Position
Name of Company
Address (no., street)
Address (city, state, zip)

Seeking Job in Arts, Museum, or Cultural Organization

Dear Exact Name of Person: (or Dear Sir or Madam if answering a blind ad.)

I would appreciate an opportunity to talk with you soon about how I could contribute to your organization through my specialized background in and enthusiasm for art education as well as my strong public relations and communication skills.

As you will see from my enclosed resume, I earned my B.F.A. (Bachelor of Fine Arts) degree from the Rochester Institute of Technology, Rochester, NY, with a concentration in photography and extensive coursework in gallery management. I am a highly competent and creative photographer. While earning my college degree, I excelled in jobs which helped me acquire experience in sales and operations management, and in one position I played a key role in organizing and implementing an arts education program which is considered a "model" for other communities.

Among my major personal strengths are my enthusiasm, creativity in both practical problem solving and in the artistic sense, as well as my ability to communicate verbally and in writing with people of all ages, social backgrounds, educational levels, and cultures or ethnic groups.

I hope you will welcome my call soon to arrange a brief meeting at your convenience to discuss your current and future needs and how I might serve them. I can provide outstanding personal and professional references which will attest to my reputation as a highly motivated self starter with boundless energy and enthusiasm. Thank you in advance for your time.

Sincerely yours,

Zelda Wilburn

Alternate last paragraph:
I hope you will call or write me soon to suggest a time convenient for us to meet and discuss your current and future needs and how I might serve them. Thank you in advance for your time.

Seeking Job in Arts, Museum, or Cultural Organization

ZELDA WILBURN

1110½ Hay Street, Fayetteville, NC 28305   •   preppub@aol.com   •   (910) 483-6611

OBJECTIVE

To offer my reputation as a dynamic and creative young professional to an organization that can benefit from my strong interest in promoting the arts throughout the community, my education in fine arts with an emphasis on photography, and my problem-solving skills.

EDUCATION

Bachelor of Fine Arts (B.F.A.) degree in Photography, Rochester Institute of Technology (RIT), Rochester, NY, 1994.
- Excelled in specialized course work including the following:

fine art photography	applied photography	photomedia survey	contemporary art
gallery management	history of photography	art in civilization	art history

SPECIAL SKILLS

Offer experience with equipment such as:
Cameras: 35 mm, Bronica medium format, and 4 X 5 Calumet and Cambo
Other equipment: B & W enlargers and Bessler color enlargers; Broncolor, White Lightning, and Lowell Tungston lighting equipment; Copal ML2000, Saunders, and Omega enlargers; Copal MSL printer; Copal CFP6550 processor
Computer skills include familiarity with the following:

Mac Write	*Microsoft Word*	*Excel*	*Aldus Pagemaker*

EXPERIENCE

Have earned a reputation as a very creative thinker, fast learner, and skilled communicator in often simultaneous jobs, internships, and volunteer positions requiring time management skills and dedication to reaching personal and professional goals.

PHOTO LAB TECHNICIAN. Photo Center, Rochester, NY (2003-present). Built on my strong educational background in photography and gained practical experience in the technical aspects of commercial photography as well as the day-to-day business side.
- Recognized as a mature and dependable individual, was selected to relieve the manager of certain daily responsibilities such as opening and closing the store.
- Assisted in activities ranging from processing film, to copying film and printing enlargements, to running the cash register, to customer service, to maintaining equipment.

ART EDUCATION PROGRAM VOLUNTEER. The Rochester Museum of Art, Rochester, NY (2003-present). Assist in a project partially sponsored by the governor's early childhood initiative Smart Start: 52 trunks will be filled with resource materials, artifacts, and literature and used as aids for teachers and parents.

SALES REPRESENTATIVE. Waldenbooks, Rochester, NY (2002). Learned about the process of ordering, displaying, and selling books and about the operation of a large retail bookseller while contributing to sales success through my personal dedication to providing answers and solutions while seeing customers were satisfied. Applied my creative ideas to develop interesting and arresting displays.

COMMUNITY ARTS PROGRAM INTERN. Art in Action for Kids, Rochester, NY (2002). Cited by the director for "quickly grasping the complexities" of an arts in education program, contributed ideas which helped expand the program and make it a success while learning how non-profit organizations are structured.
- Was exposed to all aspects of this program which links more than 130 performing, visual, and literary artists with schools and which in 2002, presented more than 3,300 workshops, performances, and artists in residence programs in 250 schools.
- Provided new artists with information on the program's history, goals, and procedures and then maintained files on each artist after they began participating.
- Used my photography skills to document various Young Audiences events.
- Volunteered as a Gallery Assistant for a visual studies workshop: gained experience in grant writing, preparing press releases, and assisting in curating exhibitions.

PHOTOGRAPHIC EQUIPMENT CLERK. RIT School of Printing, Art, and Sciences, Rochester, NY (2001-02). Increased my knowledge of the technical aspects of photography while issuing equipment to students, providing technical information, giving practical advice, and monitoring darkrooms.
- Was known for my patient attitude and willingness to help others.

PERSONAL

Feel very strongly that one of my purposes in life is to expose the joy of art and creativity to as much of the community as possible. Am very empathetic and able to communicate with people of all ages, walks of life, and cultural/ethnic backgrounds.

STUDENT

Date

Exact Name of Person
Title or Position
Name of Company
Address (no., street)
Address (city, state, zip)

Seeking Management Position After College Graduation

Dear Exact Name of Person: (or Dear Sir or Madam if answering a blind ad.)

I would appreciate an opportunity to talk with you soon about how I could contribute to your organization through my background in sales and management as well as through the outstanding planning, organizational, communication, and problem-solving skills that have made me very valuable to my current employer.

As you will see from my resume, I have excelled for the last seven years in a "track record" of promotion within the K-Mart Corporation, where I began working at the age of 19. While excelling in my full-time job, I simultaneously obtained my B.S. degree in Business Administration and also found time to donate my time to charities including the Special Olympics. In May 2003, I was promoted to manage the electronics department at one of K-Mart's largest stores, and I am being groomed for entry into the company's formal Management Training Program after completing six months as a department manager.

Although I respect the K-Mart Corporation greatly and enjoy my challenging management responsibilities, I am writing to your organization because I am attracted to your company's fine reputation and respected product line, and I feel I could make valuable contributions to your bottom line through my strong sales and management skills. I would enjoy an opportunity to meet with you to explore the possibility to putting my experience and talents to work for your company. I can provide outstanding personal and professional references; I am single and will travel and relocate according to your needs.

I hope you will welcome my call soon to arrange a brief meeting at your convenience to discuss your current and future needs and how I might serve them. Thank you in advance for your time.

Sincerely yours,

Stephen Warnock

Alternate last paragraph:
I hope you will call or write me soon to suggest a time convenient for us to meet and discuss your current and future needs and how I might serve them. Thank you in advance for your time.

Seeking Management Position After College Graduation

STEPHEN WARNOCK

1110½ Hay Street, Fayetteville, NC 28305 • preppub@aol.com • (910) 483-6611

OBJECTIVE

To contribute to the bottom line of an organization that can use a hard-working and resourceful young manager who offers proven abilities in sales, personnel supervision, and operations management and who also offers excellent planning, organizational, communication, and problem-solving skills.

EDUCATION

B.S. degree in Business Administration, the University of North Carolina at Chapel Hill, NC, May, 2003.
- Completed this degree while excelling in my full-time job in retailing.
- A member of Air Force ROTC, received the prestigious ROTC Award of Merit for leadership potential and academic excellence; was appointed to several leadership positions which involved managing up to 40 people, and completed the six-week Officer Training program.

EXPERIENCE

Began with K-Mart when I was 19 years old, and have been promoted into increasingly responsible positions; am being groomed for entry into the formal Management Training Program after I complete six months as a department manager.
- Have been appointed to serve on key corporate committees including the Promotional Committee, Hiring Committee, Safety Team, and Support Team (a support team is authorized to make decisions).

DEPARTMENT MANAGER, ELECTRONICS. K-Mart in Chapel Hill (2003-present). Was promoted to this position in May and am responsible for training, motivating, scheduling, and supervising eight employees.
- Work with dozens of vendors to negotiate terms of trade, select merchandise, develop marketing plans, and determine pricing policy.
- Develop special promotions to create consumer demand for electronics; implement modular set-ups.
- Am continuously in the process of strategic planning; plan for seasonal events and set/order special features.
- Improved the appearance of the department by organizing the risers, flagging merchandise, and assuring that every item is properly labeled.
- Have utilized my extensive computer knowledge to develop a more informed staff and to boost sales of computers and computer accessories.
- Am respected for my excellent problem-solving and decision-making skills.

SALES CLERK, ELECTRONICS. K-Mart on Second Street (2001-03). Used my computer knowledge to boost sales while stocking counters, setting features, operating the cash register, ordering merchandise, and maintaining a perpetual inventory system.
- On my own initiative, developed several new measures that established better security and which reduced theft and pilferage.
- Became known for my exceptionally strong customer service skills.

SALES CLERK, LAWN & GARDEN CENTER AND PET CENTER. K-Mart on Second Street (2000-01). While providing excellent customer service, discovered ways of preventing loss from plants dying and from exterior theft; set up modulars, ordered regular and seasonal merchandise.

SALES CLERK, HARDWARE. K-Mart on Second Street (1997-00). Handled all ordering for the paint and hardware departments.

STOCKER/SALES CLERK, HOUSEWARES DEPARTMENT. K-Mart on Morton Avenue (1996-97). Learned how to order merchandise and implement price changes and also learned how to correctly merchandise a retail department for maximum sales; provided excellent customer service while keeping the department at a stock level of 98% or higher.

VOLUNTEER WORK

Even while excelling in my full-time job and simultaneously earning my college degree, volunteered my time to worthy projects:
- *Special Olympics:* Prepared children for events; monitored the events.
- *Public Television fund raiser:* Worked telephones in Plattsburgh, NY.
- *ROTC projects:* Sponsored a needy family at Christmas, held Easter egg hunt for preschoolers, and collected canned goods for the poor.

COMPUTERS

Knowledge of Microsoft Word, Excel, Powerpoint, and dBase.

PERSONAL

Can provide outstanding personal and professional references. Will relocate. Am known for my ability to get along well with anyone.

STUDENT

Exact Name of Person
Title or Position
Name of Company
Address (no., street)
Address (city, state, zip)

Seeking First Job in Biology Field

Dear Exact Name of Person: (or Dear Sir or Madam if answering a blind ad.)

I would appreciate an opportunity to talk with you soon about how I could contribute to your organization through my education in biology and experience in small business management.

As you will see from my enclosed resume, I will receive my bachelor's degree in Biology from The University of North Carolina at Chapel Hill (UNC-CH) in December. I have completed more than 300 hours as a Lab Technician in biology, chemistry, and organic chemistry labs while in college at UNC-CH and earlier while studying Organic Chemistry at Campbell University.

Through my experience in helping build a family-owned business to increased profitability, I have gained valuable exposure to bookkeeping and finance, customer service, maintenance and groundskeeping, and public relations. During the past eight years, beginning while I was still in high school and part-time throughout my college years, I have been involved in making decisions and advanced with the business as profits increased at a 20% growth over the last five years.

I am a fast learner with knowledge of several languages. Through my adaptability, friendly personality, and initiative I have always been able to quickly earn the respect and admiration of people from employees, to peers, to members of the public.

I hope you will welcome my call soon to arrange a brief meeting at your convenience to discuss your current and future needs and how I might serve them. Thank you in advance for your time.

Sincerely yours,

Boyd Strickland

Alternate last paragraph:
I hope you will call or write me soon to suggest a time convenient for us to meet and discuss your current and future needs and how I might serve them. Thank you in advance for your time.

BOYD STRICKLAND

1110½ Hay Street, Fayetteville, NC 28305   •   preppub@aol.com   •   (910) 483-6611

OBJECTIVE
To contribute to an organization through my education in biology, my experience in small business management, as well as my exposure to public relations, customer service, and financial/accounting functions.

EDUCATION
Bachelor's degree in Biology, The University of North Carolina at Chapel Hill (UNC-CH), December 2003. Studied Organic Chemistry, Campbell University, Buies Creek, NC.

TRAINING
Completed more than 100 hours as a Lab Technician in university laboratory settings such as:
    chemistry lab and biology lab — UNC-CH
    organic chemistry lab — Campbell University

EXPERIENCE
Gained experience in all phases of small business operations and made important contributions to the growth of a family-owned motel, the Traveler's Inn, Fayetteville, NC, in this track record of advancement:
MANAGER. (2000-present). Refined my managerial skills and learned to oversee the work of others while becoming familiar with the financial aspects of taking care of the company's bookkeeping activities.

- Quickly learned the details of handling financial activities and prepared the daily figures for the accountants and wrote checks to pay various operating expenses.
- Was praised for my decision-making skills and ability to develop ideas which led to increased profitability and smoother daily operations.
- Made suggestions which helped ease the transition to a new name after the motel had operated as the Florida Motor Inn for several years.
- Refined my interpersonal communication skills dealing with a wide range of customers and employees.
- Have been recognized as a key figure in the motel's record of annual increases in income — over the past five years the business has seen a 20% increase.

DESK CLERK and **REPAIRMAN.** (1998-00). Advanced to take on a more public and active role in day-to-day operations as a front-desk clerk responsible for providing helpful and courteous service to customers and handling large sums of money.

- Maintained the swimming pool which included seeing that the proper chemical balances were reached and that the pool was clean and safe to use.
- Displayed my versatility by doing painting, roofing, and minor electrical repairs on air conditioning systems and TVs which resulted in extending the usefulness of appliances and reduced the need for outside repairs.

MAINTENANCE WORKER/GROUNDSKEEPER. (1996-98). While still in high school, began helping with building maintenance, minor repairs, and lawn maintenance.

Highlights of other experience: As a **Patient Care Volunteer** at the VA Hospital, Fayetteville, NC (2002), helped nursing staff in emergency room care such as transporting patients and assisting in preliminary check-ups.

- Learned how to operate vital computer systems and hook up equipment such as heart monitors and blood sugar checking devices as well as preparing records.

COMPUTERS
Am proficient in using Microsoft Word and Excel for word processing and recordkeeping.

LANGUAGES
As a native of India who came to the U.S. as a young teenager, can speak, read, and write in English, Hindu, and the Gujarati dialect. Also have basic knowledge of French.

HONORS
As a high school student, was named to Who's Who Among High School Students, graduated in the top 5% of my class with a 3.8 GPA, and earned Algebra Excellence Awards.

PERSONAL
Lived in three countries and attended 15 schools while growing up: always adapted to new cultures and ways of life and earned the respect of those around me.

STUDENT

Exact Name of Person
Title or Position
Name of Company
Address (no., street)
Address (city, state, zip)

Seeking to Enter Law Enforcement/Criminal Justice Field

Dear Exact Name of Person: (or Dear Sir or Madam if answering a blind ad.)

With the enclosed resume, I am formally expressing my desire to work in your organization, and I can assure you that I offer a solid commitment to the law enforcement and criminal justice field.

You will see from my resume that I excelled as a Chemical Specialist while serving my country in the U.S. Army from 1997-00. While acquiring expertise in the handling, storage, and disposal of toxic and hazardous substances, I was promoted ahead of my peers and selected to train other young people. It was during my time in the military that I decided to earn my degree in criminal justice and dedicate myself to a career in law enforcement. I believe my self control and calm temperament are well suited to police work.

After my honorable discharge in 2000, I enrolled at Fayetteville State University and then completed my B.S. degree in Criminal Justice in only three years instead of the usual four years. I give much credit for my academic success to the disciplined work habits I learned while in military service.

Most recently I have excelled as a Police Officer Intern with the Fayetteville Police Department, and during that internship I became skilled in resolving domestic/personal disputes, conducting surveillance, handling auto accidents, retrieving stolen goods, writing up police documentation, and detecting illegal activities related to drugs, shoplifting, and other areas. Obviously this brief experience in law enforcement does not make me an "expert" in any area, but I hope you will conclude from my military and academic track record that I am committed to becoming an outstanding law enforcement professional.

Please be assured that I can provide outstanding personal and professional references. I can also assure you that you would find me in person to be an enthusiastic and dedicated young person who prides myself on being the best and doing the best at all times.

I hope you will welcome my call soon to arrange a brief meeting at your convenience to discuss your current and future needs and how I might serve them. Thank you in advance for your time.

Sincerely yours,

Howard Isaacs

Alternate last paragraph:
I hope you will call or write me soon to suggest a time convenient for us to meet and discuss your current and future needs and how I might best serve them. Thank you in advance for your time.

Seeking to Enter Law Enforcement/Criminal Justice Field

HOWARD ISAACS

1110½ Hay Street, Fayetteville, NC 28305   •   preppub@aol.com   •   (910) 483-6611

OBJECTIVE

I want to work for an organization that can use a disciplined, hard-working, and resourceful young professional who offers skills related to law enforcement and the criminal justice field along with planning, management, and communication abilities transferable to any field.

EDUCATION

Earned my Bachelor of Science (B.S.) degree in Criminal Justice, Fayetteville State University (a campus of the University of North Carolina), NC, 2003.
- Completed this rigorous degree program in only three years by applying my hard-working nature as well as the disciplined habits I learned in military service.
- In the computer lab, gained familiarity with Microsoft Word, Excel and dBase.

As a military professional, completed basic training; then excelled in the Army's Chemical School studying chemical warfare and decontamination; also completed training as a Drug and Alcohol Abuse Counselor.

EXPERIENCE

POLICE OFFICER INTERN. Fayetteville Police Department, Fayetteville, NC (July 2003-August 2003). Gained experience in many aspects of police work in this internship completed after receiving my B.S. degree; was commended for demonstrating excellent judgment and exhibiting a patient approach to public relations and problem solving while working in hostile and often dangerous situations.

- *Police documentation*: Wrote citations while handling the normal duties of a police officer; learned to complete police reports and other documentation.
- *Personnel protection/transport*: Transported mental patients to and from hospitals.
- *Domestic disputes*: Refined my skills in handling domestic/family problems.
- *Stolen goods*: Retrieved stolen vehicles and coordinated their disposition.
- *Auto accidents*: Learned how to handle all aspects of auto accidents from arranging for medical help to writing up all the documentation required at accident scenes.
- *Illegal drugs*: Became knowledgeable of procedures used to detect the sale and use of illegal drugs and to apprehend suspects.
- *Property protection*: Became skilled in dealing with shoplifters and trespassers.
- *Surveillance*: Learned police surveillance techniques; attended Community Watch meetings.

ADMINISTRATIVE ASSISTANT. V.A. Hospital, Fayetteville, NC (July 2002-August 2002). While excelling in this work-study job to finance my college degree, became skilled in completing medical forms and paperwork particular to the medical field.
- Scheduled students for work study interviews and other administrative duties.
- Answered telephones in a personnel placement operation.

ALCOHOL/DRUG ABUSE COUNSELOR. V.A. Hospital, Fayetteville, NC (May 2001-January 2002). Was cited for my compassionate personality and kind nature while dealing with people experiencing multiple personal problems; screened and counseled veterans abusing alcohol and drugs and determined appropriate treatment remedies.

SALES REPRESENTATIVE. Office Max, Fayetteville, NC (June 2001-November 2001). Learned how to order and control inventory while buying/selling furniture from companies in Raleigh, Charlotte, Durham, Cary, and other cities in the region.

CHEMICAL SPECIALIST. U.S. Army, Ft. Bragg, NC, and Ft. McClellan, AL (January 1997-April 2000). Gained expertise in the handling and disposal of toxic and hazardous substances while participating in numerous field exercises and projects in the chemical field.
- Was promoted ahead of my peers, and was selected to instruct others about chemical warfare and about decontaminating vehicles; prepared lesson plans and delivered numerous classroom presentations/demonstrations.
- Became certified as a **Chemical Operations Specialist**.

PERSONAL

Am an energetic individual who has a positive outlook. Remain calm in stressful situations.

STUDENT

Exact Name of Person
Title or Position
Name of Company
Address (no., street)
Address (city, state, zip)

With Criminal Justice Degree

Dear Exact Name of Person: (or Dear Sir or Madam if answering a blind ad.)

I would appreciate an opportunity to talk with you soon about how I could contribute to your organization through my degree in Criminal Justice and strong interest in the fields of law enforcement and corrections.

I am a very mature and responsible young professional with a reputation for being articulate, hard-working, and good with people. A recent graduate from Fayetteville State University, Fayetteville, NC, with a B.S. degree in Criminal Justice, I completed specialized course work which included law enforcement, criminal law, community-based corrections, and the legal aspects of the criminal justice system. Other classes in sociology, social problems, abnormal psychology, statistics, and computer science gave me a well-rounded base of knowledge. The degree program also gave me an opportunity to participate in two internships where I observed members of the Fayetteville Police Department on duty and which gave me a practical insight into the day-to-day operations of a metropolitan police department.

As you will see from the work experience described on my resume, I am no stranger to hard work and have developed a reputation for my dedication to success as well as my skills. I am a very enthusiastic, creative, and articulate individual. I have successfully adapted to jobs which required customer service and sales abilities, attention to detail, and office operations and data processing skills as well as the ability to work in a warehouse loading trucks, tallying inventories, and operating a forklift.

I believe that through my enthusiasm, motivational abilities, empathy, and compassion for others I can make valuable contributions to an organization that seeks a professional with these qualities.

I hope you will welcome my call soon to arrange a brief meeting at your convenience to discuss your current and future needs and how I might serve them. Thank you in advance for your time.

Sincerely yours,

Philip D'Alessandro

Alternate last paragraph:
I hope you will call or write me soon to suggest a time convenient for us to meet and discuss your current and future needs and how I might serve them. Thank you in advance for your time.

PHILIP D'ALESSANDRO

1110½ Hay Street, Fayetteville, NC 28305   •   preppub@aol.com   •   (910) 483-6611

OBJECTIVE

To offer my strong interest in the field of law enforcement and my education in criminal justice to an organization that can use a mature young professional who offers strong computer, sales, and communication abilities.

EDUCATION

B.S. degree in Criminal Justice, Fayetteville State University, Fayetteville, NC, 2003.
- Completed specialized course work including the following:

principles of sociology	crime and delinquency	law enforcement
contemporary social problems	the court system	criminal law
civil rights and the constitution	abnormal psychology	juvenile justice
legal aspects of the criminal justice system		community-based corrections

Attended Pembroke State University, Pembroke, NC.

INTERNSHIPS

Completed two 40-hour Criminal Justice Internships with the Fayetteville Police Department, Fayetteville, NC, summer and fall, 2002.
- Was exposed to the day-to-day functions of the department and given an opportunity to ride in a patrol car while observing police officers on duty.

EXPERIENCE

SALES ASSOCIATE. Sam's Club, Fayetteville, NC (2003-present). Quickly earned promotion from Stocker to assist customers in the hard goods department which includes computers, electronics, sporting goods, pet supplies, and tools.

- Learned where a wide range of merchandise was located and became skilled in answering consumers' questions and helping them find what they needed.
- Provided pleasant, helpful telephone service to customers calling for information.
- As a Stocker, learned to use the computer to prepare price signs for merchandise and made sure grocery items were neatly and correctly stocked and properly priced.

Refined my time management skills while gaining practical work experience and building a reputation as a detail-oriented and hard-working young professional in these jobs while also attending college full time:
WAREHOUSE WORKER. Nordic Warehouse, Inc., Benson, NC (2002). Gained experience in operating material-handling equipment including forklifts and power jacks as well as in activities including loading trucks, preparing items for cold storage, separating items into proper categories, and cleaning a warehouse.
- Used my attention to detail while taking careful and accurate tallies of items to be exported and items that had been imported.

ADMINISTRATIVE ASSISTANT. 82nd Airborne Division Association, Inc., Fayetteville, NC (2001-02). Provided this professional association of approximately 23,500 active members throughout the world, with secretarial support which included answering phone calls and giving information about activities.
- Built up my familiarity with using Microsoft Word for wordprocessing various documents.
- Was very proud and pleasantly surprised at receiving the President's Award given at a national convention in honor of my many hours of service and dedication.

SURVEYOR. U.S. Department of Agriculture, Fayetteville, NC (summer 2000). Learned to work independently while being responsible for maintaining and operating a government vehicle and using my powers of observation and aerial maps to help locate fields of crops and inspect them for witchweed which is a parasite that consumes crops.

COMPUTER KNOWLEDGE

Offer experience in using Microsoft Word, Excel, Access, PageMaker and dBase.
Am familiar with copy machines, electronic calculators, and 10-key adding machines.

LANGUAGE

Speak and read Spanish fluently; have a fair grasp of written Spanish.

PERSONAL

Am very enthusiastic, energetic, and creative. Truly like people and enjoy meeting and getting to know and help others. Offer strong problem-solving skills and a drive to succeed.

STUDENT: Seeking First Job in Criminal Justice Field

ANTHONY OTTINGER

1110½ Hay Street, Fayetteville, NC 28305   •   preppub@aol.com   •   (910) 483-6611

OBJECTIVE

I want to contribute my problem-solving and decision-making skills to an organization that can use a creative, well-organized professional with excellent written and oral communication skills.

EDUCATION

Bachelor of Science in Criminal Justice, Fayetteville State University (a campus of the University of North Carolina), Fayetteville, NC, May 2003.
Have excelled in numerous seminars and courses related to these and other areas:
social problems in criminal justice
mediation and arbitration as problem-solving alternatives

EXPERIENCE

INTERN, DISTRICT COURT JUDGES' OFFICE. Fayetteville, NC (2003). As part of my criminal justice curriculum, was selected for a prestigious internship with the District Court Judges' Office.

- Observed nearly every type of courtroom proceeding and gained valuable insight into courtroom procedures.
- Made the acquaintance of many people within the legal system including judges, lawyers, legal assistants, and others.
- Developed an understanding of how judges arrive at their decisions and observed how they manage the courtroom, interact with lawyers, and instruct juries.

INTERN, PROBATION & PAROLE OFFICE. Fayetteville, NC (2003-present). Acted as the "right arm" and "shadow" of a very skilled parole officer who spent extensive time teaching me the nuts and bolts of probation and parole.

- Spent some time with several people on probation and parole, and earned the respect of senior probation/parole officers for my listening and counseling skills; demonstrated my ability to interact with probationers and parolees in a professional manner.
- Became knowledgeable about the paperwork and documentation which is required of probation and parole officers; assisted in completing paperwork.
- Coordinated with other law enforcement agencies about particular cases.
- Made visits to court and also conducted home visits.
- Have been invited to apply for a permanent job here.

SALES CLERK. Wal-Mart, Fayetteville, NC (2000-present). Became a valued employee and trusted co-worker of this retail giant while working to finance my college education.

- Was complimented numerous times for my excellent listening and customer service skills.
- Through my sales experience, have gained insights into consumer behavior and have learned how to "read" people in sales situations.
- Am often in situations where I must educate and counsel people about the expected benefits of certain products.
- Because of my strong analytical skills and attention to detail, have been invited to apply to the management training program of this corporation, and have been evaluated as possessing proven executive potential and outstanding communication skills.
- Have developed a business style that emphasizes listening carefully to the customer.

PERSONAL

Can provide outstanding personal and professional references upon request. Am known as a hard worker who always gives 110% to any job I take on. Can provide outstanding personal and professional references upon request. Truly enjoy a situation where I can make a positive difference in someone's life.

STUDENT: Seeking Position Involving Writing, Editing, Proofreading

LAURA MCNAIR

1110½ Hay Street, Fayetteville, NC 28305 • preppub@aol.com • (910) 483-6611

OBJECTIVE

To offer my newly minted degree, reputation for creativity, and strong interest in writing, editing, and proofreading to an organization in need of a hard-charging young professional known for the ability to motivate and guide others to achieve outstanding results.

EDUCATION

B.A., English, North Carolina State University, Raleigh, NC, December 2003.
- Excelled in a degree program which included specialized course work such as:

business writing	creative writing	editing
proofreading	technical writing	copy writing

- Played a leadership role in campus residence hall activities and developed programs which led to improvements in the quality of life for dormitory residents.

SPECIAL SKILLS

Am familiar with computer hardware and proficient with software programs including Microsoft Word. Type between 50 and 60 WPM.
Have experience with office equipment such as 10-key adding machines and copiers.

EXPERIENCE

INVENTORY ANALYST. AccuCount Inventory Service, Raleigh, NC (2003-present). In a part-time job which I held in order to partially finance my college education, applied my attention to detail and well organized nature while providing retail businesses with inventory services; through my meticulous work habits, maintained a margin of error of less than one percent.
- Was increasingly relied upon to consult with clients who used my employer's services.
- Have learned to be tolerant of others and work as a team member in a group with widely diverse backgrounds and educational levels.

HOME HEALTH AIDE. Medical Personnel Pool, Harrells, NC (2000). Offered companionship to the elderly and displayed maturity while taking full responsibility for the care of a person who was physically unable to be independent: provided 24-hour care five days a week by preparing meals and administering medications as well as transporting her to doctor's appointments and giving assistance during physical therapy.

Gained experience in student leadership at North Carolina State University, Raleigh, NC:
TREASURER. North Carolina State University Residence Hall Association (1999). Established budget preparation guidelines which are still used: the association had allowed itself to break budgets and operate with deficits in the past.
- Received an outstanding service award in recognition of my creativity and organizational skills used to establish fund raising activities which compensated for budget problems and got the association out of debt.
- Provided 15 residence halls with guidance on fund raising and budget compliance.

RESIDENCE HALL PRESIDENT. James Hall (1997-99). Motivated the residents of my hall and encouraged them to show more school spirit and pride in their residence facility so that it became a better place to live and a leader in intercampus competitions.
- Was honored for giving one of the top 10 presentations at a state-wide conference: gave a program entitled "Let Your Fingers Do the Talking" which dealt with tolerance for the hearing impaired and the use of sign language.
- Planned successful programs for homecoming and parents' weekends as well as coordinating with representatives of the Boys' and Girls' Clubs for special holiday activities.
- As liaison with campus offices, received and relayed information on campus activities and policies to dorm residents.

RESIDENCE HALL SECRETARY. James Hall (1997). Elected as president after proving my concern for others and leadership qualities in this role, assisted the president in planning programs and represented the hall at leadership conferences.

PERSONAL

Offer a reputation for determination, persistence, and attention to detail. Would relocate.

STUDENT

Date

Exact Name of Person
Title or Position
Name of Company
Address (no., street)
Address (city, state, zip)

Dear Exact Name of Person: (or Dear Sir or Madam if answering a blind ad.)

Can you use a self-starter and fast learner who offers extensive computer knowledge and sharp math skills along with proven abilities related to management and marketing?

While earning my B.S. degree in marketing, I excelled in several "real-world" projects that involved setting up a minor league baseball team, establishing a new franchise "from scratch," and analyzing the financial condition of a major electronics corporation. I am skilled at using several popular software packages.

My mathematical abilities are considered top-notch: I was ranked in the highest percentile of high school students based on my superior math S.A.T. score. I also offer some experience in sales, business management, and customer service through jobs I held prior to earning my college degree.

I am seeking to make a long-term commitment and significant "bottom-line" contribution to a company that can use a versatile and creative young leader with a capacity for hard work.

I hope you will welcome my call soon to arrange a brief meeting at your convenience to discuss your current and future needs and how I might serve them. Thank you in advance for your time.

Sincerely yours,

Clyde Dominey

Alternate last paragraph:
I hope you will call or write me soon to suggest a time convenient for us to meet and discuss your current and future needs and how I might serve them. Thank you in advance for your time.

Seeking Marketing Job in Sports Organization

CLYDE DOMINEY

1110½ Hay Street, Fayetteville, NC 28305 • preppub@aol.com • (910) 483-6611

OBJECTIVE

I want to contribute to an organization that can use a hard-working young professional who offers a proven ability to quickly learn and creatively apply information with a "bottom-line" orientation.

EXTENSIVE COMPUTER SKILLS

Have used software and programming languages including:

Pascal	Excel spreadsheets	Java
dBase III Plus	Microsoft Word	Ethernet

- Excelled in a computer Human Interface course, SIGCHI, Austin, TX, 2001.

EDUCATION

Earned Bachelor of Science (B.S.) degree in Marketing, Montana State University, Bozeman, MT, 2003.

EXPERIENCE

MARKETING TRAINEE. Montana State University, Bozeman, MT (2001-03). As a successful candidate for the Bachelor of Science degree, excelled in several "real-world" projects which enhanced my business administration and marketing skills.

- In a project for a <u>promotion</u> course, started up a Minor League baseball team for the city of Bozeman: developed advertising, prepared schedules, prepared consumer literature and discount booklets, and determined logo/team colors.
- In a project for a <u>retail management</u> course, established "from scratch" a new Putt-Putt franchise: performed extensive feasibility analysis and prepared in-depth oral/written presentations.
- For a <u>finance</u> course, performed extensive in-depth financial analysis, including ratio analysis, of the Apple Computer Company: prepared five-year and 10-year projections.
- For a <u>marketing</u> project, collected information to help determine community banking needs and the public's perception of First Interstate Bank.

ACTING STORE MANAGER/MANAGER TRAINEE. Bubba's Breakaway, Raleigh, NC (2001). Was entrusted with occasionally managing this store after learning the internal workings of this fast-food preparation and delivery business serving the Raleigh area.

Scheduled/directed drivers.	Ordered food/supplies.
Balanced daily receipts.	Answered phones/took orders.
Made bank deposits.	Prepared/delivered food.

SALES CLERK. Boulevard Pawn Shop, Fayetteville, NC (1998). Acquired excellent customer relations skills and learned valuable inventory control techniques while monitoring a diversified inventory including stereo equipment and firearms.

Other experience: Learned the importance of "attention to detail" as a dishwasher at a seafood restaurant and lifeguard at a country club pool.

MATHEMATICS KNOWLEDGE & ACADEMIC ABILITY

Scored a very high 700 on the math portion of Scholastic Aptitude Test (S.A.T).
- Was ranked in the top percentile of high school students in math mastery.

Was offered an academic scholarship by the University of South Carolina.
- Received a Presidential Academic Fitness Award for academic excellence.

PERSONAL

Was elected pledge president in my college fraternity. Enjoy racquetball, golf (l2-handicap), skiing, surfing, basketball, softball, and baseball.

STUDENT

Exact Name of Person
Title or Position
Name of Company
Address (no., street)
Address (city, state, zip)

Accounting Background

Dear Exact Name of Person: (or Dear Sir or Madam if answering a blind ad.)

I would appreciate an opportunity to talk with you soon about how I could contribute to your organization through my education in accounting as well as through my excellent math skills, adaptability, and reputation as a fast learner.

As you will see from my enclosed resume, I will receive my B.S. in Accounting from Fayetteville State University in December. I earned a full scholarship on the basis of my potential to excel academically and high SAT scores and have succeeded in maintaining a perfect 4.0 GPA throughout my college career. I was singled out to receive the Dean's Award for achieving the highest GPA of any student in the School of Business and Finance.

My work history outside the accounting field reveals my high level of creativity, resourcefulness, and adaptability. For a period of time I excelled in a variety of assignments while working for a temporary agency. Subsequently I gained entrepreneurial experience when I started a successful day care business which became known for quality service and excellent customer relations.

Recently as a tutor in the university's writing center, I have been able to teach written communication skills and computer knowledge. My computer experience includes the most commonly used programs including Microsoft Word, Excel and dBase, and I offer a proven ability to rapidly master new software and operating systems.

I am a highly motivated individual with a reputation for outstanding communication, motivational, and organizational skills along a high level of enthusiasm and energy.

I hope you will welcome my call soon to arrange a brief meeting at your convenience to discuss your current and future needs and how I might serve them. Thank you in advance for your time.

Sincerely yours,

Ginger Decker

Alternate last paragraph:
I hope you will call or write me soon to suggest a time convenient for us to meet and discuss your current and future needs and how I might serve them. Thank you in advance for your time.

Accounting Background

GINGER DECKER

1110½ Hay Street, Fayetteville, NC 28305 • preppub@aol.com • (910) 483-6611

OBJECTIVE

To contribute to an organization in need of a mature professional who can offer a keen eye for detail and high level of initiative as well as an education in accounting, excellent math skills, and the enthusiasm and energy needed to achieve superior results.

EDUCATION

Bachelor of Science (B.S.) degree in Accounting, Fayetteville State University, a campus of the University of North Carolina, Fayetteville, NC; December 2003.

- Received the Chancellor's Scholarship Award, a full scholarship given on the basis of my SAT scores and potential to excel academically.
- Have maintained a perfect 4.0 GPA throughout my college career.
- Was honored with the Dean's Award for achieving the highest GPA of any student in the School of Business and Economics.
- Earned acceptance in Delta Mu Delta National Honor Sorority in recognition of my academic excellence.
- Completed specialized course work including the following:

cost accounting	marketing	auditing
accounting theory	tax accounting	business law
money and banking	fund accounting	corporate finance

EXPERIENCE

TUTOR. Fayetteville State University, Fayetteville, NC (2001-03). Instructed other students in the university's writing center where assistance was given in the areas of essay writing, conducting research, and using computers.
- Built on my own knowledge of Word and Excel software programs and printer set up by helping others increase their skills and familiarity with the software and equipment.

PIANIST. Shaw Heights Baptist Church, Fayetteville, NC (2002-present). Offer my musical talents to provide the church congregation with piano music during regularly scheduled services and for practices as well as occasionally for funerals.
- Used my musical knowledge and creativity to write music after listening to tapes when the sheet music is not available for a particular song.

BOOKKEEPER. Murphy & Black Accountants, Fayetteville, NC (2002-03). Learned the value of being professional, tactful, and courteous while helping out in this busy accounting firm for a month over the Christmas holiday while filling in for regular employees on vacation.
- Demonstrated that I am capable of quickly mastering a job with no formal training and with no one to show me the way things "should" be done.

ENTREPRENEUR/CHILD-CARE PROVIDER. Self-employed, Germany (1991-95). Ensured that young children had a safe and caring place in which to be taken care of while their parents were working or attending school during the day.
- Discovered a capacity for patience and ability to handle stress while managing the details of a successful small business.

SECRETARY. RTH GmbH (Inc.), Stuttgart, Germany (1989-91). For a German company similar to Mega-Force in this area, worked for various companies on short-term temporary assignments.
- Displayed my adaptability by taking on assignments which included typing, filing, making cash disbursements, and customer service.

SPECIAL SKILLS

Type 50 wpm.
Am familiar with Microsoft Word and have working knowledge of Excel and dBase.

LANGUAGES

Am completely bilingual — speak, read, and write both English and German fluently.

PERSONAL

Am a well-organized individual with a creative flair. Offer a very outgoing and friendly personality. Enjoy helping others learn, live, and grow. Am eager to tackle new challenges.

STUDENT

Date

Exact Name of Person
Title or Position
Name of Company
Address (number and street)
Address (city, state, and ZIP)

Mathematics Degree Seeking Technical Environment

Dear Exact Name of Person: (or Dear Sir or Madam if answering a blind ad.)

I would appreciate an opportunity to talk with you soon about how I could contribute to your organization through my strong interest in the field of geotechnical engineering, quality control and inspection, and materials testing as well as through my experience, education, and communication skills.

You will see by my enclosed resume that while earning my B.S. in Mathematics, I gained practical experience in summer and part-time positions which included Concrete Technician and Engineering Technician. I am certified by the state of Virginia as a Concrete Technician and was promoted to Quality Control Inspector after only six months with a precast company in Virginia.

I offer well-developed communication skills partially as a result of my eight years of service in the U.S. Army where I was heavily involved in training and supervision of teams of up to nine well-trained people. I also refined my ability to communicate effectively during a period where I tutored students in mathematics at a college learning center where most of my students needed assistance in precalculus or calculus.

My computer skills include familiarity with DOS and UNIX operating systems with some experience in programming in Pascal. I enjoy technical challenges and learning new theories and mechanics.

I hope you will welcome my call soon to arrange a brief meeting at your convenience to discuss your current and future needs and how I might serve them. Thank you in advance for your time.

Sincerely yours,

David Callahan

Alternate last paragraph:
I hope you will call or write me soon to suggest a time convenient for us to meet and discuss your current and future needs and how I might serve them. Thank you in advance for your time.

Mathematics Degree Seeking Technical Environment

DAVID CALLAHAN

1110½ Hay Street, Fayetteville, NC 28305   •   preppub@aol.com   •   (910) 483-6611

OBJECTIVE

To offer my analytical and mathematical abilities to an organization that can use a technically oriented young professional with a reputation as a team player known for outstanding communication, problem-solving, and planning abilities.

EDUCATION

Bachelor of Science degree in Mathematics, Mary Washington College, Fredericksburg, VA, degree requirements completed December 2003.
- Was inducted into Pi Mu Epsilon National Mathematics Honor Society as a math major with a 3.5 GPA, spring semester 2002.
- Earned departmental honors in mathematics in recognition of my high GPA and completion of a semester of directed study with a presentation made to department faculty.
- Became a member of the Mathematical Association of America (MAA), 2003.

LICENSE

Was licensed as a Concrete Technician by the Virginia Department of Transportation.

TECHNICAL KNOWLEDGE

Am familiar with the DOS and UNIX operating systems and use computer software such as Word, Excel and dBase; have experience with programming in Pascal.

EXPERIENCE

Gained practical experience and refined my time management skills while juggling the demands of attending college full time and working to help finance my education:
CARPENTER'S HELPER. Sexton Construction, Washington, DC (2003 and 2001). Earned a reputation as a dependable and trustworthy employee while learning commercial carpentry working on ceilings and dry walls; was rehired in 2003 based on my performance during the summer of 2001.

QUALITY ASSURANCE CLERK. Roadway Package System, Hartwood, VA (2001-02). Polished customer service skills while involved in activities including redirecting packages which had been improperly routed, processing damaged parcels, maintaining various types of records and documentation, and responding to customer complaints and problems.
- Was cited as the driving force behind providing satisfactory quality assurance operations for the first time since the terminal was built.

MATHEMATICS TUTOR. Germanna Community College, Locust Grove, VA (2000-01). Applied my well-developed communication skills and mathematical abilities while helping students experiencing difficulties in subjects such as precalculus and calculus.
- Became adept at explaining technical subject matter concisely and clearly.
- Refined customer service skills while assisting in resource center operations.

ENGINEERING TECHNICIAN. Geotechnical Materials Testing, Inc. (GMTI), Stafford, VA (1998). Further enhanced my knowledge of concrete testing and learned soil testing techniques while preparing reports prior to collecting samples.

QUALITY CONTROL INSPECTOR/CONCRETE TECHNICIAN. Rotonda Pre-Cast, Fredericksburg, VA (1997-98). Promoted to Quality Control Inspector after six months, was involved in testing concrete and aggregates as well as in preparing and filing reports.
- Learned Quality Control techniques including reading blueprints and was in charge of maintaining the department's records.
- Became certified by the state as a Concrete Technician.

MILITARY EXPERIENCE: Served my country in the U.S. Army for eight years and was promoted ahead of my peers to management; supervised teams of up to nine people.

PERSONAL

Working knowledge of German. Enjoy reading scientific/technical books on subjects such as quantum mechanics. Like technical challenges and learning new theories.

Date

Exact Name of Person
Title or Position
Name of Company
Address (number and street)
Address (city, state, and zip)

**Seeking First Job in
Social Work and
Counseling**

Dear Exact Name of Person: (or Dear Sir or Madam if answering a blind ad.)

I would appreciate an opportunity to talk with you soon about how I could contribute to your organization through my education and interest in human services and my knowledge related to social work and counseling.

As you will see from my enclosed resume I graduated *magna cum laude* from the University of North Carolina at Greensboro with a Bachelor of Social Work degree. My areas of concentration included 15 credit hours in Family and Children's Services and an additional 21 hours of Psychology which included Adolescent, Child, and Developmental Psychology.

During an internship at Wilson Memorial Hospital, I was able to earn the respect of medical professionals in a hospital setting where the social work aspect of patient care was of secondary importance. During this period I gained experience in areas such as interviewing patients and their family members, assessing their needs, and networking through the community in order to make referrals to outside agencies and resources.

Through practical work experience and volunteer activities, I have become known as an empathetic and caring professional with excellent listening and analytical skills. I am very patient and nonjudgmental and respect the need for confidentiality in client care. An excellent manager of time, I am familiar with proper and accepted procedures for collecting data, identifying and assessing needs, and keeping complete and accurate records.

I hope you will welcome my call soon to arrange a brief meeting at your convenience to discuss your current and future needs and how I might serve them. Thank you in advance for your time.

Sincerely yours,

Willa Willoughby

Alternate last paragraph:
I hope you will call or write me soon to suggest a time convenient for us to meet and discuss your current and future needs and how I might serve them. Thank you in advance for your time.

Seeking First Job in Social Work and Counseling

WILLA WILLOUGHBY

1110½ Hay Street, Fayetteville, NC 28305   •   preppub@aol.com   •   (910) 483-6611

OBJECTIVE

To contribute through my education and interest in the field of social work and counseling to an organization that can benefit from my personal qualities and reputation as an empathetic and caring professional who is good at listening, interviewing, and counseling.

EDUCATION

Bachelor of Social Work (B.S.W.) degree, the University of North Carolina at Greensboro (UNCG), Greensboro, NC, 2003.
- Graduated *magna cum laude* with a 3.68 GPA from one of only three accredited schools of social work in the state.
- Was elected to membership in Phi Kappa Phi honor society in recognition of my placement in the top 5% of my class.
- Earned recognition from the Golden Key National Honor Society for my academic accomplishments.
- Completed 15 semester hours of work with a concentration in Family and Children's Services.
- Excelled in 21 hours of studies in Psychology which included courses in Adolescent Psychology, Child Psychology, and Developmental Psychology.

EXPERIENCE

ADMINISTRATIVE ASSISTANT. The Legal Connection, Greensboro, NC (2003-present). As an assistant in the Real Estate Department, have polished my communication skills while dealing on a regular basis with professionals ranging from attorneys, to real estate agents, to mortgage and insurance company personnel, to people at title companies.
- Gained knowledge of real estate law and the mortgage closing process while learning to work effectively under pressure in a fast-paced office with constant deadlines.

SOCIAL WORK INTERN. Wilson Memorial Hospital, Greensboro, NC (2003). Gained practical experience in a hospital setting by conducting interviews with patients and their families, arranging for home health care, coordinating plans for hospice care, and arranging for patients to be placed in nursing homes or rest homes.
- Became familiar with local assets and referred clients and their families to support agencies and services within the community.
- Completed paperwork and proper documentation of all interviews and actions.
- Learned the importance of following procedures for identifying and assessing needs, collecting data, interviewing, and keeping complete and accurate records.

SALES ASSOCIATE. Brody's Department Store, Greenville, NC (2003). Learned valuable time management skills while assisting with customer purchases, returns, or lay-a-way of clothing and accessories along with helping with stocking.

PHYSICAL THERAPY CLINIC VOLUNTEER. Southeastern Regional Rehabilitation Center, Fayetteville, NC (2002). Contributed more than 100 hours working with pediatric physical therapy patients by assisting the physical therapy staff members in moving the children, playing with them and giving them individual attention, and observing their physical and emotional condition.
- Gained awareness of how different each patient is and how fragile the emotional state of a child can be when forced to spend long periods of their life hospitalized.

WAITRESS. Brian's Grill, Fayetteville, NC (2001). Earned a reputation as a friendly, helpful, and cheerful individual who could be counted on to remain calm and professional even under hectic and trying circumstances.

CUSTOMER SERVICE SPECIALIST. Hecht's Department Store, Fayetteville, NC (1998-99). Learned to be adaptable and quickly master new tasks: took care of such day-to-day activities as accounting for petty cash/register money, wrapping gifts, typing, taking credit applications, processing gift certificates, and handling returned checks/lay-a-ways/complaints.

PERSONAL

Skilled at interviewing — concisely paraphrase, clarify, and summarize what others have said. Am patient and non-judgmental with respect for the importance of confidentiality.

STUDENTS: Teacher Seeking First Full-Time Teaching Position

SUZANNE WRIGHT

1110½ Hay Street, Fayetteville, NC 28305 • preppub@aol.com • (910) 483-6611

OBJECTIVE

To offer my strong desire to teach and work with young people by applying my degree in the science field as well as my creativity, motivational skills, knowledge of computer operations, and practical experience with a variety of laboratory procedures.

EDUCATION

Bachelor of Science, Biology Teaching, North Carolina State University, NC, 2003.
- Was named to the university's Chancellor's List in recognition of my academic achievements in maintaining a GPA of 3.8 or higher.
- Excelled in specialized coursework including:

methods of teaching	analytical chemistry	histology
anatomy and physiology	medical terminology	biochemistry
probability and statistics	human development	Spanish
computers in education — emphasis on Word, Excel, Powerpoint, Report Card		

- Held membership in the Science Club.

EXPERIENCE

STUDENT TEACHER. Raleigh Board of Education, Raleigh, NC (2003). Instructed a diverse student population at Wilson Smith High School while teaching Biology I and Biology II to ninth through 12th grade students.
- Applied active learning techniques while motivating students to participate in class activities and open themselves to learning.
- Implemented positive classroom management strategies to encourage proper behavior and respect for others.
- Utilized planning and organizational skills in carrying out classroom support activities including completing interesting and thorough lesson plans as well as preparing test materials and monitoring testing.
- Earned the teacher's respect for my true concern for the students, willingness to tackle hard assignments, and ability to follow through on any project taken on.
- Displayed creativity and initiative in the development of informative bulletin boards.

CASHIER. Taco Bell, Fayetteville, NC (1999-present). Refined time management skills and displayed a high level of self-motivation while working 30 hours a week to help finance my education, maintaining a high grade point average in a demanding field of study, and taking care of a home and family.
- Known for my dedication to providing high quality customer service, was entrusted with training new employees and setting an example for them to follow.
- Displayed an eye for details while independently taking on the responsibility for restocking supplies and organizing the food preparation area for the next group of employees.

LABORATORY ASSISTANT. The American Red Cross, Germany (1997-1998). As a volunteer in the chemistry department lab of a U.S. Army hospital in Germany, logged in and separated blood specimens and then ran them through the SMA-18 machine which analyzed specimens for 18 separate chemical tests.
- Assisted in drawing blood from patients and doing electrolyte testing.

Highlights of earlier experience while serving as a LABORATORY TECHNICIAN, U.S. Army:
- Processed urine specimens for military personnel throughout the Pacific area while screening for illegal substances including heroin, cocaine, barbiturates, and amphetamines.
- Conducted drug screening procedures at a facility which supported Army, Navy, and Air Force personnel based in the Philippines, Japan, Korea, and Hawaii.
- Assisted a doctor who was doing research on high blood pressure and the effects of high altitude on the human body.
- For the hematology, STAT Lab, and chemistry departments of a military hospital, ran various chemical tests on blood and urine specimens and performed blood cross matches.
- Also worked in urinalysis and parasitology; cross trained medics as lab technicians to work in outlying clinics; and shipped specimens to outside labs for analysis.

PERSONAL

Am an open water-certified SCUBA diver; received Red Cross certification in CPR and lifesaving techniques. Offer empathy for the problems and tough choices facing young people.

STUDENT: Completing Elementary Education Degree

LINDA ELMORE

1110½ Hay Street, Fayetteville, NC 28305 • preppub@aol.com • (910) 483-6611

OBJECTIVE   I want to contribute to an organization that can use a caring and hard-working professional who offers excellent teaching, counseling, and administrative skills along with a proven ability to work graciously with people of all ages.

EDUCATION   Completing B.S. degree in Elementary Education and Psychology, Pembroke State University, Pembroke, NC.
Previously attended Mount Olive College studying education.
Received Certificate in Basic Law Enforcement, Fayetteville Technical Community College, Fayetteville, NC, 2000.
Hold a Certificate as a Substitute Teacher.

EXPERIENCE   **GENERAL MANAGER.** Faircloth's Cleaning Services, Warsaw, NC (2003-present). While completing my college degree, manage a cleaning service which enjoys an excellent reputation because of its honest, reliable, professional staff.
* Have hired and trained workers.
* Handle all financial and accounting functions for the business.
* Maintain excellent relationships with residential and business customers.
* In my spare time, also work as a **SUBSTITUTE TEACHER** in a day care environment when the regular teacher has conflicts.

SUBSTITUTE TEACHER. Cumberland County Board of Education, Fayetteville, NC (2000-01). Gained a reputation as a popular substitute teacher while filling in for teachers in grades K-6 in various Cumberland County schools.
* Earned my Certificate in Substitute Teaching.
* Derived great satisfaction from helping many students with learning deficiencies overcome obstacles and establish higher personal goals for themselves.
* Was commended by several principals and teachers on my firm yet approachable style with children.
* Worked in classrooms of handicapped and behaviorally (BEH) disruptive children.
* Refined my ability to develop excellent lesson plans.

FACTORY WORKER. MegaForce, Fayetteville, NC (2000). Worked on the assembly line in the production of children's books.
* Became known as a flexible person who was willing to work on any shift.

INSPECTOR/QUALITY CONTROL COORDINATOR. Dawson Company, Warsaw, NC (1998-99). For a sewing plant, inspected the quality of sewn products in order to assure consistently high standards; maintained daily records of production output and quality performance.
* Learned valuable techniques related to quality control which would be transferrable to any industry or professional activity.

Other experience:
Industrial fabrication: At the Mohassco Furniture Company in Turkey, NC, worked as a fabricator of sofas and recliners; learned all the steps involved in furniture fabrication from start to finish.
Sales: At the Warsaw Drug Company in Warsaw, NC, operated a cash register while also acting as a sales representative for all store products.

PERSONAL   Am a creative, well-organized individual who has a sincere desire to help others.

STUDENT: Completing Management Trainee Position
CANDACE CAMERON
1110½ Hay Street, Fayetteville, NC 28305   •   preppub@aol.com   •   (910) 483-6611

OBJECTIVE

To contribute my talent for selling ideas as well as products to an organization that can use an adaptable young professional who works well under pressure while providing excellent customer service and public relations.

EDUCATION

Earned a B.S. in **Business Administration,** Wofford College, Spartanburg, SC, 2003.
- Maintained a 3.2 GPA and excelled in specialized course work including:
  principles of marketing   basic advertising
  managerial accounting   marketing management

EXPERIENCE

MANAGEMENT TRAINEE. The Jewel Tree, Inc., Spartanburg, SC (2001-present). After gaining experience as a Jewelry Sales Representative (part-time 2001-03), was selected to participate full time in the company's management training program and am continuing to refine my sales and managerial abilities.
- Am recognized as one of the elite few who consistently achieve more than $300,000 in sales annually.
- Was handpicked to be in a training video to be used company wide.
- Used my public relations knowledge and skills to implement creative marketing plans for special events.
- Handled day-to-day activities including opening and closing the store, making nightly deposits, and verifying daily business reports with customer receipts.
- Became very adept at quickly identifying customer needs and in locating and selling the merchandise that met those needs.
- Explained diamond and Rolex watch warranties to customers and ensured that they understood and maintained warranty standards.
- Follow-up with customers during and after the sale to ensure customer satisfaction and provide any special instructions for the care of high-dollar merchandise; also liaise with buyers at the home office for custom-made merchandise.
- Received and processed lay-a-way and charge account payments using computerized registers to enter the proper information.
- Became involved in the personnel aspects of the business including constantly recruiting prospective employees, interviewing, and checking references.
- Conducted training for new employees and provided continual guidance on any area needing improvement; informed staff members of company benefits and maintained the confidentiality of personal information gained while having access to personnel records.
- Scheduled employees so that overtime could be kept to a minimum and personnel used most efficiently.
- Conducted regular store meetings to keep staff members up to date on product knowledge, policy and procedural changes, and suggested sales techniques.
- Kept informed on competitors' strengths and weakness including pricing, customer service, and selection of merchandise available.
- Participated in controlling inventory by making spot checks, reporting losses immediately, and preparing for and conducting inventories.
- Worked closely with the buyer to ensure displays and advertisements were prepared on time and were exciting so that special events were maximized.
- Gained experience in bookkeeping while entering transactions in the computer, preparing daily deposits and sales figures, and overseeing credit transactions.
- Emphasized customer service and the development of personal relations so that repeat business and word-of-mouth advertising resulted in high sales levels and satisfied customers.

ADMINISTRATIVE ASSISTANT. Alcohol and Drug Control Office, Germany (1998-00). Performed regular secretarial duties such as greeting the public, answering phone and in-person inquiries, typing, filing, and word processing reports and documentation.
- Chosen to handle additional responsibilities as assistant Biochemical Test Coordinator, scheduled/ coordinated urinalysis testing of 8,000 military professionals, conducted testing of specimens, and informed commanders when their soldiers tested positive.
- Assisted the education coordinator in the development and administration of education programs focusing on self-improvement and substance abuse knowledge.

PERSONAL

Excellent personal and professional references available upon request. Am available for travel or relocation according to employer needs.

STUDENT: Seeking First Job in Finance Field After College Graduation

DAVID YUEN

1110½ Hay Street, Fayetteville, NC 28305   •   preppub@aol.com   •   (910) 483-6611

OBJECTIVE

To offer my education in finance along with my analytical, sales, and communication skills, to an organization that can benefit from my strong interest in financial planning and banking as well as from my personal reputation for integrity, high moral standards, and a strong work ethic.

EDUCATION

Am pursuing a **Bachelor of Science degree in Finance,** The University of North Carolina at Wilmington (UNCW); degree expected spring 2003.
- Placed on the university's Dean's List in recognition of my academic accomplishments.
- Received an "A" on an intensive class project: performed a company analysis on Harley-Davidson including keeping records, analyzing price and volume data as well as technical data, gathering and analyzing information about the industry, and making determinations on the economic outlook for the company and industry as a whole.
- Completed specialized course work such as Finance 330 (principles of finance, stock valuation, options, etc.) and Finance 331 (real estate investing).

EXPERIENCE

Learned to manage time wisely while maintaining at least a 3.0 GPA thus far in my college career and excelling in demanding part-time jobs including this track record of accomplishments with Macy's Department Store, Wilmington, NC:

LOSS PREVENTION DETECTIVE. (October 2003-present). In only 18 months with the company, have progressed to the highest level available to a part-time employee based on my maturity, willingness to take on hard work, and communication skills.
- Increased apprehensions of shoplifters 50% thereby greatly reducing losses from theft.
- Displayed the ability to remain calm and in control and act as an arbitrator under intense conditions.
- Provided security for the store premises, researched discrepancies in cash accounts, and generated surveillance programs.
- Gained a thorough understanding of the importance of confidentiality while guarding privileged information.

FRONT-LINE SUPERVISOR. (April-October 2003). Supervised approximately 50 employees in order to ensure that customers received the highest quality of service and satisfaction.
- Opened cash drawers and initiated changeovers while register contents were transferred as well as changing large denominations of bills for smaller ones as needed.
- Approved refunds, lay-a-ways, and purchases by associates.
- Conducted new employee orientation which included such areas as cash handling procedures, customer service techniques, and company policy.
- Was honored as "Associate of the Quarter" by management and other associates.

CASH OFFICE ASSOCIATE. (January-April 2003). Was given the opportunity to apply my knowledge gained in college in a real-life situation while handling day-to-day retail store office activities including:

inputting financial data into computers	creating and filing financial reports
auditing cash variances of sales associates	preparing reports for the home office
auditing and making daily cash deposits	balancing registers with cash in vault
determining and reporting weekly after-tax cash sales totals	

- Learned the value of accuracy and attention to detail.

CASHIER. (June 2002-January 2003). Became skilled in handling refunds and sales accurately and quickly while becoming responsible for large amounts of cash transactions.
- Was known for my ability to greet and assist customers as well as for my keen eye for possible cases of switching tickets and theft by customers.

TRAINING

Completed several seminars and training programs including a Excel spreadsheets and loss prevention training (detecting losses, detaining suspects, and making reports).

PERSONAL

Keep up with stock market and read "The Wall Street Journal" regularly. Familiar with Microsoft Word and the Internet. Graduated from high school with honors.

PART FOUR:

People Changing Careers

CHANGING CAREERS

Date

Mrs. Janet Faircloth
Office Manager
Smith and Smith Associates
P.O. Box 80734
Atlanta, GA 30331

**From Sales to
Dental Assisting**

Dear Mrs. Faircloth:

I would appreciate an opportunity to talk with you soon about how I could contribute to your organization through my sincere desire to work as a dental assistant. At 25 years of age, I can show you in person that my natural drive, hard-working nature, and proven sales/customer service skills would enable me to rapidly master your requirements and become a valuable asset to you.

You will see from my resume that I maintained a 4.0 GPA while completing three years of college. I hope that you will provide some glimpse into my highly dedicated personality as well as my natural intelligence.

Experienced in using computers and most standard office equipment, I have excelled in jobs in photographic sales, insurance sales, and optical sales. After considerable thought, I have decided that I want to work toward a career in dentistry, and I am hopeful that you will see my potential and offer me my first job in this field. I am a proven performer and you would not be taking a chance!

Please consider me for this position. I am confident that I could demonstrate during an interview that I am the person you are looking for and could count on. I hope I will hear from you so that we can set up a meeting at your convenience to discuss your current and future needs and how I might serve them. Thank you in advance for your time.

Sincerely yours,

Victoria Braswell

VICTORIA BRASWELL

1110½ Hay Street, Fayetteville, NC 28305 • preppub@aol.com • (910) 483-6611

OBJECTIVE
To benefit an organization seeking an enthusiastic, energetic, and highly motivated professional skilled in sales and public relations who possesses sound bottom-line judgment along with excellent communication, time management, and planning abilities.

EXPERIENCE
SALES REPRESENTATIVE and **COMMERCIAL PHOTOGRAPHER.** PCA International, Inc., Atlanta, GA (2002-03). Consistently exceeded the organization's performance and sales standards while ensuring customers were treated properly and received the highest quality photographic products in this busy high-volume studio.
- Established new sales records and maintained a volume approximately 30% above corporate standards.
- Earned the distinction of being the first person in the company's history to receive "excellent" evaluations in all rated performance categories during my initial periodic evaluation.
- Excelled in dealing with customers no matter how tired and difficult they became by applying my talent for establishing rapport with people of all ages and cultures.
- Earned the respect of district executives and was soon entrusted with the sole responsibility for opening and closing the studio.
- Gained practical experience in using a digital point-of-sale computer system to ring up sales and receive payments from customers.
- Was cited for my ability to adapt to changing circumstances and remain courteous and in control at all times.

COLLEGE STUDENT. Fayetteville State University, Fayetteville, NC (2000-present). Completed almost three years of college course work with honors while polishing my time management skills coordinating school and work.

INSURANCE SALES REPRESENTATIVE. Western-Southern Life Insurance Company, Fayetteville, NC (1999-00). Consistently led the district in sales as a licensed life and health insurance agent.
- Used my communication skills and ability to deal with others on their level while making cold calls on prospective clients and collecting premiums from existing clients.
- Was selected to attend a 48-hour training program on policy types and terminology for life and health insurance sales.

OPTICIAN'S ASSISTANT and **SALES REPRESENTATIVE.** Ft. Bragg Optical Shop, Ft. Bragg, NC (1996-98). Became highly aware of the importance of attending to details while making certain to take exact measurements so that customers' eye wear was made and fitted correctly.
- Cited for my maturity and rapport with others, worked independently while providing high quality services and support.
- Handled technical areas such as fabricating lenses and making adjustments and repairs.

Highlights of other experience: **OPTICIAN'S ASSISTANT** and **SALES REPRESENTATIVE.** Professional Opticians, Fayetteville, NC. Became highly skilled in guaranteeing customer satisfaction with services and products while taking order requests, closing sales, and assisting customers in their selections in this part-time job while attending college.

EDUCATION
Have completed three years of course work toward a degree in Education, Fayetteville State University, Fayetteville, NC.
- Placed on the National Dean's List with a 4.0 GPA.
Studied Business and Education, Fayetteville Technical Community College.

SPECIAL SKILLS
Am familiar with a wide range of computers and office equipment including:
calculators   typewriters — type 50 wpm   fax machines   copiers

PERSONAL
Enjoy working with children — was a volunteer teacher's assistant at an elementary school. Am a good listener and quick learner who adapts easily to new ideas and circumstances.

CHANGING CAREERS

Date

Pendleton's Food Chain
Box 897
Grove City, PA 16127

**From Dental Assisting
to Retail Sales**

Dear Sir or Madam:

I am responding to the ad you recently placed in the *Grove City-Times* for an Assistant Manager. I would appreciate an opportunity to talk with you soon about how I could contribute to your organization through my experience related to food service management as well as retail sales and customer service.

With a reputation as a fast learner with an energetic and enthusiastic manner, I feel that two of my greatest strengths are my flexibility and adaptability. Known as a good listener, I am very effective at developing a sense of team work among employees and motivating them to provide high quality service. In every company I've worked for, I have been effective in finding ways to contribute to increased productivity while working my way up to higher levels of responsibility.

For instance, I began working at Godfather's Pizza at 16 and rapidly displayed a talent for handling customer service and motivating other employees through my personal example. I was promoted to Shift Supervisor and found ways to improve morale, make deliveries run more smoothly, and increase profitability. More recently as a Dental Assistant and Medical Supply Specialist, I was placed in charge of more experienced technicians and instructed professional development classes.

I feel confident that I could make valuable contributions to your organization through my managerial, supervisory, and customer service skills combined with my personality and enthusiasm.

I hope you will call or write me soon to suggest a time convenient for us to meet and discuss your current and future needs and how I might serve them. Thank you in advance for your time.

Sincerely yours,

Ryan Teague

from Dental Assisting to Retail Sales

RYAN TEAGUE

1110½ Hay Street, Fayetteville, NC 28305   •   preppub@aol.com   •   (910) 483-6611

OBJECTIVE

To contribute to an organization that can use an adaptable, flexible, and motivated young professional who offers a reputation as a fast learner who is articulate, can deal with people, and is knowledgeable of management, inventory control, and customer service activities.

EXPERIENCE

Became skilled and earned a reputation as a dedicated hard worker in jobs in the dental/ medical field, U.S. Government, Department of Defense, Germany:

SENIOR DENTAL ASSISTANT. (2003). Earned the respect of the dentists and was selected to oversee the work of personnel with much more experience because of my ability to quickly learn new procedures and provide the care and expertise which helped make patients more relaxed and comfortable.

- Lightened the supervisor's responsibilities by jumping in and taking on extra work.
- Learned to be effective and take charge of technical professionals while conducting continuing education classes.

MEDICAL SUPPLY CLERK. (2002-03). Became skilled in the methods for properly sterilizing dental instruments and was chosen to present classes which successfully taught other dental clinic employees safe and thorough methods to use.

DENTAL ASSISTANT. Quickly became known as a highly competent hard worker while assisting dentists in a variety of operative and surgical procedures and by also becoming familiar with functional activities including proper sterilization and cleanup procedures.

- Learned to take x-rays, make appointments, and use proper infection control methods as well as learning CPR and medical and dental terminology.

SALES ASSOCIATE. AAFES (Army and Air Force Exchange System), Germany (2001). Used my sales and communication skills in a retail environment by helping customers make choices on shoe styles, colors, and sizes.

- Applied my creativity to design attractive displays.
- Learned to use a 10-key register to complete sales.

SALES AND INVENTORY CONTROL SPECIALIST. Wal-Mart, Fayetteville, GA (2000). Contributed to the store's reputation for friendly, fast service by providing leadership which added to the spirit of team work and ensured that questions were answered and problems solved.

- Gained experience in stock control by ordering special items for individual customers, moving merchandise from receiving to the sales floor, and ordering and stocking merchandise for different departments.

SHIFT SUPERVISOR. Godfather's Pizza, Decatur, IL (1997-00). Began working as a Counter Person at age 16 and soon became the manager's right hand while helping the restaurant grow, become profitable, and build a strong customer base.

- Was promoted to Shift Supervisor after proving my maturity and dedication during 1-1/2 years of taking orders and helping customers.
- Built the store to where it was taking in an average of from $900 to $2,500 and serving more than 100 customers each day.
- Kept labor costs below 13% and food costs under 28%.
- Handled daily functions including opening and closing, setting up the register for sales, scheduling from five to 12 employees, and interviewing and training new employees.
- Ordered food, condiments, and supplies and ensured adequate amounts were on hand.
- Became very skilled in developing employee relations and in defusing difficult situations such as with customers who became hostile or rude.

TRAINING

Received on-the-job training in the areas of food service management, customer service, inventory control procedures, and dental clinic operations and support activities.

PERSONAL

Am a very enthusiastic and energetic individual who works well with others as a team member or in supervisory roles. Enjoy working with figures and forecasting financial trends.

CHANGING CAREERS

Mr. Bill Martin
Spaulding Products Division
P.O. Box 2560
Marietta, GA 30062

**From Golf Pro
to Sales**

Dear Mr. Martin:

I would appreciate an opportunity to talk with you soon about how I could contribute to your organization through my strong desire to represent your product line throughout eastern North Carolina and southeast Virginia.

As you will see from my resume, since earning my B.A. degree in 1994, I have been promoted to increasing responsibilities at Pinehurst Country Club. I began as an Assistant Golf Professional, was promoted to Head Golf Professional, and am currently Director of Golf Operations. Although many clubs and organizations have approached me over the years with other employment opportunities, I was determined to remain at Pinehurst Country Club until I developed its golf program to the highest possible standard. By every measure, I have achieved that goal and, in the process, have gained a reputation as an exceptionally strong communicator and motivator. I have frequently been called a "born salesman" and have become skilled in retail management while owning and managing the golf shop which grosses $165,000 annually.

As a lifetime resident of eastern North Carolina, I am well acquainted with the region and have an extensive network of contacts who know of my fine personal and professional reputation. I believe my name would make an excellent "calling card" for Spaulding, and I am certain I could contribute to your goals and continued success. I am an enthusiastic advocate of Spaulding already, and I would enjoy the opportunity to talk with you about the position of sales representative which is available. Of course I can provide outstanding personal and professional references.

I hope you will call or write me soon to suggest a time convenient for us to meet and discuss your current and future needs and how I might serve them. Thank you in advance for your time.

Sincerely yours,

Tom Wilson

TOM WILSON

1110½ Hay Street, Fayetteville, NC 28305 • preppub@aol.com • (910) 483-6611

OBJECTIVE

To contribute to an organization through my expertise as a golf professional, outstanding personal and professional reputation, exceptionally strong communication and sales skills, as well as my proven ability to manage operations, budgets, people, events, and assets.

EDUCATION

Bachelor of Arts (B.A.) degree in History, Grinnell College, Grinnell, Iowa, 1994.
- Areas of concentration were Business Administration, Psychology, and Sociology.

EXPERIENCE

Pinehurst Country Club, Pinehurst, NC (1994-present). On numerous occasions, have been approached by other clubs and organizations, but have steadfastly remained at Pinehurst Country Club in order to achieve the goal of elevating this golf program to the highest standard; have been promoted in the following progression:

DIRECTOR OF GOLF OPERATIONS. (2003-present). At this 625-member private club, own and operate a retail shop grossing $165,000 annually and supervise its four employees while also managing all aspects of golf operations, including supervising a staff of eight performing course maintenance.
- Combined my creativity and writing skills to improve communication with members through the monthly newsletter.
- Directed installation of a state-of-the-art irrigation system tee-to-green.
- Added senior tees, which was greatly appreciated by the members.

HEAD GOLF PROFESSIONAL. (1996-02). Planned and administered a $130,000 operational budget for golf shop operations while promoting, supervising, directing, and coordinating the overall golf program.
- Trained and supervised four employees retailing products in the golf shop.
- Created and directed a Junior Golf League which began as a four-club league in 1996 and grew to 15 member clubs in three divisions by 2002.
- Established and created a Junior Golf Association.
- Was golf coach for Pinehurst High School, 1999-03.
- Was featured in *Golf World Magazine* for walking and playing a 100-hole golf marathon for Junior Golf, July 2000.
- Coordinated numerous tournaments and golf promotions.

ASSISTANT GOLF PROFESSIONAL. (1994-96). After graduating from college, served as apprentice under Maynard Griffin, PGA Professional, while planning and conducting golf clinics and club tournaments, coordinating the junior golf program, and serving as Secretary of the Men's Golf Association.
- On my own initiative, organized a junior golf team to compete with area clubs.

PROFESSIONAL BACKGROUND & AFFILIATIONS

- PGA National Education Committee, 2003
- Carolinas PGA Section involvement:
  Tournament Committee Chairman, 2003
  Junior Golf Committee Chairman, 2002
  Playing Ability Workshop Instructor, 2002
  Area VI Board of Directors 2000, 2001, 2002, & 2003
  Special Events Chairman, 2001
  Area VI Winter Events Coordinator, 2000 & 2001
  Section Host Pro Workshop, 1999
- PGA Business School II, 1997, and PGA Business School I, 1996

PLAYING BACKGROUND

Winner of eight Pro-Ams and qualified for PGA Club Pro Championship, 1999 & 2003
- CPGA Winter Seminar Pro-Am Champion, 2003
- Birchwood Pro-Lady, 2002
- Duck Woods Pro-Am Champion, 2002
- Pepsi-Brook Valley Country Club Pro-Am Champion, 2003
- Pizza Inn-Willow Springs Pro-Am Champion, 2003
- Willow Springs Pro-Am Champion, 2002
- Carolinas PGA Section Pro-Junior Champion, 1999
- Scotfield Country Club Pro-Am Champion, 1999

CHANGING CAREERS

Date

Exact Name of Person
Title or Position
Name of Company
Address (number and street)
Address (city, state, and zip)

**From Oil Company
Operations to Other
Management**

Dear Exact Name of Person: (or Dear Sir or Madam if answering a blind ad.)

I would appreciate an opportunity to talk with you soon about how I could benefit your organization through my well-developed managerial abilities along with my reputation as a self-motivated, versatile professional who is knowledgeable in administrative, technical, supervisory, safety, emergency management, and profit-and-loss functions.

During the past ten years as Operations Manager for a large oil distributor, I have played a key role in the company's growth while working with federal, state, and county regulators. I was routinely involved in decision making related to waste disposal, central services administration, purchasing, vehicle maintenance, property inspections, and emergency management. In addition to performing liaison with the EPA in all compliance matters, I was the company's Safety Officer and conducted meetings to assure compliance with OSHA and company regulations. I am proud of the fact that our company has not had a compliance problem during my ten years of employment, and I believe strict attention to detail was critical to our success in this area.

As Operations Manager I also have been effective in reducing operating expenses, increasing business finding new sources of revenue, and improving the moral and efficiency of the company as a whole. I played a key role in the company's growth from 600 to 900 customers and from 17 to 24 bulk fuel locations, and I personally handled any customer problems pertaining to those 900 customers.

With a bachelor's degree and a strong background in management, I also offer a reputation for loyalty, intelligence, and dedication. I have been effective in analyzing organizational goals and in finding solutions for stubborn problems.

I hope you will welcome my call soon to arrange a brief meeting at your convenience to discuss your current and future needs and how I might serve them. Thank you in advance for your time.

Sincerely yours,

Doyle Campbell

Alternate last paragraph:
I hope you will call or write me soon to suggest a time convenient for us to meet and discuss your current and future needs and how I might serve them. Thank you in advance for your time.

from Oil Company Operations to Other Management

DOYLE CAMPBELL

1110½ Hay Street, Fayetteville, NC 28305   •   preppub@aol.com   •   (910) 483-6611

OBJECTIVE

To offer managerial experience to an organization that can use a self-motivated professional with experience in operational areas including administration, supervision, technical activities, and purchasing along with the proven ability to lead others in achieving organizational goals while applying excellent analytical and problem-solving skills.

EXPERIENCE

OPERATIONS MANAGER. Eaton Oil Company, Westchester, OH (1993-03). Joined the company at a time when it had 600 customers and 17 bulk fuel locations, and played a key role in its growth to 900 customers and 24 locations; in the midst of its growth, provided major input into strategic decisions about which dealers/customers to retain and which to eliminate due to cost/payback considerations.

- Was involved in decision making related to waste disposal, central services administration, purchasing, vehicle maintenance, property inspections, and emergency management; worked with federal, county, and local government officials.
- Provided customer service for 900 customers and personally handled any complaints that arose; applied my effective communication and organizational skills in maintaining lines of communication between the company owner and employees.
- Accounted for approximately $6-7 million annually in operating costs.
- Increased business 18% by implementing changes in operating procedures.
- Reduced operating expenses 15% by leading the owner and employees to work as a team to find ways to eliminate unnecessary expenditures and waste.
- Reduced the amount of on-hand inventory for each station to an eight or nine-day supply from the previous 15-day supply thereby freeing capital which could be used to fill other operating needs.
- Controlled inventories of petroleum products and maintained gain/loss records for 24 gasoline outlets; performed liaison with EPA in all compliance matters.
- As the company's Safety Officer, conducted meetings with employees to assure compliance with OSHA and company regulations; our company was never cited for a violation during my 10-year tenure.
- Supervised six employees including office, product delivery, and service personnel.
- Oversaw functional operations including appliance sales, account collections, and weekly billing of each of the 24 locations for gasoline purchases.
- Searched for and recruited new independent dealers.
- Oversaw a project to install electronic point-of-sale terminals in each of the stations.
- Learned all aspects of staffing, operating, and ensuring profitability in a small business.

Highlights of earlier experience: refined technical knowledge and inventory control skills while developing a reputation as a dependable and adaptable quick learner in jobs including the following:
As an **Apprentice Electrician,** learned safe procedures for installing and maintaining power boards for outdoor construction projects as well as gaining experience in inventory control, BE&K Construction at Federal Paper Board in Lancaster, PA.
As an **Apprentice Pipe Fitter,** learned to use specialized tools and maintain inventories of tools and related equipment, Power Plant Maintenance in Lancaster, PA.
As a **Tool Room Attendant,** contributed to team efforts in a nuclear power plant where my main areas of responsibility included issuing and receiving tools as well as measuring them for excess radiation after each shift, Yeargin Construction at BSEP, Pittsburgh, PA.

EDUCATION & TRAINING

B.A. in Sociology, Pembroke State University, NC, 1989.
Completed extensive training related to EPA, OSHA, and other government regulations.
Attended several NC Petroleum Marketers Association workshops with an emphasis on effective customer service techniques and the refinement of managerial skills.

PERSONAL

Am a permanent resident of Westchester. Have been selected by the membership of my church to hold offices as a trustee and deacon. Am tenacious and will not give up on anything I attempt to accomplish until it is done to the best of my ability.

CHANGING CAREERS

Date

Attn: Personnel
EI Dupont de Nemours & Co.
P.O. Drawer Z
Fayetteville, NC 28302-1770

Dear Sir or Madam:

I would appreciate an opportunity to talk with you soon about how I could contribute to your organization through my experience in production management as well as through my initiative, resourcefulness, and highly dedicated nature.

After earning my Bachelor of Science degree in Industrial Technology, I excelled as a machine operator in a plastics company and then as a production worker in a food processing plant, where I was quickly promoted into production line supervision. I have been commended for the creative way I apply my extensive technical knowledge as well as for my ability to communicate with people at all levels. I offer knowledge of several software programs used for data analysis and problem solving in industrial situations.

In my current job as an Assistant Supervisor, I make out the weekly rotation schedules for employees in five departments and oversee food processing operations from initial receipt of raw material through packing and shipping. I have become respected for keen attention to detail as well as for my ability to instill a "quality control" attitude in all employees. I strongly believe that quality control is not "a job at the end" but an attitude that all employees bring to their jobs, because it is a quality job at each stage of production that results in quality end products as well as lowest-possible production costs.

Single and willing to relocate or travel as needed, I am writing to you because I am impressed with your company's reputation and product line, and I believe I could become a valuable asset to your team. I can provide outstanding personal and professional references.

I hope you will welcome my call soon to arrange a brief meeting at your convenience to discuss your current and future needs and how I might serve them. Thank you in advance for your consideration.

Sincerely yours,

George Fairley

from Livestock Production to Manufacturing

GEORGE FAIRLEY

1110½ Hay Street, Fayetteville, NC 28305 • preppub@aol.com • (910) 483-6611

OBJECTIVE

To benefit an industrial organization that can use a resourceful problem solver who offers extensive experience in production operations and who is known for strong communication, technical, and supervisory skills as well as expert planning and organizational abilities.

EDUCATION

B.S., Industrial Technology, Elizabeth City State University, Elizabeth City, NC, 1995-00.

COMPUTER KNOWLEDGE

Am proficient in solving industrial problems by applying knowledge of the following:
Microsoft Excel   Fortran   Pascal-Turbo

TECHNICAL TRAINING

Completed courses in the following subject areas:
Dynamics   Quality Assurance   Statics
Motion & Time Study   Fluids Technology   Production Engineering
- Gained expert skills in testing the strength of wood, metal, and plastic materials.

EXPERIENCE

SUPERVISOR. Carroll's Foods, Laurinburg, NC (2003-present). Am being groomed to oversee the breeding of livestock.
- Supervise the breeding and farrowing of 2,400 sows, including direct mating and artificial insemination; have managed breeding, farrowing, and finishing for 1,200 sows.

Was promoted into production supervision after rapidly mastering production line tasks and demonstrating the communication skills, leadership ability, and problem-solving know-how essential to management success, Rocco Turkey of North Carolina, St. Pauls, NC (2001-03).
ASSISTANT SUPERVISOR. Consistently achieved or exceeded production goals while overseeing five different departments in the plant including the breast line, drums line, thigh line, and transfer line; coordinated operations from food processing to packing and shipping and assisted the plant manager in solving a wide range of problems.
- *Production scheduling*: Coordinated production work simultaneously in five departments, each employing 35 to 40 workers; prepared weekly employee rotation schedule.
- *Data analysis*: Analyzed data and rendered decisions regarding manpower and resource requirements.
- *Quality control*: Implemented quality assurance/quality control measures to guarantee production schedule deadlines and accurate job performance.
- *Multiple project management*: Oversaw activities ranging from line preparation, to weighing and shipping, to machine maintenance.
- *Government regulations*: Gained knowledge of sanitation, health, and fire regulations.

PRODUCTION WORKER. Started as a production worker on the transfer line and applied my creativity and problem-solving skills to ensure that goods processed were of consistently high quality in the most cost effective manner; learned to cut turkeys, run turkeys through a leg processor, and pack necks and tails.
- Was handpicked for promotion to the job above after mastering all nine jobs on the production line; was commended for my ability to communicate with workers.
- Reduced production time and costs by applying common sense and technical skills.

MACHINE OPERATOR. Wright's Plastic Company, Atlanta, GA (2000-01). Manufactured products according to precise specifications and performed operator-level maintenance on my machine; learned how plastic is made.

Other experience: Held several positions to help finance college education.
MASTER CONTROL OPERATOR. WKFT-TV 40 (Fayetteville). Operated the switchboard, recorded and produced on-the-air promotions and commercials, and maintained log.
MAINTENANCE WORKER. Burlington Industries (St. Pauls). Performed plant maintenance.
SHIPPING CLERK. Len-Howe Corp., Inc. (St. Pauls). Handled the shipping and receiving of material, maintained traffic/distribution logs, and controlled inventory.

PERSONAL

A motivated self-starter, have attended approximately 30 hours of continuing education courses on the principles of supervision and being an effective leader. Willing to go "the extra mile."

CHANGING CAREERS

Date

Exact Name of Person
Title or Position
Name of Company
Address (no., street)
Address (city, state, zip)

**From Principal to
Corporate Marketing**

Dear Exact Name of Person: (or Dear Sir or Madam if answering a blind ad.)

Can you use an articulate executive and creative administrator who offers a proven ability to solve problems, find new opportunities, and achieve quality results in all functional areas?

As you will see from my resume, I have distinguished myself in the academic arena, having excelled as a principal at three different schools. I am very proud of the contributions I have made to quality learning, and I am highly regarded in my profession.

I believe my creative approach to programming and my strong administrative skills in implementing new programs could also be valuable in a business environment, and I would like to explore the possibility of joining your organization and applying my top-notch organizational and communication skills in the achievement of your goals. As a principal I have worked with numerous budgets and have become known for my ability to "make things happen" with scarce resources, both human and financial resources. I am capable of meeting the challenges of assuming managerial roles where I could make important contributions to a company's bottom line and continual high quality customer service. With my enthusiasm, motivational abilities, and leadership I can make valuable contributions to your organization, and I would take great pride in helping you maximize your profitability, market share, and customer satisfaction.

I hope you will welcome my call soon to arrange a brief meeting at your convenience to discuss your current and future needs and how I might serve them. Thank you in advance for your time.

Sincerely yours,

Myrna Macias

Alternate last paragraph:
I hope you will call or write me soon to suggest a time convenient for us to meet and discuss your current and future needs and how I might serve them. Thank you in advance for your time.

MYRNA MACIAS

1110½ Hay Street, Fayetteville, NC 28305   •   preppub@aol.com   •   (910) 483-6611

OBJECTIVE   To benefit a company that can use a dynamic and articulate communicator who offers a proven ability to initiate new programs and implement organizational change, communicate effectively with and motivate people at all levels, as well as enthusiastically market new ideas and concepts.

EDUCATION   Completed **36 hours towards an Ed.D. in Administration**, South Carolina State University, Orangeburg, SC; attended a Summer Institute related to this program at Cornell University, NY.
Master's degree in Education Administration, Campbell University, Buies Creek, NC, 1989.
B.S. degree in Elementary Education, Southern Nazarene University, Bethany, OK, 1978.
As a principal, have attended professional development programs related to employee supervision, time management, creative leadership, and other areas.

EXPERIENCE   *Have established a reputation as an innovative leader and powerful motivator while excelling in this track record of promotion within the educational field:*
PRINCIPAL. (1991-present). Have served as principal of three different schools at the world's largest U.S. military base, Ft. Bragg, NC:
- In 2002 was selected for my current position, replacing a principal who had served this 400-student school for 30 years; have provided strong leadership in the midst of a fluid situation in which nearly half the staff will change after the 2002-03 school year because of redistricting and a new school.
- From 1994-02 as the principal and "chief operating officer" of Murray School, became known as a resourceful and visionary leader while developing an attitude of teamwork among the staff and implementing exciting new programs.
- Authored a grant which provided money for a center that allows students to write and publish books.
- Used my writing and interpersonal skills to obtain grant money from Hallmark, Nestle's, and other major corporations for a literacy program which distributed free books three times a year.
- Wrote a grant and received funds from Chrysler Corp. for this new program; was flown to Washington, DC, to participate in a "think tank" with 11 other program coordinators from all over the nation.
- Developed a new after-school program in which children were involved in writing and producing videos.
- Promoted the concept of "a sound mind in a sound body" through numerous programs and events teaching wellness and honoring fitness.
- Promoted to Principal after serving as Assistant Principal from 1989-91; was involved in long-range strategic planning and goal setting related to curriculum and staff development and earned a name as a visionary thinker and effective manager/motivator.

TEACHER and **PROGRAM DIRECTOR.** (1978-87). Taught school and managed educational programs in international environments where English was a second language for many of the teachers and most of the students.
- Became respected among my peers as an innovative and enthusiastic leader, and was encouraged to utilize my talents in management roles within the educational field.

PERSONAL   Familiar with Microsoft Word, Excel and PageMaker software programs. Can provide excellent personal and professional references.

CHANGING CAREERS

Date

Exact Name of Person
Title or Position
Name of Company
Address (number and street)
Address (city, state, and zip)

From Teaching to Private Industry

Dear Exact Name of Person: (or Dear Sir or Madam if answering a blind ad.)

Can you use an energetic, and intelligent young professional who offers a reputation as a talented and persuasive communicator who can sell ideas and concepts to others? I am known as a detailed-oriented individual who is determined to excel and provide a business with sound ideas and the organizational skills to carry those ideas to their successful completion.

As you will see from my enclosed resume, I have been effective in positions and volunteer roles which called for the ability to relate to others and often to persuade them to listen to my suggestions. With a keen eye for detail and strong time management abilities, I feel that my experience as an educator has given me a chance to hone skills which would effectively transfer to other industries.

While attending The University of North Carolina at Chapel Hill where I was a Dean's List student, I refined my time management skills while strengthening my public relations, communications, and project management abilities as a junior high school math tutor, coordinator, for freshmen orientation activities, and volunteer in the pediatric section of the UNC Hospitals.

From my resume you will gather the facts about my success as an educator, what may not be as obvious is the fact that I possess a strong interest in sales and marketing. I feel that the very qualities that have made me effective are readily transferable to other fields: a persuasive and informative style of communication, the ability to feel at ease and make others at ease in a variety of situations, and the dedication to quality apparent in everything I attempt.

I hope you will welcome my call soon to arrange a brief meeting at your convenience to discuss your current and future needs and how I might serve them. Thank you in advance for your time.

Sincerely yours,

Fortuna Ramos

Alternate last paragraph:
I hope you will call or write me soon to suggest a time convenient for us to meet and discuss your current and future needs and how I might serve them. Thank you in advance for your time.

from **Teaching to Private Industry**

FORTUNA RAMOS

1110½ Hay Street, Fayetteville, NC 28305   •   preppub@aol.com   •   (910) 483-6611

___

OBJECTIVE

To offer a reputation as a detail-oriented, well-organized professional with excellent written and verbal communication and sales skills to a business in need of a quick thinker who is known as a talented manager of human, material, and fiscal resources.

EXPERIENCE

ADMINISTRATIVE AND PLANNING SPECIALIST and **CLASSROOM TEACHER.** Culbreth Primary School, Chapel Hill, NC (2003-present). As a fifth grade teacher, handle a wide variety of administrative, budgeting, public relations, and management activities in addition to preparing lessons and working with approximately 26 students on a daily basis.
- Helped prepare an annual operating budget: conducted research and prioritized needs resulting in $134,570 being allocated for personnel and $7,630 for maintenance.
- Wrote material which was used on local radio stations and excelled in selling my ideas on numerous subjects to others.
- Planned and organized lessons for integrated units and developed a discipline plan.
- Supervised and oversaw the performance of one assistant.
- Applied organizational skills and patience while coordinating various field trips.
- Conducted twice-weekly tutoring sessions for students with problems.
- Maintained open communication with parents of my students so that accomplishments and problem areas could be fully discussed and acted on.
- Applied my organizational skills planning and carrying out seasonal parties for 72 faculty and staff members as well as an awards banquet for 200 people including 75 students.

Strengthened public relations, communications, and organizational abilities while learning to manage my time effectively in part-time and volunteer positions while attending college:
STUDENT TEACHER. Chapel Hill, NC (2003). Learned how to manage classroom activities for a 28-student fourth grade classroom at Frank Porter Graham Elementary School.
- Gained a strong base of experience with Macintosh computers with CD-ROM as well as VCRs and camcorders used to make presentations and conduct classroom activities.

TUTOR. Culbreth Middle School, Chapel Hill, NC (2002). As a volunteer for seventh grade math classes, prepared lessons and worked with at-risk students to help them improve their skills and learn how to develop good study habits.

ORIENTATION COUNSELOR. The University of North Carolina at Chapel Hill (2002). Was selected to help in a program which provided incoming freshmen with guidance while they were becoming adjusted to college life: gave tours, provided information about campus facilities and activities, and addressed their questions and concerns.
- On my own initiative, approached representatives of major area companies to solicit contributions; gathered materials and assembled welcome packets.

PATIENT RELATIONS VOLUNTEER. The University of North Carolina Hospitals, Chapel Hill, NC (2001). Was cited as a caring and compassionate individual while interacting with the parents of children who were hospital in-patients; organized games and spent time with children while also helping the parents by providing comfort and reassurance to parents.

EDUCATION & TRAINING

B.A., Psychology and Education, The University of North Carolina at Chapel Hill, 2003.
- Placed on the Dean's List with a GPA above 3.5 for three semesters.
Excelled in more than 300 hours of training in areas including conflict resolution as well as in special techniques for teaching both gifted and learning disabled students.

SKILLS

Operate standard office equipment including telephones, typewriters, copiers, and computers using Microsoft Word, MECC, and Print Shop software; am familiar with audiovisual equipment such as projectors, laser disc panels, and camcorders.

PERSONAL

Have a working knowledge of the French language. Easily adapt to changing situations and can relate to people of all ages and socioeconomic levels. Will relocate.

CHANGING CAREERS

Date

Exact Name of Person
Title or Position
Name of Company
Address (no., street)
Address (city, state, zip)

From Teaching to Sales/Public Relations

Dear Exact Name of Person: (or Dear Sir or Madam if answering a blind ad.)

Can you use an energetic and enthusiastic young professional who offers strong communication skills and a persuasive and diplomatic manner, along with sales experience?

As you will see from my enclosed resume, I recently received my bachelor's degree from the College of Atlanta, Atlanta, GA. While attending college I refined my time management skills and displayed my adaptability in part-time and seasonal jobs requiring strong sales, communication, and instructional skills.

My experience as a student teacher was both challenging and rewarding. I was required to develop lesson plans which motivated and instructed the children while also making learning fun and interesting. I am very proud of my accomplishments in living up to the expectations of a very demanding supervising teacher. I feel that among my greatest strengths are my tact and listening skills — I am able to hear both sides of an issue and diplomatically explain my views. You would find me to be an optimistic and creative individual with a talent for selling ideas and concepts as well as products and services.

Although I love children and enjoyed my student teaching, I have decided that I wish to use my strong communication, organizational, and management skills in a business environment. I am certain that I will be able to apply in a business situation many of the concepts and techniques I learned while completing a degree oriented toward teaching.

I hope you will welcome my call soon to arrange a brief meeting at your convenience to discuss your current and future needs and how I might serve them. Thank you in advance for your time.

Sincerely yours,

Annabelle Vines

Alternate last paragraph:
I hope you will call or write me soon to suggest a time convenient for us to meet and discuss your current and future needs and how I might serve them. Thank you in advance for your time.

ANNABELLE VINES

1110½ Hay Street, Fayetteville, NC 28305   •   preppub@aol.com   •   (910) 483-6611

OBJECTIVE   To apply my sales and communication abilities to an organization in need of a mature young professional who offers a talent for training and teaching others as well as a reputation as a creative thinker and good listener with a high level of enthusiasm and energy.

EDUCATION   Bachelor's degree, Elementary Education, the College of Atlanta, Atlanta, GA, 2003.

EXPERIENCE   *Learned to manage my time while juggling the demands of attending college full time and excelling in often simultaneous part-time and seasonal jobs requiring strength in the areas of sales, public relations, and providing instruction:*
STUDENT TEACHER. Macon Elementary School, Macon, GA (2003). After spending a short period of time observing the teacher's interactions with a class of third graders, took over all classroom activities including planning and carrying out daily activities for the children.
- Became skilled in planning lessons which called for a variety of learning styles and were interesting enough to motivate the students.
- Created a classroom management plan which was challenging enough to meet the standards of a very exacting supervisory teacher.
- Applied my creativity, optimism, and enthusiasm to make learning fun for children.
- Learned the importance of being patient and listening to the children's concerns.

STOCKER. Talbot's, Washington, DC (2002). Applied my attention to detail while seeing that new merchandise was properly ticketed and also helped with unloading shipments and tagging merchandise for sale.

SALES REPRESENTATIVE. The Post and Courier, Charleston, SC (2001-02). Learned to use my persuasiveness and sales abilities while calling customers on the phone and letting them know the cost of subscriptions.
- Gained valuable experience in applying persistence and thoroughness when trying to sell a service.

HOSTESS/WAITRESS. The Captain's Restaurant, Wrightsville Beach, NC (summers 2001-02). Contributed a cheerful attitude and patience while greeting customers and managing a waiting list that often stretched to two to three hours at this popular restaurant.
- Displayed the ability to work hard and still remain diplomatic and positive even when things were very hectic.
- Helped with daily activities including answering phone inquiries, serving drinks, and assisting in supporting other staff members to provide quality customer service.

SALES REPRESENTATIVE. The House of Hug'ems, Charleston, SC (2002). Refined my sales skills working independently by setting up a booth and making attractive displays and then demonstrating different puppets for sale.
- Displayed creative talents by finding interesting and new ways to make the puppets attractive to potential buyers.

PERSONAL   Am proud of a recent accomplishment in helping an older woman trust me and relax in my instructional methods to overcome her fear of the water and swim. Quickly pick up new ideas and concepts. Excel in motivating others to learn and grow.

CHANGING CAREERS

Date

Exact Name of Person
Title or Position
Name of Company
Address (number and street)
Address (city, state, and ZIP)

From Food Service
Management to
Other Management

Dear Exact Name of Person: (or Dear Sir or Madam if answering a blind ad.)

Can you use an articulate, detail-oriented professional who offers outstanding abilities in the areas of sales program development and management, financial management, and the training and supervision of employees?

You will see by my enclosed resume that I have built a track record of accomplishments with Holiday Inn Management Services where I am currently the Account Director at the University of North Carolina campus in Chapel Hill, NC. During my six years in this position I have reduced labor costs and increased auxiliary sales while overseeing a program with a $900,000 annual operating budget. I oversee two supervisors and a 30-person staff which provides resident dining, catering, conference, and retail dining services on a private college campus.

In addition to my business, inventory control, personnel, and human resources management responsibilities, I also am heavily involved in the development and management of promotional materials and programs. I have refined natural verbal and written communication skills while acting as liaison between corporate headquarters and the university, training and dealing with employees, and handling customer service activities.

I believe that you would find me to be an articulate professional with the ability to learn quickly and apply my organizational skills and common sense approach.

I hope you will welcome my call soon to arrange a brief meeting at your convenience to discuss your current and future needs and how I might serve them. Thank you in advance for your time.

Sincerely yours,

Callahan Warren

Alternate last paragraph:
I hope you will call or write me soon to suggest a time convenient for us to meet and discuss your current and future needs and how I might serve them. Thank you in advance for your time.

from Food Service Management to Other Management

CALLAHAN WARREN

1110½ Hay Street, Fayetteville, NC 28305 • preppub@aol.com • (910) 483-6611

OBJECTIVE

To offer my expertise in reducing costs as well as increasing profits and customer satisfaction while displaying exceptional sales, leadership, and financial management abilities and refining organizational, training, and time management skills.

EXPERIENCE

Built a track record of accomplishments with Holiday Inn Management Services at University of North Carolina at Chapel Hill, NC:

ACCOUNT DIRECTOR. (2003-present). During a six-year period in this role, have reduced total labor costs more than $96,000 while operating a $900,000 program providing this campus with resident dining, catering, conference, and retail dining services.

- Provided outstanding customer satisfaction in all areas of dining services with a staff of two supervisors and approximately 30 employees.
- Increased Operating Profit Contributions (OPC) from $25,000 to $90,000 and auxiliary sales to more than $228,000 over a six-year period by identifying opportunities, developing strategy, and implementing new plans.
- Polished managerial abilities while developing budgets and business plans along with making revisions in procedures which led to increases in sales and production.
- Managed a procurement program for more than 1,000 line items.
- Reconciled profit and loss statements and balance sheet management.
- Supervised accounts payable and receivable, payroll, and weekly financial reports sent to the corporate office as well as acting as liaison between the corporation and client.
- Assisted the regional sales director in the development of sales proposals by using sales and cost analysis modules.
- Used my communication skills to prepare brochures, calendars, and other promotional materials as well as in the development of a client communication manual.

FOOD SERVICE MANAGER. (2002-03). Gained exposure to a wide range of day-to-day operational activities related to campus dining, catering, and conference food services.

- Applied time management and organizational skills overseeing fiscal areas of operations which included purchasing as well as inventory, labor cost, and cash-handling controls.
- Handled additional activities ranging from vendor specifications, to menu development and implementation, to promotions and marketing, to catering, to sanitation and safety.
- Updated the automated procedures which reduced unit labor costs.
- Implemented a computerized system used to handle associate payroll, accounts payable, accounts receivable, and billing.

MANAGEMENT TRAINEE. (2002). As a food service management trainee, became familiar with customer service, scheduling, and employee training.

STUDENT MANAGER. Holiday Inn Management Services, Davidson University, Augusta, SC (2001). Hired by the corporation while attending the university, was in charge of food handling controls and supervised 10 part-time employees.

EDUCATION & TRAINING

B.A., Business Administration (minor in Marketing and Finance), Davidson University, SC.
Completed extensive corporate training programs in major areas of emphasis including:

public relations	safety training	management
human resource management	sales & cost analysis	Microsoft Excel
internal accounting systems	labor productivity I and II	diversity/sensitivity training
Total Quality Management 1 and II	food handling & food-borne illness	
Hazard Analysis Critical Control Points (HACCP)		

CERTIFICATIONS

Am a licensed food handler with certification in food-borne illness.

PERSONAL

Am a fast learner who is capable of easily adjusting to new environments. Enjoy using my well-developed communication skills to impact on productivity and customer satisfaction.

CHANGING CAREERS

Date

Exact Name of Person
Title or Position
Name of Company
Address (number and street)
Address (city, state, and ZIP)

**From Teaching to
Business**

Dear Exact Name of Person: (or Dear Sir or Madam if answering a blind ad.)

I would appreciate an opportunity to talk with you soon about how I could contribute to your organization through my strong communication and interpersonal skills as well as through my sales/customer service abilities and management potential.

As you will see from my enclosed resume, I graduated with honors in 2001 from the University of North Carolina at Chapel Hill with a degree in English language and literature. Although I became certified to teach, and actually excelled after graduation in positions teaching 10th and 8th graders, I have decided that I wish to utilize my professional skills in a business rather than an academic environment. I believe my creativity, warm personality, and well organized approach to work could make me a valuable asset to an organization seeking highly motivated self starters.

Prior to and while earning my degree I excelled in jobs as a waitress, and I credit those jobs with helping me acquire my excellent public relations and customer service skills. While working as a waitress and customer service coordinator from 1994-01, I became part of the restaurant's management team and handled responsibilities including training new employees, coordinating major events and banquets, and overseeing food/bar operations.

I feel certain you would find me in person to be a congenial individual who prides myself on my attention to detail, excellent memory, and ability to get along with anyone. I can provide outstanding personal and professional references.

I hope you will welcome my call soon to arrange a brief meeting at your convenience to discuss your current and future needs and how I might serve them. Thank you in advance for your time.

Sincerely yours,

Jessica Wheeler

Alternate last paragraph:
I hope you will call or write me soon to suggest a time convenient for us to meet and discuss your current and future needs and how I might serve them. Thank you in advance for your time.

JESSICA WHEELER

1110½ Hay Street, Fayetteville, NC 28305   •   preppub@aol.com   •   (910) 483-6611

OBJECTIVE

To offer outstanding communication and planning skills along with an eye for detail to an organization that can benefit from my strong work ethic, excellent memory, and ability to relate to and get along with people while selling them on ideas and concepts.

EDUCATION

Earned a B.S. degree in English Language and Literature, University of North Carolina at Chapel Hill, NC, 2001.
- Was named to the Chancellor's List on two occasions in recognition of my academic accomplishments in maintaining a perfect 4.0 GPA.
- Earned membership in Sigma Tau Delta Honor Society for maintaining a high GPA in my area of concentration.
- Refined my time management and organizational abilities while meeting the demands of working full time, taking care of a home and family, and meeting high academic standards as a full-time college upperclassman.

EXPERIENCE

COMMUNICATION SKILLS INSTRUCTOR. Southview Middle School, Cumberland County Schools, Hope Mills, NC (2002-03). Applied expertise in coordinating and planning lessons for two levels of students as well as using my creativity to develop a course of instruction for a study program which had no textbook to follow.
- Gained an awareness of the importance of establishing a plan and structure for a course of instruction and keeping close to it.

HIGH SCHOOL ENGLISH TEACHER. Southview Senior High School, Fayetteville, NC (2001-02). Taught both regular and honors English classes while developing my planning skills and refining my public speaking abilities.

CUSTOMER SERVICE COORDINATOR/WAITRESS. The Sea Restaurant, Fayetteville, NC (1994-01). Was chosen to train new employees at this exclusive restaurant while handling a variety of activities including greeting and seating customers, serving food and bar beverages, and running the cash registers.
- Displayed a creative approach to making suggestions to the owner, many of which were adopted and directly impacted on customer service and profitability.
- Handled the details of coordinating large events for as many as 60 people to include taking the initial reservation and arranging and helping in the selection of food and drink choices and prices.
- Became adept at dealing with difficult customers and in ensuring that all customers were provided with the best quality of food and service.

WAITRESS. Luigi's Restaurant and Deno's Steak House, Fayetteville, NC (1990-93). Learned to manage my time effectively and deal with the public while simultaneously working the lunch period at a popular Italian family-style restaurant and the dinner period at a steak house where I frequently handled banquets and large groups.

COMPUTERS

Familiar with Microsoft Word and Excel; type 50 wpm.

LICENSE

Am licensed by the State Department of Public Instruction to teach at the secondary level.

PERSONAL

Am open minded and eager to learn. Believe that I offer strong personal ethics and a willingness to do whatever is needed to get the job done right.

CHANGING CAREERS

Date

Exact Name of Person
Title or Position
Name of Company
Address (no., street)
Address (city, state, zip)

**From College Teaching
to Management**

Dear Exact Name of Person: (or Dear Sir or Madam if answering a blind ad.)

I would appreciate an opportunity to talk with you soon about how I could contribute to your organization through my proven analytical and problem-solving skills as well as through my strong planning and management abilities.

As you will see from my resume, I recently earned my M.A. degree from the University of North Carolina, where I achieved a 3.5 GPA in a rigorous master's degree program while also working nearly full time to finance my education. While enrolled in this graduate program, I have earned a reputation as an insightful analyst, articulate communicator, and dedicated hard worker.

You will also see from my resume that I excelled in a "track record" of accomplishment as a military professional prior to graduate school. While serving in the U.S. Army, I was handpicked for jobs which required a young leader who could implement new concepts and pioneer new ventures. In one job I established a new unit "from scratch" and in another job I implemented a new concept in tactical voice intercept. I am known for my ability to anticipate problems, foresee obstacles, and predict major obstacles.

With strong technical and problem-solving skills, I am knowledgeable of software including Microsoft Word, Excel, dBase IV, SAS statistical software, and SYSTAT. I offer a proven ability to rapidly master new software.

I can provide outstanding personal and professional references, and I am single and willing to relocate anywhere, according to your needs.

I hope you will welcome my call soon when I try to arrange a brief meeting with you to discuss your needs and goals and how I might serve them. Thank you in advance for your time.

Sincerely,

Harold Walkup

Alternate last paragraph:
I hope you will welcome my call soon to arrange a brief meeting at your convenience to discuss your current and future needs and how I might serve them. Thank you in advance for your time.

HAROLD WALKUP

1110½ Hay Street, Fayetteville, NC 28305   •   preppub@aol.com   •   (910) 483-6611

OBJECTIVE

To benefit an organization that can use a versatile young professional who offers outstanding planning, organizational, and management abilities refined through work experience along with exceptional analytical and problem-solving skills.

EDUCATION

Master of Arts (M.A.), Political Science and Public Administration, University of North Carolina at Chapel Hill (UNC-CH), NC; December 2002.
- Excelled academically; graduated with a 3.5 GPA.

Bachelor of Arts (B.A.), Political Science and Public Administration, UNC-CH, 1998.

LANGUAGE & TECHNICAL TRAINING

Received a diploma after completing studies in the Korean Language, Defense Language Institute, The Presidio, Monterey, CA, 1994.
- Graduated *with honors*.

Graduated *with honors* from the U.S. Air Force Intelligence School, Goodfellow AFB, TX, 1995, and *first* in my U.S. Army Basic Training Course, Ft. Leonard Wood, MO, 1993.

COMPUTER SKILLS

Knowledgeable of software including Microsoft Word, Excel, dBase IV, SAS statistical software, and SYSTAT.

EXPERIENCE

COLLEGE INSTRUCTOR. Methodist College, Fayetteville, NC (2003-present). As a Lecturer of Political Science, teach a class in state and local government which examines their framework and evaluates their contributions to the federal government with an emphasis on North Carolina state government in comparison to other states.

SECURITY OFFICER. Campbell University, Buies Creek, NC (1998-02). While completing my undergraduate and graduate degrees, worked nearly full-time at this large college with 2,500 students and a 250-person staff; oversaw the overall safety and security of people and assets; planned and organized security for special functions.
- Utilized the extensive electronics training I gained in military service to devise and carry out security plans that have made this campus one of the safest in the nation.

ASSISTANT TO THE ASSISTANT CITY MANAGER (INTERN). City of Southern Pines, NC (Jan 1998-Apr 1998). Became familiar with city accounting procedures for grants, municipal bond sales, and special projects while assisting the Assistant City Manager for Administration and Finance and working with the Manager for Grants and Special Projects.
- Was formally praised for my tireless efforts in helping the city move its offices to a new location; ordered materials such as room partitions and scheduled meetings with city officials and building contractors to monitor the project's critical path.

Advanced in leadership and project management roles, U.S. Army:

GENERAL MANAGER. Ft. Sill, OK (1997). Was handpicked for this job which placed me in an essentially entrepreneurial role coordinating the start-up of a new unit and creating "from scratch" a language maintenance program; received a respected medal for my work in establishing procedures for operations and training, scheduling testing for language proficiency, and overseeing the accomplishment of voice intercept and electronic interference activities.

TEAM LEADER. Korea (1995-96). Was specially selected to play a key leadership role in implementing a new concept in tactical voice intercept; was commended for my excellent decision-making and problem-solving skills while leading a team of eight people in rugged field environments in the organization's first-ever Low Level Voice Intercept (LLVI) team.

MATH/ENGLISH/COMPUTER SCIENCE TUTOR. Fayetteville State University Center for Continuing Education, Fayetteville, NC (1989-90). While earning my B.A. degree, was a popular tutor of math, English, and computer science.

PERSONAL

Offer a reputation as a tactful and articulate communicator who excels in working with people at all levels. Can provide outstanding references. Single. Held Top Secret security clearance.

CHANGING CAREERS

Exact Name of Person
Title or Position
Name of Company
Address (number and street)
Address (city, state, and zip)

From Medical to Manufacturing

Dear Exact Name of Person: (or Dear Sir or Madam if answering a blind ad.)

I would appreciate an opportunity to talk with you soon about how I could contribute to your organization through my well-developed planning skills, attention to detail, customer service orientation, and knowledge of production scheduling and quality control in manufacturing environments.

Known for my dedication to high quality, I have always been effective in supervising production workers and leading them to reach or exceed production quotas while keeping costs down. As you will see from my resume, I excelled as a Production Supervisor and Shipping Supervisor for several area manufacturing firms.

A quick learner who easily becomes familiar with new procedures and methods, I can then pass my knowledge on to others. Highly effective in developing subordinates, I have often been recognized for my ability to provide an example of fairness and honesty for others to follow and for being able to pass my own high performance standards and ethics on to others.

I hope you will welcome my call soon to arrange a brief meeting at your convenience to discuss your current and future needs and how I might serve them. Thank you in advance for your time.

Sincerely yours,

Marcella Wetzig

Alternate last paragraph:
I hope you will call or write me soon to suggest a time convenient for us to meet and discuss your current and future needs and how I might serve them. Thank you in advance for your time.

MARCELLA WETZIG

1110½ Hay Street, Fayetteville, NC 28305   •   preppub@aol.com   •   (910) 483-6611

OBJECTIVE   To offer my strong planning and organizational skills to a business that can use a mature individual who excels in jobs that require the ability to develop and maintain good relations with the public as well as motivate employees to provide outstanding customer service and high levels of productivity.

EXPERIENCE   **MEDICAL THERAPIST.** Winston-Salem Dialysis Center, Winston-Salem, NC (2003-present). Am known for my caring attitude and ability to put people at ease while dealing with the specialized aspect of medical care for hemodialysis patients.

- Worked with an average daily patient load of ten people while administering treatment and providing individual care.
- Took patient's vital signs and processed the special needs of those with weight problems in addition to setting up equipment prior to treatment.
- Observed all related safety requirements for patients as well as those applying to staff members.

NURSING ASSISTANT. Cape Fear Nursing Center, Wake Forest, NC (2003). Applied communication skills while dealing on a daily basis with 12 patients requiring long-term nursing care.

PRODUCTION SUPERVISOR. Calibre Apparel Company, Canaveral, NC (1998-02). Earned a reputation as an effective supervisor with the ability to produce high quality products and keep costs down while monitoring the work flow of 40 employees.

- Hired, trained, and supervised employees.
- Evaluated employee skills and assigned them according to their strengths.
- Applied knowledge of quality control standards while corresponding with contract buyers and ensuring compliance in the orders they had received.
- Polished my analytical, mathematical, and reasoning skills.

SHIPPING SUPERVISOR. Kennedy Sportswear, Inc., Wilmington, NC (1994-96). For a manufacturer of leisure wear, handled day-to-day activities ranging from production scheduling, to supervising 25 employees involved in tagging and packing merchandise for shipment to distributors, to processing correspondence with contract buyers.

- Applied my attention to detail and math skills while processing invoices for shipping and receiving as well as during the preparation of quarterly tax returns.
- Kept track of employee time cards and tallied payroll figures for 100 employees.
- Refined my communication and human resource management skills while earning recognition for my dedication to producing quality products.

PRODUCTION SUPERVISOR. Lori Lee Manufacturing, Inc., Clinton, NC (1985-94). Oversaw quality control support while training and supervising 25 employees and leading them to reach production levels for this manufacturer.

- Assigned employees to work areas so that production goals could be met.
- Was promoted on the basis of my dedication and dependability after going to work for this company at age 17 and being trained to operate an industrial sewing machine.

TRAINING   Am studying computer applications at Sampson Community College, Sampson, NC.
Attended various medical training programs which resulted in certification as a Hemodialysis Therapist, Nursing Assistant, and Phlebotomist.

REGISTRATION   Am licensed by the State of North Carolina as a Nurse's Aide I.

PERSONAL   Have a reputation for being very fair and not expecting others to do more than I can do myself. Am very quality conscious and dedicated to achieving results. Thrive on challenges. Can handle pressure and deadlines with authority.

CHANGING CAREERS

Date

Exact Name of Person
Title or Position
Name of Company
Address (no., street)
Address (city, state, zip)

From Parole Services to
Program Management

Dear Exact Name of Person: (or Dear Sir or Madam if answering a blind ad.)

With the enclosed resume and this letter of introduction, I would like to begin the process of formally applying for the job you recently advertised as a program manager.

As I believe you will see from my resume, I offer the skills, experience, and personal qualities which you are seeking. Since graduating with my B.A. degree, I have excelled in what is generally considered one of the most high-stress jobs in the world: administering parole services. While handling a large caseload of 150 clients, I supervise a wide variety of parole conditions and assist people in finding employment, obtaining help for substance abuse problems, managing their personal affairs and finances, and generally reorganizing their lives in creative and productive ways. I believe my positive and cheerful attitude has been the key to my excelling in a profession known for its high "burnout" and turnover rate.

I have become skilled in finding creative solutions for difficult problems, and I can provide strong personal and professional references describing my character and professional abilities. Computer literate, I offer a reputation as a tactful and diplomatic communicator with excellent writing skills. I have become adept at working with law enforcement officials at all levels, from judges to police officers, while also performing liaison with attorneys, prison administrators, business managers and private sector employers, and federal/state assistance programs of every kind.

You would find me to be a warm and enthusiastic professional who offers an exceptionally creative approach to program/case management, office and operations administration, and law enforcement/community relations.

I hope you will write or call me soon to arrange a brief meeting at your convenience to discuss your current and future needs and how I might serve them. I feel certain I could become a valuable asset to your organization, and I would enjoy an opportunity to show you in person that I am the qualified individual you are seeking.

Yours sincerely,

Cynthia Willis

from Parole Services to Program Management

CYNTHIA WILLIS

1110½ Hay Street, Fayetteville, NC 28305 • preppub@aol.com • (910) 483-6611

OBJECTIVE

I want to contribute to an organization that can use an experienced administrator and program manager who offers proven decision-making and problem-solving skills along with a reputation as a resourceful, creative, well-organized professional with excellent written and oral communication skills.

EDUCATION

Bachelor of Arts in Sociology and **Business Administration**, the University of North Carolina at Chapel Hill, NC, 1991.
Have excelled in numerous seminars and courses related to these and other areas:

case management	law enforcement administration
human resources administration	budget management
computer operations	effective counseling strategies
sexual harassment prevention	emergency first aid
management of sex offenders	alcohol and drug abuse prevention
adolescent counseling/crisis intervention	schizophrenia
impact of child abuse	advanced probation and parole
substance abuse counseling	family therapy/family counseling

Completed extensive training at the N.C. Justice Academy, Salem, NC.

EXPERIENCE

Have become known for my ability to communicate well with others and to assist others in developing realistic strategies for solving their life problems, finding suitable employment, developing career goals, and becoming productive members of society:
ADULT PAROLE SERVICES CASE MANAGER. Department of Corrections, Raleigh, NC (2003-present). Am extremely knowledgeable of how to network and "get things done" within the legal, law enforcement, business, and social services communities and apply that knowledge while managing a caseload of 150 clients comprised of offenders released from prison by the Parole Commission.

- Assist parolees in all aspects of life management including seeking help for substance abuse problems, prospecting for and obtaining suitable employment, managing personal finances as well as personal relationships, and generally finding a "focus" in life that is meaningful and motivating.
- Am known for my compassionate attitude as well as for my tough, creative, and practical approach to solving difficult problems.
- Work with law enforcement officials at all levels, from judges to police officers, while also performing liaison with attorneys, prison administrators, business managers and employers in the private sector, and federal assistance programs of every kind.
- Excel in a job which requires constant attention to detail as I supervise numerous conditions of parole including compliance with community service, debt and fee payment obligations, and other matters.
- Have acquired excellent "crisis management" skills while dealing routinely with incidents such as threatened suicides and other volatile, high-risk situations.

ADULT PROBATION SERVICES CASE MANAGER. Department of Corrections, Wilmington, NC (1996-03). Became skilled in the counseling and supervision of offenders placed on probation by the court system; enforced conditions of parole.

- Became known for my tact and diplomacy as well as for my excellent writing skills.
- Excelled in a profession generally regarded as very stressful and which has a very high turnover and "burnout" rate.
- Established an impressive track record of success in assisting dysfunctional people.

CERTIFICATIONS

Am Department of Corrections certified in unarmed self defense.
Am CPR certified.
Certified in Arrest, Search, and Seizure.

SKILLS

Am computer literate and experienced in working with various types of software.
Am skilled in operating electronic house arrest equipment.

PERSONAL

Pride myself on my positive and cheerful attitude, and believe that a healthy mental attitude is the key to dealing with life's difficulties in a positive manner. Can provide excellent references.

CHANGING CAREERS

Director of Human Resources
Wake County Community College
2200 Airport Road
Raleigh, NC 28374

From Hairdresser to
Technical College
Instructor

Dear Sir or Madam:

I would appreciate an opportunity to talk with you soon about how I could contribute to Wake County Community College as an instructor.

As you will see from my resume, I was previously hired by Tar Heel Community College to set up its cosmetology program "from scratch," which included ordering equipment, supplies, textbooks, and educational materials. In the first year after I started the program, I trained many students who won state and national awards based on their ability to create total fashion looks. I also established the National Cosmetology Association in that area of the country.

I am interested in becoming an instructor within your cosmetology program and feel my most recent experience in founding and managing a successful beauty salon would make me a valuable asset to your students. Through setting up and managing this business while simultaneously holding elected positions in numerous state and local professional associations, I have acquired valuable insights into business management which I feel could be of great value to your students. With a reputation as a talented and dynamic communicator, I enjoy sharing my knowledge and take great pride in the fact that I have helped many people become very successful through my ability to train and develop people. Well known statewide for the contributions I have made to improving professional standards in the industry, I am skilled at communicating concepts ranging from hairstyling techniques to management principles.

You would find me in person to be a warm and caring person who could enhance the excellent reputation your college already enjoys. I am confident that my teaching ability and extensive experience could combine to give your students the "competitive edge" in the marketplace. I have studied with some of the leading hairstyling experts worldwide, and I would enjoy the challenge of making sure your graduates can compete with the best.

I hope you will call or write me soon to suggest a time convenient for us to meet and discuss your current and future needs and how I might best serve them. Thank you in advance for your time.

Sincerely yours,

Penelope Gaillard

248   Resumes And Cover Letters That Have Worked, Revised Edition

from Hairdresser to Technical College Instructor

PENELOPE GAILLARD

1110½ Hay Street, Fayetteville, NC 28305 • preppub@aol.com • (910) 483-6611

OBJECTIVE

To contribute to the quality of teaching and instruction in an organization which can use a successful business woman with a dynamic personality who combines extensive entrepreneurial and business management experience with the proven ability to communicate the theory, concepts, and techniques that will be of most value to students.

HIGHLIGHTS OF ACHIEVEMENTS

- Set up and taught the first Cosmetology Department at Tar Heel Community College, Southern Pines, NC; was instrumental in establishing the National Hairdressers Association in that area.
- Trained numerous competition winners within the cosmetology schools and salons and have won many competitions based on my ability to create a total fashion look "from head to toe."
- Appointed by the Governor of North Carolina to serve on the State Board of Cosmetic Art, and was elected vice-chairman of that committee; served as President of the National Hairdressers Association of Burlington and chairman of the Continuing Education Committee for N.C.
- Am the inventor of and patent holder for a new process/system in the beauty industry.
- Oversaw nationwide sales for a four-year period, including organizing and coordinating trade show presentations and giving sales presentations to corporate leaders to introduce products; initial order form from Redken Laboratories was $500,000.
- Featured in a national magazine for my teamwork skills and incentive programs.
- Held numerous elected positions in state associations and committees, and played a key role in establishing new units for national associations.

EXPERIENCE

INSTRUCTOR. Jordan Matthews High School, Siler City, NC (2001-03). As a part-time instructor, taught all phases of cosmetology to high school students.
- Served on the Advisory Board of the High School Division for Chatham County.

GENERAL MANAGER. The Chic Salon, Garden City, NC (1994-03). Started "from scratch" and then managed a hair salon business which grew into a popular hair salon grossing a quarter of a million dollars annually in a town with 5,000 people.
- Was featured in a national magazine for my teamwork skills and incentive programs I established in a cosmetology business I founded and managed.
- Published an article entitled "If You Don't Like Criticism, Do Something to Change" in a national magazine.
- Used my training to become a respected professional in the hairdressing industry: won numerous national and local competitions; served as President of the National Hairdressers Association and served as Educator for the association; became well-known for my contributions to improving professional standards within this industry.
- As an appointed member of the State Board of Cosmetic Art, traveled all over the state setting up and administering Board Exams; became involved in rewriting the state exam.
- Trained and developed dozens of employees who became successful business people.

Highlights of other experience:
TRAINING COORDINATOR. Leon's Beauty School, Greensboro, NC. Was in charge of the advanced training program that licensed hairdressers attended in order to upgrade their skills and knowledge of latest techniques and current fashion.

INSTRUCTOR. Tar Heel Community College, Southern Pines, NC. Was hired by this community college to set up its cosmetology program "from scratch," which included ordering equipment, supplies, textbooks, and educational materials; in the first year after I started the program, trained many students who won state and national awards based on their ability to create total fashion looks.
- Established the National Cosmetology Association in this area of the country.
- Achieved a 100% pass rate of students taking the State Board Exam.

INSTRUCTOR. Carolina Beauty Systems, High Point, NC. Joined this chain of schools as an instructor and, after one month, was put in charge of recruiting; brought this school from "last" to "first" place in the chain in the number of students enrolled.

EDUCATION

Graduate of Burlington Beauty School and earned certificates from:

Vidal Sassoon — San Francisco	Pivot Point — Chicago	Sebastian International — LA
Carol Lynn Smith — Atlanta	Midwest Show — Chicago	Clairol — New York

CHANGING CAREERS

Date

Mr. William Monroe
Gruber Properties
222 McPherson Church Rd.
Charlotte, NC 27803

**From Store Management
to Real Estate Sales**

Dear Mr. Monroe:

I would appreciate an opportunity to talk with you soon about how I could contribute to your organization through my sales and management experience along with my formal education and technical training related to real estate.

As you will see from the enclosed resume, I am licensed by the North Carolina Real Estate Commission as a sales person and am currently completing Brokers Certification courses. I completed the "North Carolina Fundamentals of Real Estate Course" at The Charlotte School of Real Estate.

My resume also will show you my "track record" of achievement in sales and management. Although I was born and raised in the Charlotte area and am living here permanently, most recently I worked in Ft. Lauderdale and Jacksonville, FL, as a Store Manager for Camelot Music. I managed other employees, decreased inventory shrinkage, opened new stores, converted acquisition stores to Camelot systems and procedures, and was specially selected to manage a new "superstore" of more than 10,000 square feet.

I am sending you this resume because, after conducting extensive research of real estate companies, your company is the one I would most like to be associated with. I hope you will find some time in your schedule for us to meet at your convenience to discuss your needs and goals and how I might serve them. I shall look forward to hearing from you, and thank you in advance for your time.

Yours sincerely,

William Maas

from Store Management to Real Estate Sales

WILLIAM MAAS

1110½ Hay Street, Fayetteville, NC 28305   •   preppub@aol.com   •   (910) 483-6611

OBJECTIVE

To contribute to an organization that can use a resourceful and congenial sales professional with excellent customer relations skills who offers a proven "track record" of accomplishment in both sales and operations management.

SUMMARY OF EXPERIENCE

- Eight years of restaurant and retail management experience.
- Skilled in hiring, training, scheduling, and maintaining sales staff dedicated to superior customer relations.
- Proven commitment to meeting deadlines and serving customers.
- Exceptionally strong analytical and problem-solving skills.
- Known for my positive attitude and cheerful disposition.

EXPERIENCE

STORE MANAGER. Camelot Music, Jacksonville, FL, and Ft. Lauderdale, FL (1999-03). Earned a reputation as a skilled store manager who was equally effective in starting up new retail operations, "turning around" existing stores experiencing sales and profitability problems, and managing "superstores."

- After managing three Camelot Music retail stores in Jacksonville and Ft. Lauderdale, was selected to manage a new 10,000 square foot freestanding "superstore."
- Was responsible for opening new stores and converting acquisition stores to Camelot's procedures, methods, and systems.
- Devised and implemented effective merchandising techniques.
- Specialized in maintaining superior inventory conditions.
- Achieved consistent sales increases and ranked among the chain's highest volume stores.
- Diminished shrinkage and substantially increased profits.
- Implemented effective off-site sales locations utilizing radio and television as well as popular musicians and bands at successful local events.

Other experience:
After earning my Associate of Arts degree, excelled in restaurant management and was selected for management training programs.

- Worked in Hardees and was selected for their corporate training program; was selected as co-manager of a Hardees at Myrtle Beach.
- Worked in Quincy's Restaurant as an assistant manager after completing their corporate training program.

EDUCATION

Associate of Arts degree in Restaurant and Hotel Management, Baltimore's International Culinary College, 1996-98.
Completed renowned management training programs with established restaurants, Hardee's and Quincy's.
Completed high school at Hargrave Military Academy and Flora McDonald Academy.

REAL ESTATE

- Licensed by North Carolina Real Estate Commission as sales person.
- Currently completing Brokers Certification courses.
- Completed "North Carolina Fundamentals of Real Estate Course" at the Fayetteville School of Real Estate.

PERSONAL

Am an accomplished guitarist and musical collector. Was born and raised in the Fayetteville area. Born 1978. Excellent health. Single. 6'3". 175 lbs.

CHANGING CAREERS

Date

Ms. Frances McGillen
Sprint Communications
256 South Fayetteville Road
Charlotte, NC 27809

From Insurance to Sales and Customer Service

Dear Ms. McGillen:

I would appreciate an opportunity to talk with you soon about how I could contribute to your organization through my versatile customer relations, bookkeeping, computer operation, sales, and office management skills.

As you will see from my resume, I excelled academically while earning my Bachelor of Science degree in Economics and was named to the Chancellor's List and to Phi Theta Kappa Society. In an internship while earning my degree I worked for the Clerk of the Court and was involved in handling administrative duties for the Sheriff's Department and court system.

Prior to enrolling in college, I had extensive experience as a bookkeeper and office manager. I offer skills related to performing bookkeeping, preparing payroll, developing financial statements, and handling accounts receivable/payable. While in college, I acted as treasurer for the Business and Economics Club and, since 1994, I have volunteered my spare time as treasurer of a youth association, helping this outstanding youth service organization account for its yearly cash flow of $120,000.

In addition to proven intelligence and bookkeeping knowledge, I have also excelled in sales situations. While working as a Sales Representative for a Dallas-based company which markets products through home demonstrations, I ranked in the top of all sales people every year. I enjoy working with people and offer the ability to get along with just about anyone.

You would find me to be a hard worker who is confident I can excel in anything. While working for a plumbing company several years ago, I studied for and obtained my license as a plumbing contractor and, most recently, I studied for and obtained my license as a Property and Casualty Agent in the state of North Carolina.

I know you would find me to be a reliable and dedicated employee who would take great pride in being a part of your organization and helping you achieve your goals. I hope you will write or call me soon to suggest a time when we might meet to discuss your needs and how I might fit into them. Thank you in advance for your time.

Sincerely yours,

Veronica Nepstad

VERONICA NEPSTAD

1110½ Hay Street, Fayetteville, NC 28305   •   preppub@aol.com   •   (910) 483-6611

OBJECTIVE	To benefit an organization that can use a dedicated professional who offers strong personal qualities of loyalty, initiative, and resourcefulness along with excellent office administrative skills, proven sales and customer service abilities, and extensive bookkeeping knowledge.
EDUCATION	**Bachelor of Science** (B.S.) degree, **Economics**, The University of North Carolina at Chapel Hill, Chapel Hill, NC, 2002; **3.6 GPA**.

- Was named to the Chancellor's List and Phi Theta Kappa Society.
- Served as **Treasurer**, Business and Economics Club, 2000-02.

Associate of Applied Science (A.S.) degree, **Business Administration**, Fayetteville Technical Community College, Fayetteville, NC, 2000; **3.9 GPA**.

EXPERIENCE

INSURANCE AGENT. Nationwide Insurance Agency, Stedman, NC (2003-present). Passed the state licensing exam after completing Insurance Systems of North Carolina Licensing Procedures and a class for Property and Casualty Insurance; currently assist customers in completing application information and then write insurance policies while also handling a wide range of office duties: answer phones, make bank deposits, open and respond to mail, receive/collect payments, and work with national insurers.

- Am a Licensed Property and Casualty Agent.

SALES REPRESENTATIVE. Elegant Interiors & Gifts (home office: Dallas, TX), Fayetteville, NC (1996-present). Work as an independent contractor and decorating consultant in my spare time for a Dallas-based company which markets decorating accessories in at-home demonstrations; have exceeded my personal sales and marketing goals every year.

- Was the Junior Top Sales Person in my first year with the company.
- Have been named to the Top Sales Court every year since 1996.
- Refined my public speaking skills by demonstrating merchandise; refined my business management skills while ordering/delivering merchandise, maintaining records, recruiting and training other sales associates, and contributing to weekly sales meetings.

INTERNSHIP: CLERK OF THE COURT. County Clerk of the Court, Chapel Hill, NC (May 2002-July 2002). In an internship related to earning my B.S. degree in Economics, handled administrative duties for the Sheriff's Department and court system; processed paperwork and worked with the public researching files involving civil suits.

- Was commended for poise, professionalism, courtesy, and reliability; received the highest ratings on all skills and abilities measured on a formal rating, which also contained the comment that "no evaluation would be high enough for her."

PLUMBING CONTRACTOR/BOOKKEEPER. Smith Plumbing Company, Fayetteville, NC (1994-96). Obtained my N.C. State Plumbing and Heating License; hired and trained employees and made job assignments while also acting as bookkeeper/accountant for the business; bid on plumbing jobs, handled billing, collected receivables, prepared payroll, and performed bookkeeping.

- Ordered plumbing materials and supervised work performed on site.

OFFICE MANAGER/BOOKKEEPER. Smith Plumbing Co., Fayetteville, NC (1980-94). Performed bookkeeping, payroll, and collections for a small business.

Volunteer experience. (1994-present).
TREASURER. Stedman Youth Association. Maintain this youth organization's financial records and handle its bookkeeping; prepare and present monthly and annual financial statements showing the disposition of an annual cash flow of more than $120,000.

COMPUTERS	Proficient with Microsoft Word; familiar with Excel and PageMaker.
PERSONAL	Am known for my cheerful disposition and ability to work well with others. Believe that persistence, dedication, and reliability are the keys to accomplishment in life.

CHANGING CAREERS

Date

Exact Name of Person
Title or Position
Name of Company
Address (number and street)
Address (city, state, and ZIP)

From Teaching to Administration

Dear Exact Name of Person: (or Dear Sir or Madam if answering a blind ad.)

I would appreciate an opportunity to talk with you soon about how I could benefit your organization through my outstanding work ethic, people skills, and dedication.

You will see by my enclosed resume that I have well-developed organizational and planning skills and am known for being reliable, punctual, and productive. Through my degree in Public Administration as well as earlier course work emphasizing law enforcement, I have gained exposure to a wide range of subjects including human relations management, budgeting, finance and accounting, and the social sciences. I am a good judge of people and am skilled in communicating with people of all ages and socioeconomic levels through my versatile work experience.

Since 1998 I have been a Teacher's Aide for the Spartanburg Board of Education providing supportive teaching and tutoring to individual students as well as small groups. I have earned the respect of the teachers, staff members, and principals at each of the schools for my warmth and concern for the students as well as my professionalism. Although I am excelling in my job, I feel that my administrative skills are underutilized in a teaching environment, and I am confident that my excellent organizational and management abilities could be of enormous value to an organization such as yours.

Through my experience I have gained familiarity with a wide range of office machines and equipment and have always been effective in organizing and carrying out projects which require attention to detail and motivational abilities.

I hope you will welcome my call soon to arrange a brief meeting at your convenience to discuss your current and future needs and how I might serve them. Thank you in advance for your time.

Sincerely yours,

Rosalind Yurek

Alternate last paragraph:
I hope you will call or write me soon to suggest a time convenient for us to meet and discuss your current and future needs and how I might serve them. Thank you in advance for your time.

ROSALIND YUREK

1110½ Hay Street, Fayetteville, NC 28305   •   preppub@aol.com   •   (910) 483-6611

OBJECTIVE

To contribute a positive attitude and enthusiasm for helping others to an organization that can benefit from my skills in motivating and communicating with people of all ages as well as my versatility and willingness to dedicate my efforts toward progress and productivity.

EDUCATION

Earned an Associate of Applied Science degree in **Public Administration,** Fayetteville Technical Community College, NC, 2002.
- Completed course work in areas including:

financial accounting	composition	business law
police organizations	data processing	public financing
criminal investigation	public budgeting	macroeconomics
accounting for managers	oral communication	ethics in government
human resource management	state/local government	business organization

EXPERIENCE

TEACHER'S AIDE. Spartanburg Board of Education, Spartanburg, SC (1998-present). As an Instructional Aide for kindergarten through high school, assist classroom teachers by providing supportive teaching and tutoring to individuals or small groups in the county's exceptional children's programs.

- Have gained valuable experience working with students who are categorized as having "special needs," including tutoring 9 to 12-year-olds in the Willie M program who are emotionally, mentally, behaviorally, and/or physically handicapped.
- Earned the respect of each of the various teachers I assisted for my warmth and true concern for the students as well as my willingness to take on hard work.
- Displayed patience and the ability to handle stress while working with small groups of learning disabled children and those who have trouble adapting socially and who have come from backgrounds which have included receiving intensive youth services.
- Was known for my adaptability while being placed in different schools throughout the county and quickly learning the routines and expectations of the teachers, staff, and principal of each.
- Monitored students during enrichment activities including computer time and provided supervision on the playgrounds, in the lunch room, and on the bus.
- Applied my organizational and planning skills while assisting teachers in the preparation of test material and during testing.
- Learned to deal with situations unique to exceptional children who deviate from what is considered the norm in mental capacity, physical limitations, or behavioral patterns.
- Was honored with an Outstanding Performance Award, 2003.

Highlights of earlier experience: Displayed adaptability in jobs including the following:
Production Worker: learned to work under pressure and remain calm while meeting deadlines and working with a team to meet production quotas.
Preschool Teacher's Assistant: gained time management skills and refined my organizational abilities while planning and carrying out learning and recreational activities.
File Clerk: became aware of the importance of confidentiality while contributing to smooth office operations while processing and filing data for the CIA.
Food Service Worker: contributed good work habits and dependability in the hectic atmosphere of a hospital cafeteria.

SPECIAL SKILLS

Through my work experience, have become familiar with office equipment and aids including:

typewriters	calculators	copy machines
overhead projectors	multi-line phones	transparency makers
software: some knowledge of Microsoft Word, Excel and Access		

AFFILIATIONS

Held membership in the NC Association for Teacher's Assistants.

PERSONAL

Have assumed numerous leadership roles in my church including teaching an adult class for about seven years. Enjoy seeing people pull together as a team to achieve their goals.

CHANGING CAREERS

Date

Exact Name of Person
Title or Position
Name of Company
Address (number and street)
Address (city, state, and ZIP)

Dear Exact Name of Person: (or Dear Sir or Madam if answering a blind ad.)

I would appreciate an opportunity to talk with you soon about how I could contribute to your organization through my formal education in social work as well as my versatile experience in social services, business management, office operations, and transportation management.

As you will see from my resume, I recently completed the B.A. in Social Work degree which I started several years ago and was unable to complete quickly because my husband was being relocated worldwide as a military professional. I am especially proud that, through my persistence and determination, I was able to complete my degree in late 2002 even while managing a successful and fast-growing small business which I started "from scratch" and directed until recently, when we relocated to Washington.

In a previous job in the human services/social work field prior to receiving my degree, I worked as an Eligibility Specialist for the County of San Bernardino and was involved in interviewing clients and assessing their needs. I gained a reputation as a caring counselor and respected co-worker, and I was encouraged to apply for a social work position in the county if we were ever again residing in San Bernardino.

From my work experience in the Air Force and in office environments, I am accustomed to dealing graciously with the public while working under tight deadlines and solving difficult problems. I offer a naturally compassionate personality along with an ability to handle large volumes of work efficiently and accurately. I can provide outstanding personal and professional references.

I hope you will welcome my call soon to arrange a brief meeting at your convenience to discuss your current and future needs and how I might serve them. Thank you in advance for your time, and I will look forward to meeting you.

Sincerely yours,

Marlene Routhier

from House Cleaning Management to Social Work

MARLENE ROUTHIER

1110½ Hay Street, Fayetteville, NC 28305 • preppub@aol.com • (910) 483-6611

OBJECTIVE

I want to contribute to an organization that can use a cheerful hard worker who offers an education related to social work and human services along with experience which includes proudly serving my country in the U.S. Air Force.

EDUCATION

Bachelor of Arts (B.A.) degree in Social Work, California State Polytechnic University, Pomona, CA, December 2002; worked at night to finish this degree while managing a business during the day.
Studied Social Work at Northwestern State University, Natchitoches, LA, 1988-90 and 1996.
Excelled in supervisory and management training sponsored by the U.S. Air Force, 1990-95.

EXPERIENCE

GENERAL MANAGER. Marlene's Cleaning Service, Fayetteville, NC (2001-03). On my own initiative and with only a fifty-dollar initial investment, set up "from scratch" a business which provided cleaning services for residential and commercial property; hired and supervised clerical and cleaning personnel while personally establishing the company's 18 major accounts.
- Only two months after starting the business, generated monthly cash flow of $1700 and personally handled the finances including accounts receivable/payable, financial reporting, tax preparation, and collections.
- Was frequently commended for my gracious style of dealing with people by telephone and in person.

ELIGIBILITY WORKER. County of San Bernardino, San Bernardino, CA (2000-02). Performed assessments of clients to determine eligibility for medical assistance in the form of Medicare and Medicaid.
- Became acquainted with the vast interlocking network of social services organizations, and referred clients to those agencies and organizations as appropriate.
- Assisted clients in preparing personal budgets and strengthened their ability to manage their finances.
- Earned a reputation as a compassionate counselor and effective motivator while treating people from all walks of life with dignity and respect.
- Became skilled in handling a heavy case load and became known for my accuracy in preparing large volumes of paperwork.

OFFICE MANAGER'S ASSISTANT. M.T.S. Insurance Service, Brea, CA (1998-00). Worked as the "right arm" of a busy office manager in a fast-paced insurance office, and excelled in activities ranging from word processing, to invoicing, to customer service.

DATA ENTRY OPERATOR. The Broadway, Los Angeles, CA (1996-98). Operated a computer in order to input data provided by sales associates; worked with customers in establishing delivery dates, and verified financial/accounting transactions.

PASSENGER & HOUSEHOLD GOODS SPECIALIST. U.S. Air Force, McGuire AFB, NJ (1990-95). While serving my country in the Air Force, specialized in managing the transportation of people and property all over the globe.
- Developed expertise in working with commercial airlines and shipping operations.
- Expertly processed every kind of paperwork related to making reservations for domestic and international travel, issuing tickets, coordinating shipments of personal goods, and preparing monthly reports and bills of lading.
- Learned to solve problems creatively and resourcefully in the process of locating "lost" people and property worldwide.
- Received two prestigious medals for exceptional performance and exemplary service.

COMPUTERS

Have used Microsoft Word for word processing, and can rapidly master new software.

PERSONAL

Am a patient, calm person who can handle a heavy work load and not get stressed out by tight deadlines. Have been told many times that I am a gifted counselor and communicator. Can provide outstanding personal and professional references upon request.

ABOUT THE EDITOR

Anne McKinney holds an MBA from the Harvard Business School and a BA in English from the University of North Carolina at Chapel Hill. A noted public speaker, writer, and teacher, she is the senior editor for PREP's business and career imprint, which bears her name. Early titles in the Anne McKinney Career Series (now called the Real-Resumes Series) published by PREP include: *Resumes and Cover Letters That Have Worked, Resumes and Cover Letters That Have Worked for Military Professionals, Government Job Applications and Federal Resumes, Cover Letters That Blow Doors Open,* and *Letters for Special Situations.* Her career titles and how-to resume-and-cover-letter books are based on the expertise she has acquired in 20 years of working with job hunters. Her valuable career insights have appeared in publications of the "Wall Street Journal" and other prominent newspapers and magazines.

PREP Publishing Order Form

You may purchase any of our titles from your favorite bookseller! Or send a check or money order or your credit card number for the total amount*, plus $4.00 postage and handling, to PREP, 1110 1/2 Hay Street, Fayetteville, NC 28305. You may also order our titles on our website at www.prep-pub.com and feel free to e-mail us at preppub@aol.com or call 910-483-6611 with your questions or concerns.

Name: _____

Phone #:_____

Address: _____

E-mail address:_____

Payment Type: ☐ Check/Money Order   ☐ Visa   ☐ MasterCard

Credit Card Number: _____ Expiration Date: _____

Put a check beside the items you are ordering:

☐ Free—Packet describing PREP's professional writing and editing services

☐ $16.95—REAL-RESUMES FOR RESTAURANT, FOOD SERVICE & HOTEL JOBS. Anne McKinney, Editor

☐ $16.95—REAL-RESUMES FOR MEDIA, NEWSPAPER, BROADCASTING & PUBLIC AFFAIRS JOBS. Anne McKinney, Editor

☐ $16.95—REAL-RESUMES FOR RETAILING, MODELING, FASHION & BEAUTY JOBS. Anne McKinney, Editor

☐ $16.95—REAL-RESUMES FOR HUMAN RESOURCES & PERSONNEL JOBS. Anne McKinney, Editor

☐ $16.95—REAL-RESUMES FOR MANUFACTURING JOBS. Anne McKinney, Editor

☐ $16.95—REAL-RESUMES FOR AVIATION & TRAVEL JOBS. Anne McKinney, Editor

☐ $16.95—REAL-RESUMES FOR POLICE, LAW ENFORCEMENT & SECURITY JOBS. Anne McKinney, Editor

☐ $16.95—REAL-RESUMES FOR SOCIAL WORK & COUNSELING JOBS. Anne McKinney, Editor

☐ $16.95—REAL-RESUMES FOR CONSTRUCTION JOBS. Anne McKinney, Editor

☐ $16.95—REAL-RESUMES FOR FINANCIAL JOBS. Anne McKinney, Editor

☐ $16.95—REAL-RESUMES FOR COMPUTER JOBS. Anne McKinney, Editor

☐ $16.95—REAL-RESUMES FOR MEDICAL JOBS. Anne McKinney, Editor

☐ $16.95—REAL-RESUMES FOR TEACHERS. Anne McKinney, Editor

☐ $16.95—REAL-RESUMES FOR CAREER CHANGERS. Anne McKinney, Editor

☐ $16.95—REAL-RESUMES FOR STUDENTS. Anne McKinney, Editor

☐ $16.95—REAL-RESUMES FOR SALES. Anne McKinney, Editor

☐ $16.95—REAL ESSAYS FOR COLLEGE AND GRAD SCHOOL. Anne McKinney, Editor

☐ $25.00—RESUMES AND COVER LETTERS THAT HAVE WORKED, Revised Ed. McKinney. Editor

☐ $25.00—RESUMES AND COVER LETTERS THAT HAVE WORKED FOR MILITARY PROFESSIONALS. McKinney, Ed.

☐ $25.00—RESUMES AND COVER LETTERS FOR MANAGERS. McKinney, Editor

☐ $25.00—GOVERNMENT JOB APPLICATIONS AND FEDERAL RESUMES: Federal Resumes, KSAs, Forms 171 and 612, and Postal Applications. McKinney, Editor

☐ $25.00—COVER LETTERS THAT BLOW DOORS OPEN. McKinney, Editor

☐ $25.00—LETTERS FOR SPECIAL SITUATIONS. McKinney, Editor

☐ $16.95—REAL-RESUMES FOR NURSING JOBS. McKinney, Editor

☐ $16.95—REAL-RESUMES FOR AUTO INDUSTRY JOBS. Patty Sleem

☐ $24.95—REAL KSAS--KNOWLEDGE, SKILLS & ABILITIES--FOR GOVERNMENT JOBS. McKinney, Editor

☐ $24.95—REAL RESUMIX AND OTHER RESUMES FOR FEDERAL GOVERNMENT JOBS. McKinney, Editor

☐ $24.95—REAL BUSINESS PLANS AND MARKETING TOOLS ... Samples to use in starting, growing, marketing, and selling your business

_____ **TOTAL ORDERED**

_____ **(add $4.00 for shipping and handling)**

_____ **TOTAL INCLUDING SHIPPING**

PREP offers volume discounts on large orders. Call us at (910) 483-6611 for more information.

THE MISSION OF PREP PUBLISHING IS TO PUBLISH
BOOKS AND OTHER PRODUCTS WHICH ENRICH
PEOPLE'S LIVES AND HELP THEM OPTIMIZE THE
HUMAN EXPERIENCE. OUR STRONGEST LINES ARE
OUR JUDEO-CHRISTIAN ETHICS SERIES AND OUR
REAL-RESUMES SERIES.

Would you like to explore the possibility of having PREP's writing
team create a resume for you similar to the ones in this book?

For a brief free consultation, call 910-483-6611
or send $4.00 to receive our Job Change Packet to
PREP, 1110 1/2 Hay Street, Fayetteville, NC 28305. Visit our
website to find valuable career resources: www.prep-pub.com!

QUESTIONS OR COMMENTS? E-MAIL US AT PREPPUB@AOL.COM